BLOODY KISS

VOLUME 2

BY KAZUKO FURUMIYA

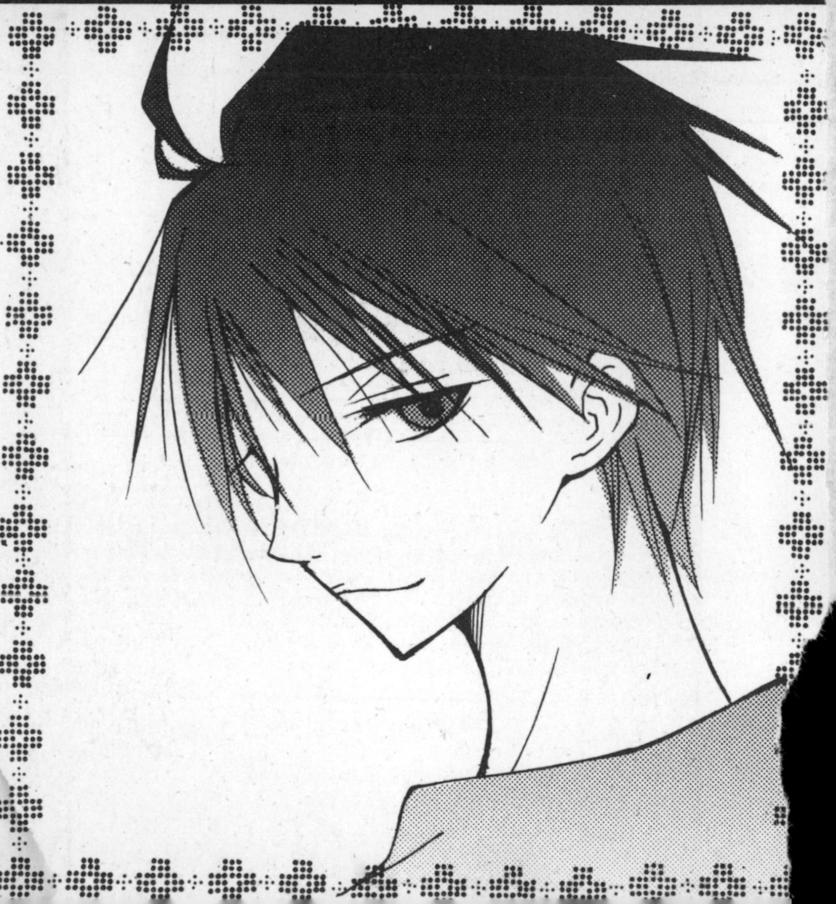

Bloody Kiss Volume 2
Created by Kazuko Furumiya

Translation - Monica Seya Chin
English Adaptation - Magda Erik-Soussi
Retouch and Lettering - Star Print Brokers
Production Artist - Rui Kyo
Graphic Designer - Chelsea Windlinger

Editor - Cindy Suzuki
Print Production Manager - Lucas Rivera
Managing Editor - Vy Nguyen
Senior Designer - Louis Csontos
Director of Sales and Manufacturing - Allyson De Simone
Associate Publisher - Marco F. Pavia
President and C.O.O. - John Parker
C.E.O. and Chief Creative Officer - Stu Levy

A 🐸 TOKYOPOP® Manga

TOKYOPOP Inc.
5900 Wilshire Blvd. Suite 2000
Los Angeles, CA 90036

E-mail: info@TOKYOPOP.com
Come visit us online at www.TOKYOPOP.com

ISBN: 978-1-4278-1580-4

First TOKYOPOP printing: November 2009
10 9 8 7 6 5 4 3 2 1
Printed in the USA

BLOODY KISS

VOLUME 2

CREATED BY
KAZUKO FURUMIYA

HAMBURG // LONDON // LOS ANGELES // TOKYO

Contents

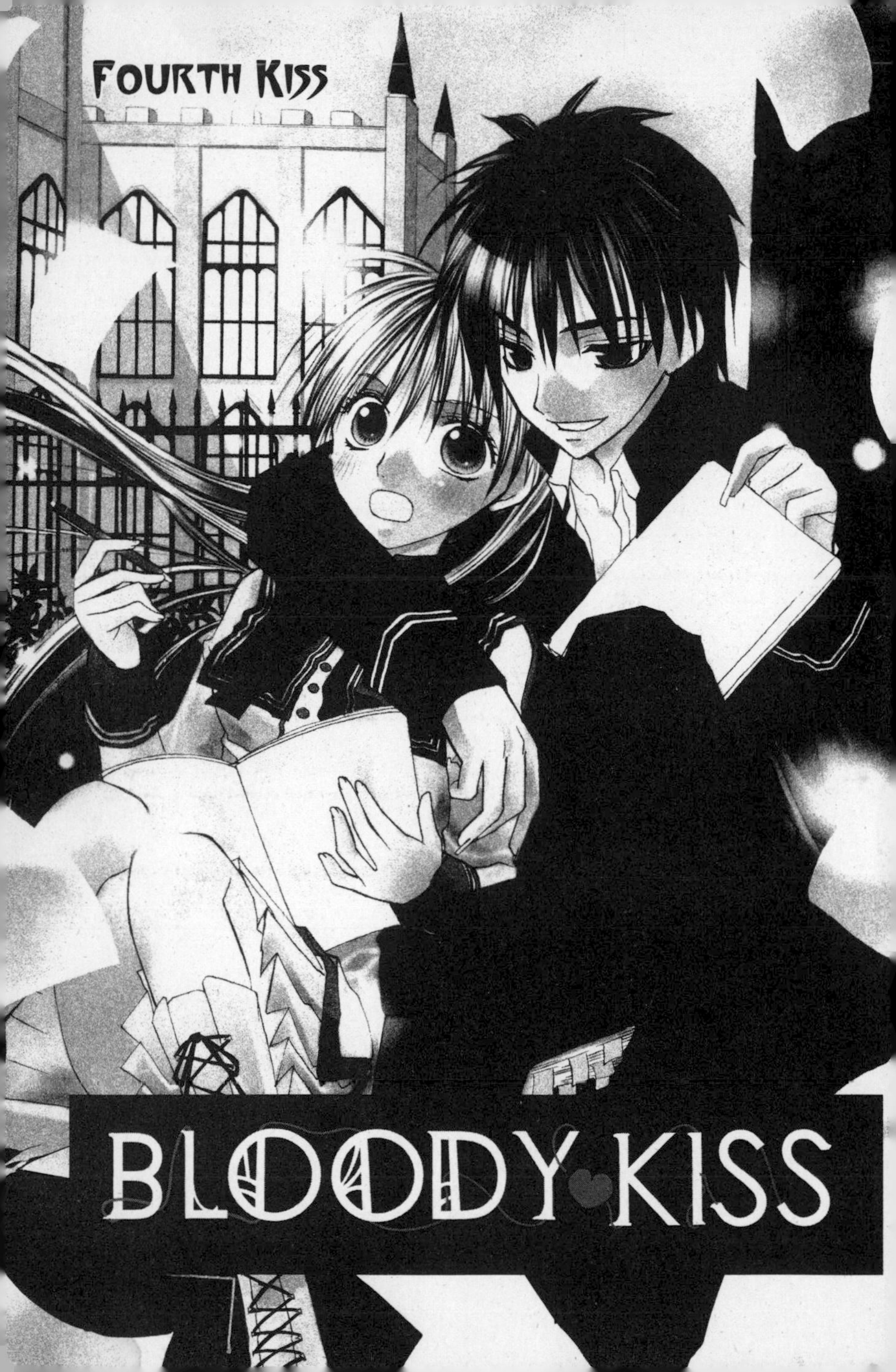
FOURTH KISS
BLOODY KISS

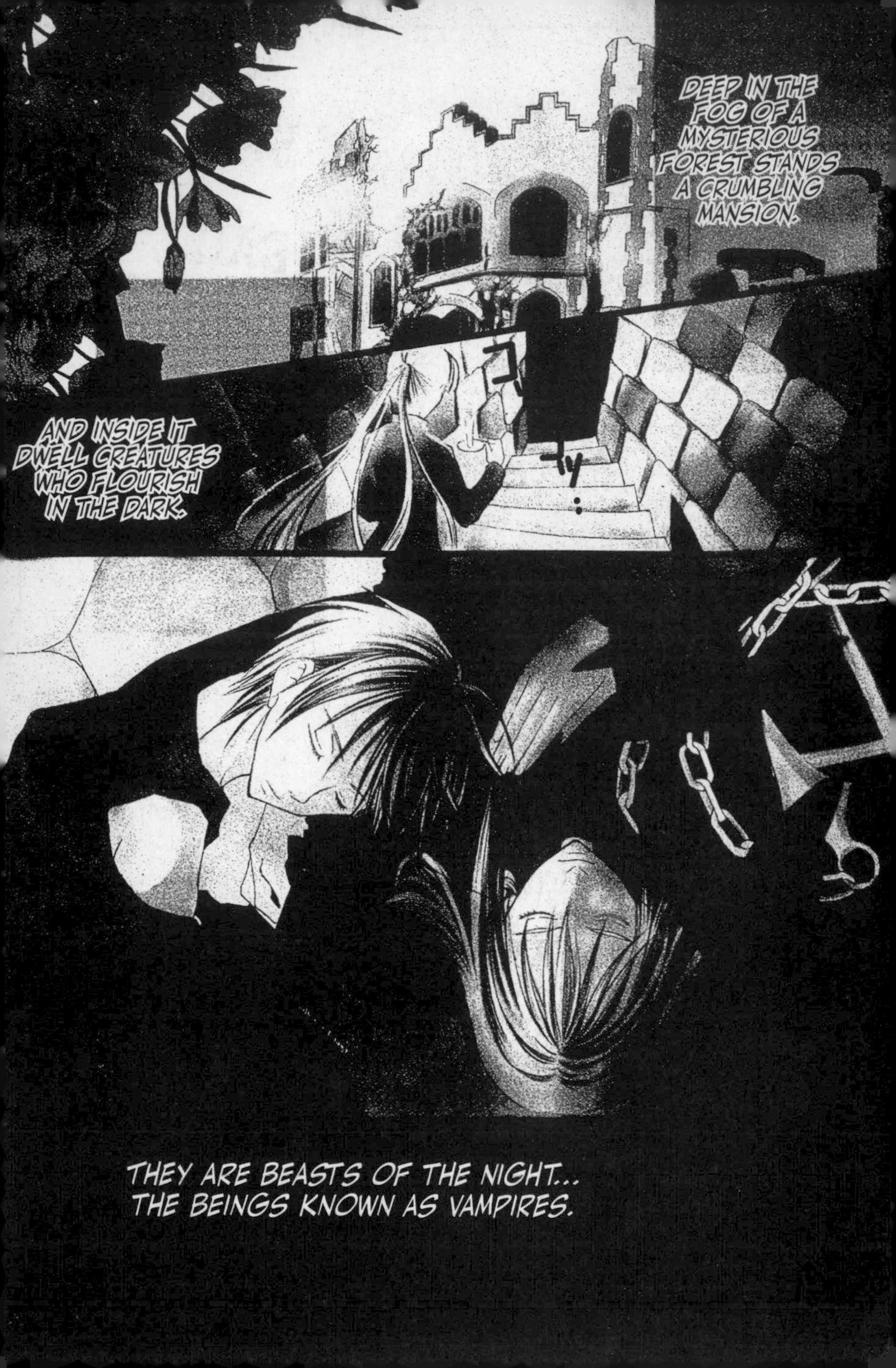
DEEP IN THE FOG OF A MYSTERIOUS FOREST STANDS A CRUMBLING MANSION.
AND INSIDE IT DWELL CREATURES WHO FLOURISH IN THE DARK.
THEY ARE BEASTS OF THE NIGHT... THE BEINGS KNOWN AS VAMPIRES.

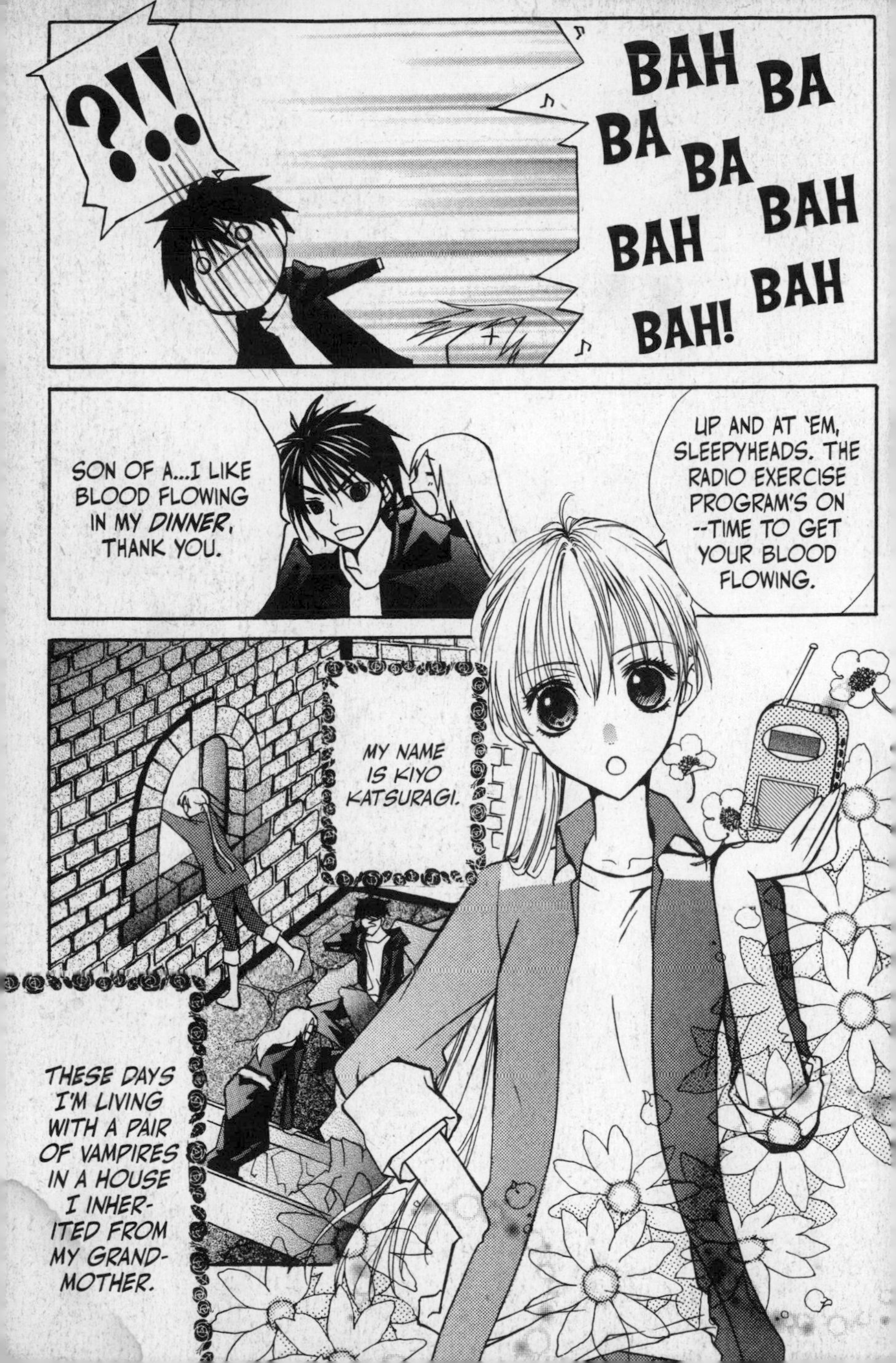
BAH BA BA BA BAH BAH BAH BAH!
?!!
UP AND AT 'EM, SLEEPYHEADS. THE RADIO EXERCISE PROGRAM'S ON --TIME TO GET YOUR BLOOD FLOWING.
SON OF A...I LIKE BLOOD FLOWING IN MY *DINNER*, THANK YOU.
MY NAME IS KIYO KATSURAGI.
THESE DAYS I'M LIVING WITH A PAIR OF VAMPIRES IN A HOUSE I INHERITED FROM MY GRANDMOTHER.

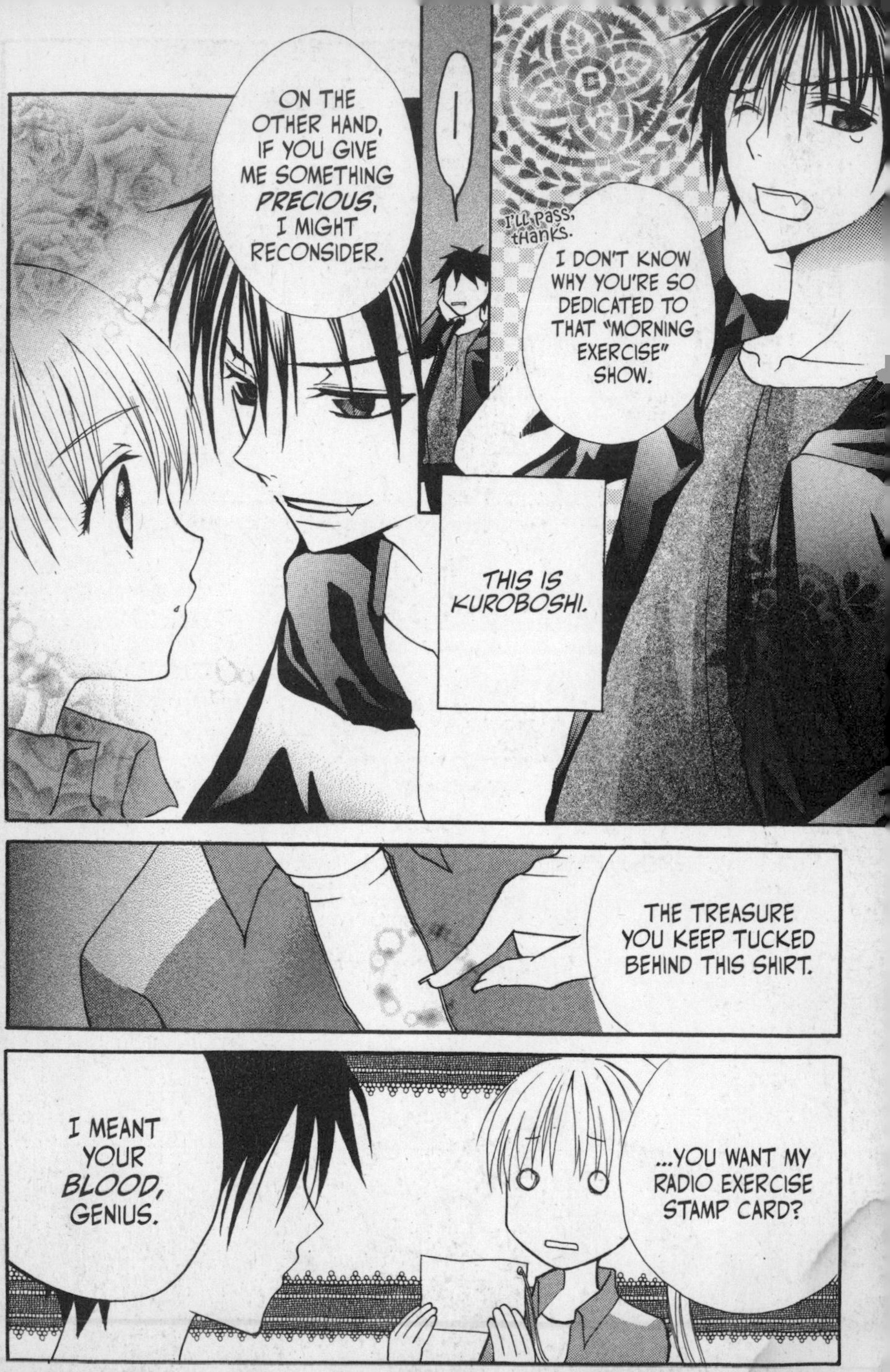
I DON'T KNOW WHY YOU'RE SO DEDICATED TO THAT "MORNING EXERCISE" SHOW.
I'll pass, thanks.
THIS IS KUROBOSHI.
!
ON THE OTHER HAND, IF YOU GIVE ME SOMETHING *PRECIOUS*, I MIGHT RECONSIDER.
THE TREASURE YOU KEEP TUCKED BEHIND THIS SHIRT.
...YOU WANT MY RADIO EXERCISE STAMP CARD?
I MEANT YOUR *BLOOD*, GENIUS.

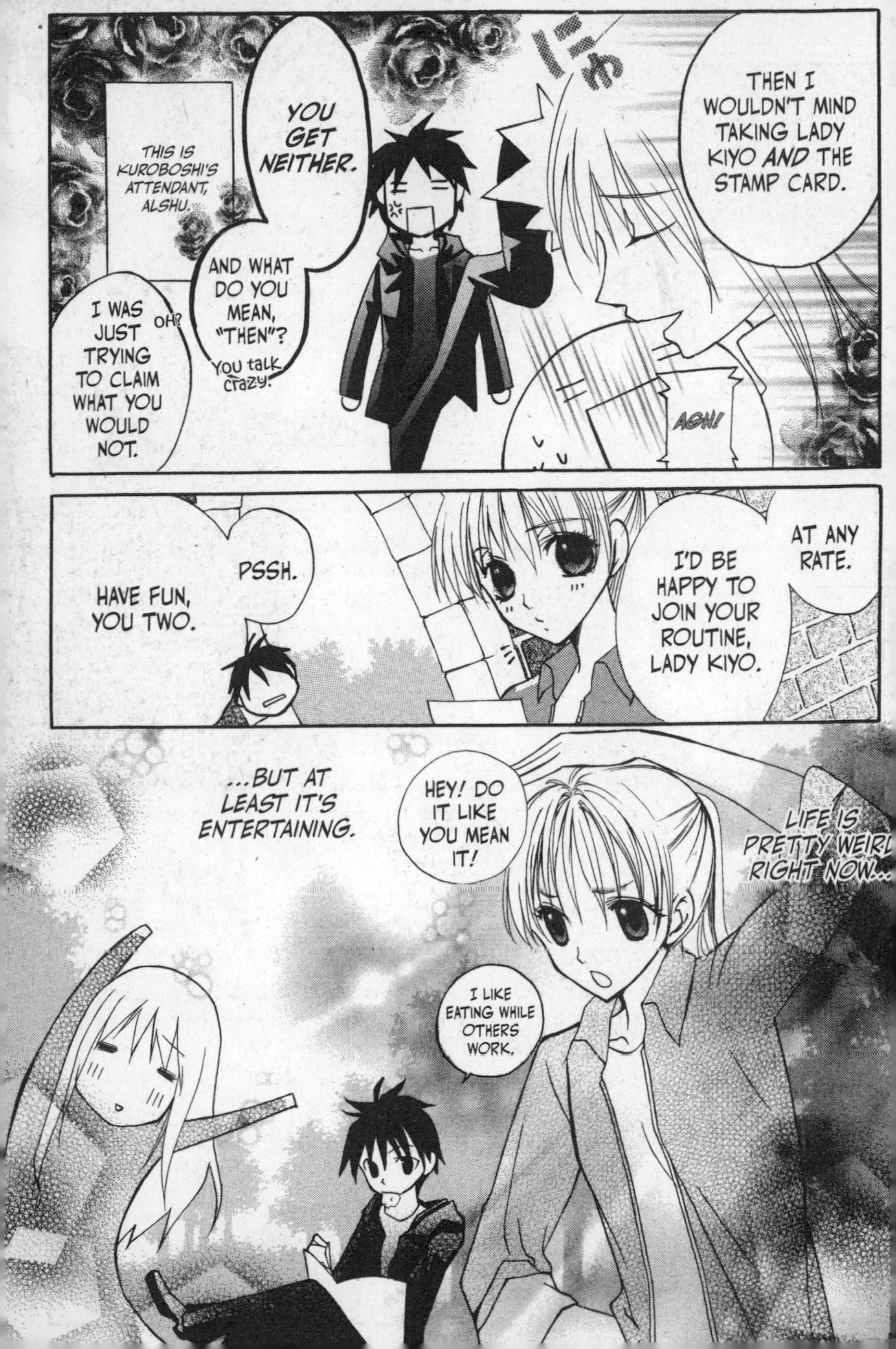
THEN I WOULDN'T MIND TAKING LADY KIYO AND THE STAMP CARD.
AGH!
YOU GET NEITHER.
AND WHAT DO YOU MEAN, "THEN"?
You talk crazy!
OH?
I WAS JUST TRYING TO CLAIM WHAT YOU WOULD NOT.
THIS IS KUROBOSHI'S ATTENDANT, ALSHU.
AT ANY RATE.
I'D BE HAPPY TO JOIN YOUR ROUTINE, LADY KIYO.
PSSH.
HAVE FUN, YOU TWO.
LIFE IS PRETTY WEIRD RIGHT NOW...
HEY! DO IT LIKE YOU MEAN IT!
...BUT AT LEAST IT'S ENTERTAINING.
I LIKE EATING WHILE OTHERS WORK.

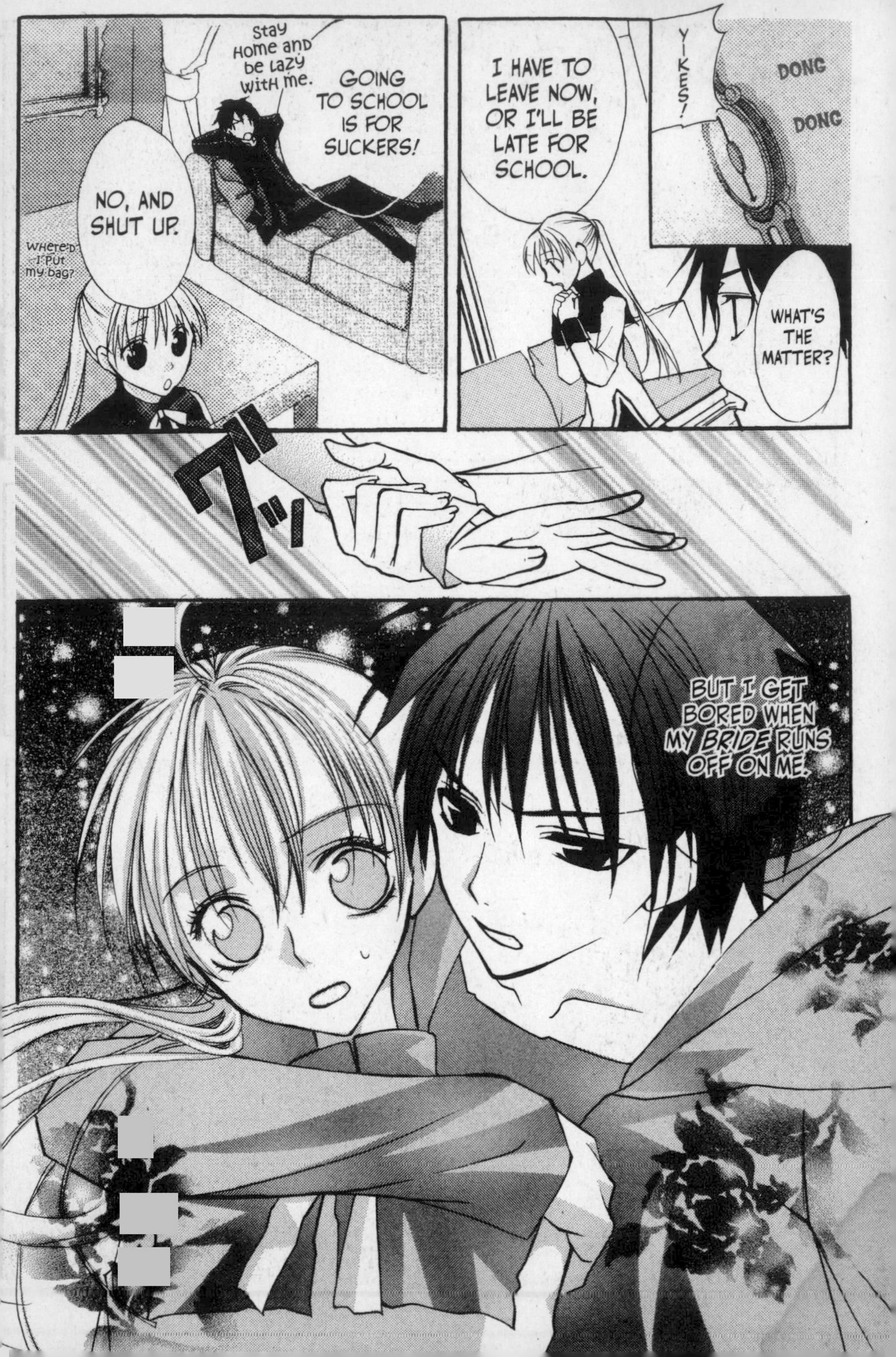
DONG
DONG
YIKES!
I HAVE TO LEAVE NOW, OR I'LL BE LATE FOR SCHOOL.
WHAT'S THE MATTER?
GOING TO SCHOOL IS FOR SUCKERS!
Stay Home and be lazy with me.
NO, AND SHUT UP.
Where'd I put my bag?
グッ
BUT I GET BORED WHEN MY BRIDE RUNS OFF ON ME.

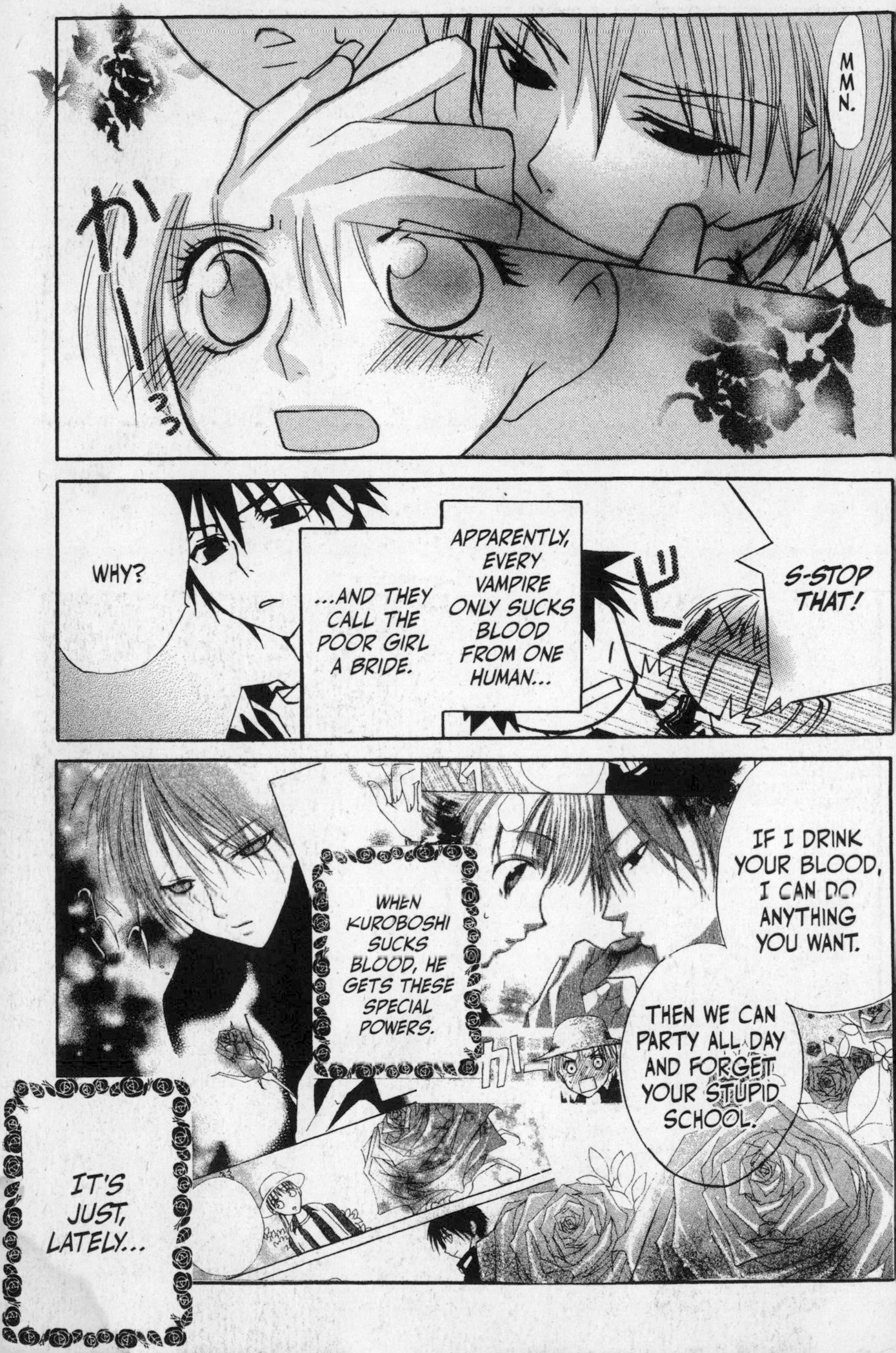
MMN.
S-STOP THAT!
APPARENTLY, EVERY VAMPIRE ONLY SUCKS BLOOD FROM ONE HUMAN...
...AND THEY CALL THE POOR GIRL A BRIDE.
WHY?
IF I DRINK YOUR BLOOD, I CAN DO ANYTHING YOU WANT.
THEN WE CAN PARTY ALL DAY AND FORGET YOUR STUPID SCHOOL.
WHEN KUROBOSHI SUCKS BLOOD, HE GETS THESE SPECIAL POWERS.
IT'S JUST, LATELY...

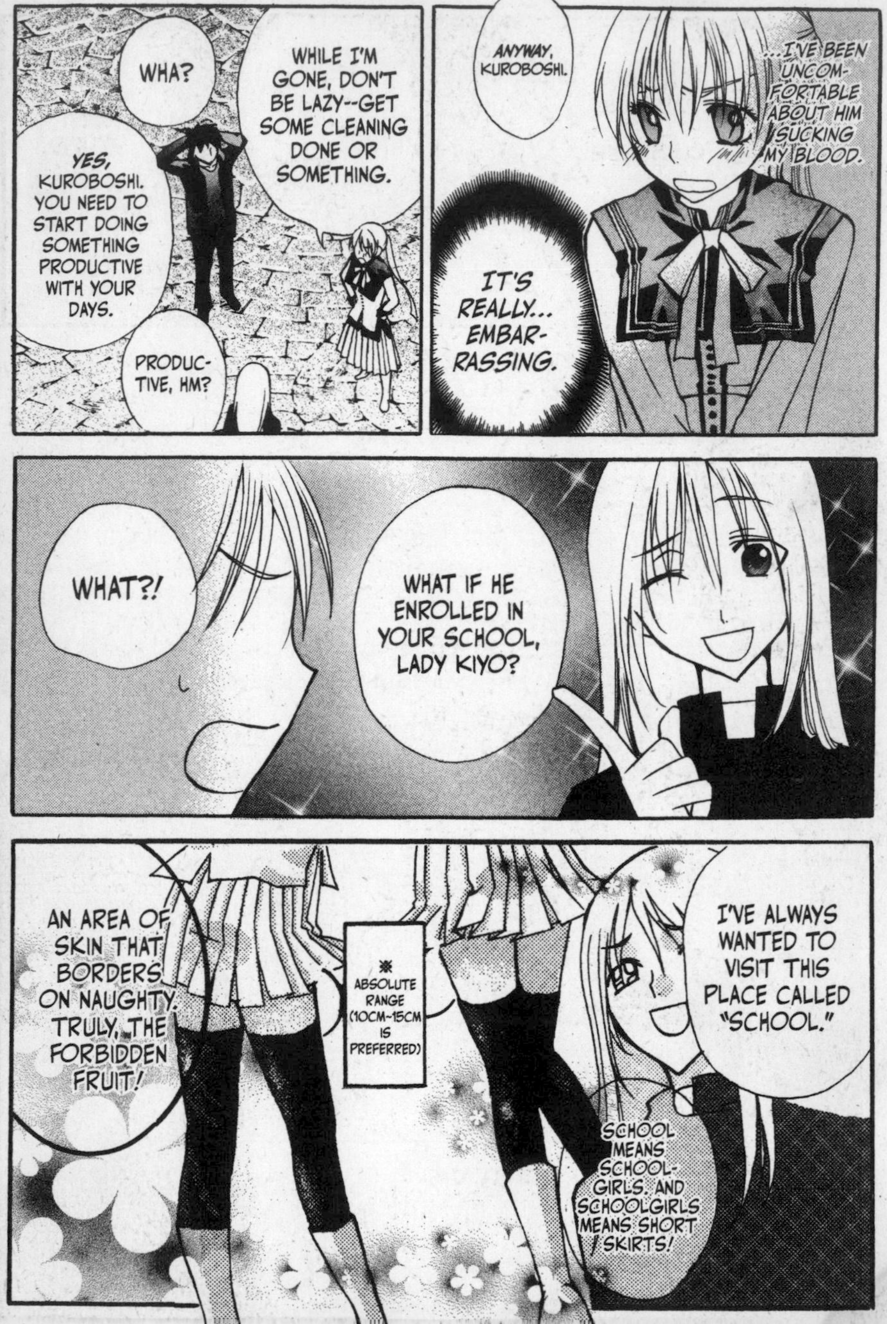

ANYWAY, KUROBOSHI.
...I'VE BEEN UNCOMFORTABLE ABOUT HIM SUCKING MY BLOOD.
IT'S REALLY... EMBARRASSING.
WHILE I'M GONE, DON'T BE LAZY--GET SOME CLEANING DONE OR SOMETHING.
WHA?
YES, KUROBOSHI. YOU NEED TO START DOING SOMETHING PRODUCTIVE WITH YOUR DAYS.
PRODUCTIVE, HM?
WHAT IF HE ENROLLED IN YOUR SCHOOL, LADY KIYO?
WHAT?!
I'VE ALWAYS WANTED TO VISIT THIS PLACE CALLED "SCHOOL."
SCHOOL MEANS SCHOOLGIRLS, AND SCHOOLGIRLS MEANS SHORT SKIRTS!
※ ABSOLUTE RANGE (10CM~15CM IS PREFERRED)
AN AREA OF SKIN THAT BORDERS ON NAUGHTY. TRULY, THE FORBIDDEN FRUIT!

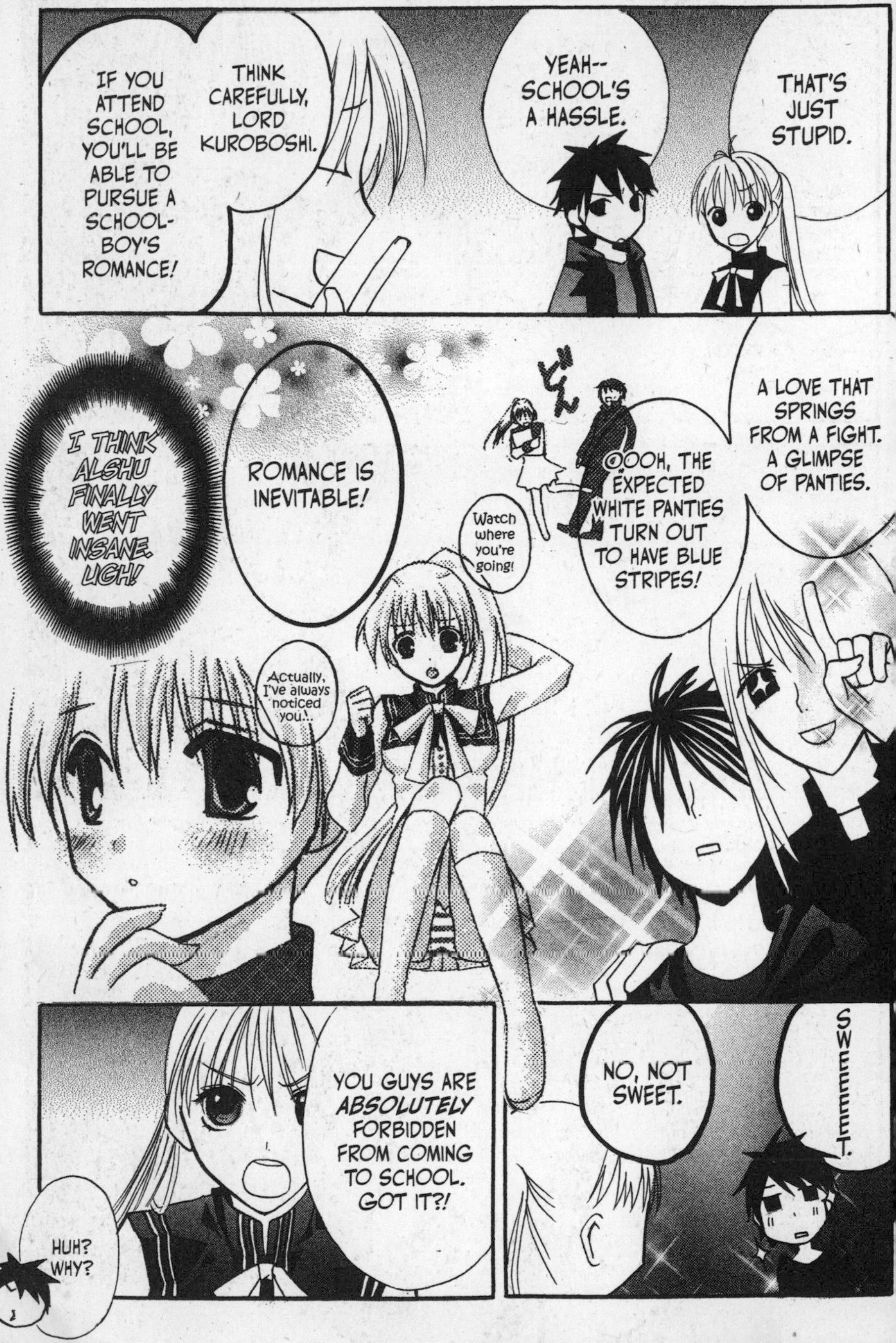
THAT'S JUST STUPID.
YEAH-- SCHOOL'S A HASSLE.
THINK CAREFULLY, LORD KUROBOSHI.
IF YOU ATTEND SCHOOL, YOU'LL BE ABLE TO PURSUE A SCHOOL-BOY'S ROMANCE!
A LOVE THAT SPRINGS FROM A FIGHT. A GLIMPSE OF PANTIES.
どん
OOOH, THE EXPECTED WHITE PANTIES TURN OUT TO HAVE BLUE STRIPES!
Watch where you're going!
ROMANCE IS INEVITABLE!
Actually, I've always noticed you...
I THINK ALSHU FINALLY WENT INSANE. UGH!
SWEEEET.
NO, NOT SWEET.
YOU GUYS ARE ABSOLUTELY FORBIDDEN FROM COMING TO SCHOOL. GOT IT?!
HUH? WHY?

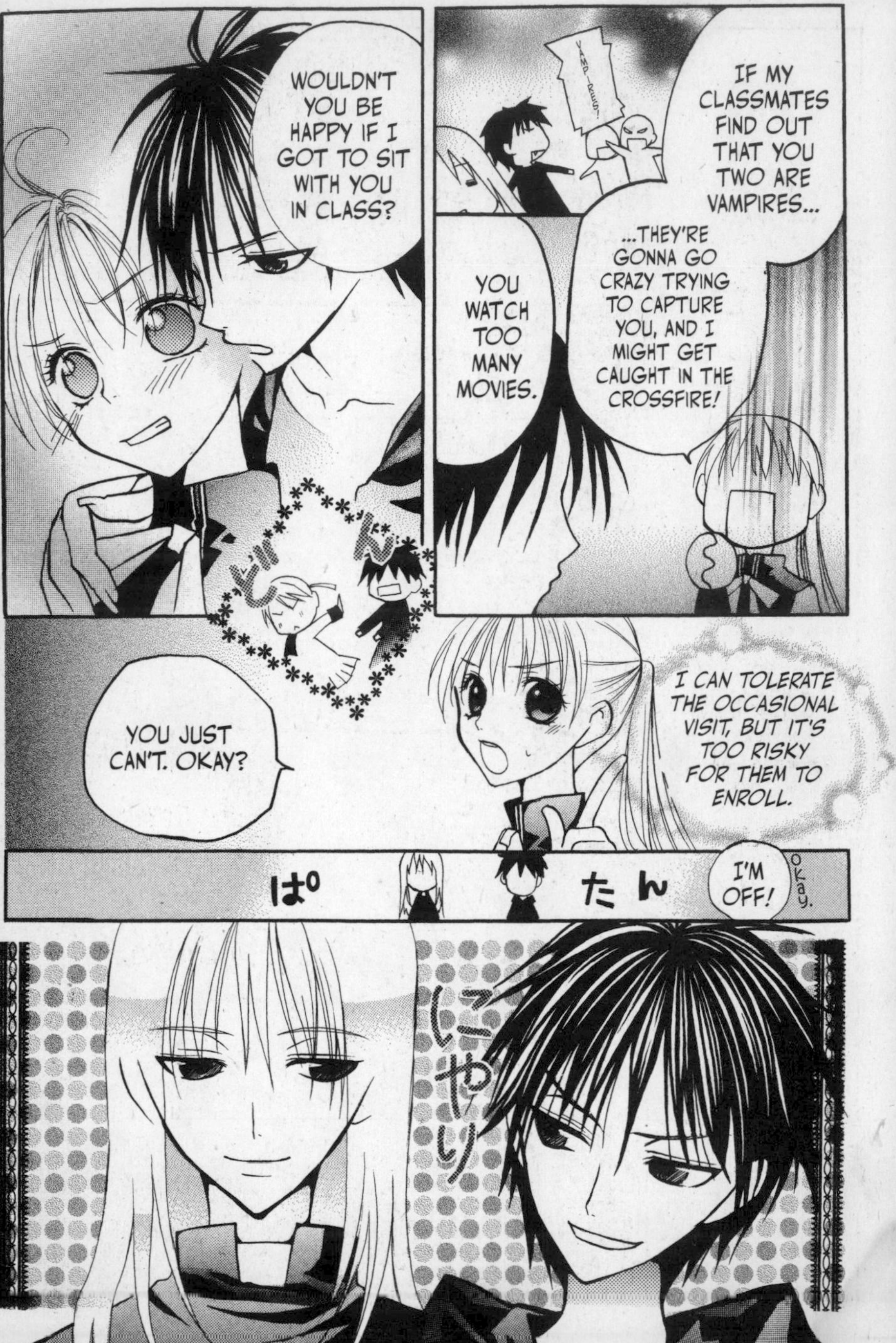
VAMPIRES!
IF MY CLASSMATES FIND OUT THAT YOU TWO ARE VAMPIRES...
...THEY'RE GONNA GO CRAZY TRYING TO CAPTURE YOU, AND I MIGHT GET CAUGHT IN THE CROSSFIRE!
YOU WATCH TOO MANY MOVIES.
WOULDN'T YOU BE HAPPY IF I GOT TO SIT WITH YOU IN CLASS?
どどん
I CAN TOLERATE THE OCCASIONAL VISIT, BUT IT'S TOO RISKY FOR THEM TO ENROLL.
YOU JUST CAN'T. OKAY?
Okay.
I'M OFF!
ぱたん
にやり

Morning!
SIIIGH.
ARE YOU OKAY?
OH, HEY.
I JUST HAD TO SHED SOME BAGGAGE BEFORE COMING HERE.
I CAN'T BELIEVE THEY WOULD EVEN THINK OF COMING TO SCHOOL.
"WOULDN'T YOU BE HAPPY IF I GOT TO SIT WITH YOU IN CLASS?"
THINKING ABOUT THIS IS BAD FOR MY HEART.
ARGH!
I HAVE TO FOCUS. FOCUS!
OKAY!
IT'S ALMOST CLASS MATCH TIME.
WE'RE GOING TO DECIDE ON THE TOPICS IN HOMEROOM TODAY.
OH, YEAH?

Hello, everyone-- This is Kazuko Furumiya. I'm here to deliver "Bloody Kiss" Volume 2. It's blocky, as usual, but please bear with me until the end. I, um, have seven free spaces for author's notes this time. I wish I had something to talk about.

I was thinking I might just discuss my favorite body parts and my least favorite body parts.

People might think that's really weird... so for those who are uninterested, feel free to keep your head down and move on along.

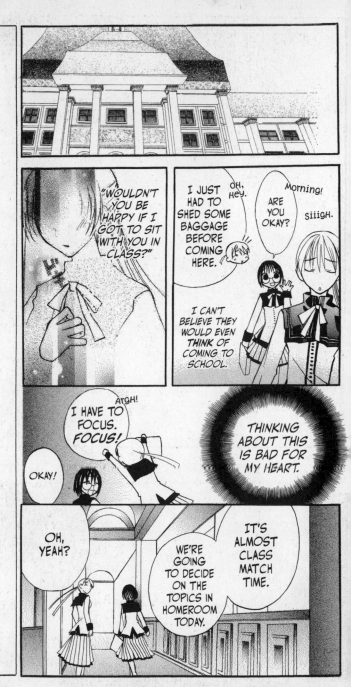

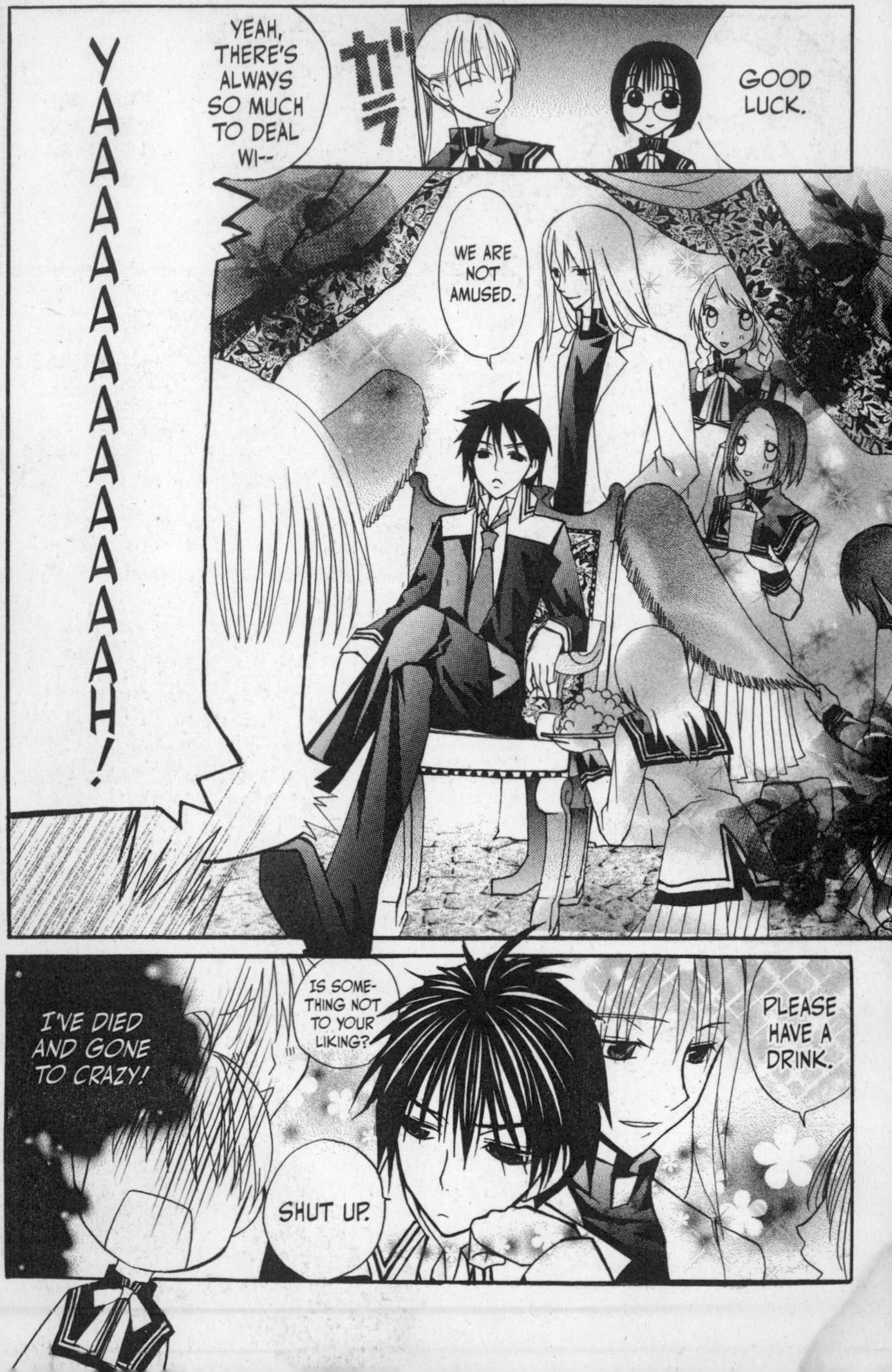
GOOD LUCK.
ガラ
YEAH, THERE'S ALWAYS SO MUCH TO DEAL WI--
YAAAAAAAAAAAAAAAH!
WE ARE NOT AMUSED.
PLEASE HAVE A DRINK.
IS SOME-THING NOT TO YOUR LIKING?
I'VE DIED AND GONE TO CRAZY!
SHUT UP.

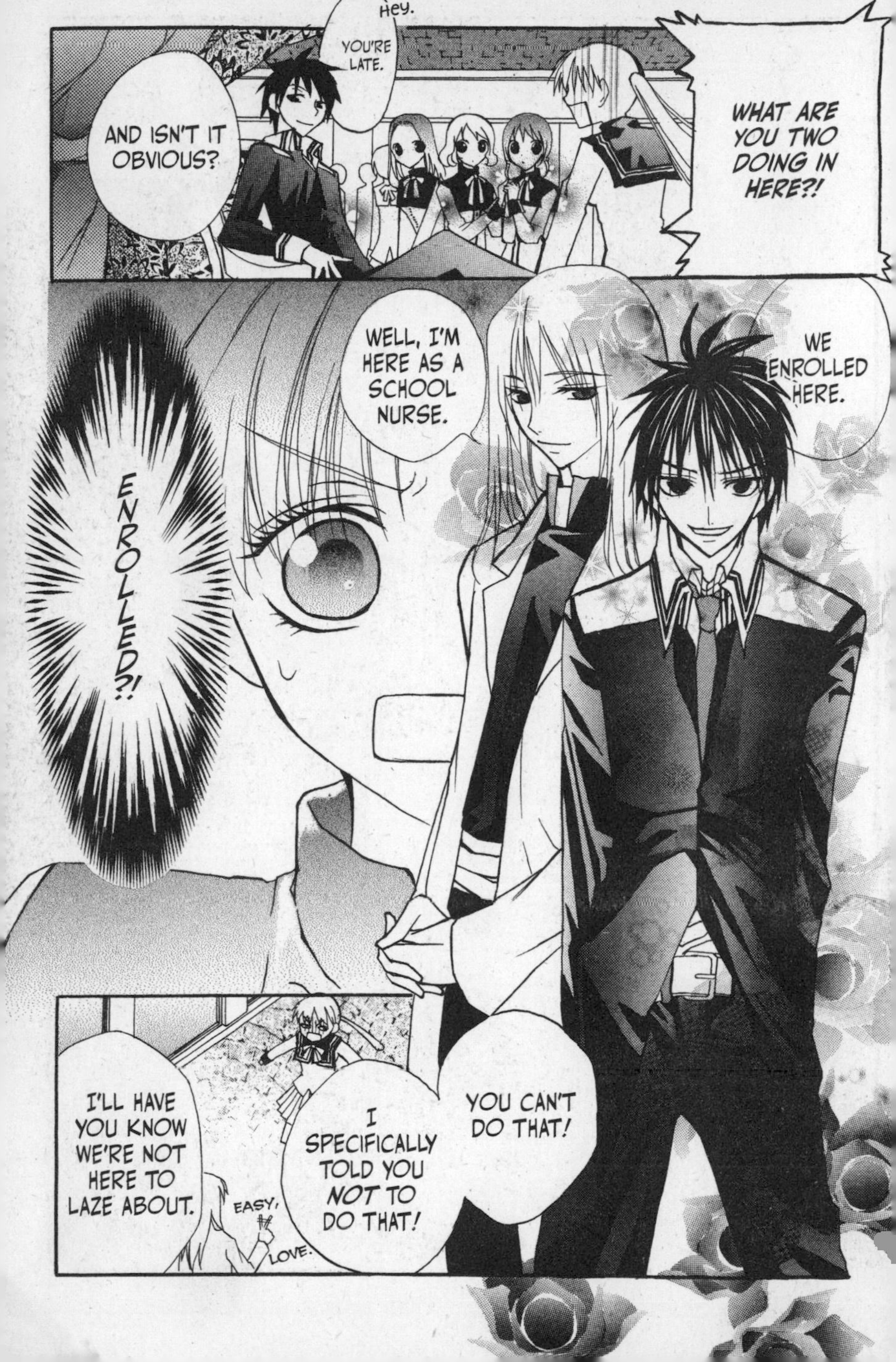
WHAT ARE YOU TWO DOING IN HERE?!
Hey.
YOU'RE LATE.
AND ISN'T IT OBVIOUS?
WE ENROLLED HERE.
WELL, I'M HERE AS A SCHOOL NURSE.
ENROLLED?!
YOU CAN'T DO THAT!
I SPECIFICALLY TOLD YOU *NOT* TO DO THAT!
I'LL HAVE YOU KNOW WE'RE NOT HERE TO LAZE ABOUT.
EASY, LOVE.

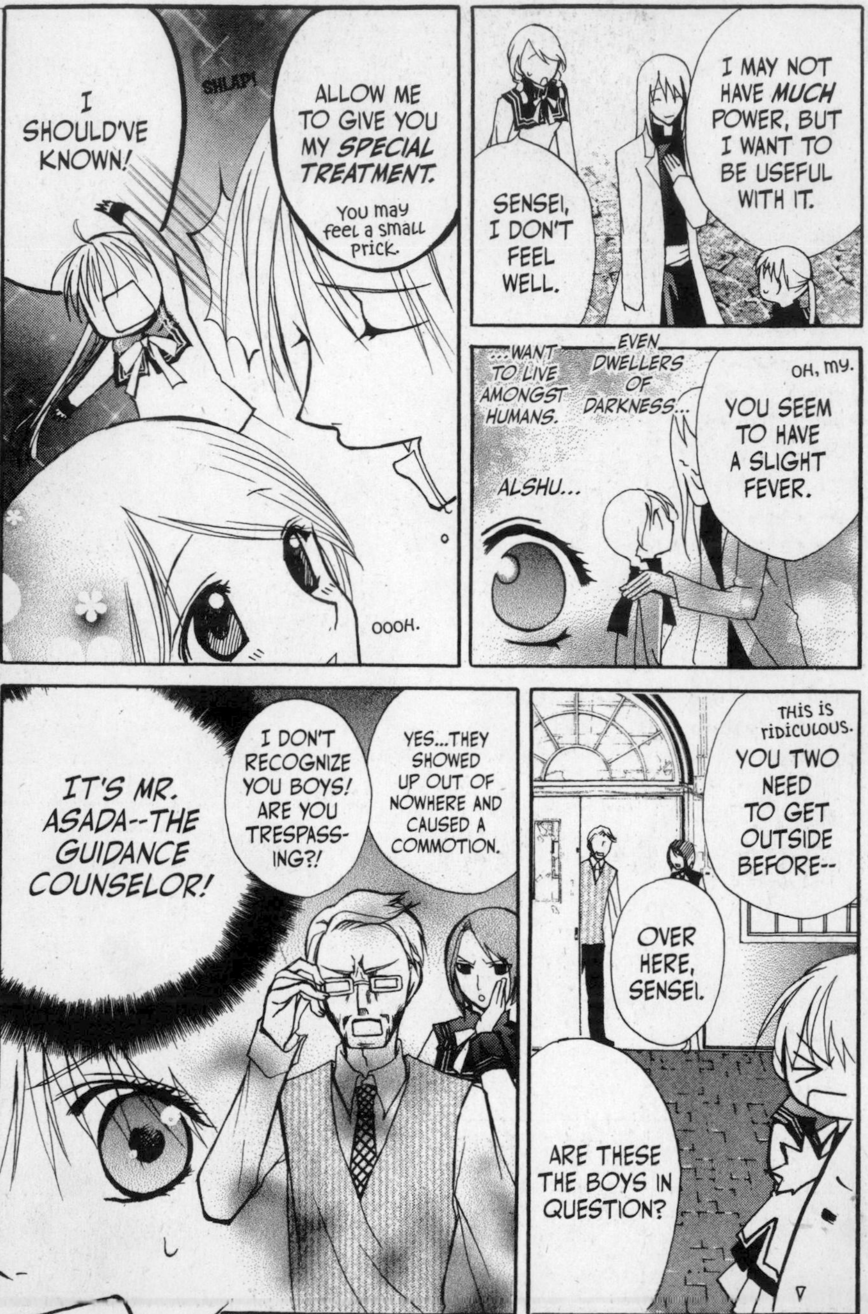
I MAY NOT HAVE MUCH POWER, BUT I WANT TO BE USEFUL WITH IT.
SENSEI, I DON'T FEEL WELL.
OH, MY.
YOU SEEM TO HAVE A SLIGHT FEVER.
EVEN DWELLERS OF DARKNESS...
...WANT TO LIVE AMONGST HUMANS.
ALSHU...
ALLOW ME TO GIVE YOU MY SPECIAL TREATMENT.
You may feel a small prick.
SHLAP!
I SHOULD'VE KNOWN!
OOOH.
This is ridiculous.
YOU TWO NEED TO GET OUTSIDE BEFORE--
OVER HERE, SENSEI.
ARE THESE THE BOYS IN QUESTION?
YES...THEY SHOWED UP OUT OF NOWHERE AND CAUSED A COMMOTION.
I DON'T RECOGNIZE YOU BOYS! ARE YOU TRESPASS-ING?!
IT'S MR. ASADA--THE GUIDANCE COUNSELOR!

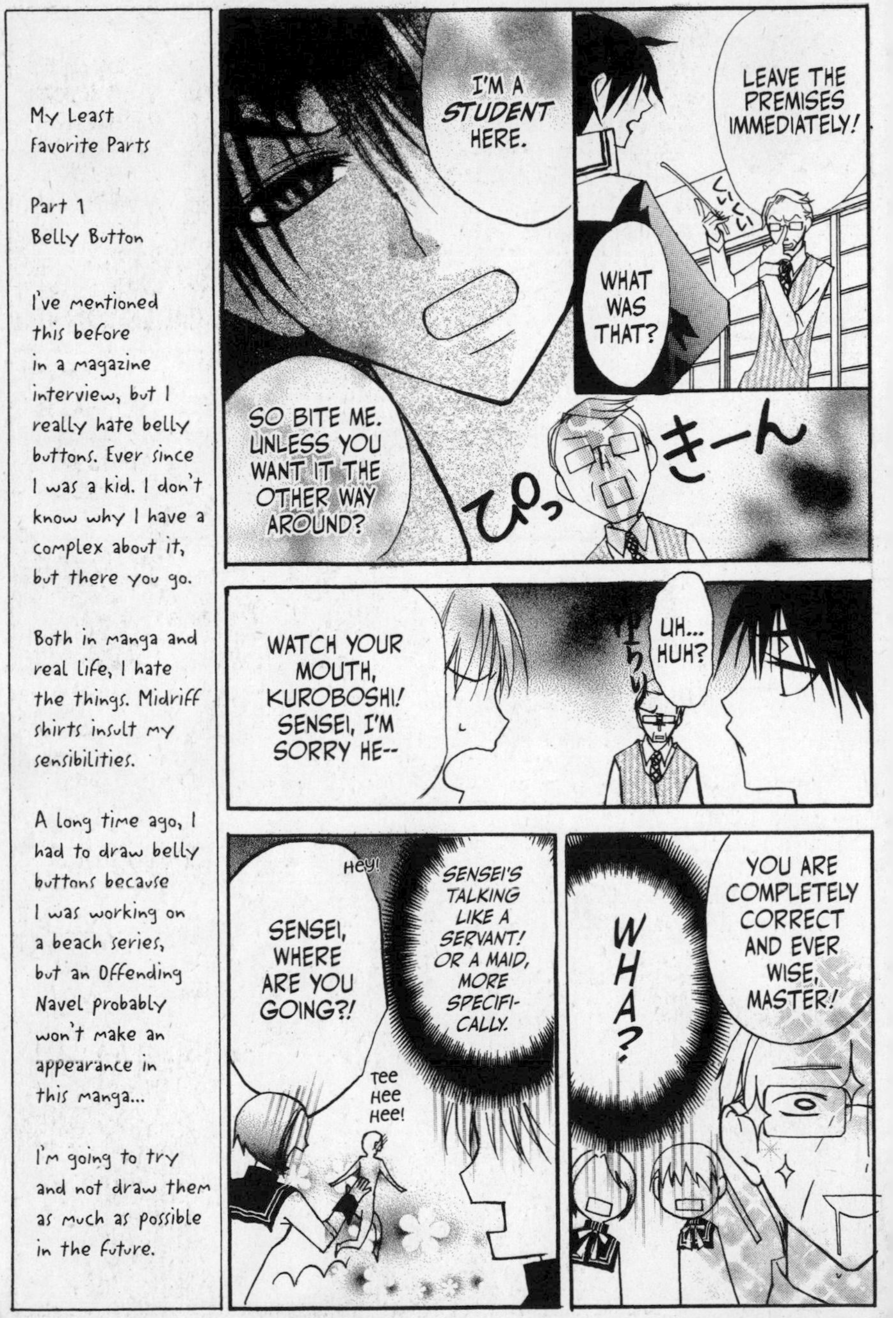
LEAVE THE PREMISES IMMEDIATELY!
WHAT WAS THAT?
きーん
ぴっ
I'M A STUDENT HERE.
SO BITE ME. UNLESS YOU WANT IT THE OTHER WAY AROUND?
UH... HUH?
WATCH YOUR MOUTH, KUROBOSHI! SENSEI, I'M SORRY HE--
YOU ARE COMPLETELY CORRECT AND EVER WISE, MASTER!
WHA?
SENSEI'S TALKING LIKE A SERVANT! OR A MAID, MORE SPECIFI-CALLY.
HEY!
SENSEI, WHERE ARE YOU GOING?!
TEE HEE HEE!

My Least Favorite Parts

Part 1
Belly Button

I've mentioned this before in a magazine interview, but I really hate belly buttons. Ever since I was a kid. I don't know why I have a complex about it, but there you go.

Both in manga and real life, I hate the things. Midriff shirts insult my sensibilities.

A long time ago, I had to draw belly buttons because I was working on a beach series, but an Offending Navel probably won't make an appearance in this manga...

I'm going to try and not draw them as much as possible in the future.

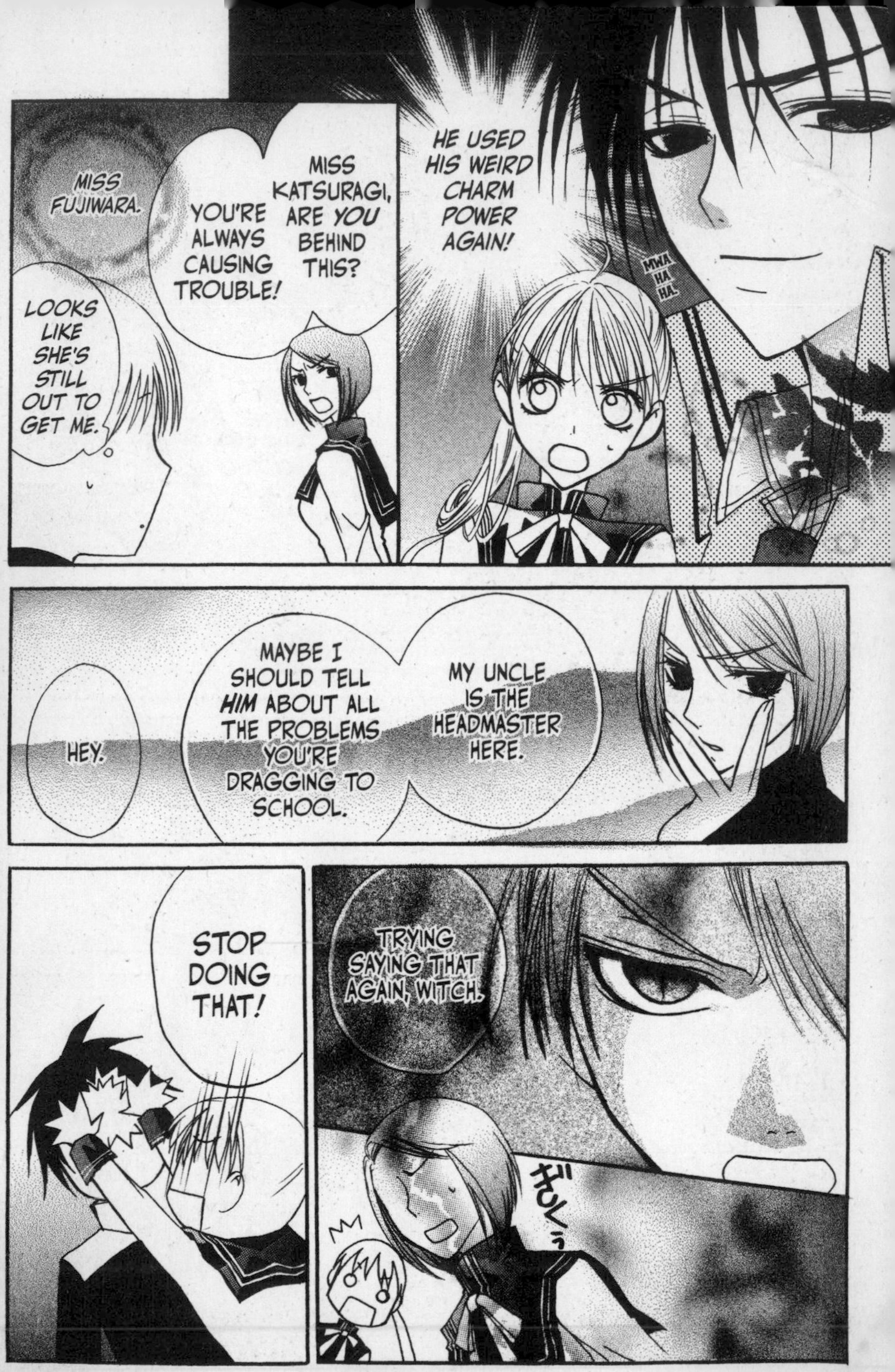
HE USED HIS WEIRD CHARM POWER AGAIN!
MWA HA HA.
MISS KATSURAGI, ARE *YOU* BEHIND THIS?
YOU'RE ALWAYS CAUSING TROUBLE!
MISS FUJIWARA.
LOOKS LIKE SHE'S STILL OUT TO GET ME.
MY UNCLE IS THE HEADMASTER HERE.
MAYBE I SHOULD TELL ***HIM*** ABOUT ALL THE PROBLEMS YOU'RE DRAGGING TO SCHOOL.
HEY.
TRYING SAYING THAT AGAIN, WITCH.
STOP DOING THAT!

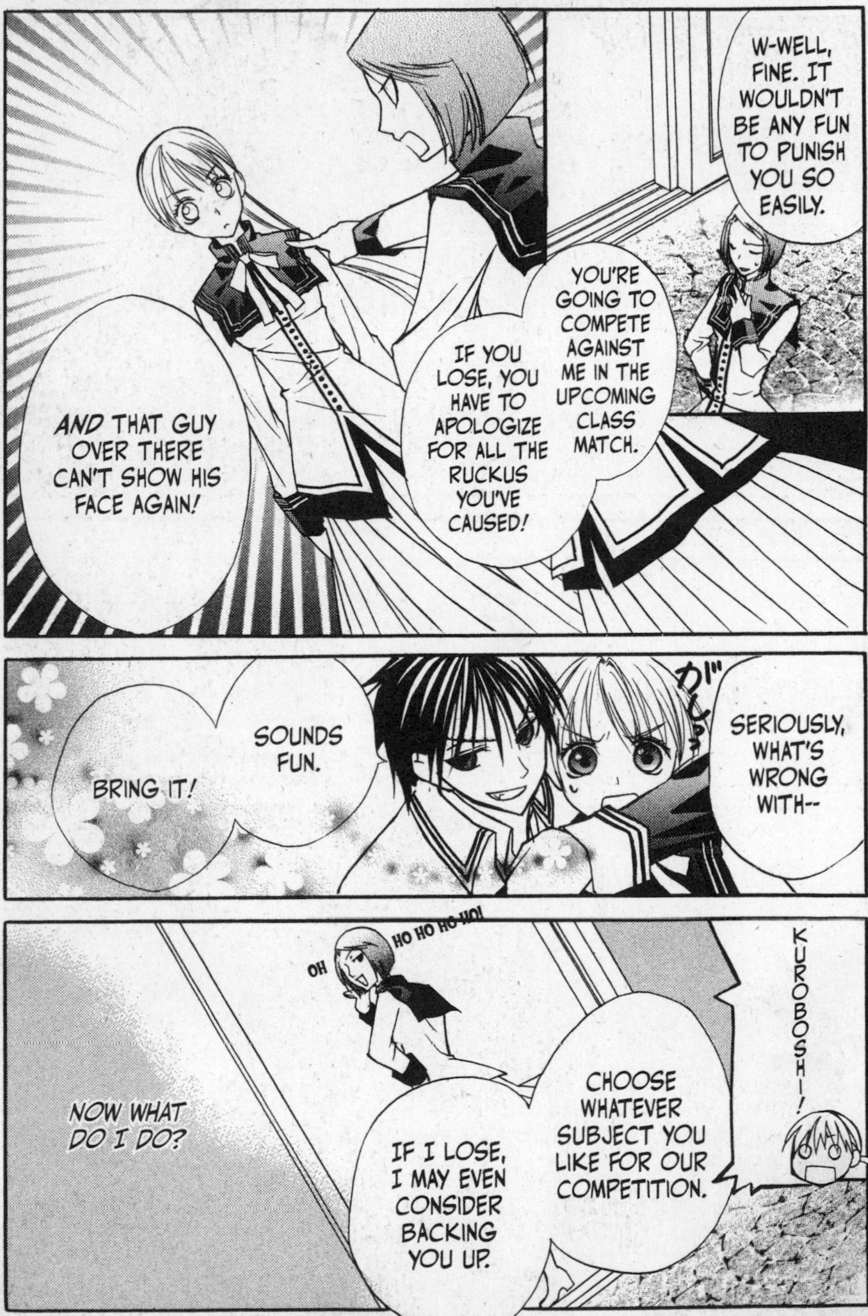
W-WELL, FINE. IT WOULDN'T BE ANY FUN TO PUNISH YOU SO EASILY.
YOU'RE GOING TO COMPETE AGAINST ME IN THE UPCOMING CLASS MATCH.
IF YOU LOSE, YOU HAVE TO APOLOGIZE FOR ALL THE RUCKUS YOU'VE CAUSED!
AND THAT GUY OVER THERE CAN'T SHOW HIS FACE AGAIN!
SERIOUSLY, WHAT'S WRONG WITH--
SOUNDS FUN.
BRING IT!
KUROBOSHI!
OH HO HO HO HO!
CHOOSE WHATEVER SUBJECT YOU LIKE FOR OUR COMPETITION.
IF I LOSE, I MAY EVEN CONSIDER BACKING YOU UP.
NOW WHAT DO I DO?

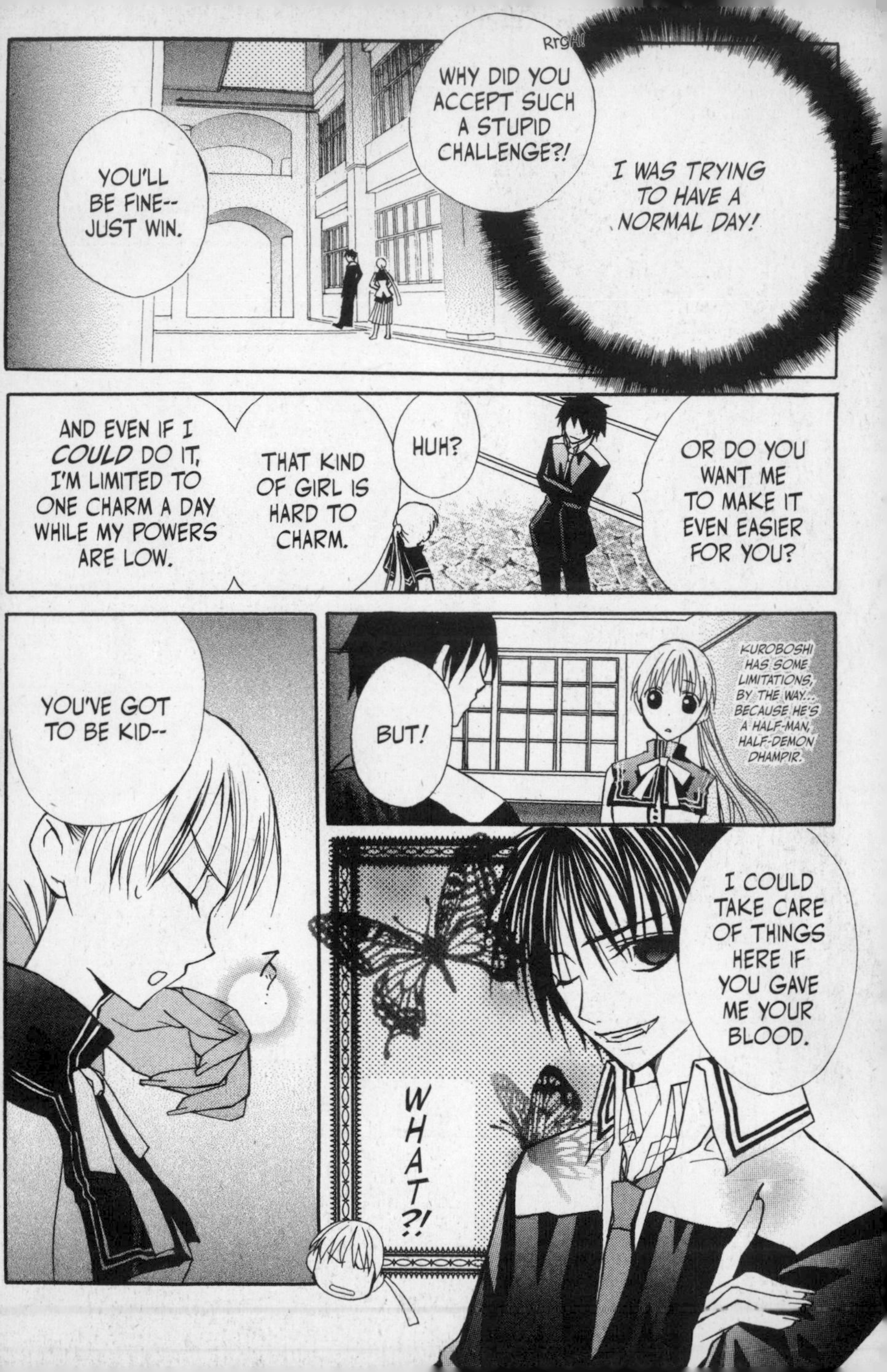

RRGH!
WHY DID YOU ACCEPT SUCH A STUPID CHALLENGE?!
I WAS TRYING TO HAVE A NORMAL DAY!
YOU'LL BE FINE-- JUST WIN.
OR DO YOU WANT ME TO MAKE IT EVEN EASIER FOR YOU?
HUH?
THAT KIND OF GIRL IS HARD TO CHARM.
AND EVEN IF I *COULD* DO IT, I'M LIMITED TO ONE CHARM A DAY WHILE MY POWERS ARE LOW.
KUROBOSHI HAS SOME LIMITATIONS, BY THE WAY... BECAUSE HE'S A HALF-MAN, HALF-DEMON DHAMPIR.
BUT!
I COULD TAKE CARE OF THINGS HERE IF YOU GAVE ME YOUR BLOOD.
WHAT?!
YOU'VE GOT TO BE KID--

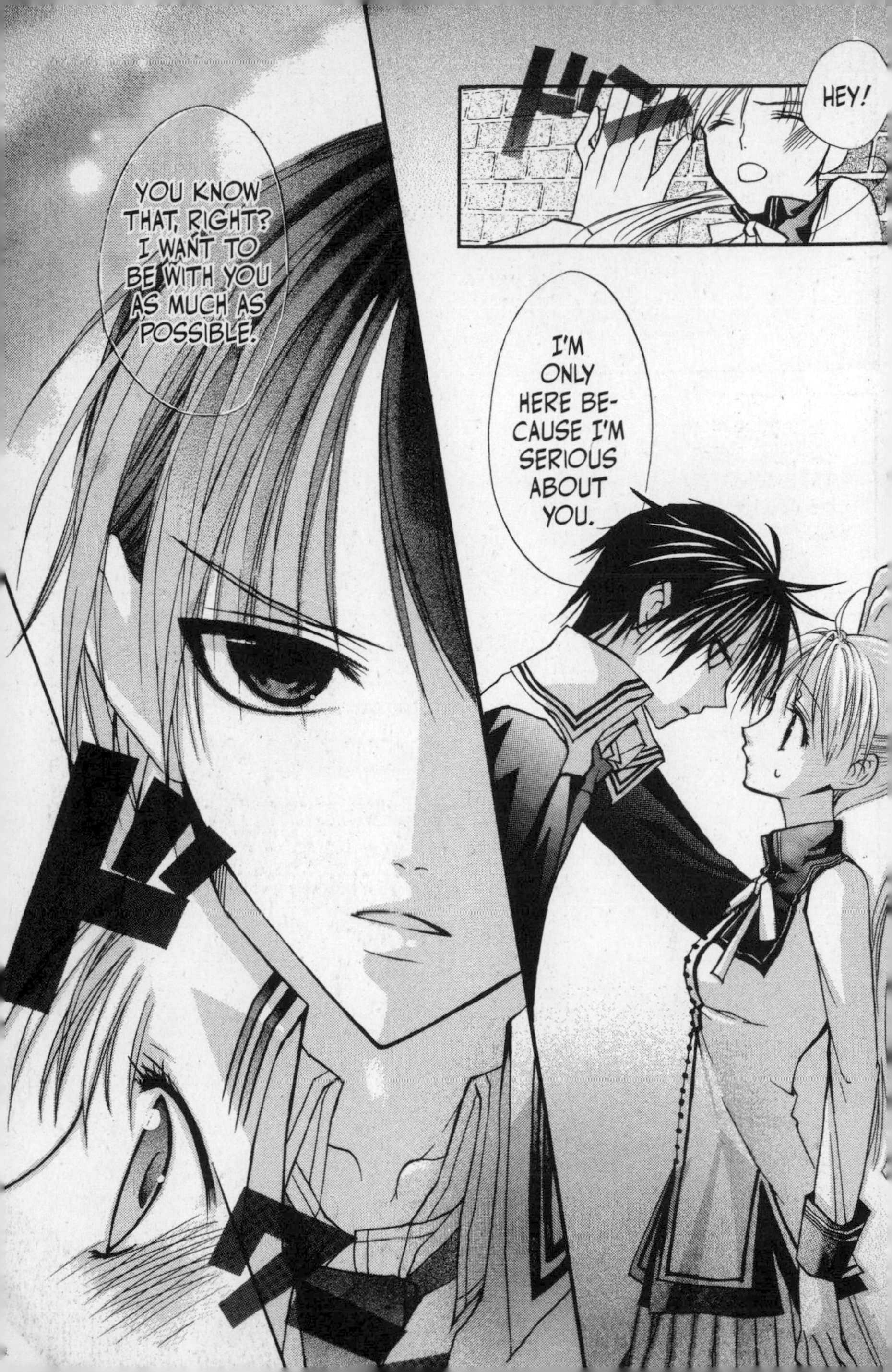
HEY!
I'M ONLY HERE BE- CAUSE I'M SERIOUS ABOUT YOU.
YOU KNOW THAT, RIGHT? I WANT TO BE WITH YOU AS MUCH AS POSSIBLE.

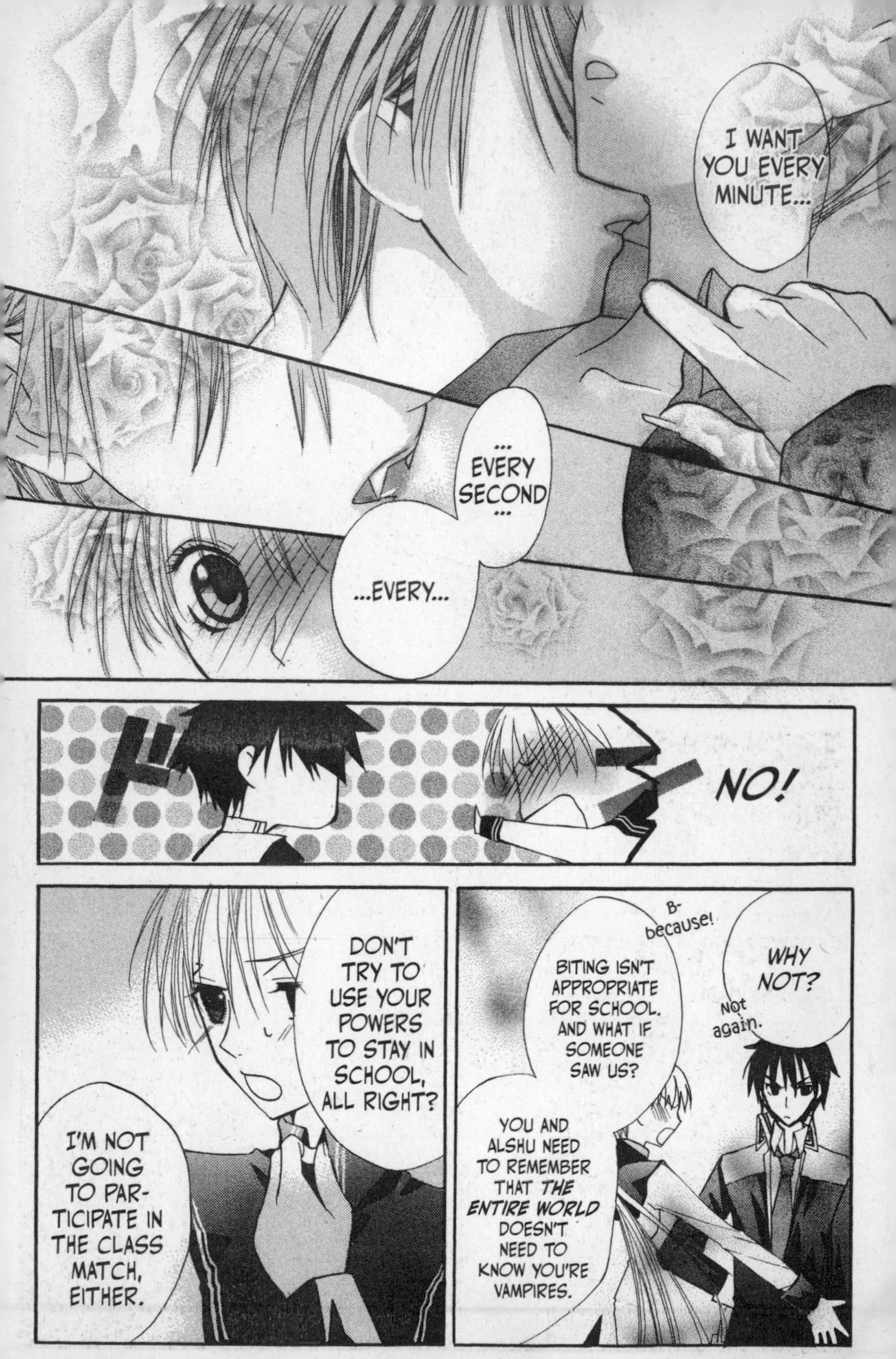
I WANT YOU EVERY MINUTE...
... EVERY SECOND ...
...EVERY...
NO!
WHY NOT?
B-because!
Not again.
BITING ISN'T APPROPRIATE FOR SCHOOL. AND WHAT IF SOMEONE SAW US?
YOU AND ALSHU NEED TO REMEMBER THAT *THE ENTIRE WORLD* DOESN'T NEED TO KNOW YOU'RE VAMPIRES.
DON'T TRY TO USE YOUR POWERS TO STAY IN SCHOOL, ALL RIGHT?
I'M NOT GOING TO PAR-TICIPATE IN THE CLASS MATCH, EITHER.

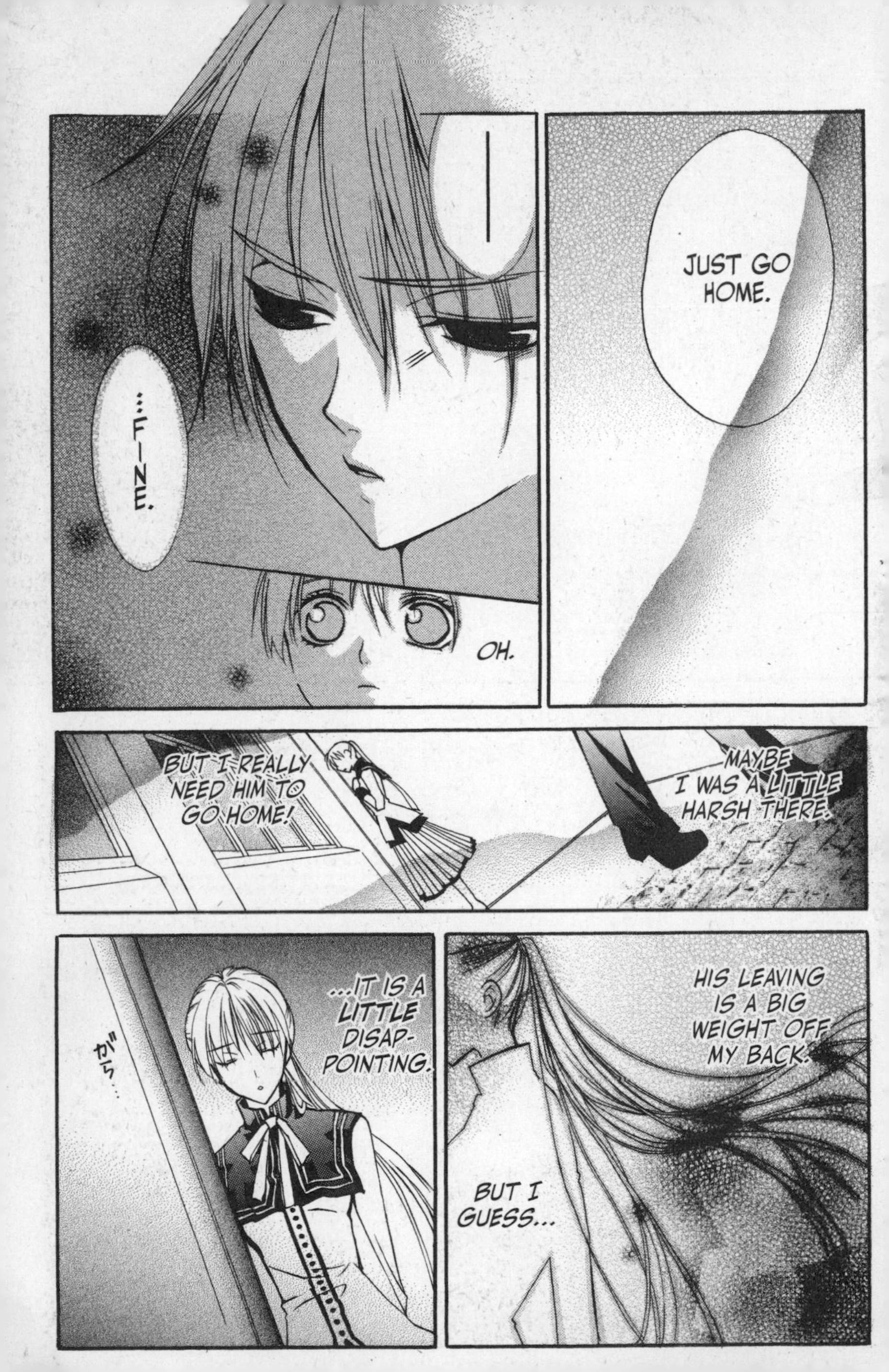
JUST GO HOME.
—
...FINE.
OH.
MAYBE I WAS A LITTLE HARSH THERE.
BUT I REALLY NEED HIM TO GO HOME!
HIS LEAVING IS A BIG WEIGHT OFF MY BACK.
BUT I GUESS...
...IT IS A LITTLE DISAP-POINTING.
がら...

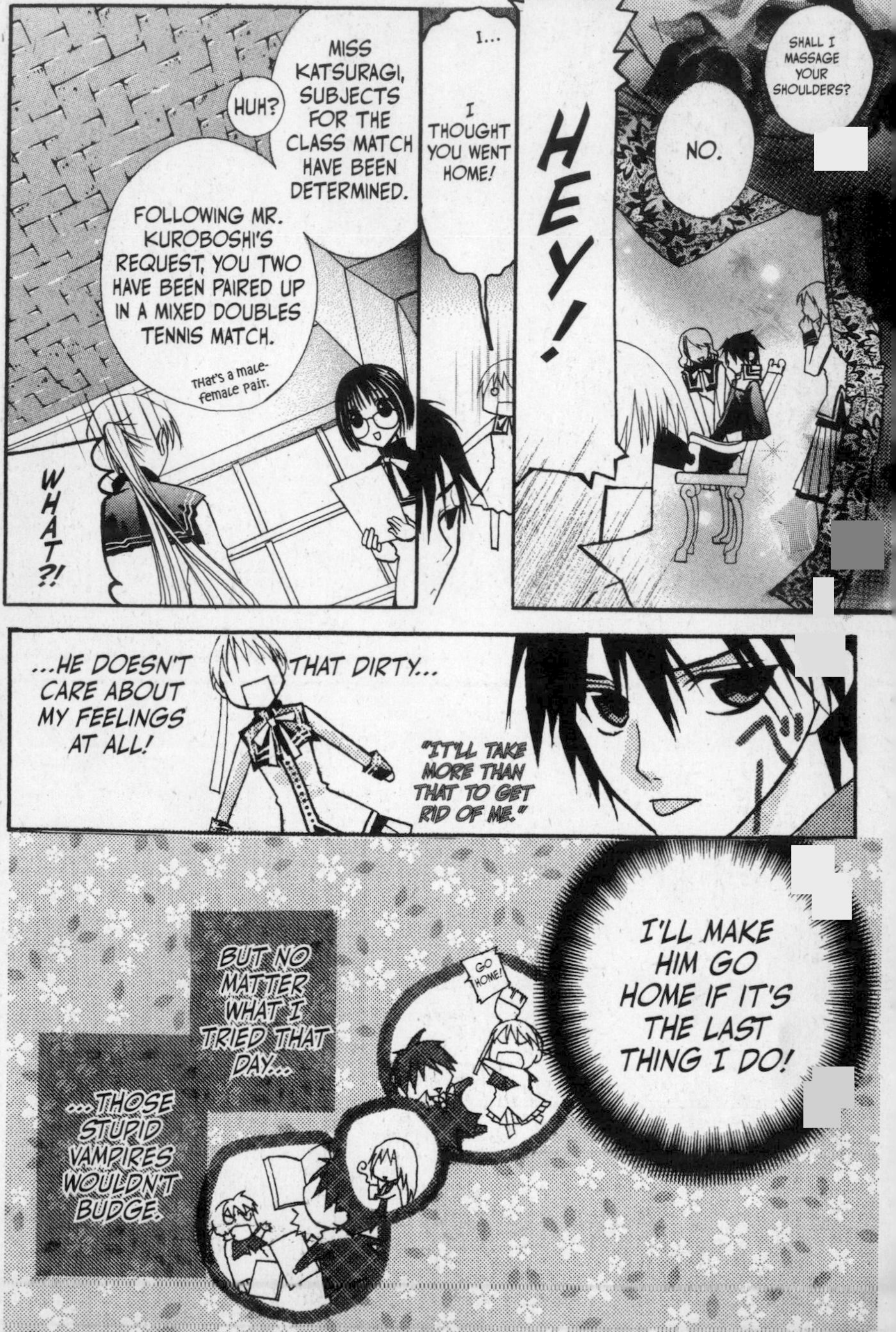
SHALL I MASSAGE YOUR SHOULDERS?
NO.
HEY!
I...
I THOUGHT YOU WENT HOME!
MISS KATSURAGI, SUBJECTS FOR THE CLASS MATCH HAVE BEEN DETERMINED.
HUH?
FOLLOWING MR. KUROBOSHI'S REQUEST, YOU TWO HAVE BEEN PAIRED UP IN A MIXED DOUBLES TENNIS MATCH.
That's a male-female pair.
WHAT?!
"IT'LL TAKE MORE THAN THAT TO GET RID OF ME."
THAT DIRTY...
...HE DOESN'T CARE ABOUT MY FEELINGS AT ALL!
I'LL MAKE HIM GO HOME IF IT'S THE LAST THING I DO!
GO HOME!
BUT NO MATTER WHAT I TRIED THAT DAY...
...THOSE STUPID VAMPIRES WOULDN'T BUDGE.

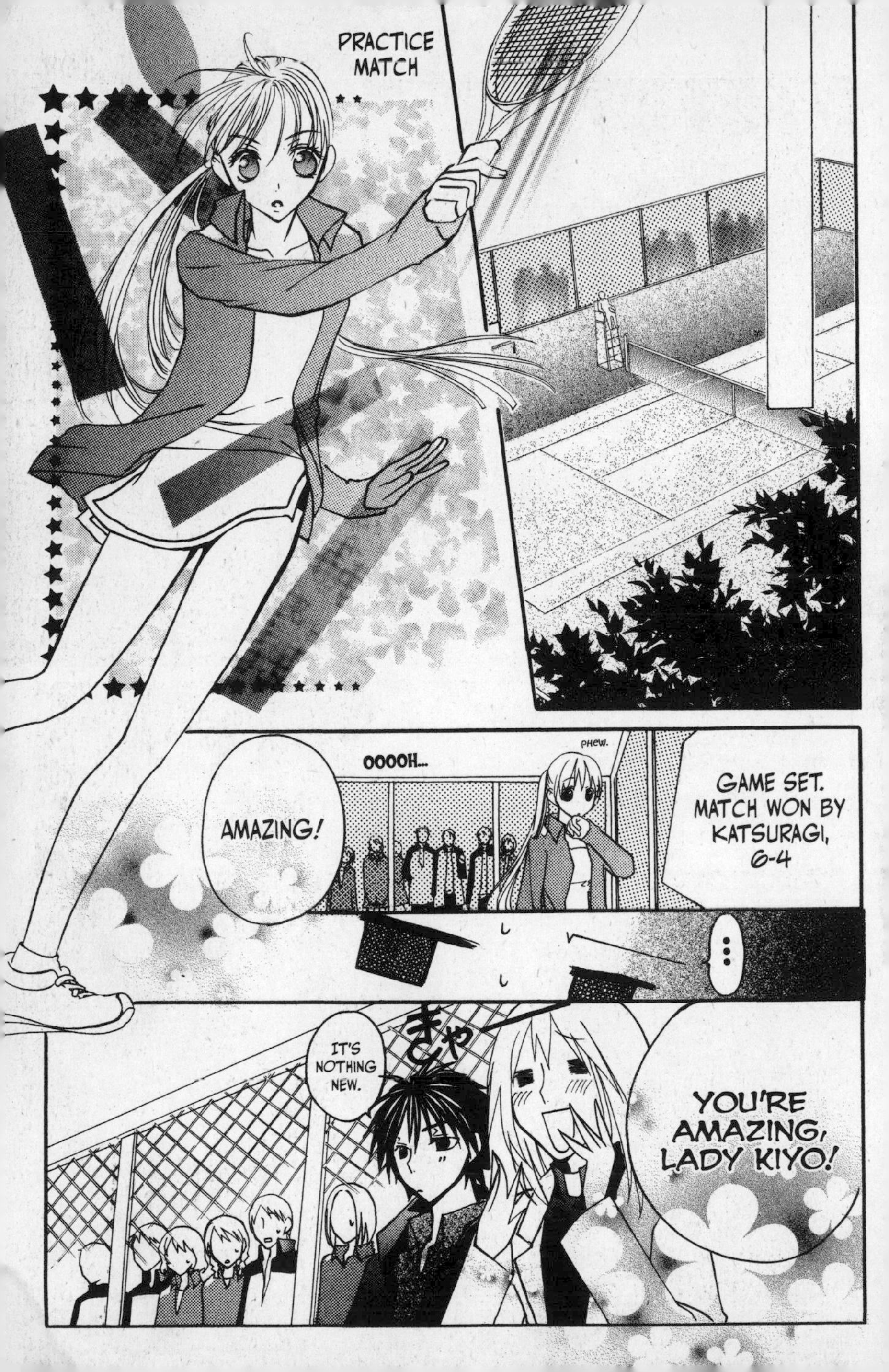
PRACTICE MATCH
GAME SET. MATCH WON BY KATSURAGI, 6-4
PHEW.
OOOOH...
AMAZING!
...
YOU'RE AMAZING, LADY KIYO!
IT'S NOTHING NEW.

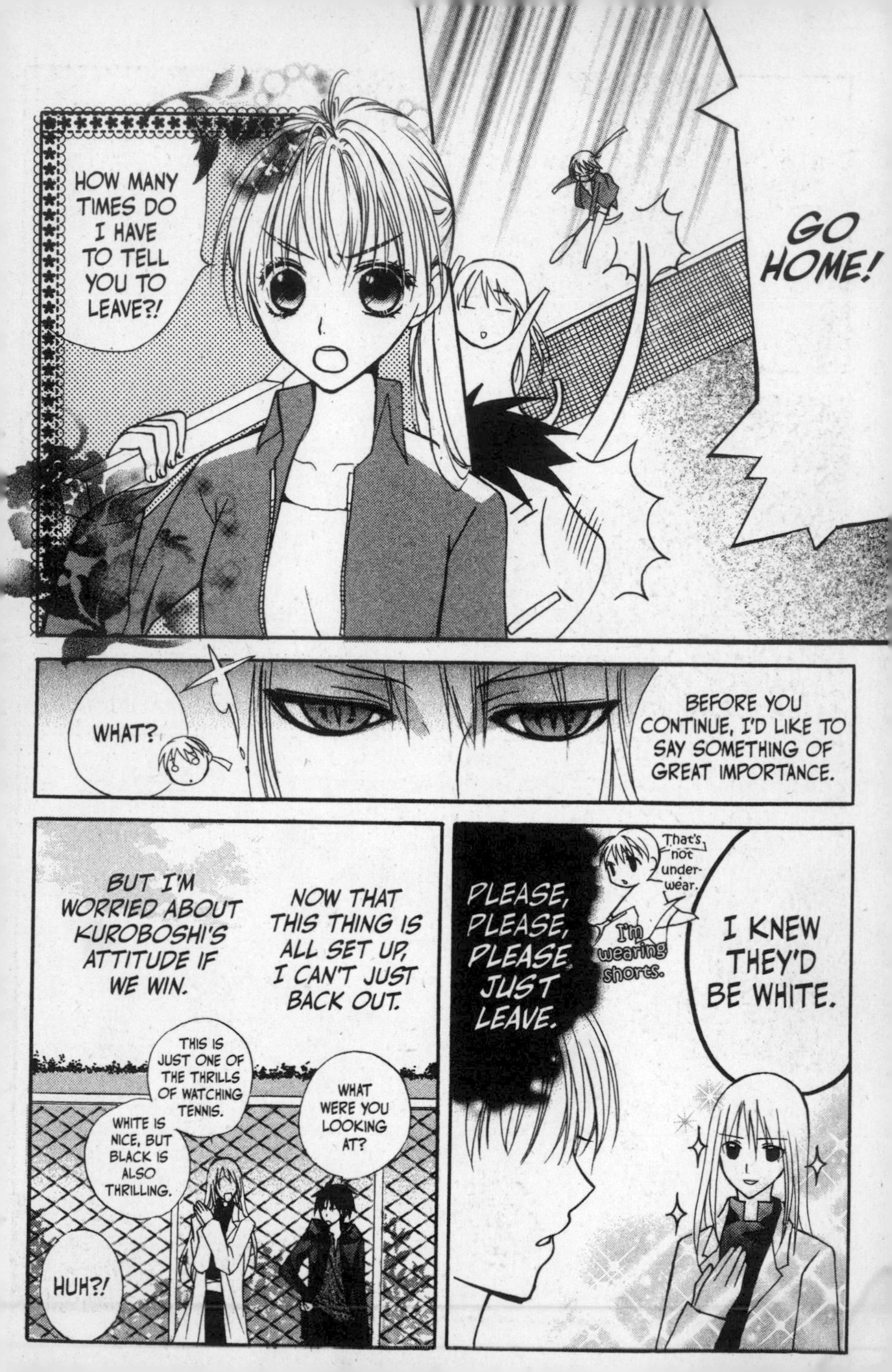
GO HOME!
HOW MANY TIMES DO I HAVE TO TELL YOU TO LEAVE?!
BEFORE YOU CONTINUE, I'D LIKE TO SAY SOMETHING OF GREAT IMPORTANCE.
WHAT?
I KNEW THEY'D BE WHITE.
That's not underwear.
I'm wearing shorts.
PLEASE, PLEASE, PLEASE JUST LEAVE.
NOW THAT THIS THING IS ALL SET UP, I CAN'T JUST BACK OUT.
BUT I'M WORRIED ABOUT KUROBOSHI'S ATTITUDE IF WE WIN.
WHAT WERE YOU LOOKING AT?
THIS IS JUST ONE OF THE THRILLS OF WATCHING TENNIS.
WHITE IS NICE, BUT BLACK IS ALSO THRILLING.
HUH?!

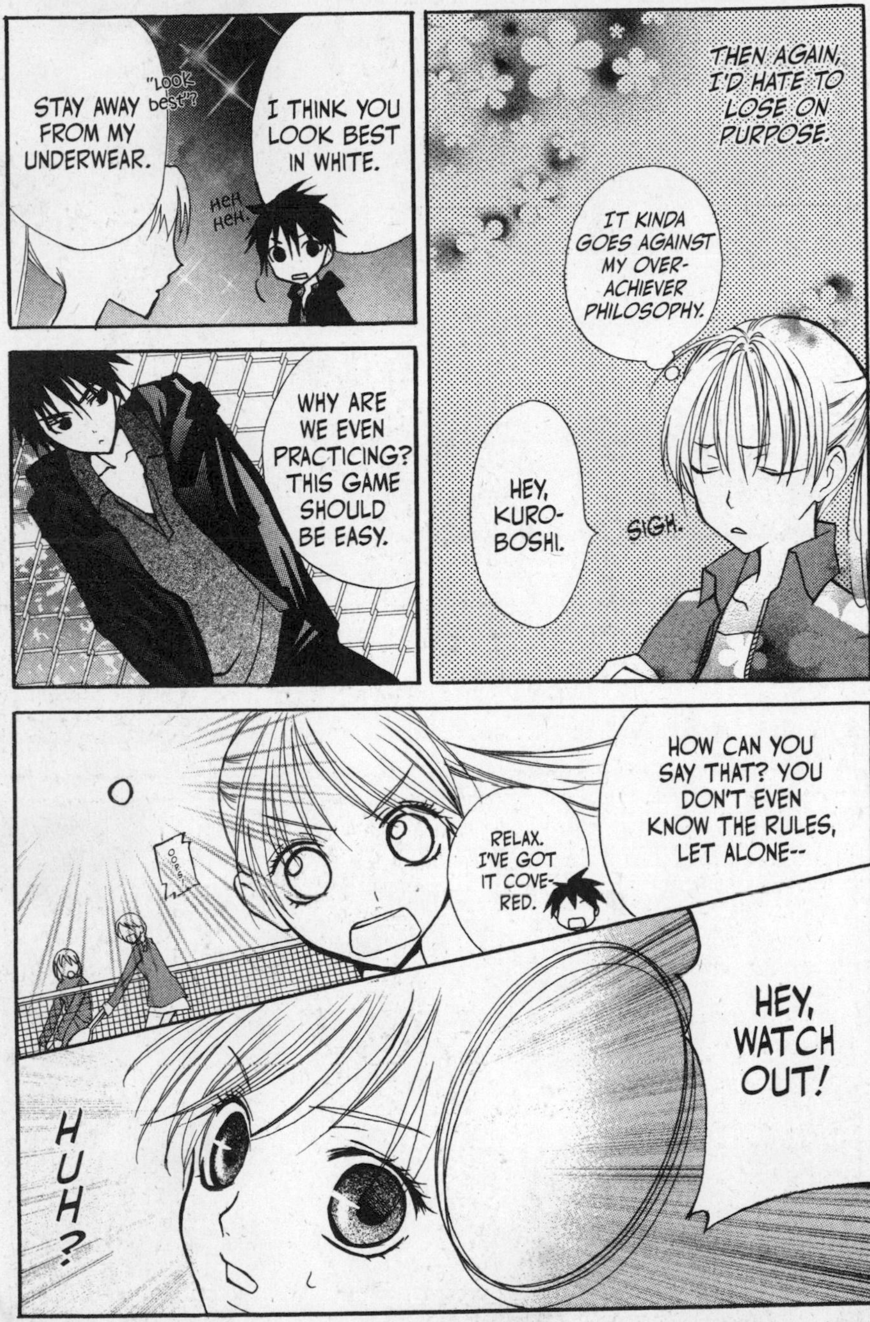

THEN AGAIN, I'D HATE TO LOSE ON PURPOSE.
IT KINDA GOES AGAINST MY OVER-ACHIEVER PHILOSOPHY.
SIGH.
HEY, KURO-BOSHI.
I THINK YOU LOOK BEST IN WHITE.
"LOOK best"?
HEH HEH.
STAY AWAY FROM MY UNDERWEAR.
WHY ARE WE EVEN PRACTICING? THIS GAME SHOULD BE EASY.
HOW CAN YOU SAY THAT? YOU DON'T EVEN KNOW THE RULES, LET ALONE--
RELAX. I'VE GOT IT COVE-RED.
OOPS!
HEY, WATCH OUT!
HUH?

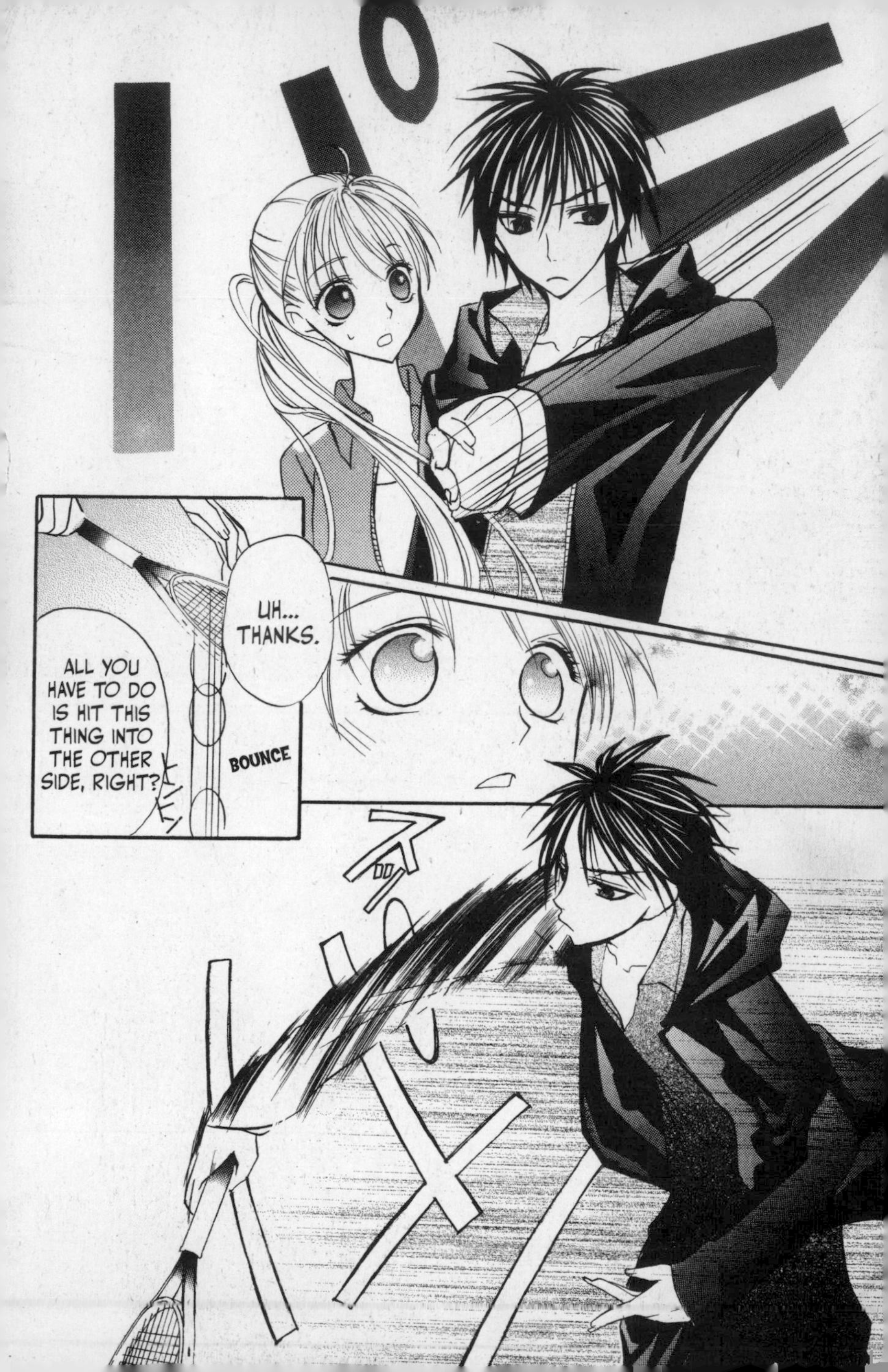
UH... THANKS.
ALL YOU HAVE TO DO IS HIT THIS THING INTO THE OTHER SIDE, RIGHT?
BOUNCE

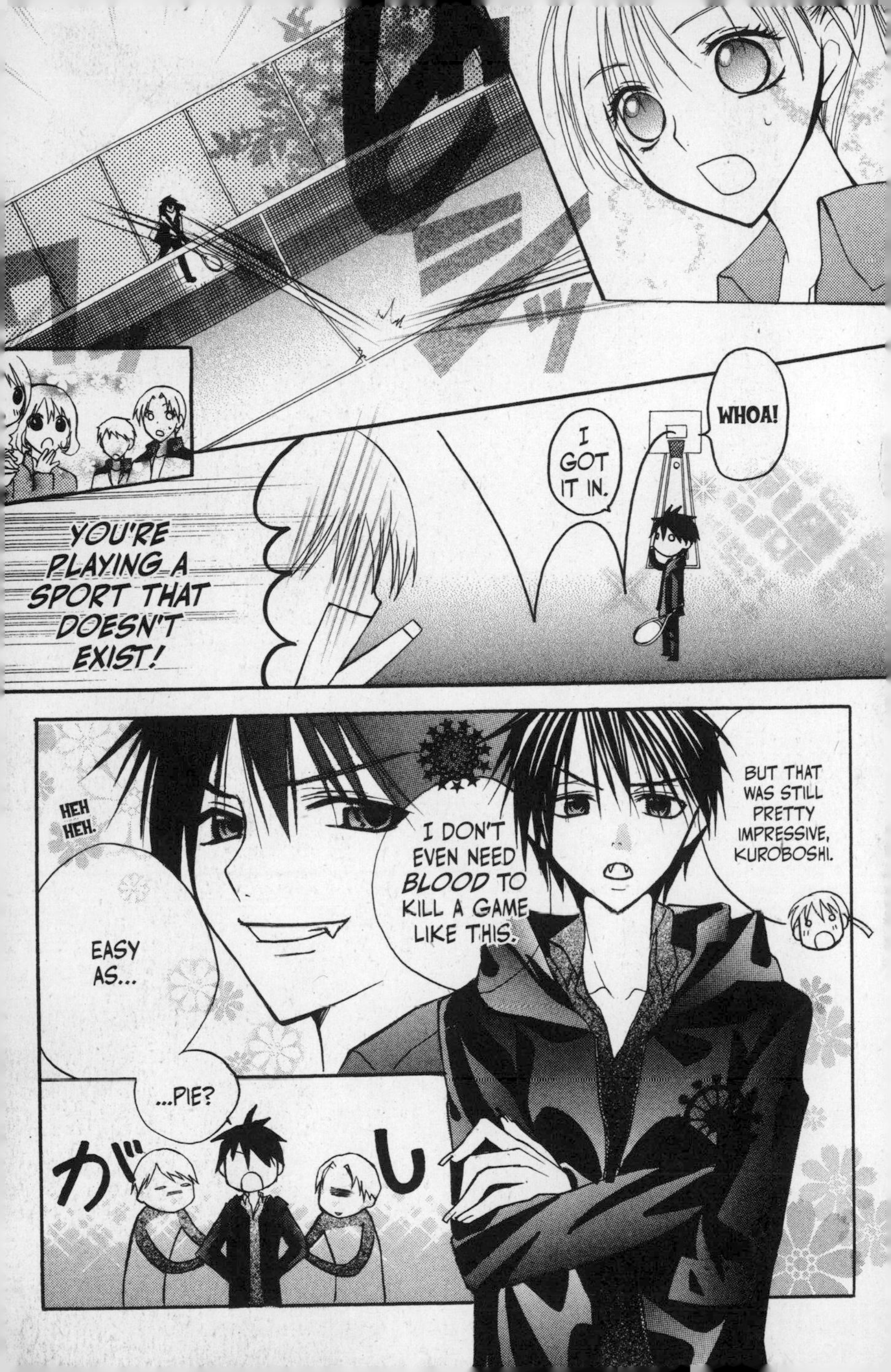
WHOA!
I GOT IT IN.
YOU'RE PLAYING A SPORT THAT DOESN'T EXIST!
BUT THAT WAS STILL PRETTY IMPRESSIVE, KUROBOSHI.
I DON'T EVEN NEED *BLOOD* TO KILL A GAME LIKE THIS.
HEH HEH.
EASY AS...
...PIE?
がし

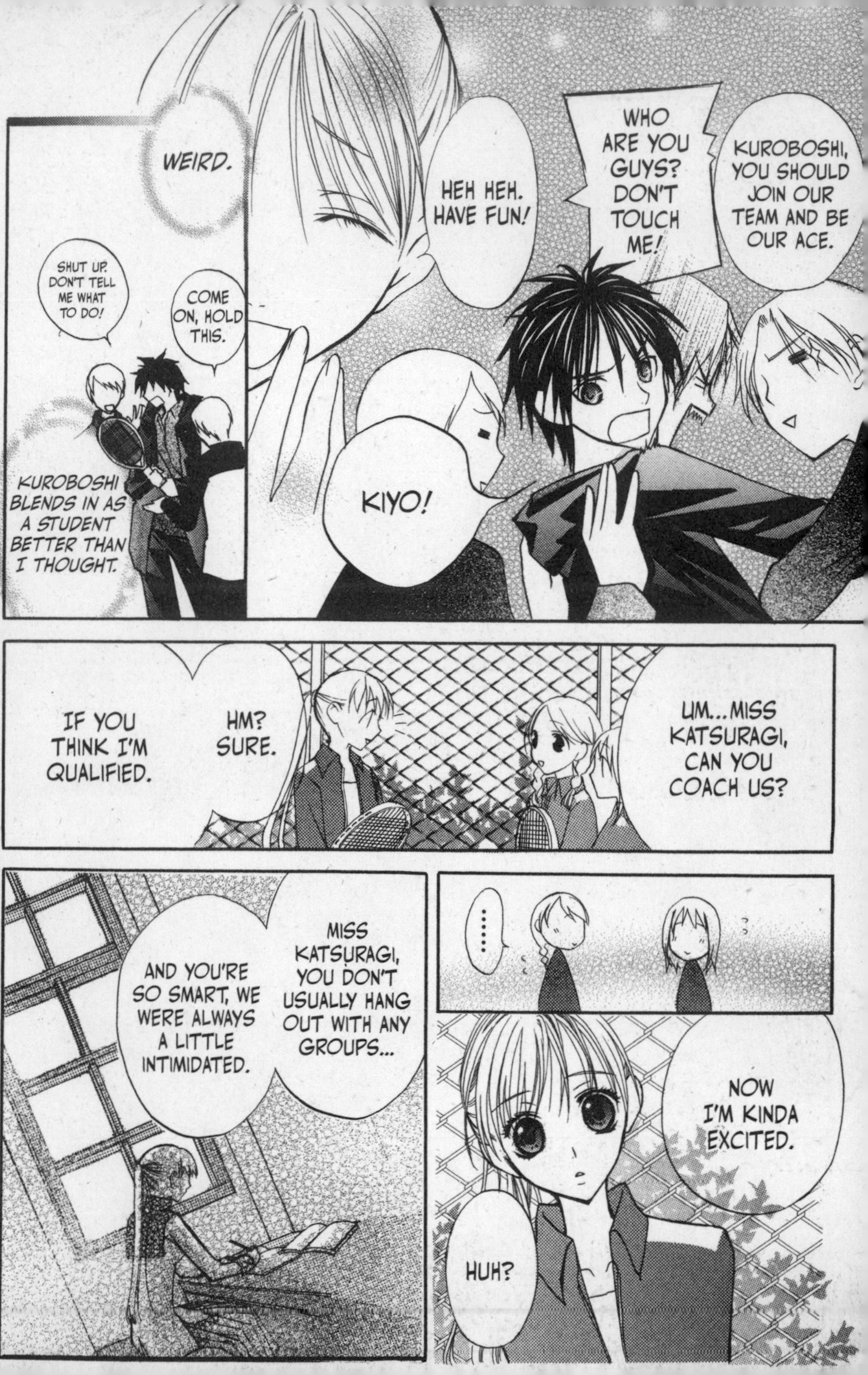
KUROBOSHI, YOU SHOULD JOIN OUR TEAM AND BE OUR ACE.
WHO ARE YOU GUYS? DON'T TOUCH ME!
HEH HEH. HAVE FUN!
KIYO!
WEIRD.
COME ON, HOLD THIS.
SHUT UP. DON'T TELL ME WHAT TO DO!
KUROBOSHI BLENDS IN AS A STUDENT BETTER THAN I THOUGHT.
UM...MISS KATSURAGI, CAN YOU COACH US?
HM? SURE.
IF YOU THINK I'M QUALIFIED.
......
NOW I'M KINDA EXCITED.
HUH?
MISS KATSURAGI, YOU DON'T USUALLY HANG OUT WITH ANY GROUPS...
AND YOU'RE SO SMART, WE WERE ALWAYS A LITTLE INTIMIDATED.

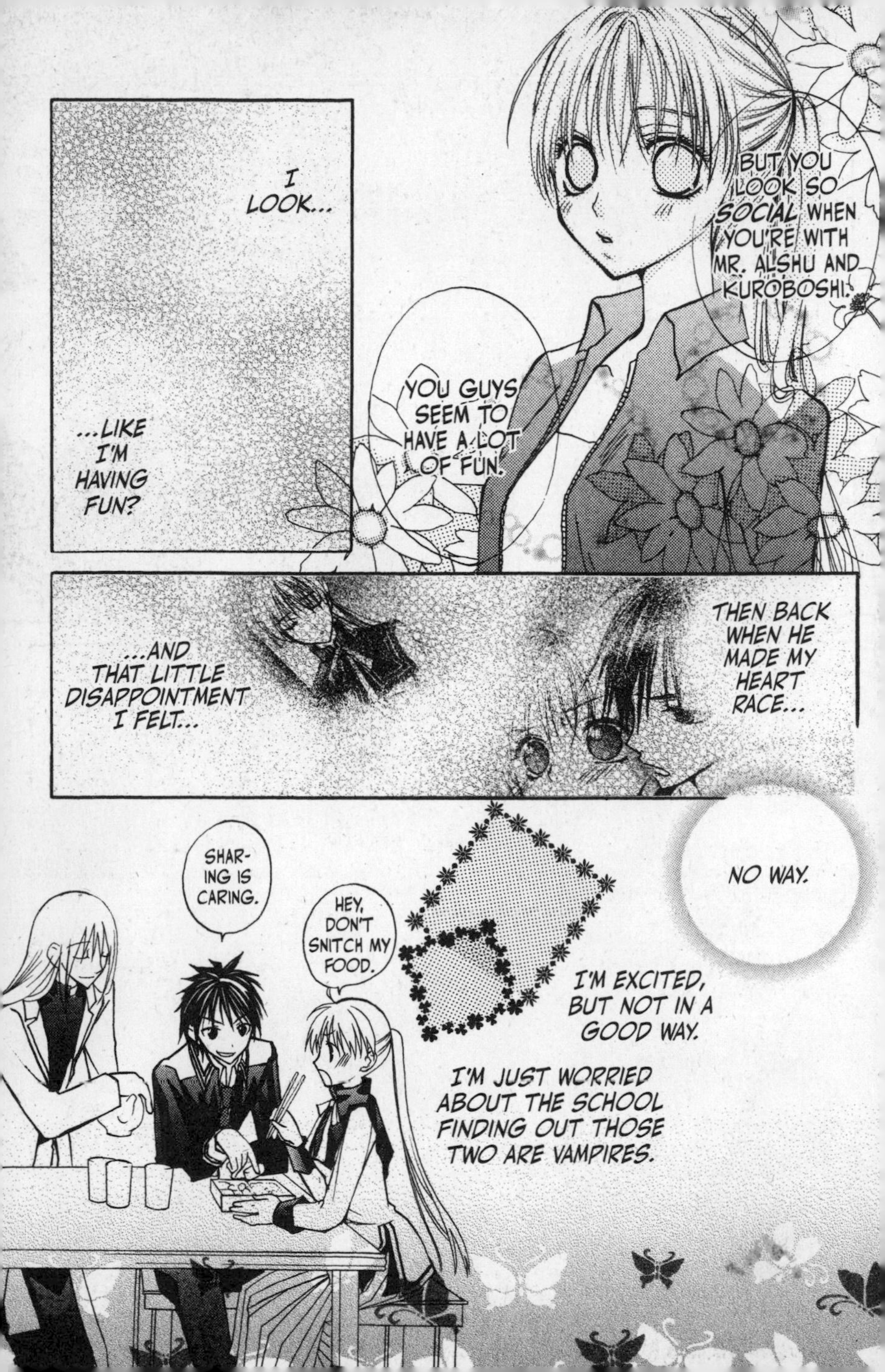

BUT YOU LOOK SO SOCIAL WHEN YOU'RE WITH MR. ALSHU AND KUROBOSHI.
YOU GUYS SEEM TO HAVE A LOT OF FUN.
I LOOK...
...LIKE I'M HAVING FUN?
THEN BACK WHEN HE MADE MY HEART RACE...
...AND THAT LITTLE DISAPPOINTMENT I FELT...
NO WAY.
I'M EXCITED, BUT NOT IN A GOOD WAY.
I'M JUST WORRIED ABOUT THE SCHOOL FINDING OUT THOSE TWO ARE VAMPIRES.
HEY, DON'T SNITCH MY FOOD.
SHARING IS CARING.

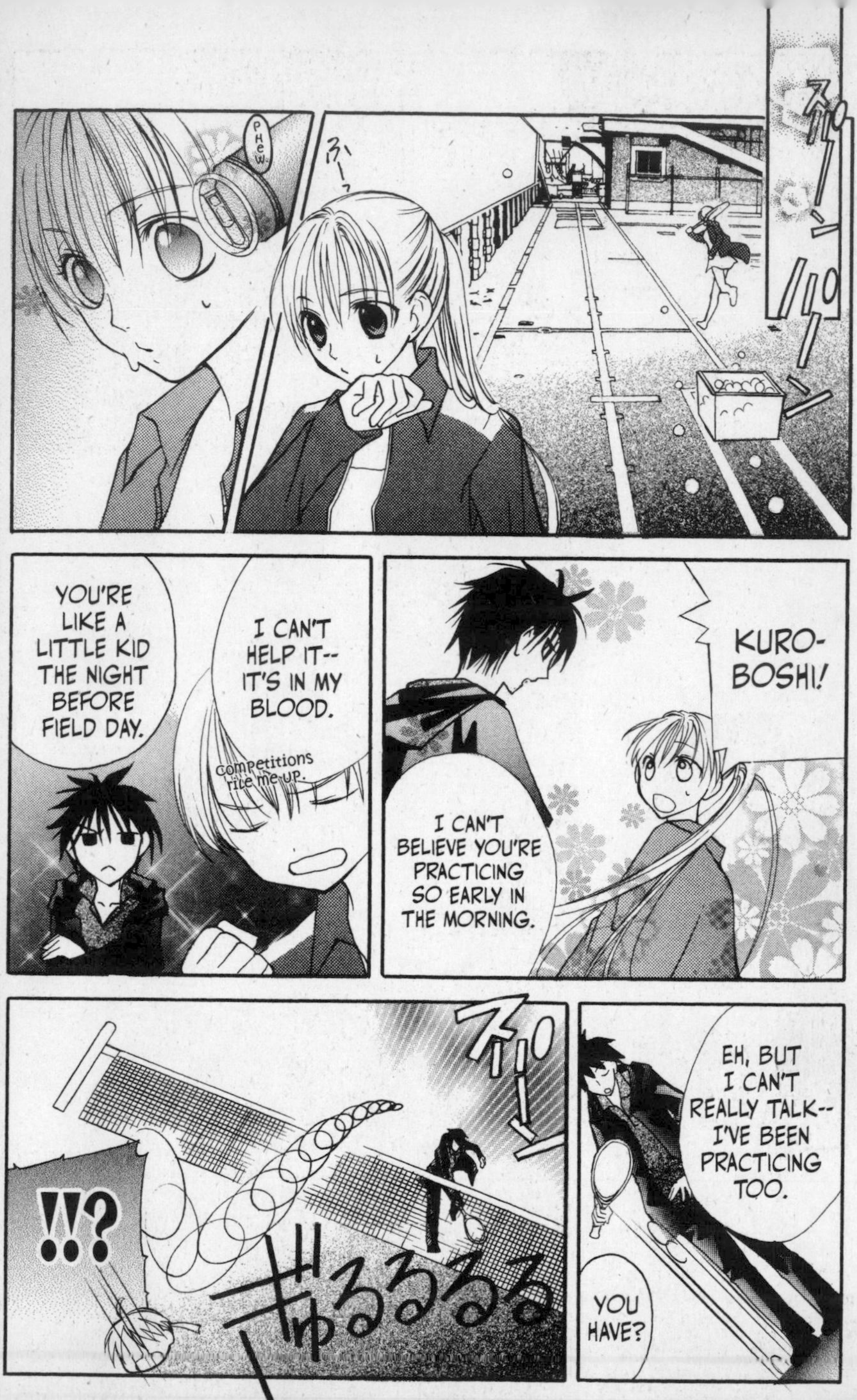

ふー
PHEW
KURO-BOSHI!
I CAN'T BELIEVE YOU'RE PRACTICING SO EARLY IN THE MORNING.
YOU'RE LIKE A LITTLE KID THE NIGHT BEFORE FIELD DAY.
I CAN'T HELP IT-- IT'S IN MY BLOOD.
competitions rile me up.
EH, BUT I CAN'T REALLY TALK-- I'VE BEEN PRACTICING TOO.
YOU HAVE?
ぎゅるるるるる
!!?

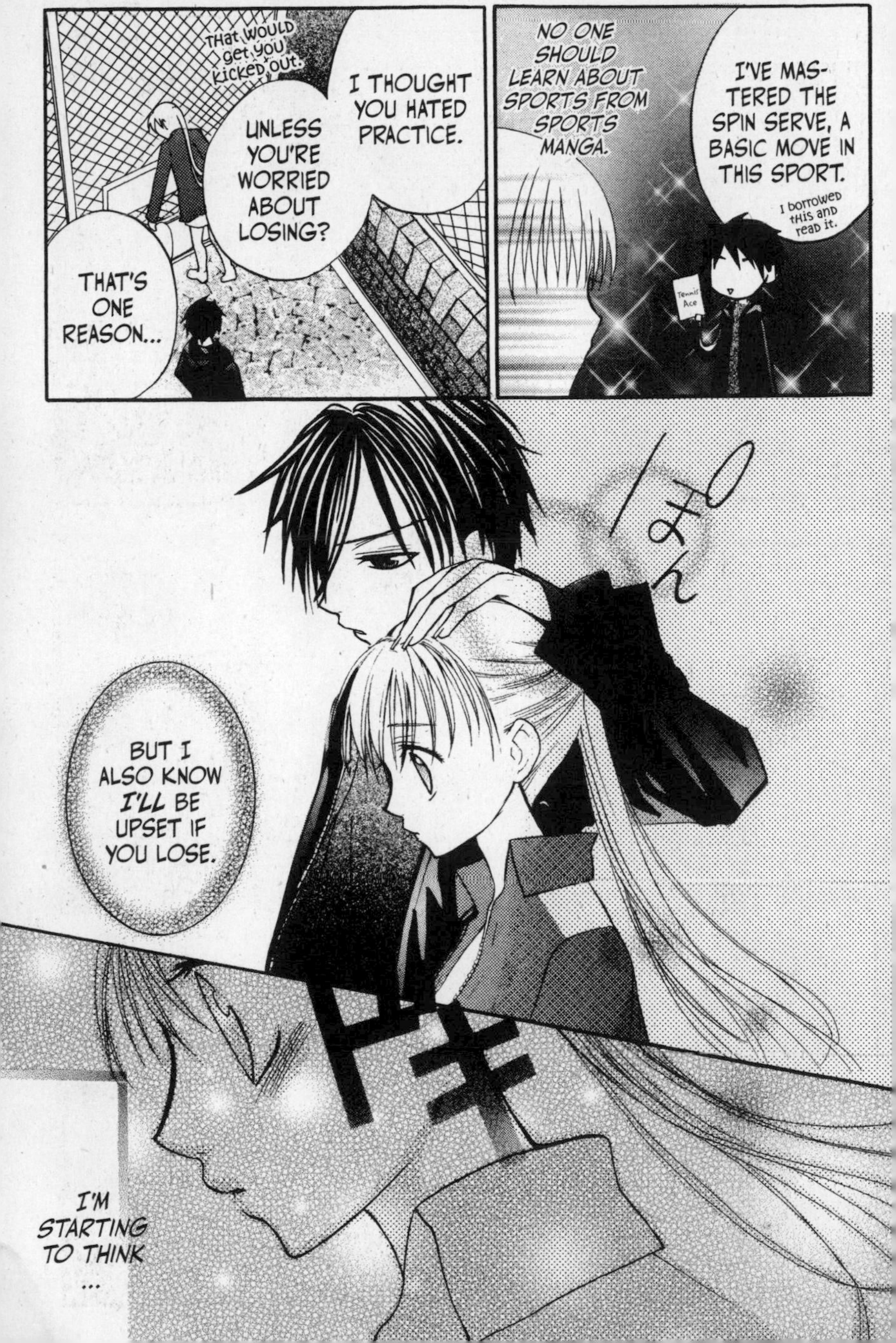
I'VE MAS-TERED THE SPIN SERVE, A BASIC MOVE IN THIS SPORT.
NO ONE SHOULD LEARN ABOUT SPORTS FROM SPORTS MANGA.
I borrowed this and read it.
Tennis Ace
I THOUGHT YOU HATED PRACTICE.
That would get you kicked out.
UNLESS YOU'RE WORRIED ABOUT LOSING?
THAT'S ONE REASON...
ぽん
BUT I ALSO KNOW *I'LL* BE UPSET IF YOU LOSE.
ドキ
I'M STARTING TO THINK ...

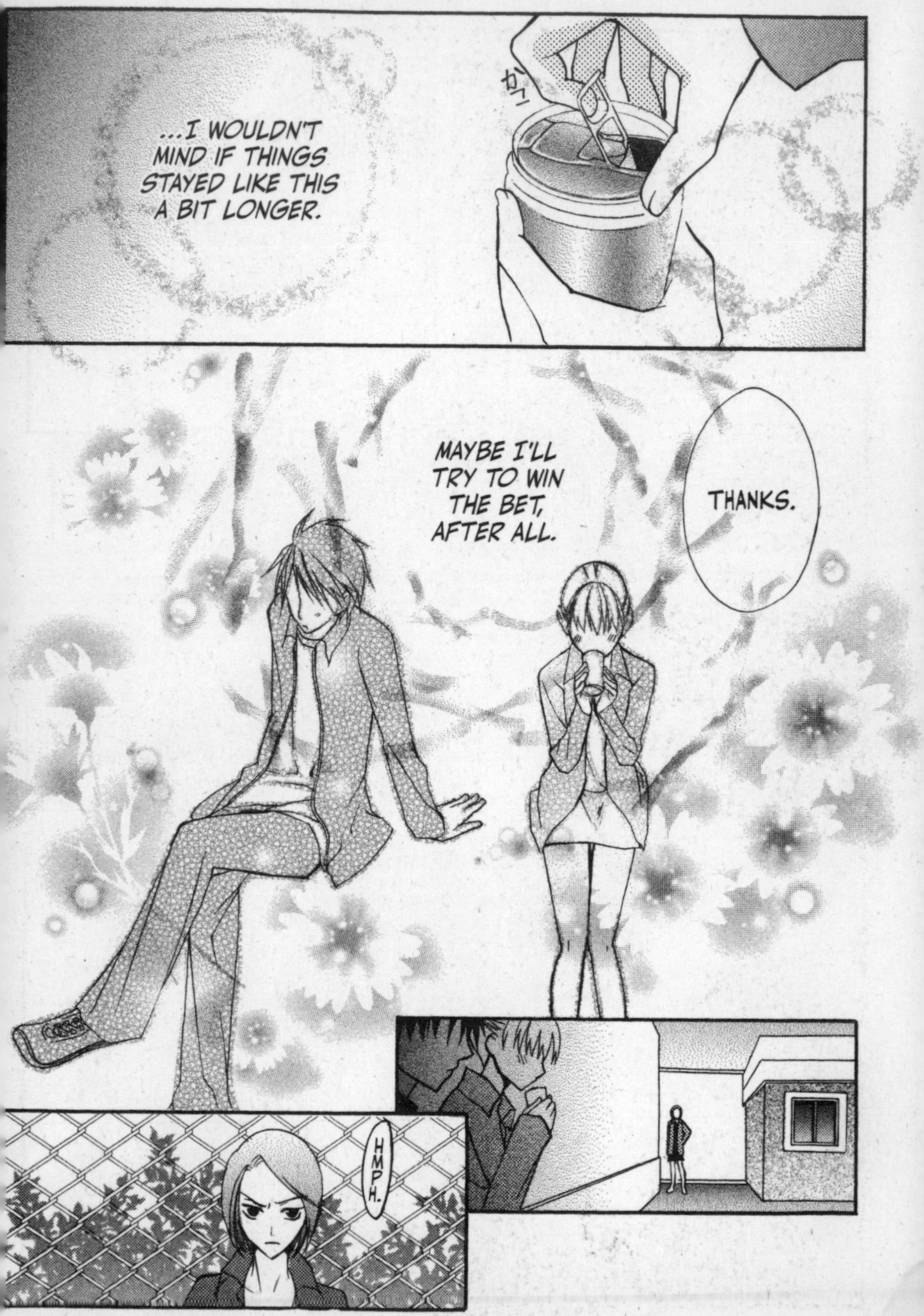
ガッ
...I WOULDN'T MIND IF THINGS STAYED LIKE THIS A BIT LONGER.
THANKS.
MAYBE I'LL TRY TO WIN THE BET, AFTER ALL.
HMPH.

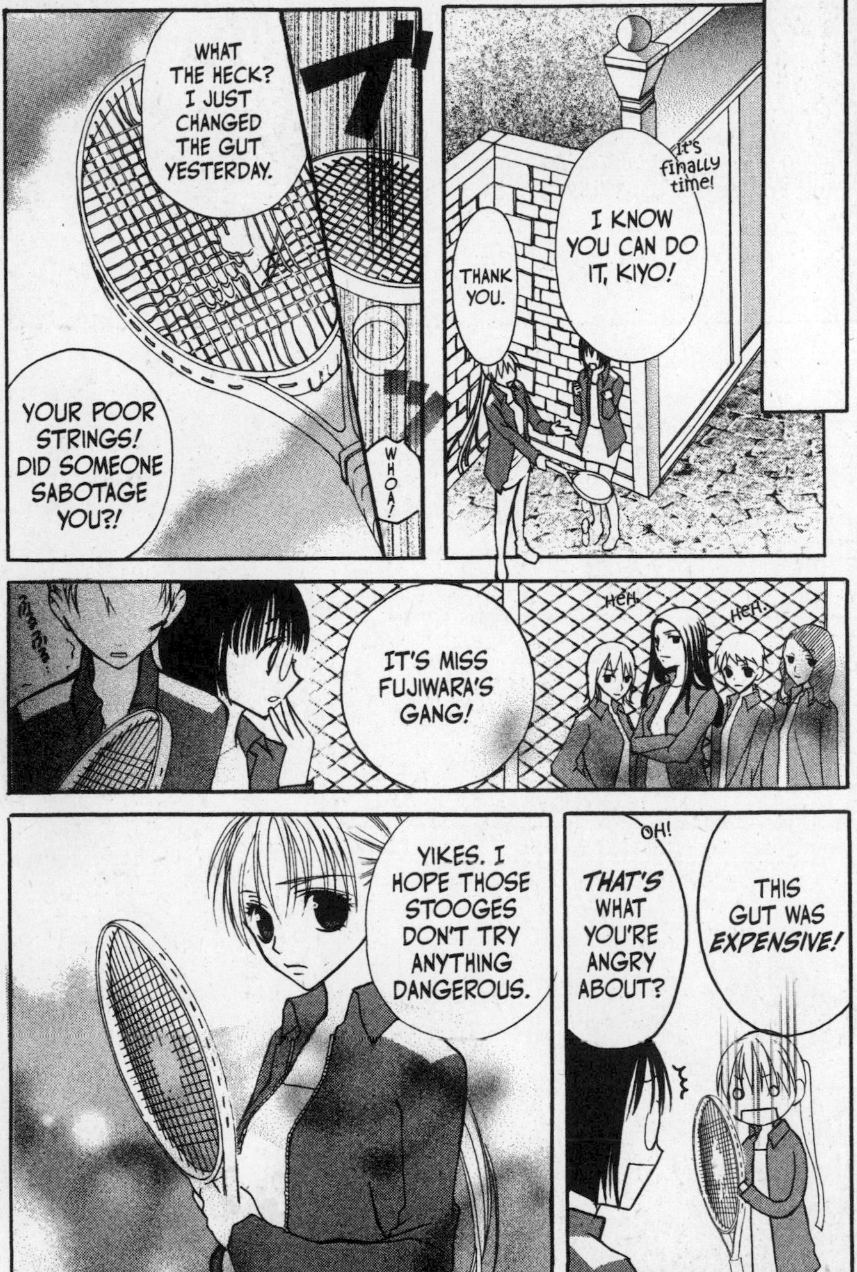
It's finally time!
I KNOW YOU CAN DO IT, KIYO!
THANK YOU.
WHAT THE HECK? I JUST CHANGED THE GUT YESTERDAY.
WHOA!
YOUR POOR STRINGS! DID SOMEONE SABOTAGE YOU?!
HEH.
HEH.
IT'S MISS FUJIWARA'S GANG!
THIS GUT WAS *EXPENSIVE!*
OH!
THAT'S WHAT YOU'RE ANGRY ABOUT?
YIKES. I HOPE THOSE STOOGES DON'T TRY ANYTHING DANGEROUS.

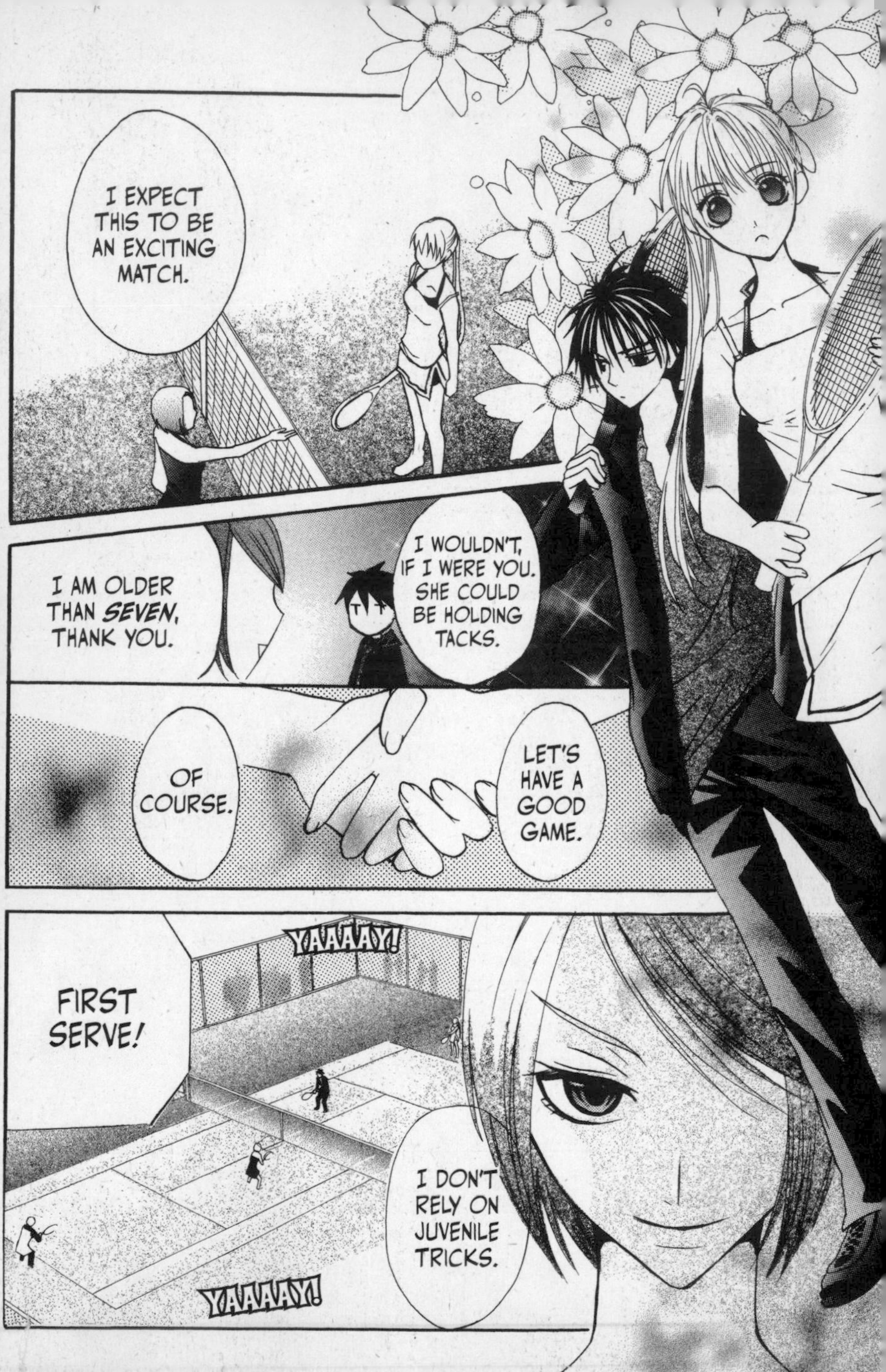
I EXPECT THIS TO BE AN EXCITING MATCH.
I WOULDN'T, IF I WERE YOU. SHE COULD BE HOLDING TACKS.
I AM OLDER THAN *SEVEN*, THANK YOU.
LET'S HAVE A GOOD GAME.
OF COURSE.
I DON'T RELY ON JUVENILE TRICKS.
YAAAAY!
FIRST SERVE!
YAAAAY!

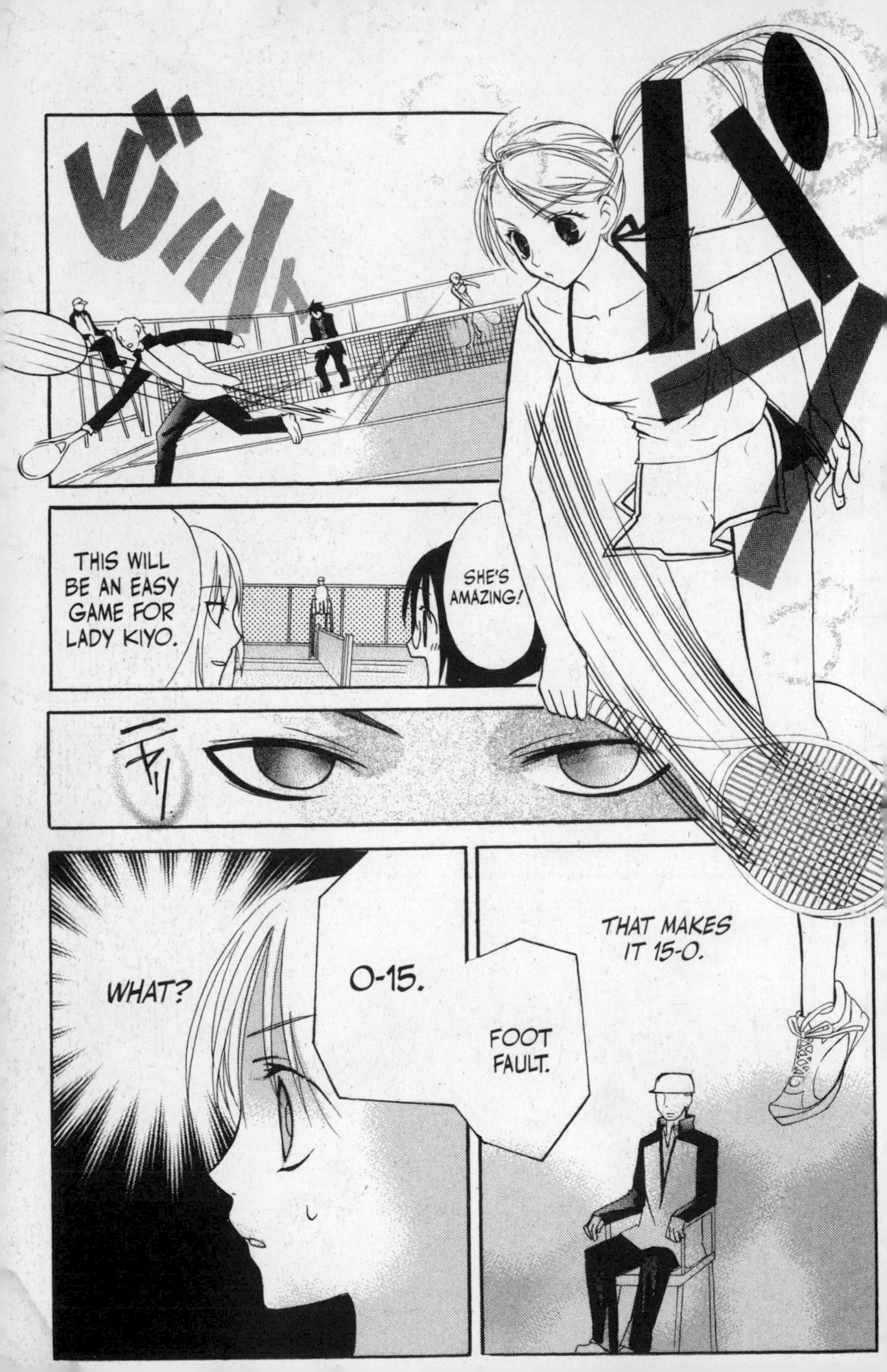
SHE'S AMAZING!
THIS WILL BE AN EASY GAME FOR LADY KIYO.
THAT MAKES IT 15-0.
FOOT FAULT.
0-15.
WHAT?

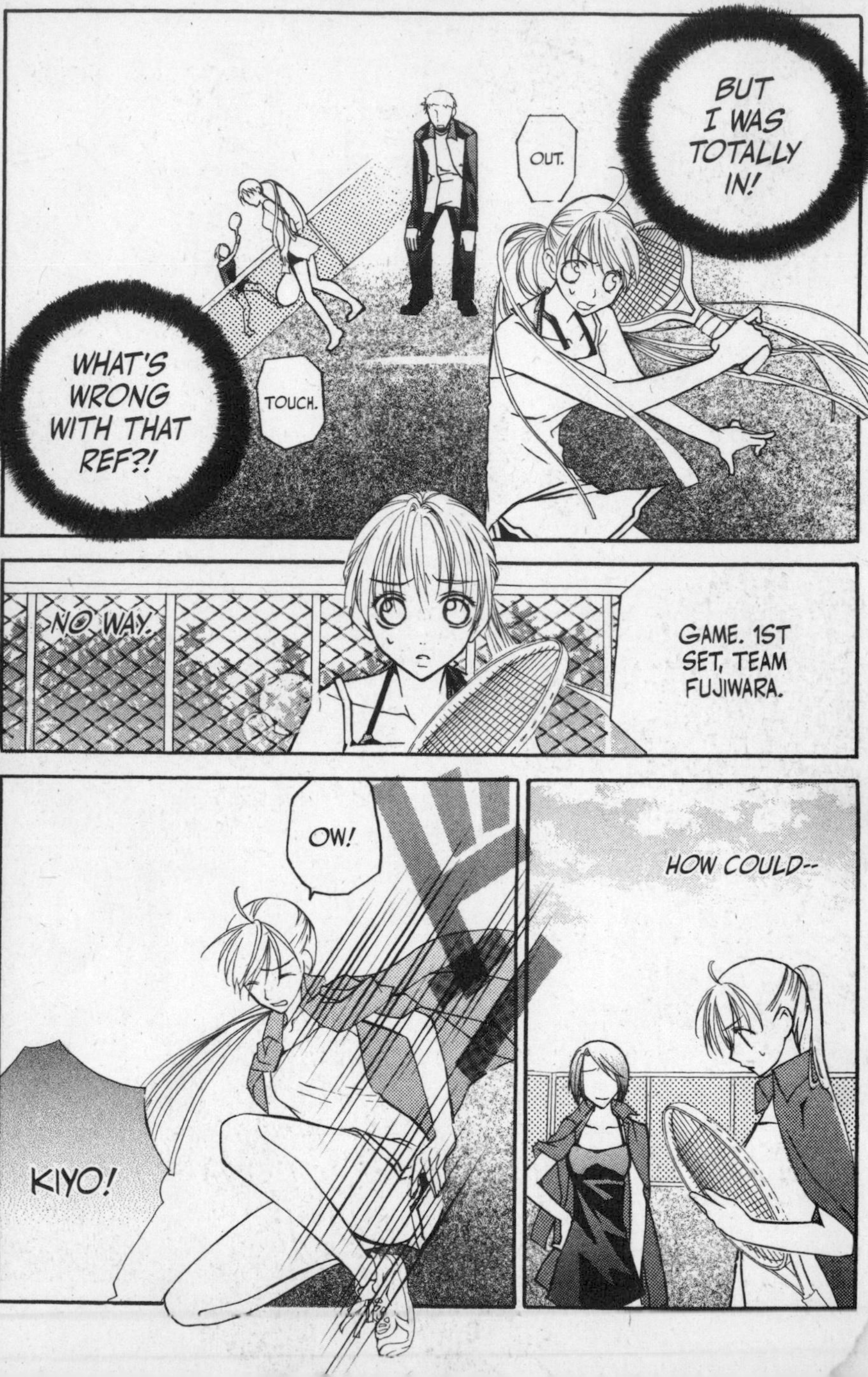
BUT I WAS TOTALLY IN!
OUT.
TOUCH.
WHAT'S WRONG WITH THAT REF?!
GAME. 1ST SET, TEAM FUJIWARA.
NO WAY.
HOW COULD--
OW!
KIYO!

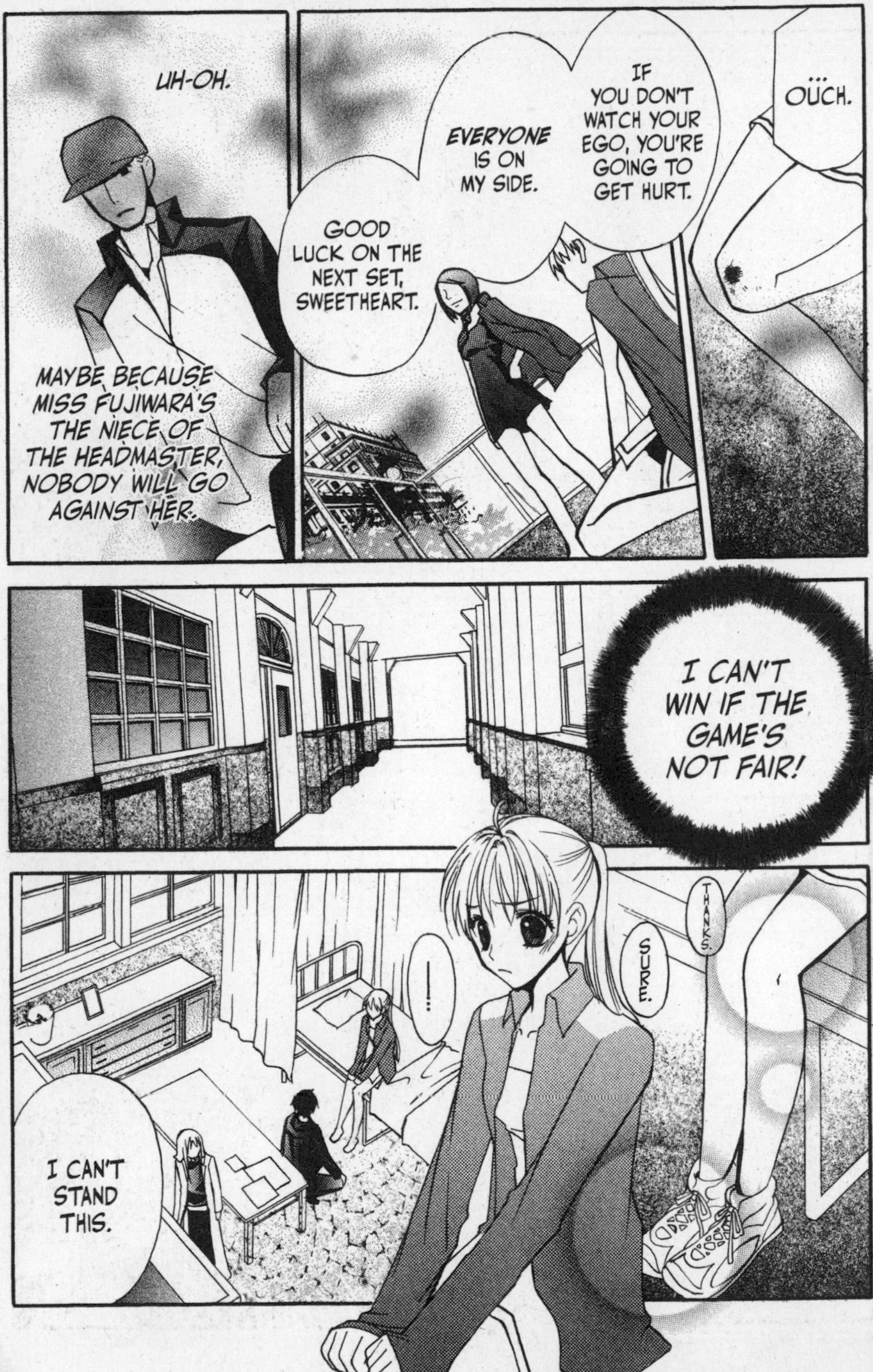
...OUCH.
IF YOU DON'T WATCH YOUR EGO, YOU'RE GOING TO GET HURT.
EVERYONE IS ON MY SIDE.
GOOD LUCK ON THE NEXT SET, SWEETHEART.
UH-OH.
MAYBE BECAUSE MISS FUJIWARA'S THE NIECE OF THE HEADMASTER, NOBODY WILL GO AGAINST HER.
I CAN'T WIN IF THE GAME'S NOT FAIR!
THANKS.
SURE.
!
I CAN'T STAND THIS.

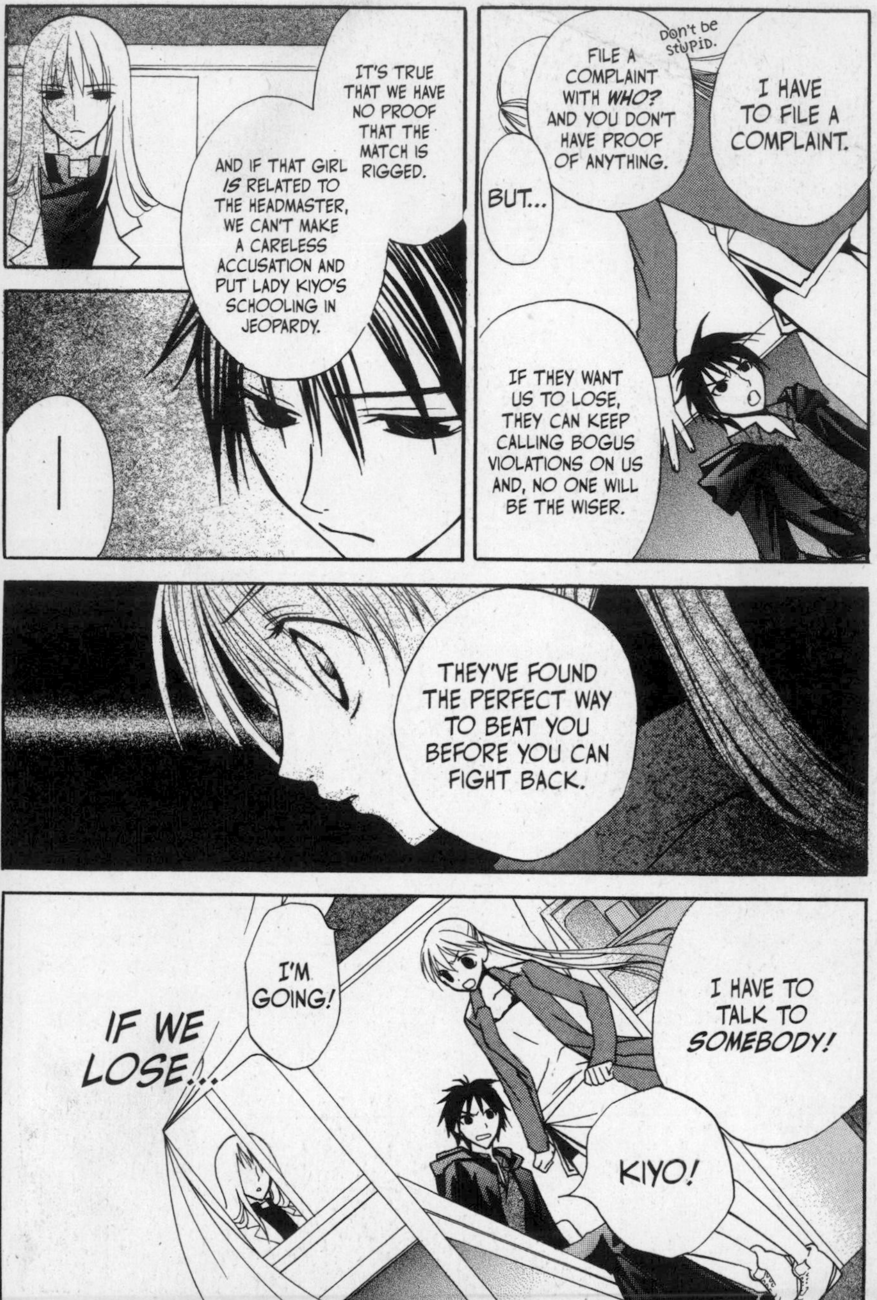
I HAVE TO FILE A COMPLAINT.
Don't be stupid.
FILE A COMPLAINT WITH *WHO?* AND YOU DON'T HAVE PROOF OF ANYTHING.
BUT...
IF THEY WANT US TO LOSE, THEY CAN KEEP CALLING BOGUS VIOLATIONS ON US AND, NO ONE WILL BE THE WISER.
IT'S TRUE THAT WE HAVE NO PROOF THAT THE MATCH IS RIGGED.
AND IF THAT GIRL *IS* RELATED TO THE HEADMASTER, WE CAN'T MAKE A CARELESS ACCUSATION AND PUT LADY KIYO'S SCHOOLING IN JEOPARDY.
THEY'VE FOUND THE PERFECT WAY TO BEAT YOU BEFORE YOU CAN FIGHT BACK.
I HAVE TO TALK TO *SOMEBODY!*
I'M GOING!
KIYO!
IF WE LOSE...

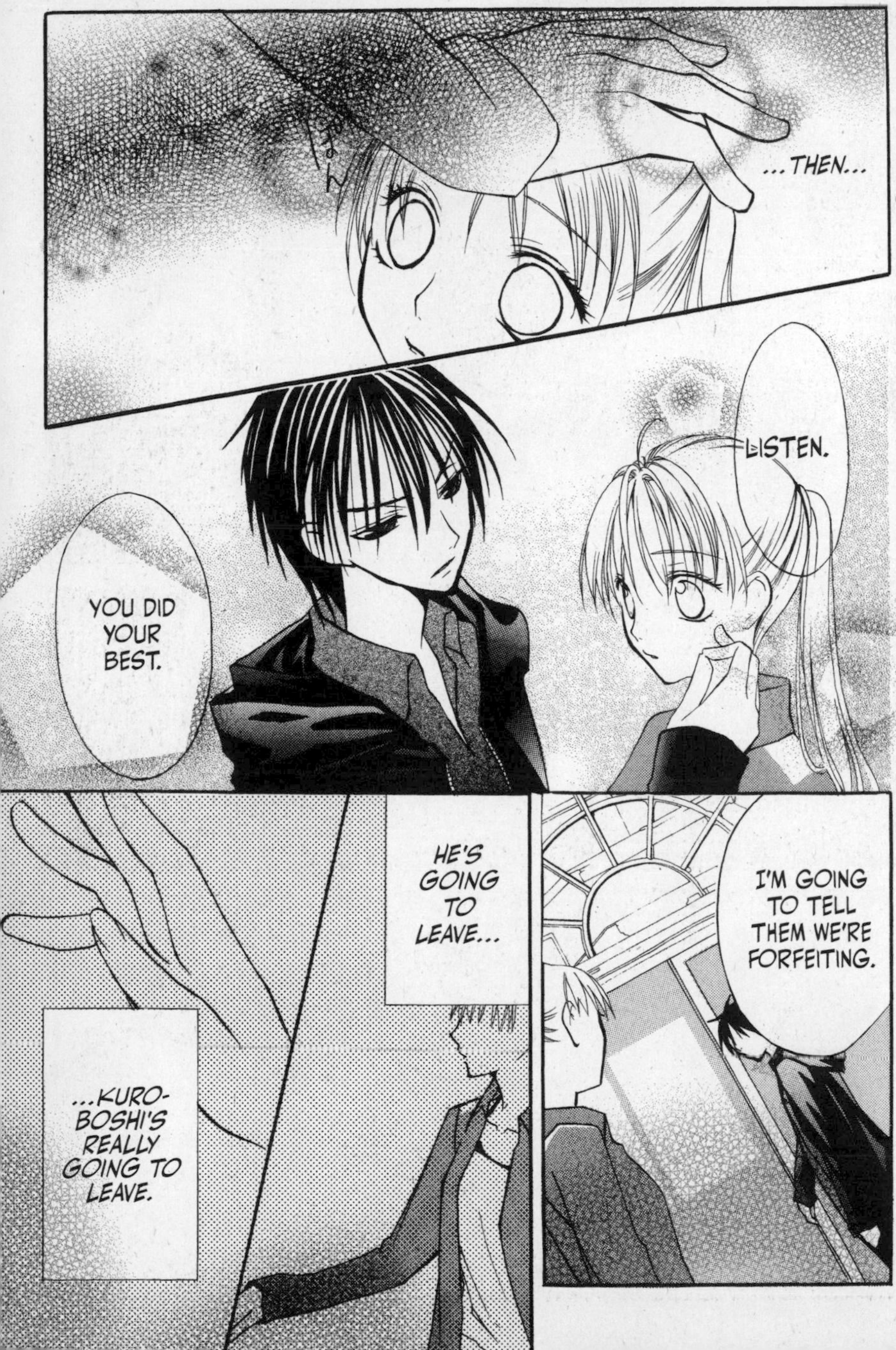
...THEN...
LISTEN.
YOU DID YOUR BEST.
I'M GOING TO TELL THEM WE'RE FORFEITING.
HE'S GOING TO LEAVE...
...KURO-BOSHI'S REALLY GOING TO LEAVE.

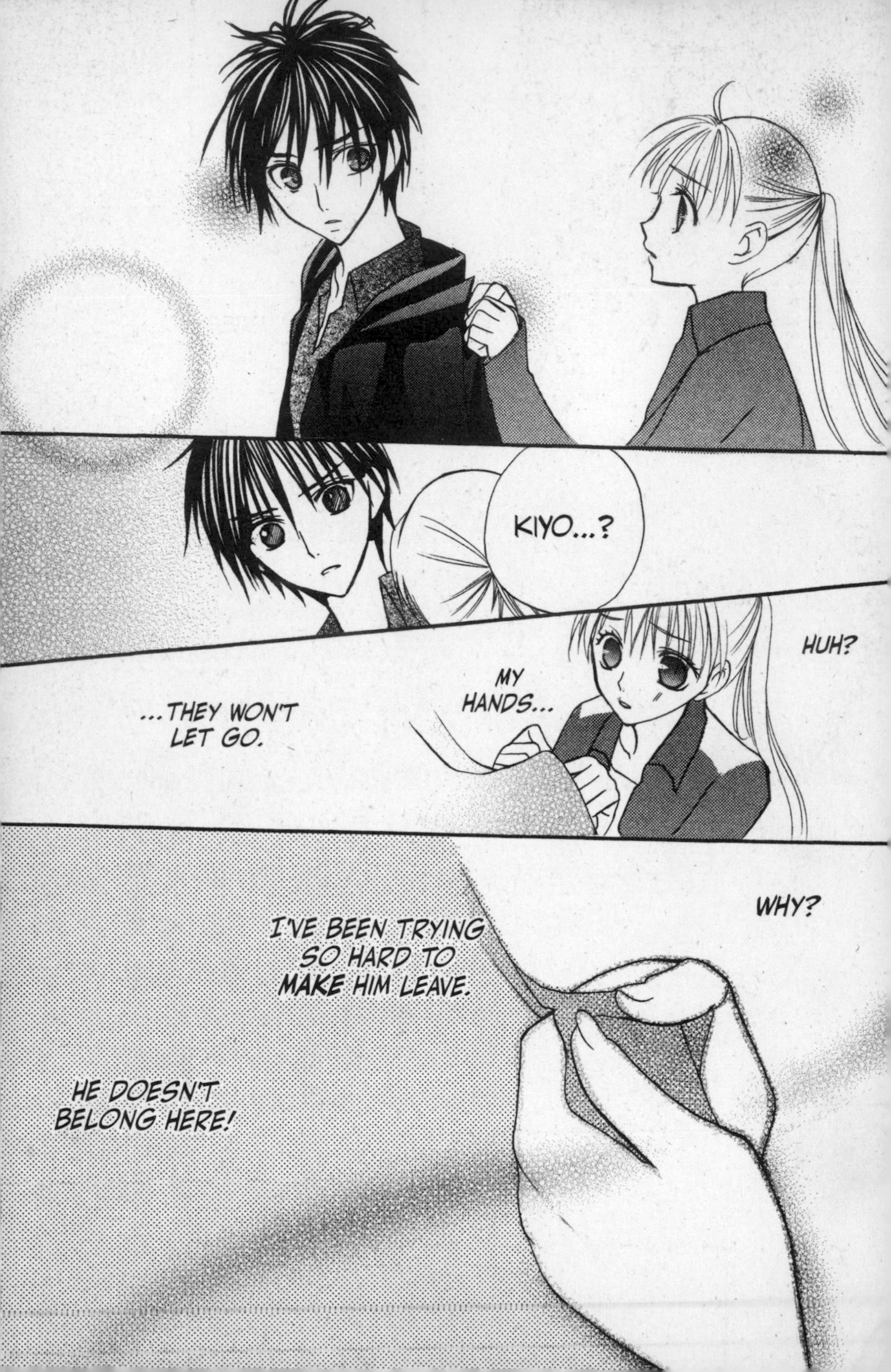
KIYO...?
HUH?
MY HANDS...
...THEY WON'T LET GO.
WHY?
I'VE BEEN TRYING SO HARD TO MAKE HIM LEAVE.
HE DOESN'T BELONG HERE!

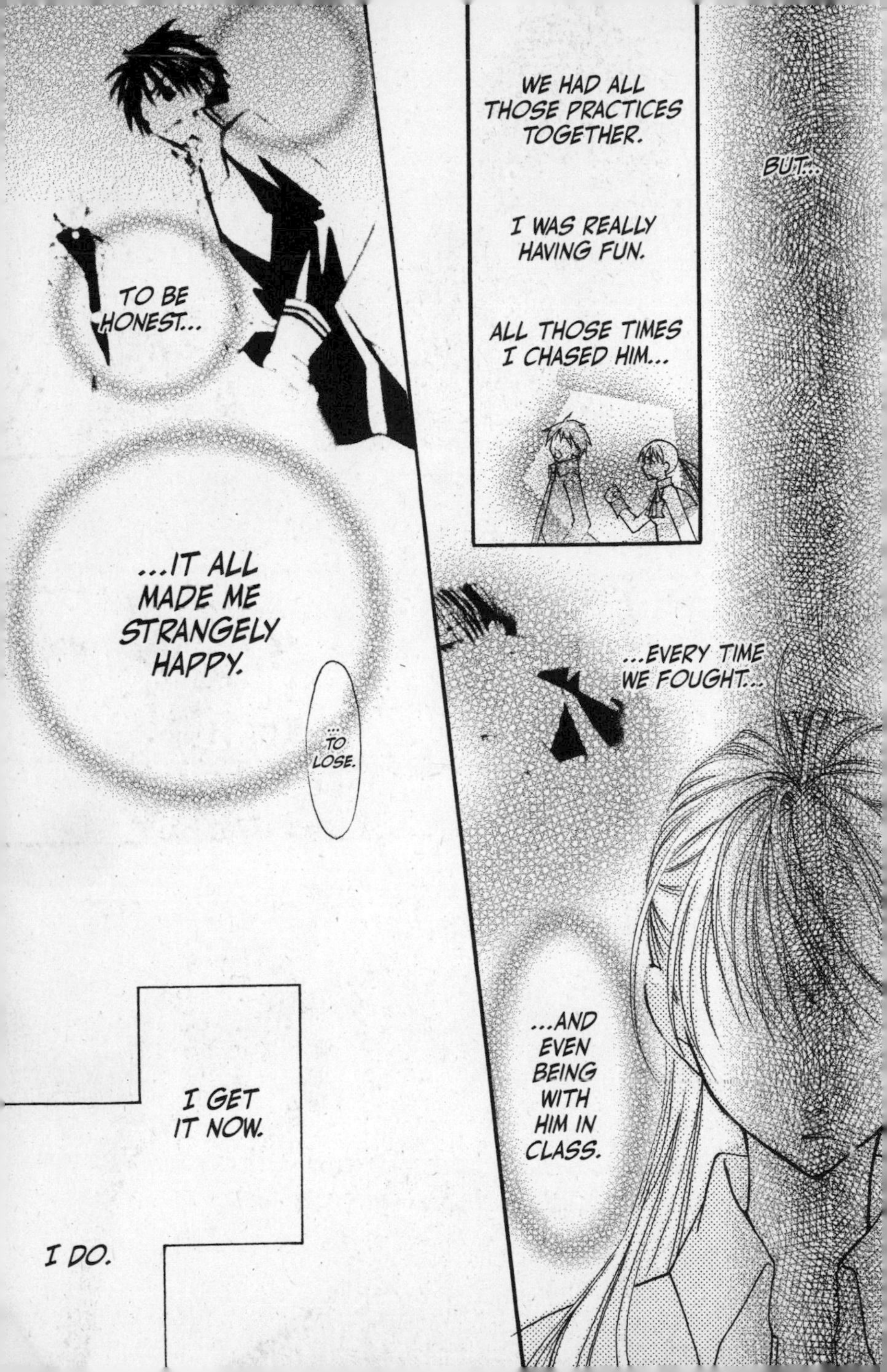
WE HAD ALL THOSE PRACTICES TOGETHER.
I WAS REALLY HAVING FUN.
ALL THOSE TIMES I CHASED HIM...
...EVERY TIME WE FOUGHT...
...AND EVEN BEING WITH HIM IN CLASS.
BUT...
TO BE HONEST...
...IT ALL MADE ME STRANGELY HAPPY.
...TO LOSE.
I GET IT NOW.
I DO.

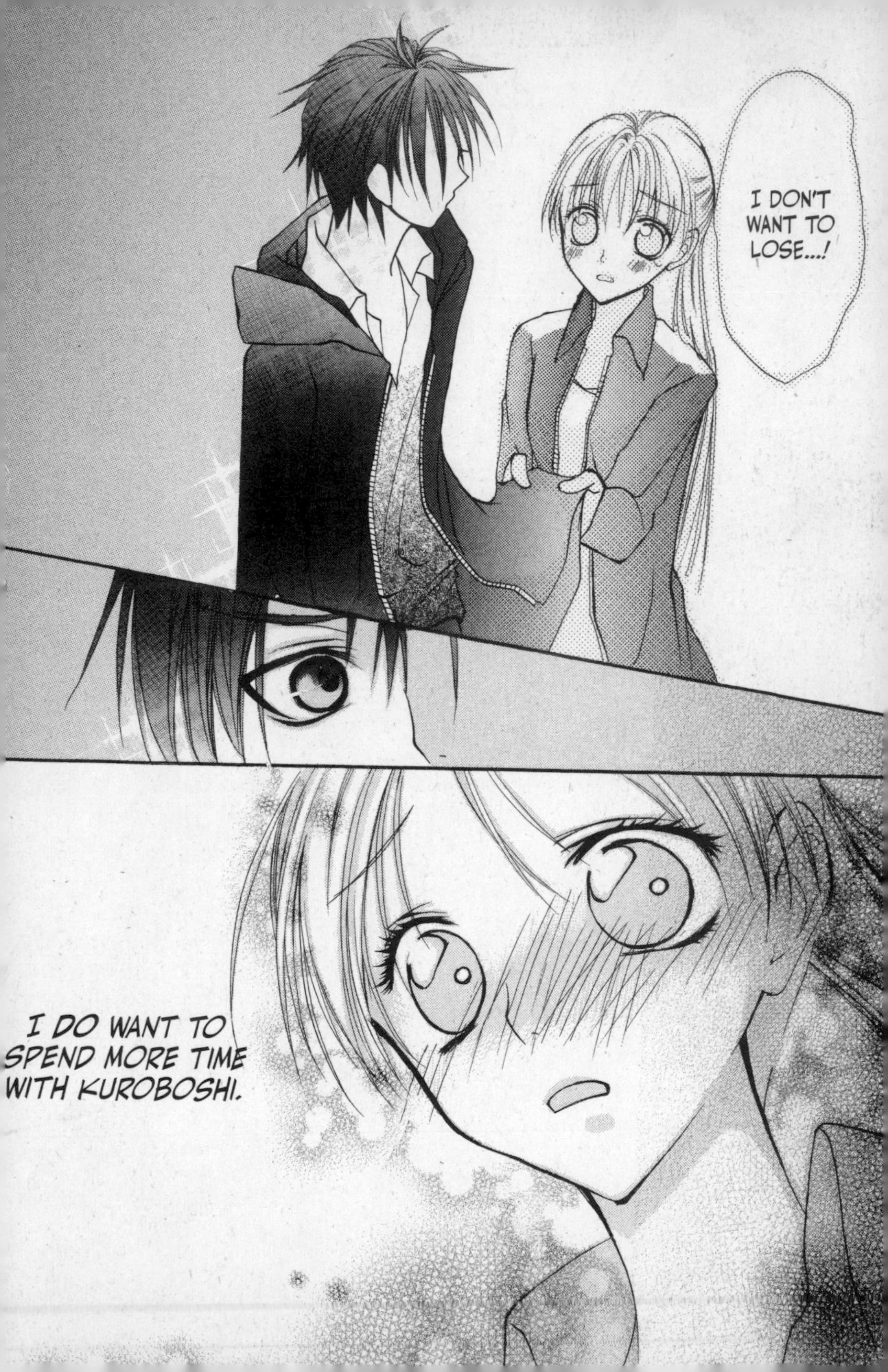
I DON'T WANT TO LOSE...!
I DO WANT TO SPEND MORE TIME WITH KUROBOSHI.

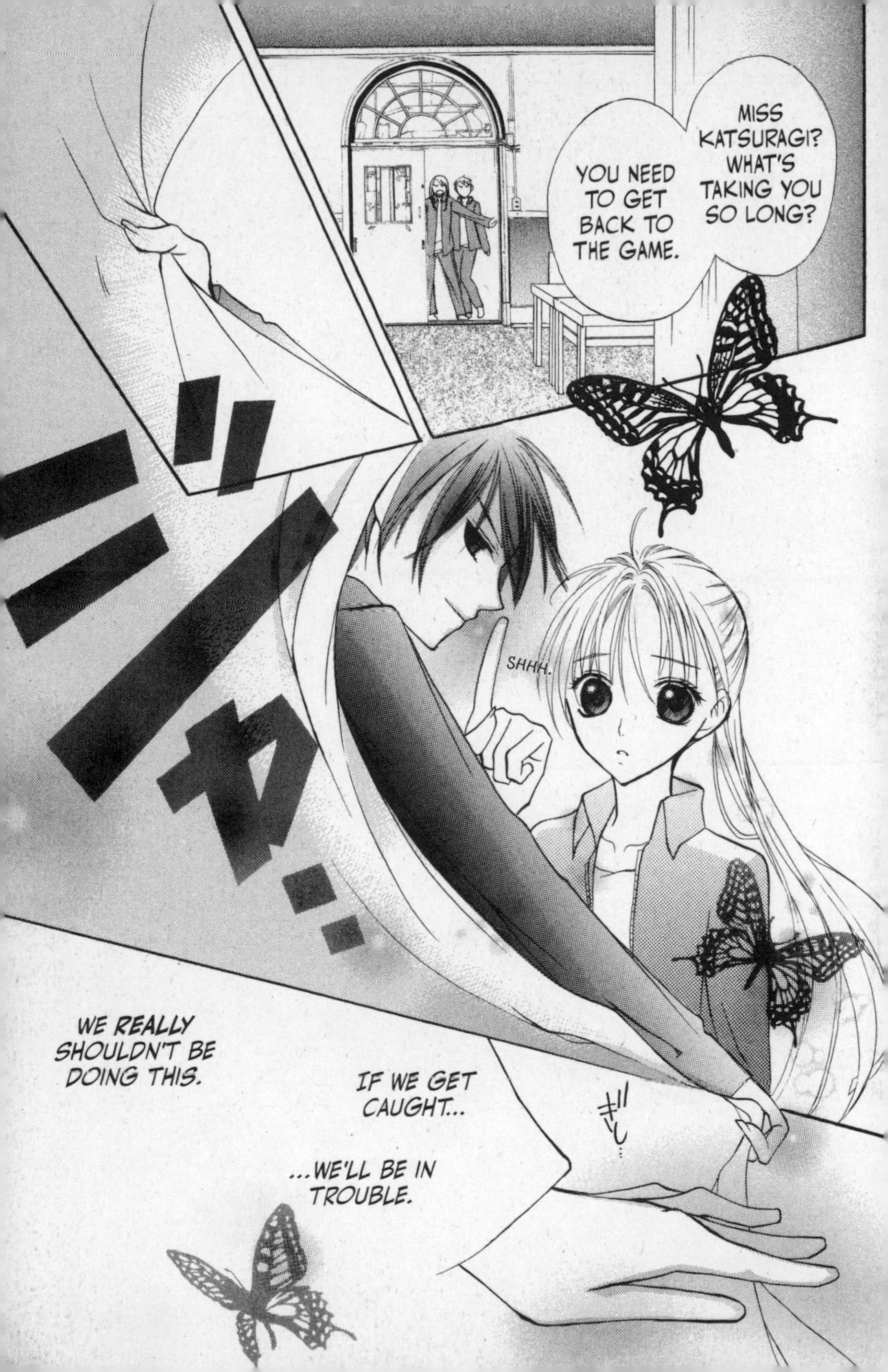
MISS KATSURAGI? WHAT'S TAKING YOU SO LONG?
YOU NEED TO GET BACK TO THE GAME.
SHHH.
WE REALLY SHOULDN'T BE DOING THIS.
IF WE GET CAUGHT...
...WE'LL BE IN TROUBLE.

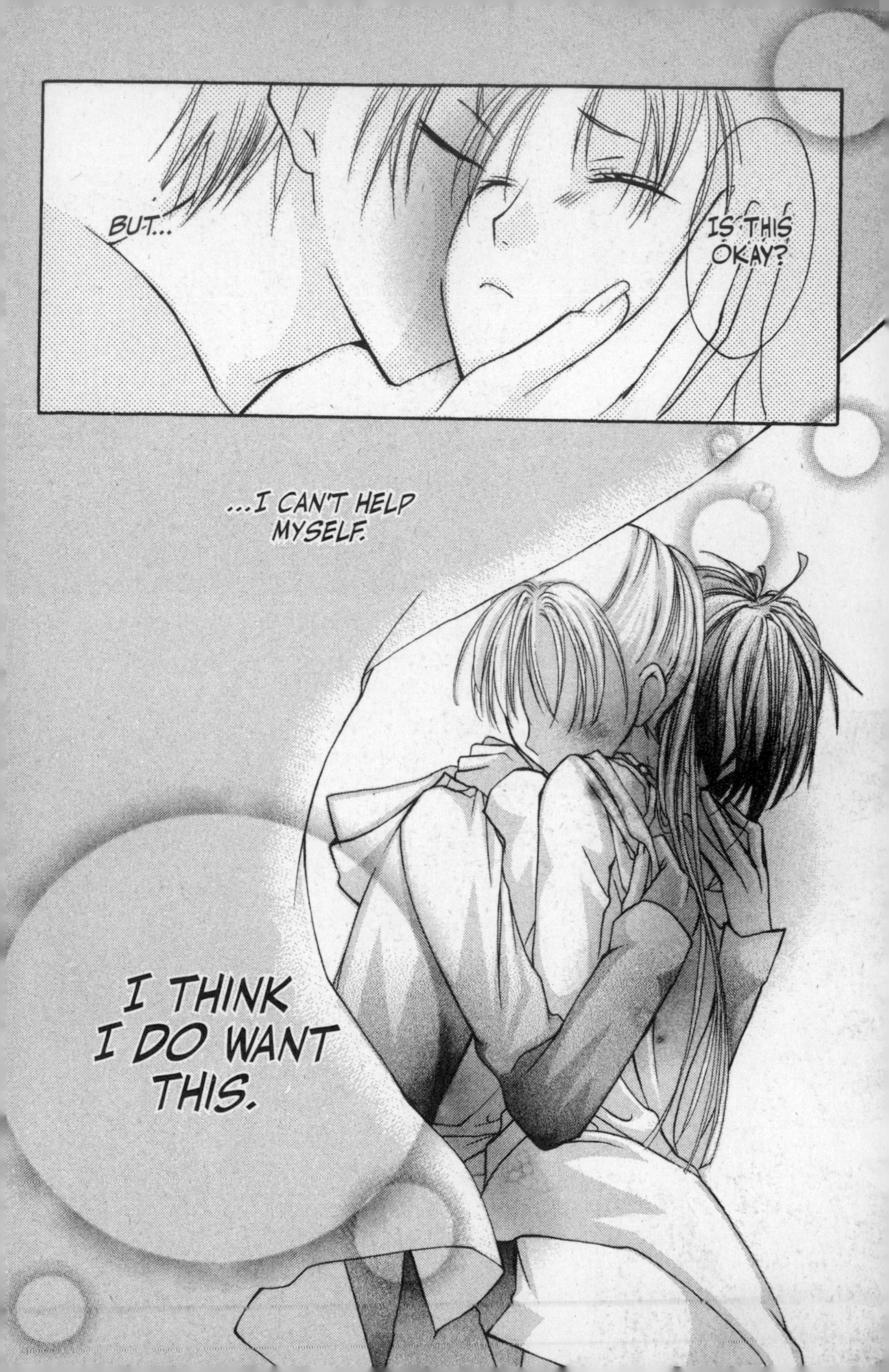
IS THIS OKAY?
BUT...
...I CAN'T HELP MYSELF.
I THINK I DO WANT THIS.

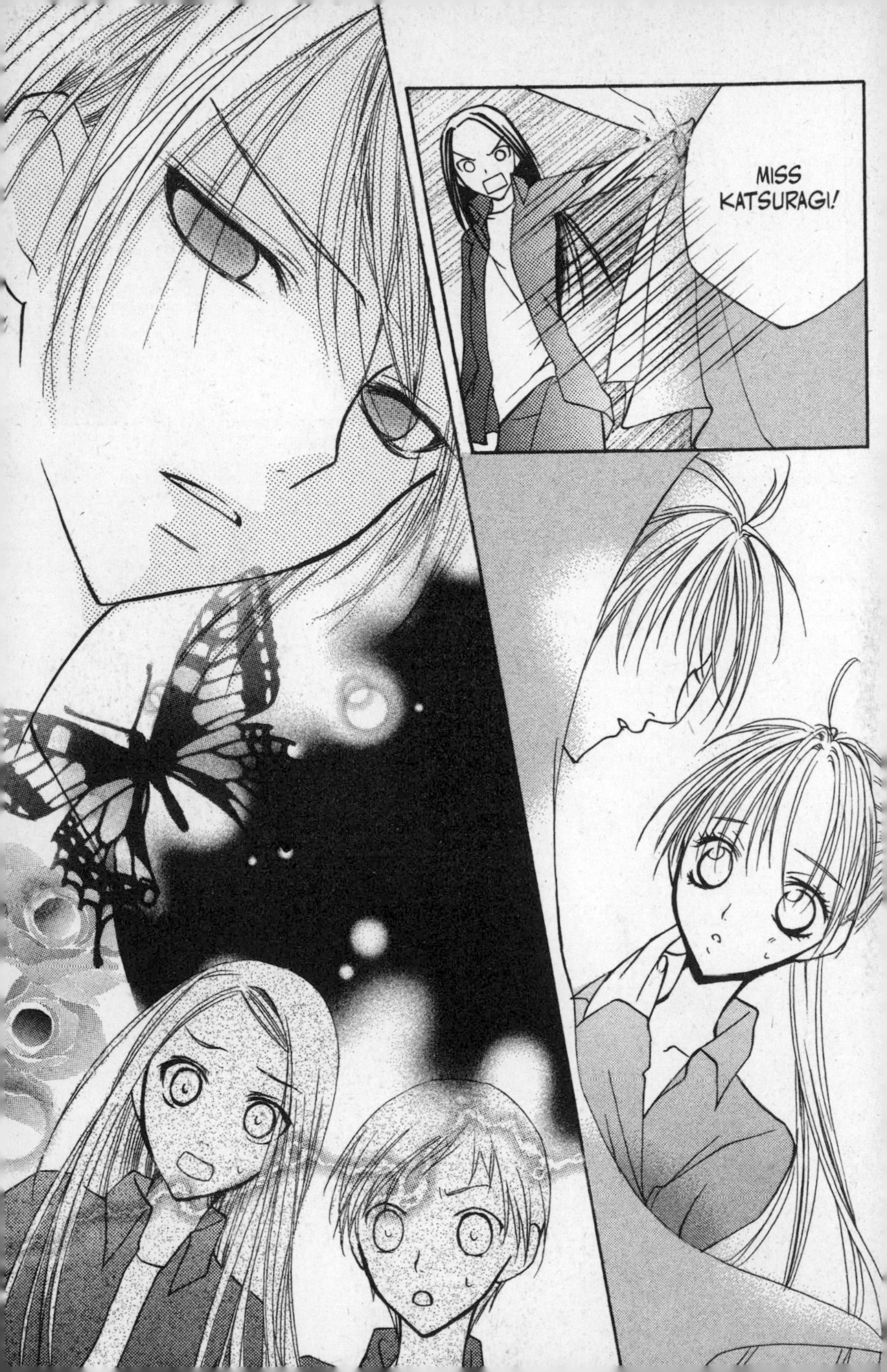
MISS KATSURAGI!

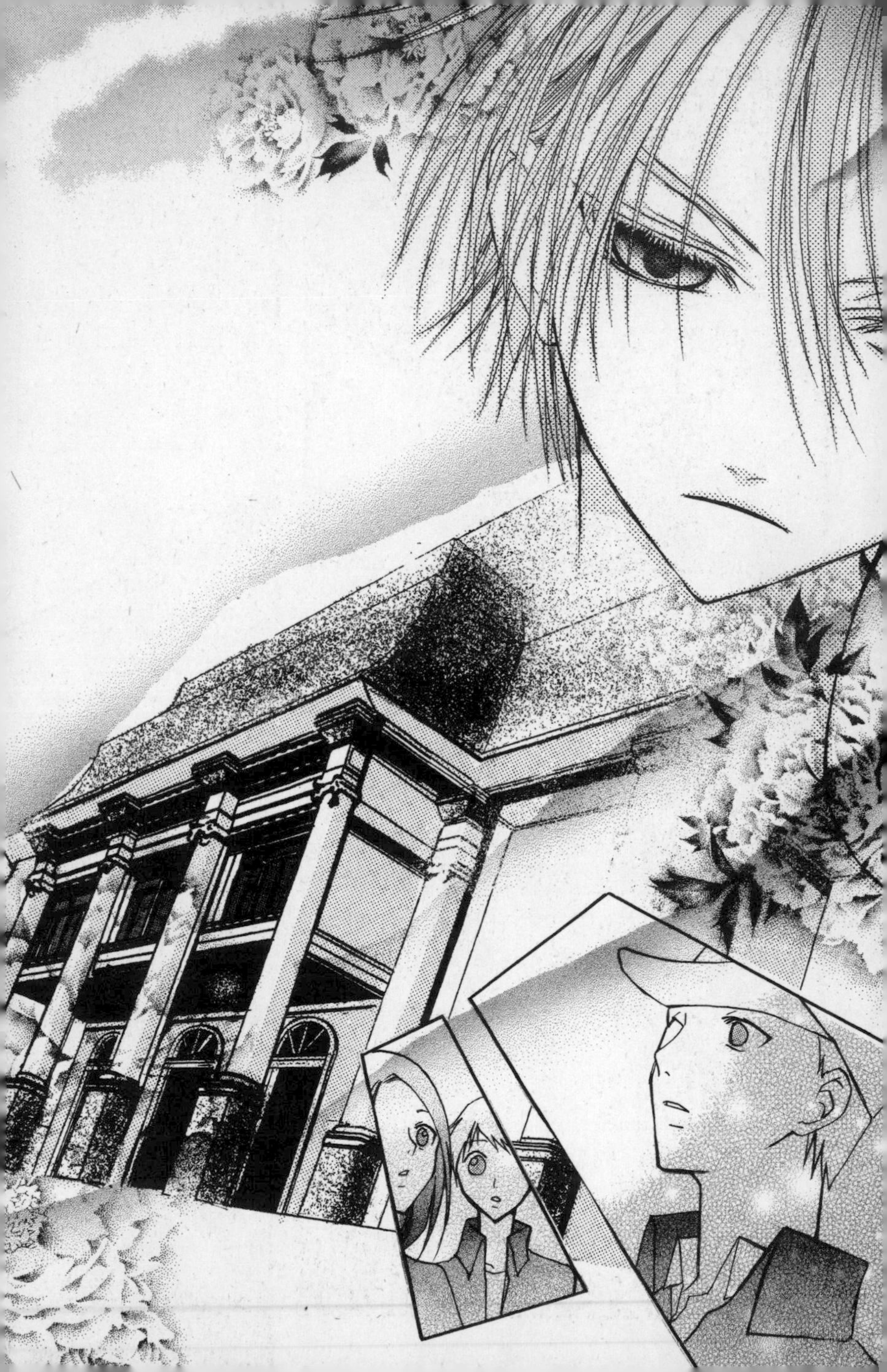

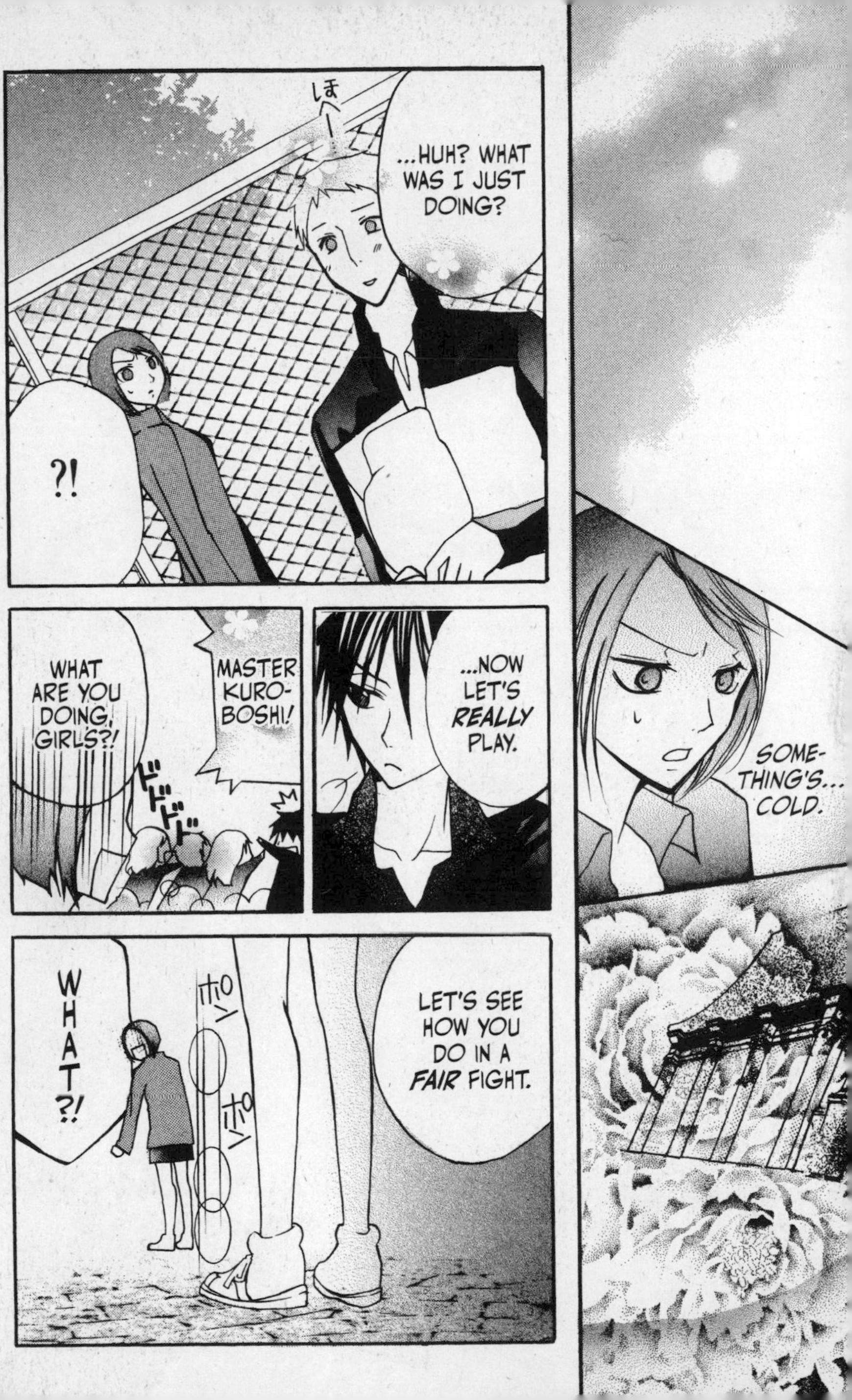
SOME-THING'S... COLD.
ほへ~
...HUH? WHAT WAS I JUST DOING?
?!
...NOW LET'S REALLY PLAY.
MASTER KURO-BOSHI!
WHAT ARE YOU DOING, GIRLS?!
ドドドド
LET'S SEE HOW YOU DO IN A FAIR FIGHT.
ポン
ポン
WHAT?!

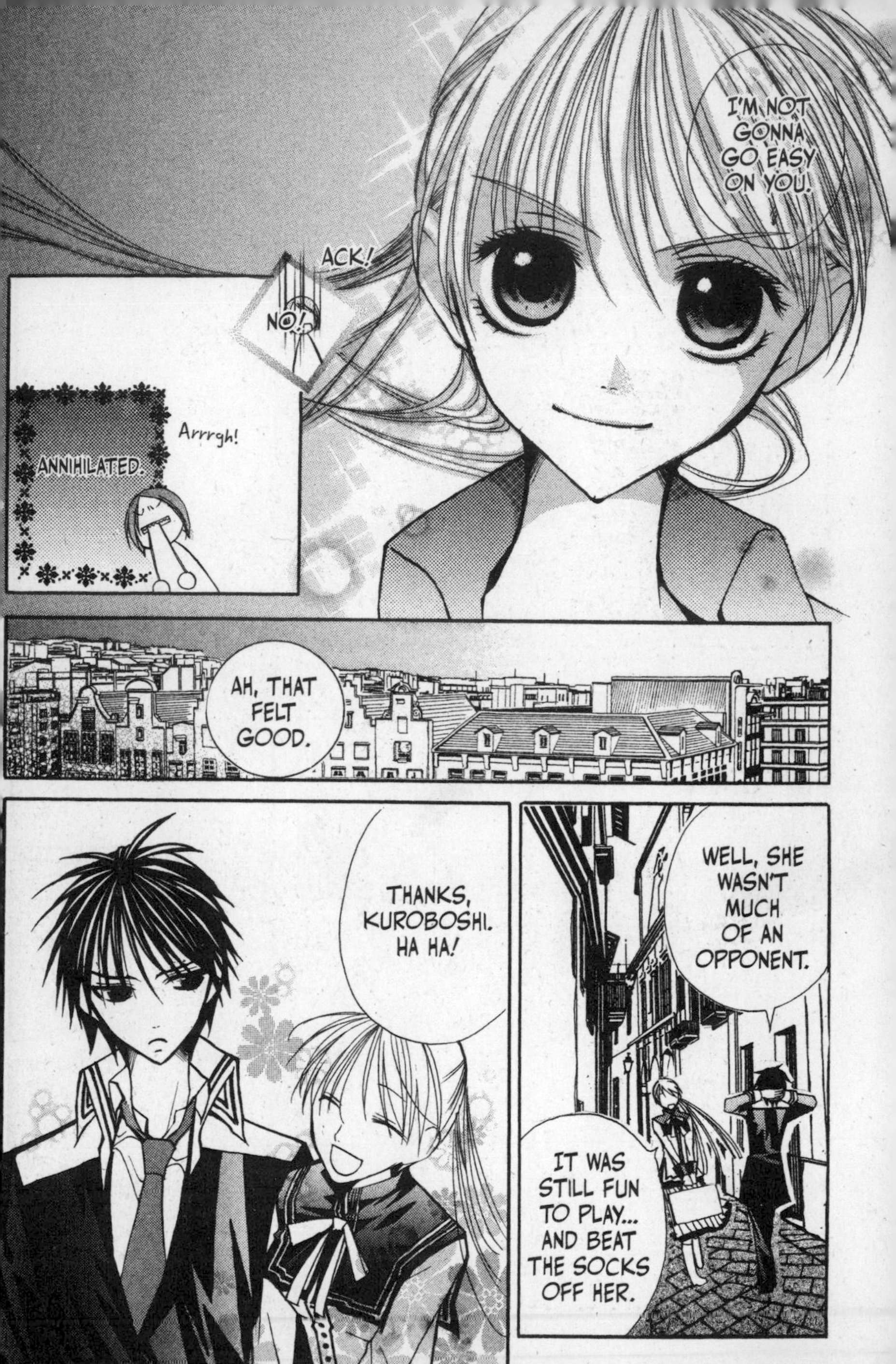
I'M NOT GONNA GO EASY ON YOU.
ACK!
NO!
Arrrgh!
ANNIHILATED.
AH, THAT FELT GOOD.
WELL, SHE WASN'T MUCH OF AN OPPONENT.
IT WAS STILL FUN TO PLAY... AND BEAT THE SOCKS OFF HER.
THANKS, KUROBOSHI. HA HA!

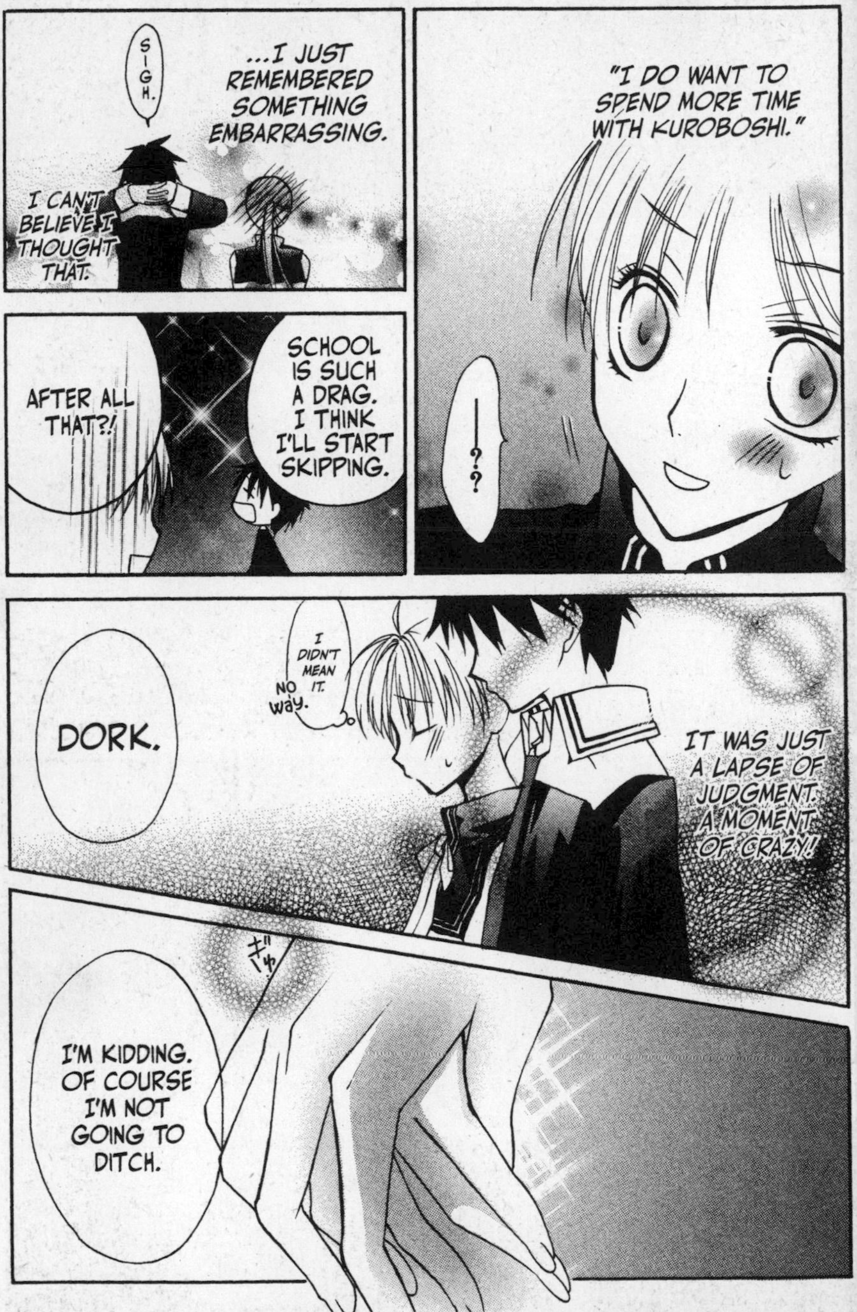
"I DO WANT TO SPEND MORE TIME WITH KUROBOSHI."
—??
SIGH.
...I JUST REMEMBERED SOMETHING EMBARRASSING.
I CAN'T BELIEVE I THOUGHT THAT.
SCHOOL IS SUCH A DRAG. I THINK I'LL START SKIPPING.
AFTER ALL THAT?!
IT WAS JUST A LAPSE OF JUDGMENT. A MOMENT OF CRAZY!
I DIDN'T MEAN IT.
NO WAY.
DORK.
ぎゅ
I'M KIDDING. OF COURSE I'M NOT GOING TO DITCH.

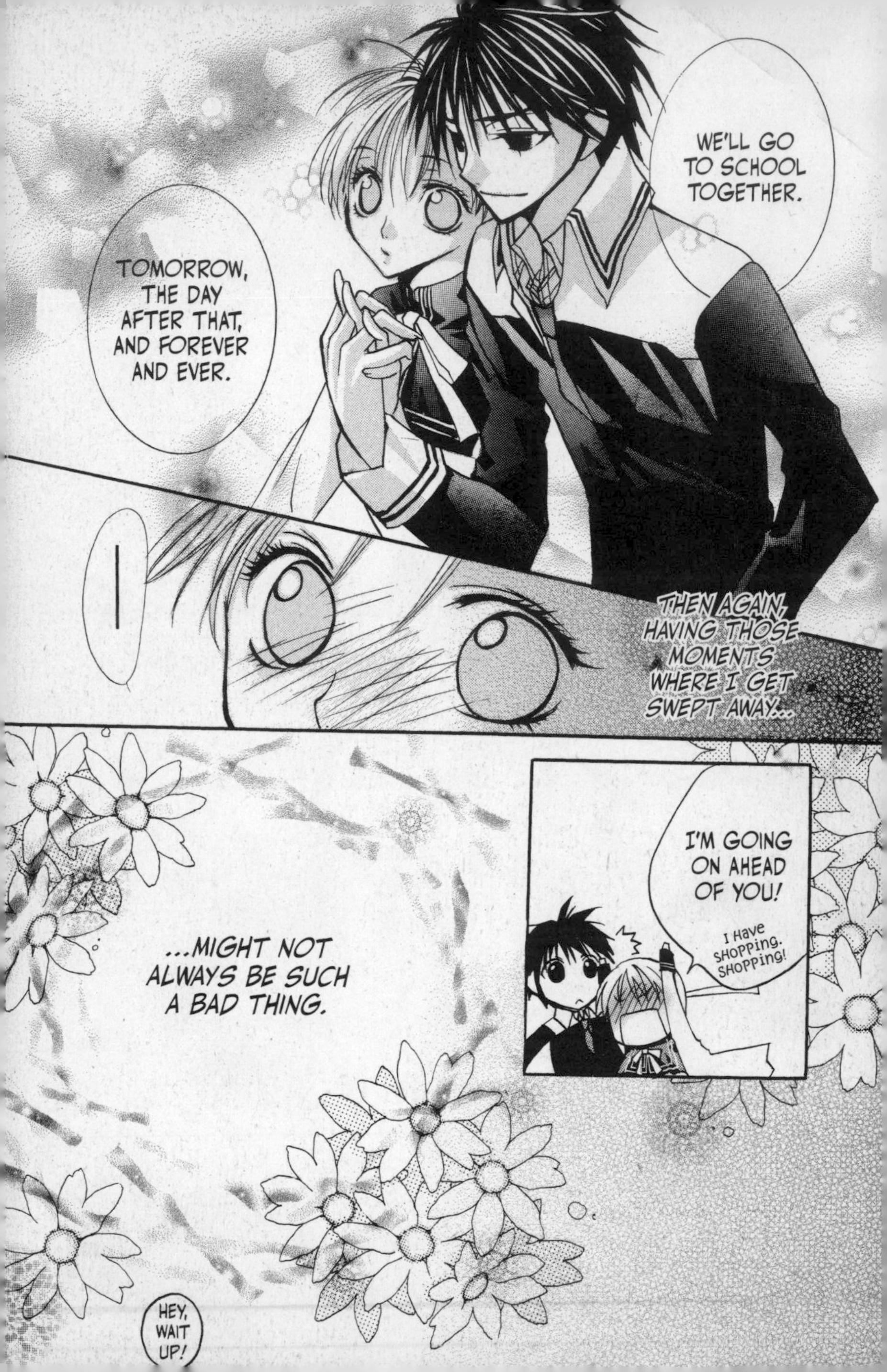
WE'LL GO TO SCHOOL TOGETHER.
TOMORROW, THE DAY AFTER THAT, AND FOREVER AND EVER.
THEN AGAIN, HAVING THOSE MOMENTS WHERE I GET SWEPT AWAY...
!
I'M GOING ON AHEAD OF YOU!
I Have SHOPPING. SHOPPING!
...MIGHT NOT ALWAYS BE SUCH A BAD THING.
HEY, WAIT UP!

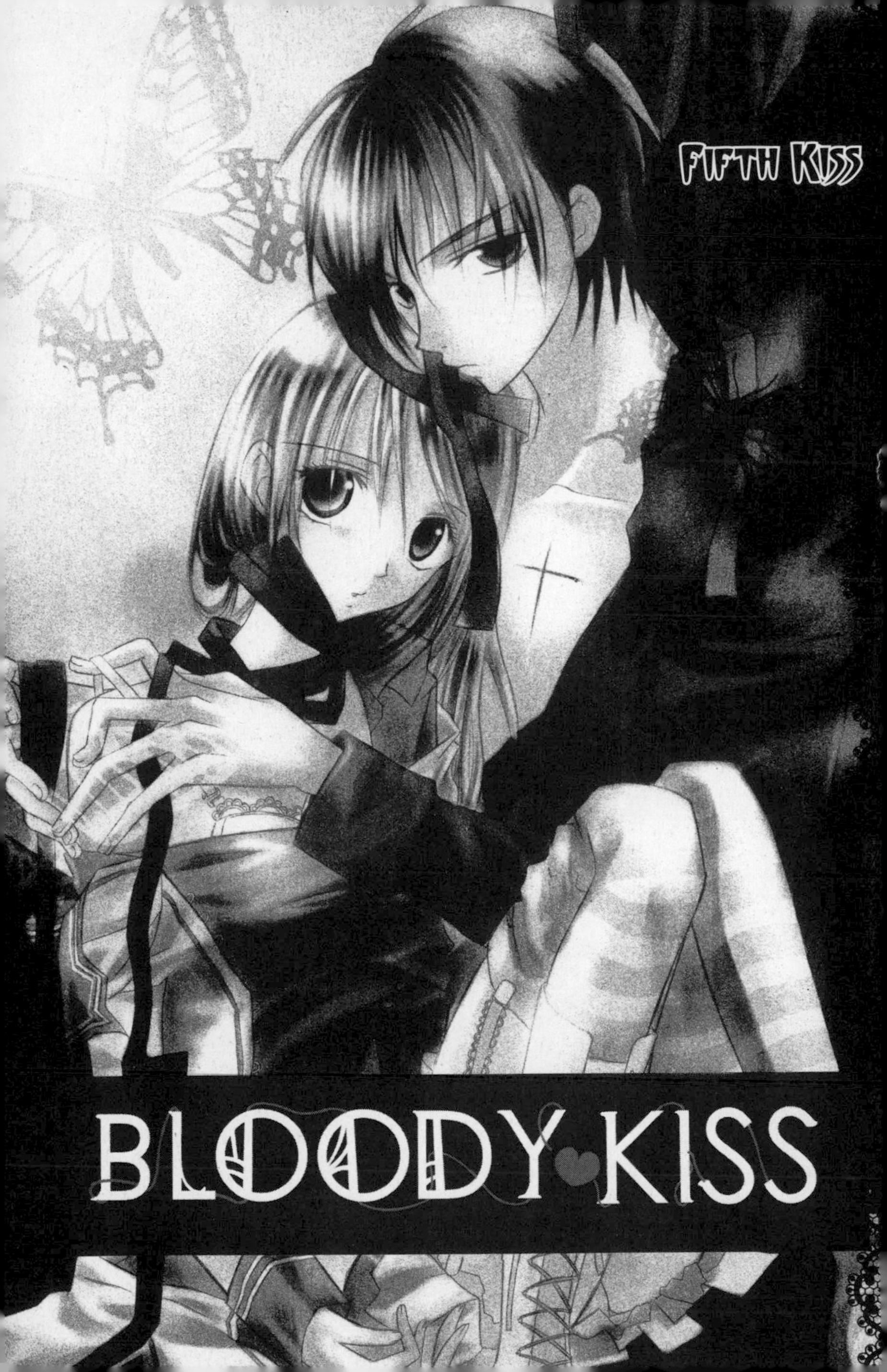
FIFTH KISS
BLOODY KISS

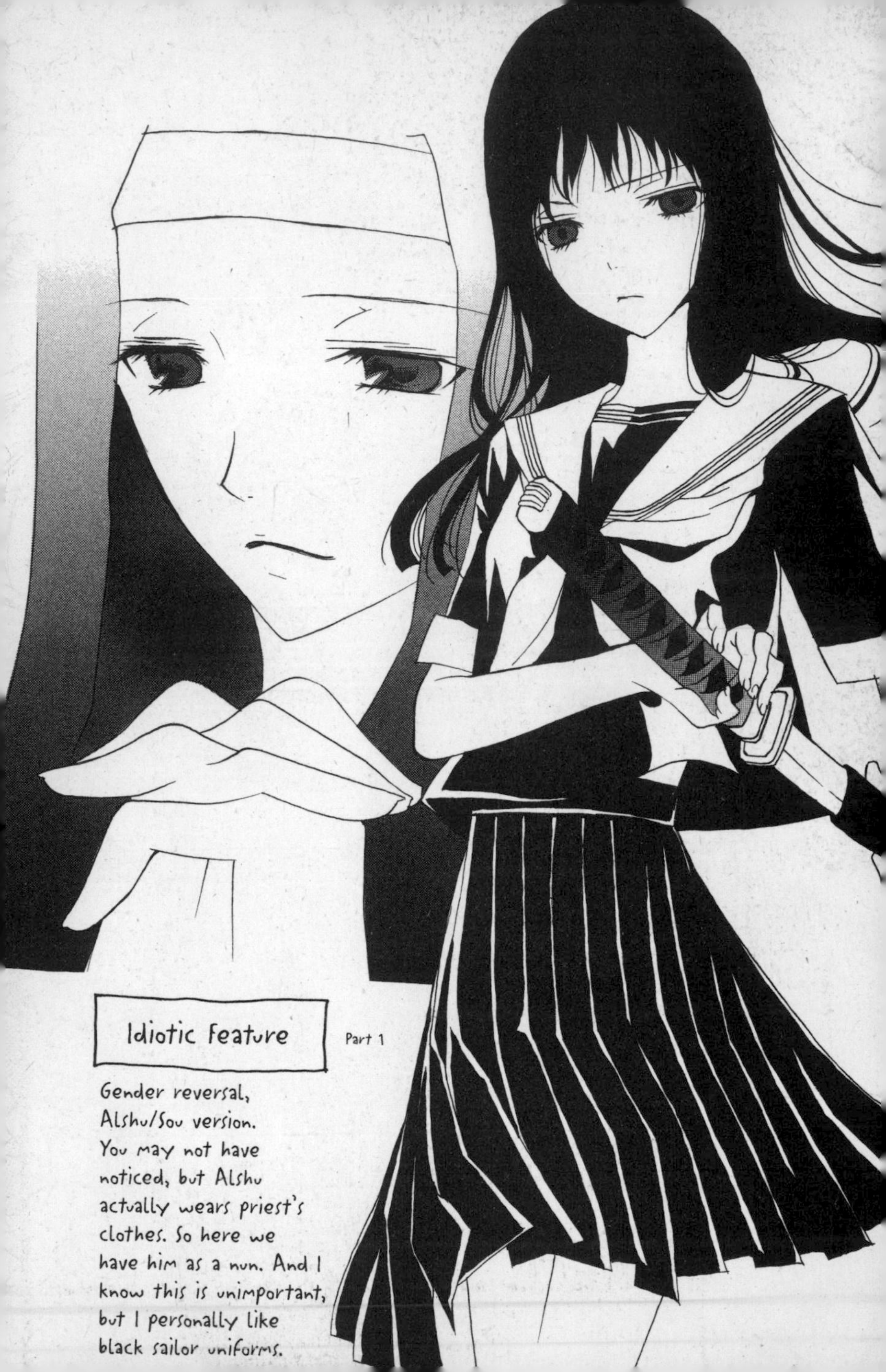
Idiotic Feature
Part 1
Gender reversal, Alshu/Sou version. You may not have noticed, but Alshu actually wears priest's clothes. So here we have him as a nun. And I know this is unimportant, but I personally like black sailor uniforms.

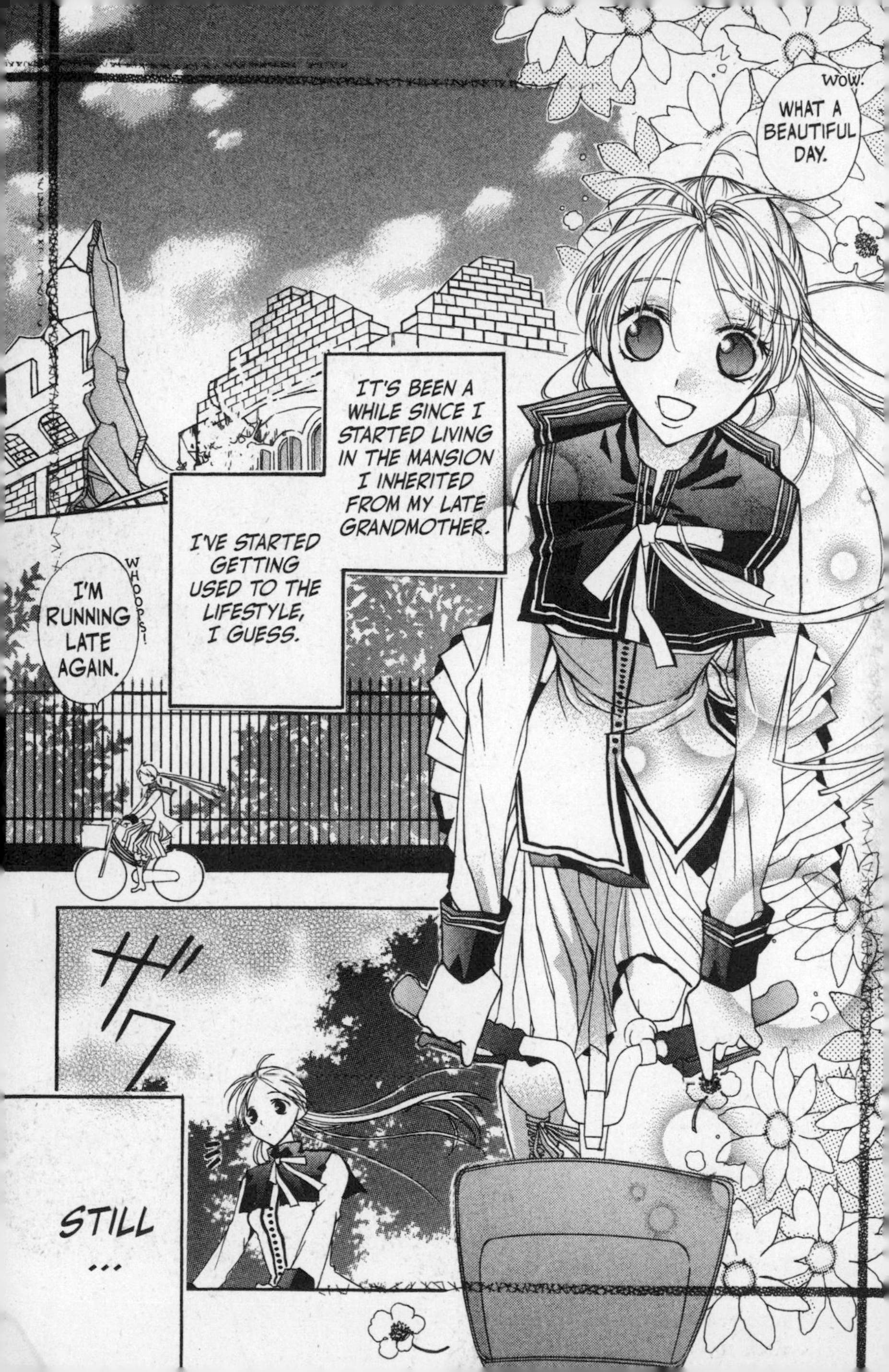
WOW! WHAT A BEAUTIFUL DAY.
IT'S BEEN A WHILE SINCE I STARTED LIVING IN THE MANSION I INHERITED FROM MY LATE GRANDMOTHER.
I'VE STARTED GETTING USED TO THE LIFESTYLE, I GUESS.
WHOOPS!
I'M RUNNING LATE AGAIN.
STILL ...

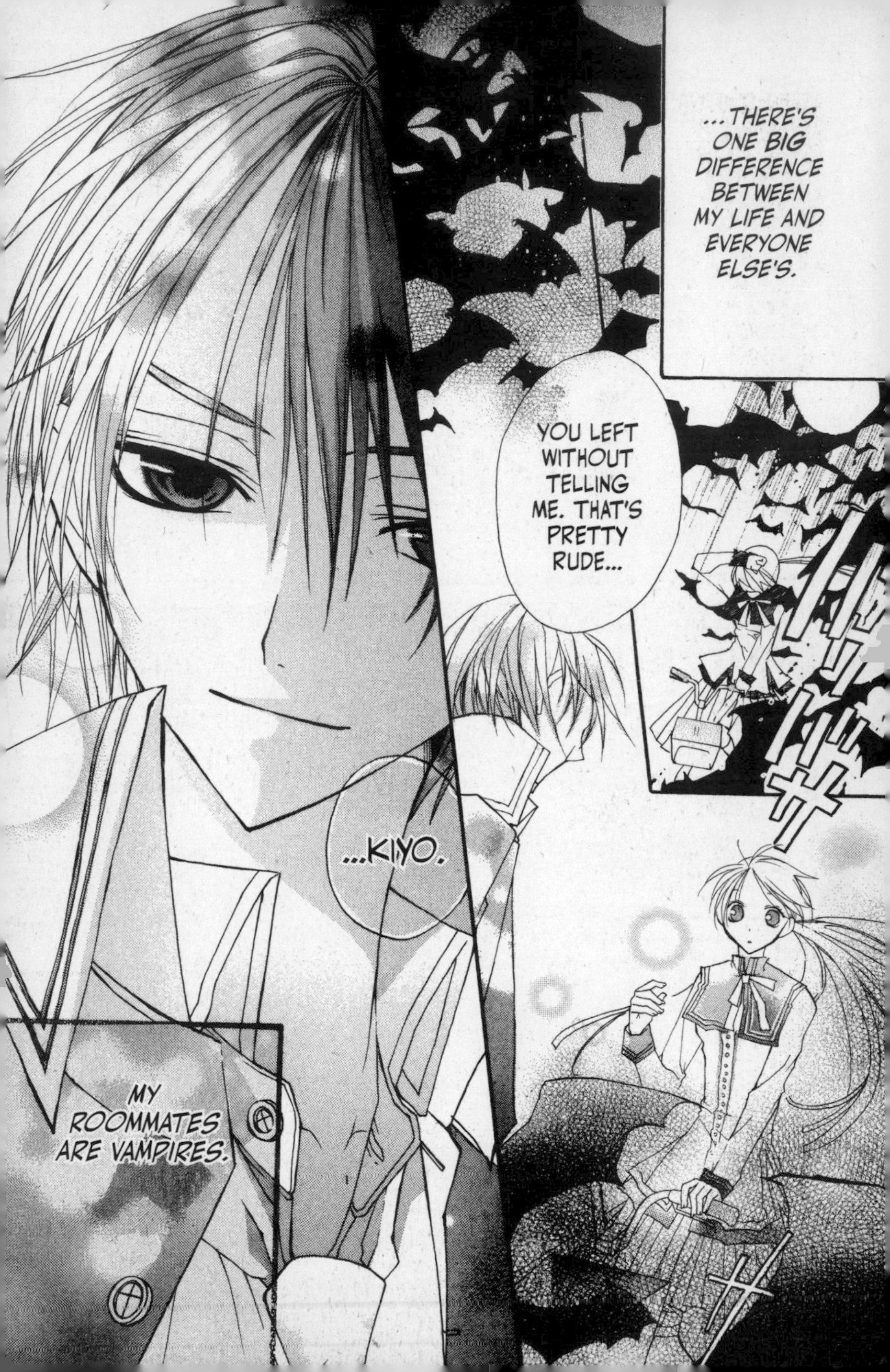
...THERE'S ONE BIG DIFFERENCE BETWEEN MY LIFE AND EVERYONE ELSE'S.
YOU LEFT WITHOUT TELLING ME. THAT'S PRETTY RUDE...
...KIYO.
MY ROOMMATES ARE VAMPIRES.

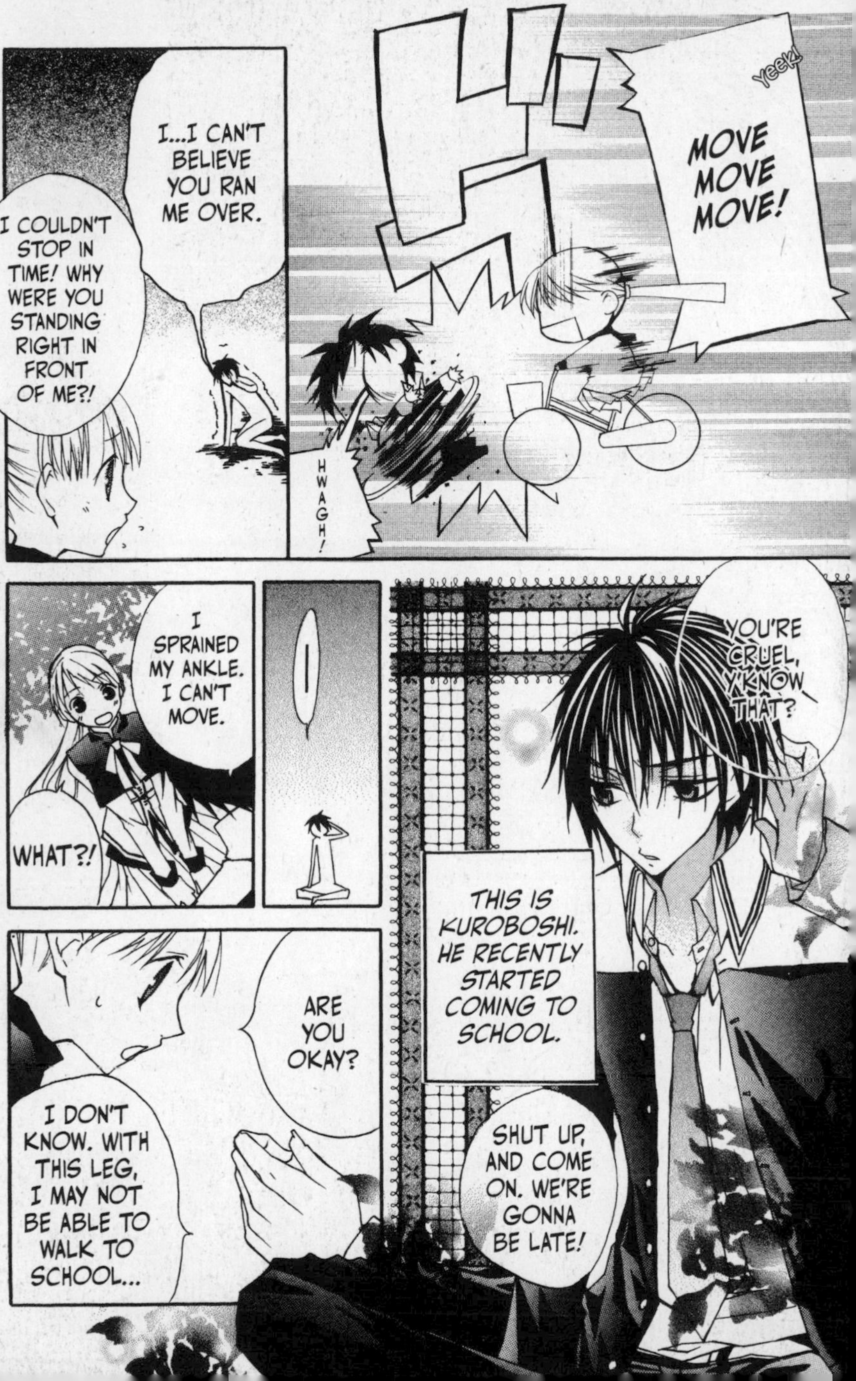
YEEK!
MOVE MOVE MOVE!
HWAGH!
I...I CAN'T BELIEVE YOU RAN ME OVER.
I COULDN'T STOP IN TIME! WHY WERE YOU STANDING RIGHT IN FRONT OF ME?!
YOU'RE CRUEL, Y'KNOW THAT?
THIS IS KUROBOSHI. HE RECENTLY STARTED COMING TO SCHOOL.
SHUT UP, AND COME ON. WE'RE GONNA BE LATE!
!
I SPRAINED MY ANKLE. I CAN'T MOVE.
WHAT?!
ARE YOU OKAY?
I DON'T KNOW. WITH THIS LEG, I MAY NOT BE ABLE TO WALK TO SCHOOL...

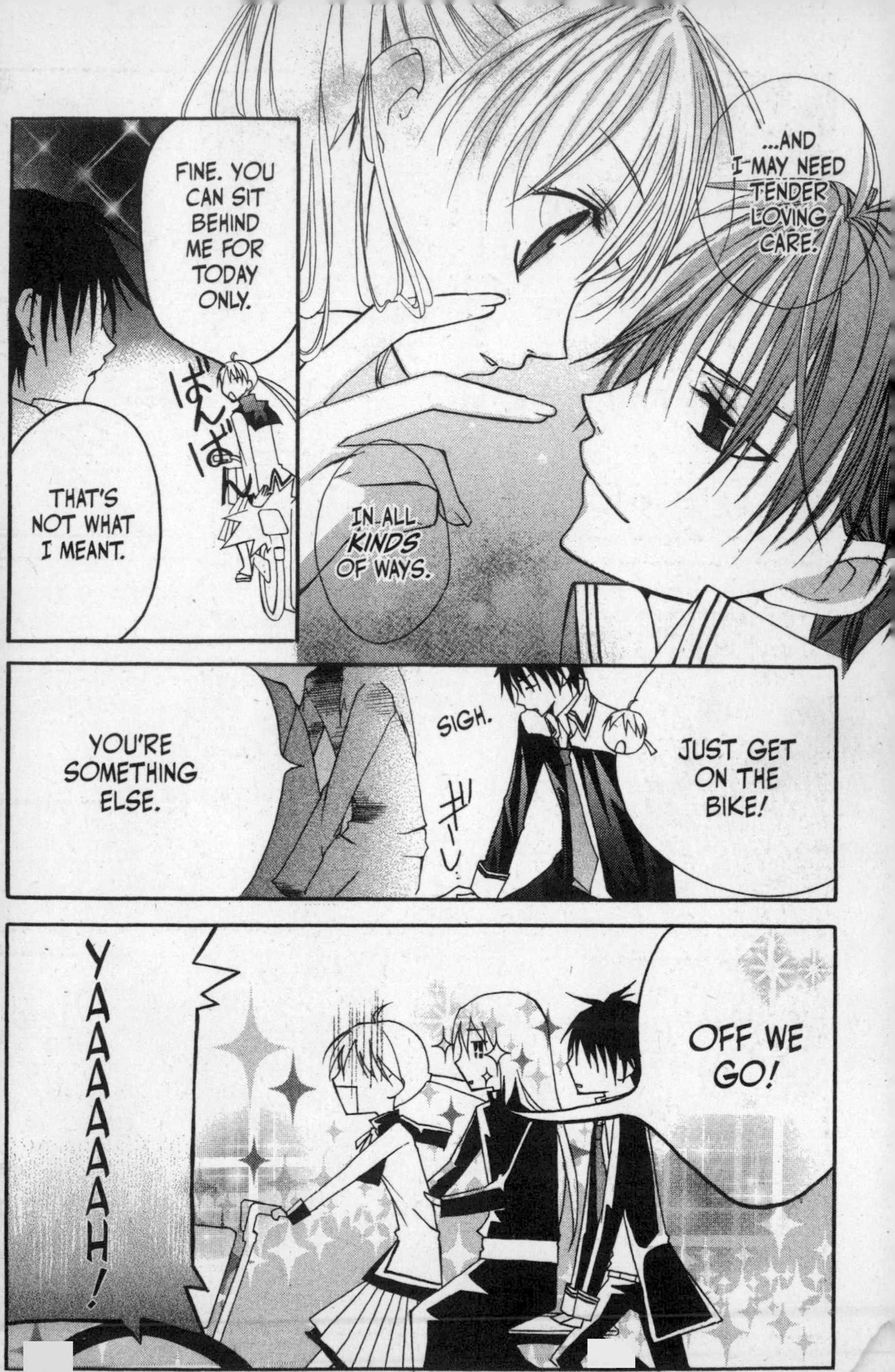
...AND I MAY NEED TENDER LOVING CARE.
IN ALL KINDS OF WAYS.
FINE. YOU CAN SIT BEHIND ME FOR TODAY ONLY.
ばんばん
THAT'S NOT WHAT I MEANT.
JUST GET ON THE BIKE!
SIGH.
YOU'RE SOMETHING ELSE.
OFF WE GO!
YAAAAAAH!

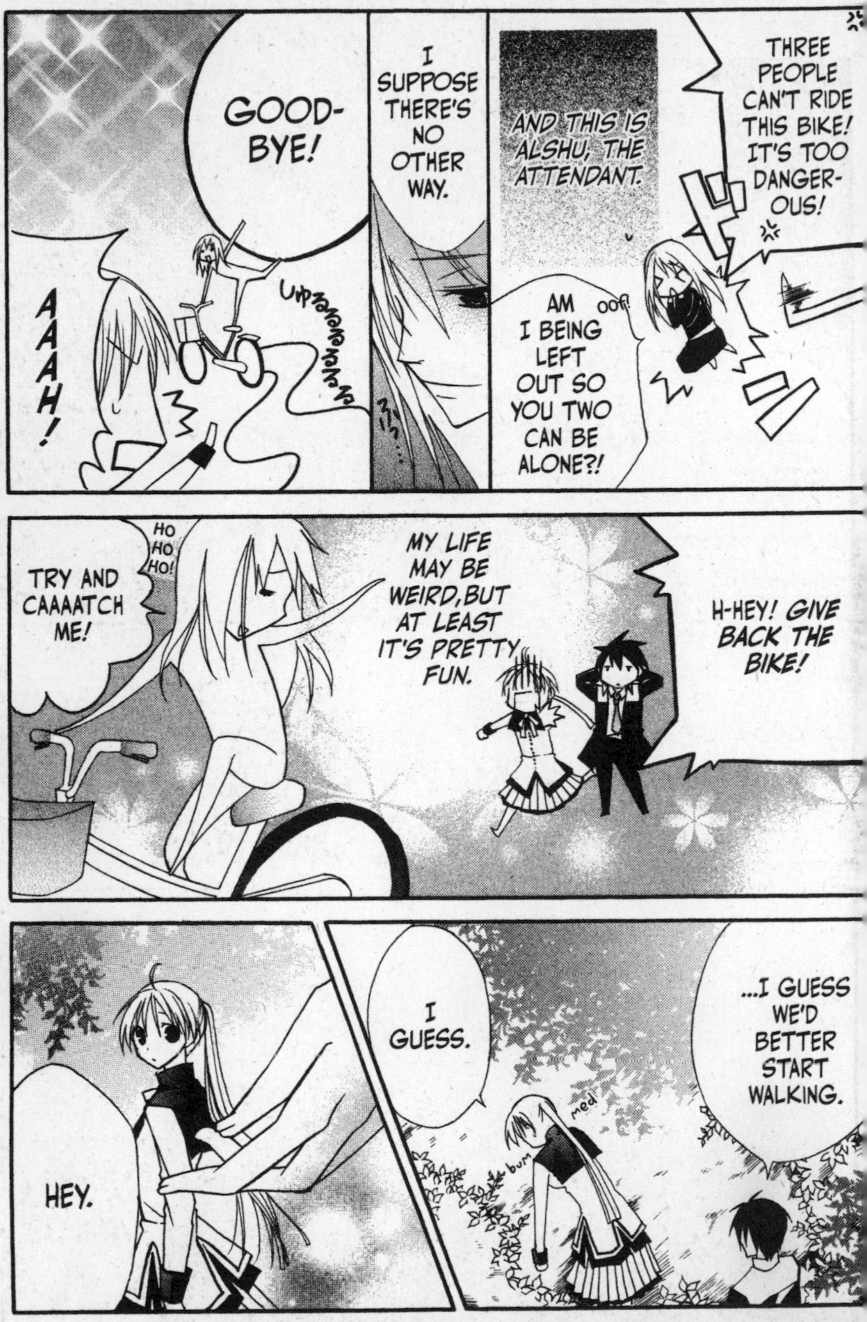
THREE PEOPLE CAN'T RIDE THIS BIKE! IT'S TOO DANGER-OUS!
AND THIS IS ALSHU, THE ATTENDANT.
OOF!
AM I BEING LEFT OUT SO YOU TWO CAN BE ALONE?!
I SUPPOSE THERE'S NO OTHER WAY.
GOOD-BYE!
AAAH!
H-HEY! GIVE BACK THE BIKE!
MY LIFE MAY BE WEIRD, BUT AT LEAST IT'S PRETTY FUN.
HO HO HO!
TRY AND CAAAATCH ME!
...I GUESS WE'D BETTER START WALKING.
I GUESS.
med
bum
HEY.

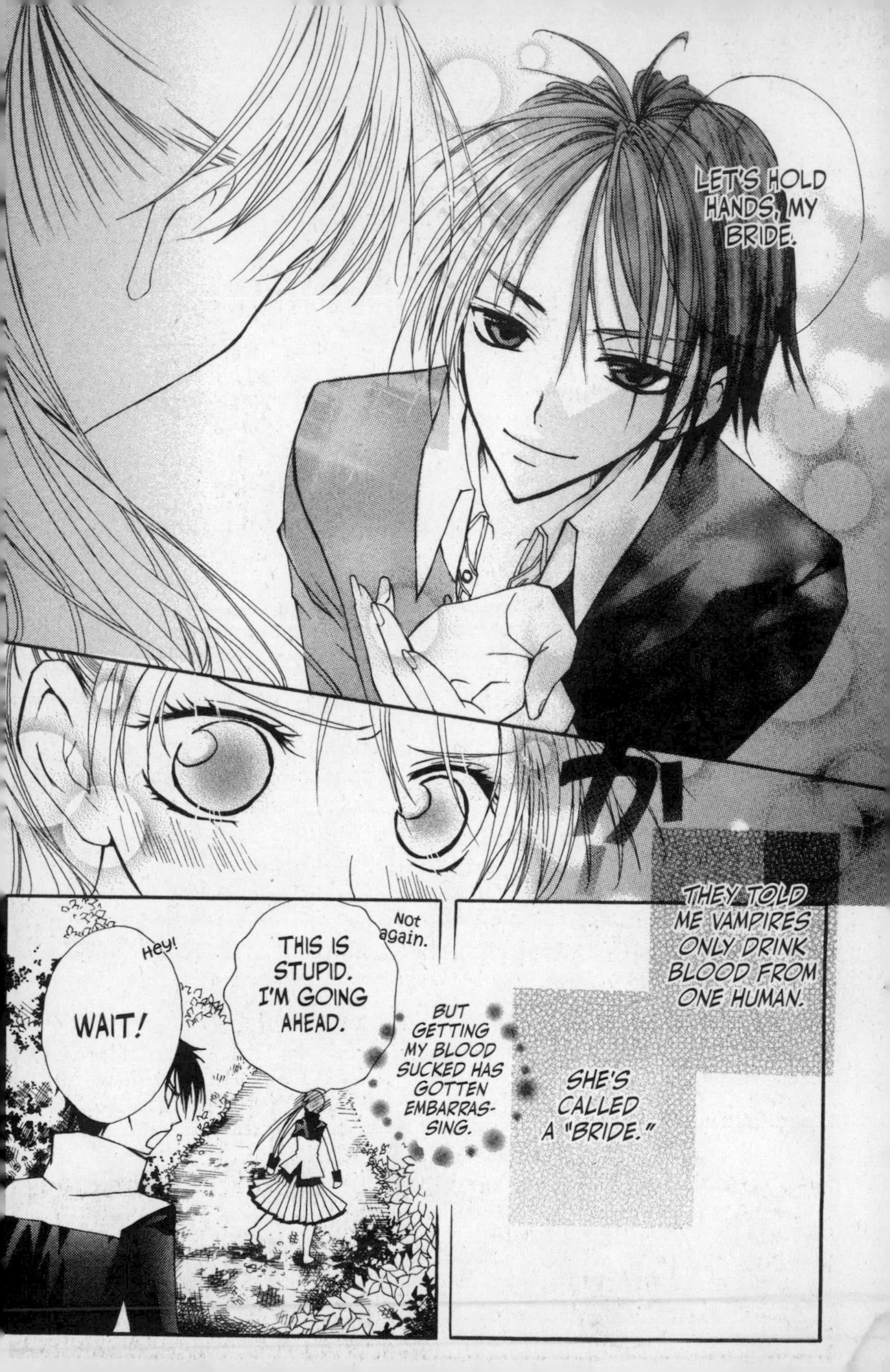
LET'S HOLD HANDS, MY BRIDE.
THEY TOLD ME VAMPIRES ONLY DRINK BLOOD FROM ONE HUMAN.
SHE'S CALLED A "BRIDE."
BUT GETTING MY BLOOD SUCKED HAS GOTTEN EMBARRAS-SING.
Not again.
THIS IS STUPID. I'M GOING AHEAD.
Hey!
WAIT!

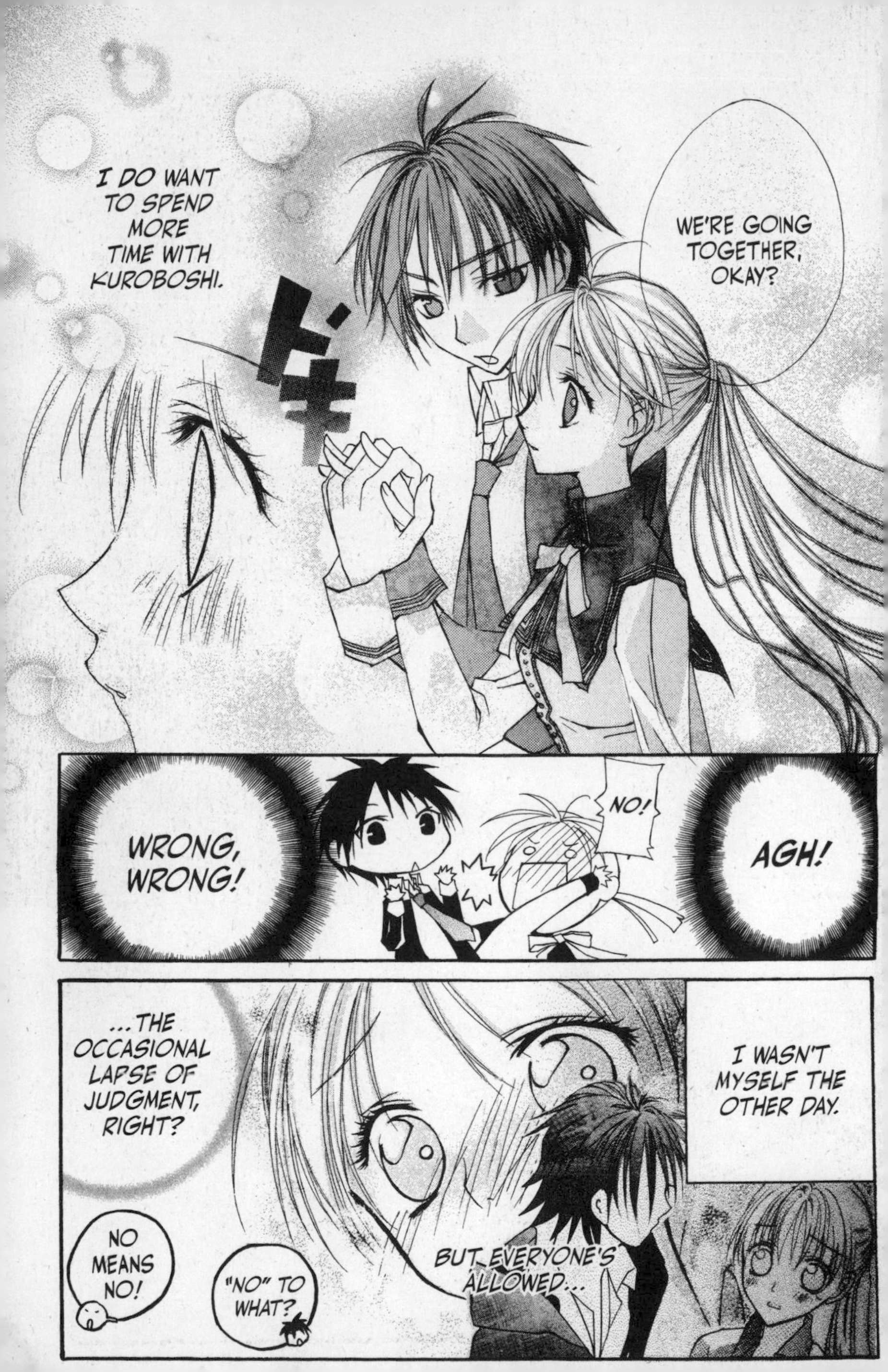

WE'RE GOING TOGETHER, OKAY?
ドキ
I DO WANT TO SPEND MORE TIME WITH KUROBOSHI.
AGH!
NO!
WRONG, WRONG!
I WASN'T MYSELF THE OTHER DAY.
BUT EVERYONE'S ALLOWED...
...THE OCCASIONAL LAPSE OF JUDGMENT, RIGHT?
"NO" TO WHAT?
NO MEANS NO!

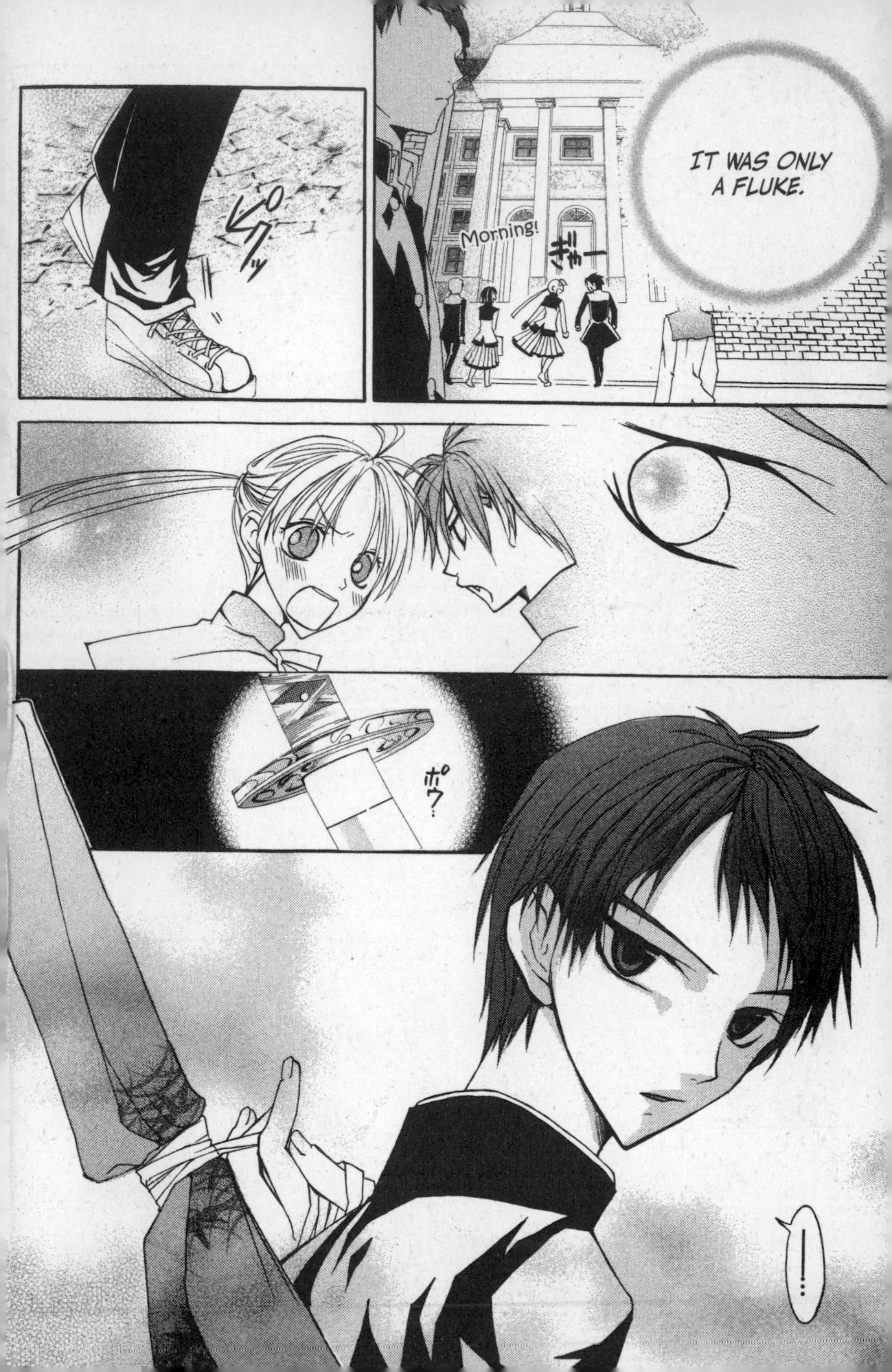
IT WAS ONLY A FLUKE.
Morning!
ぎゃー
ピクッ
ポウ…
…!

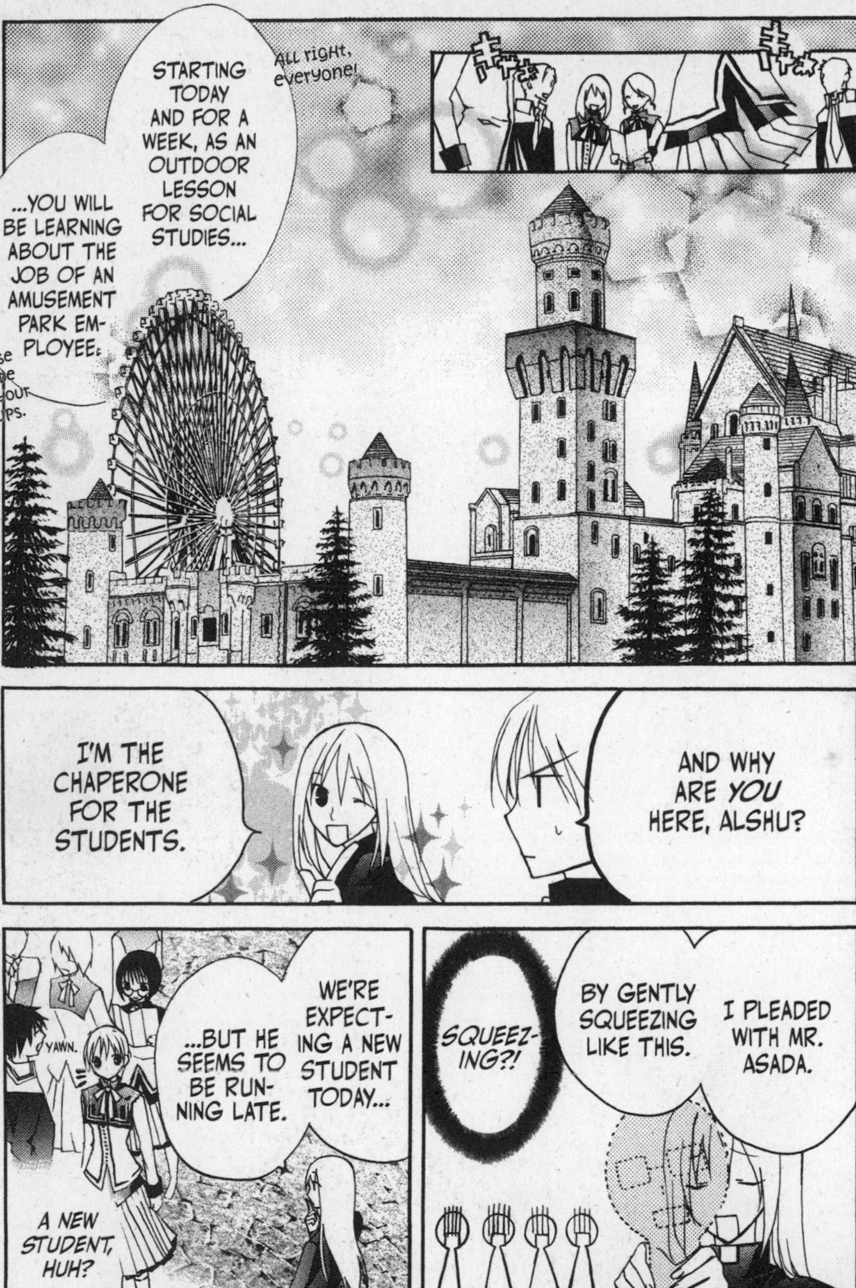
All right, everyone!
STARTING TODAY AND FOR A WEEK, AS AN OUTDOOR LESSON FOR SOCIAL STUDIES...
...YOU WILL BE LEARNING ABOUT THE JOB OF AN AMUSEMENT PARK EMPLOYEE.
Please divide into your groups.
AND WHY ARE YOU HERE, ALSHU?
I'M THE CHAPERONE FOR THE STUDENTS.
I PLEADED WITH MR. ASADA.
BY GENTLY SQUEEZING LIKE THIS.
SQUEEZING?!
WE'RE EXPECTING A NEW STUDENT TODAY...
...BUT HE SEEMS TO BE RUNNING LATE.
YAWN.
A NEW STUDENT, HUH?

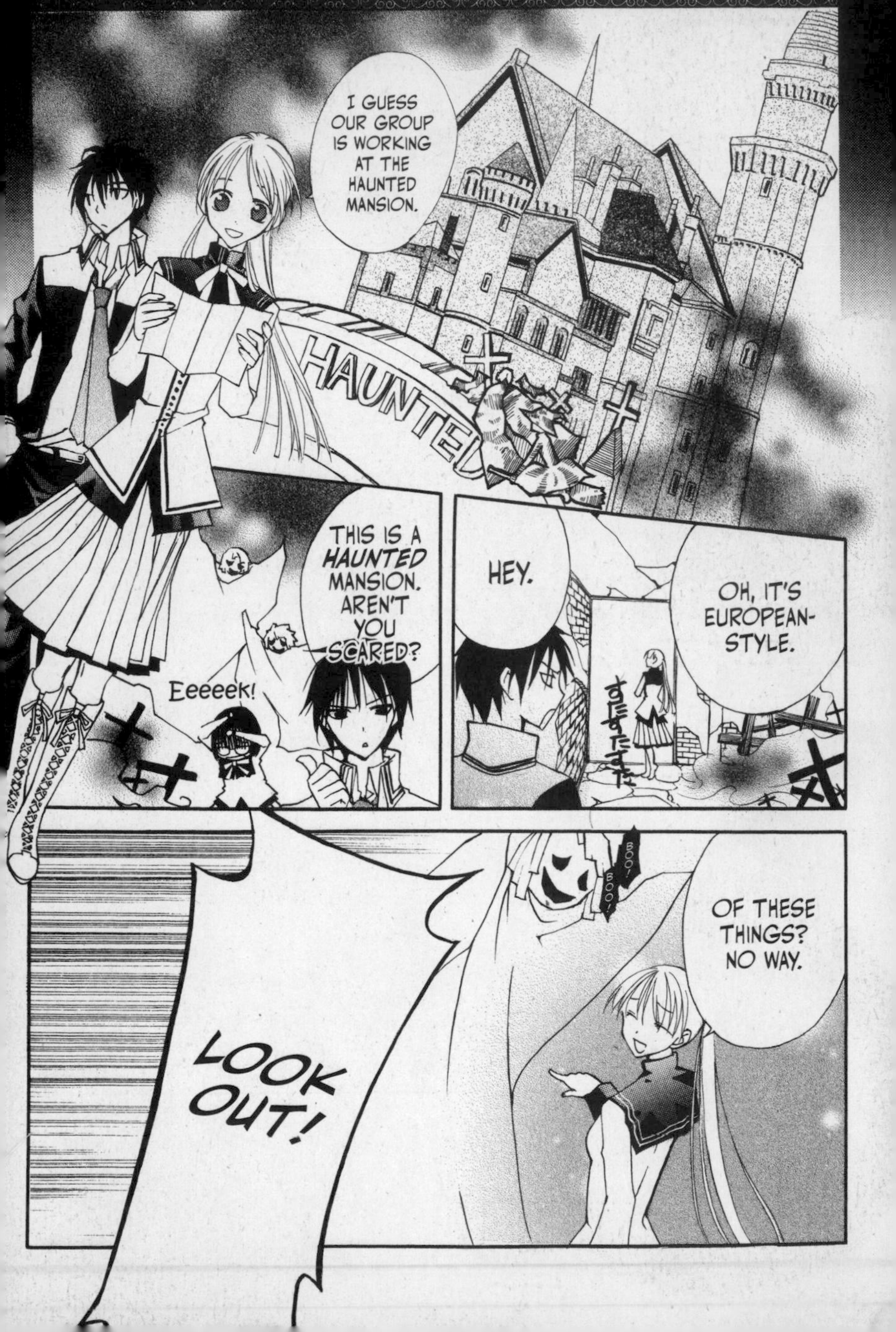
I GUESS OUR GROUP IS WORKING AT THE HAUNTED MANSION.
OH, IT'S EUROPEAN-STYLE.
HEY.
すたすたすた
THIS IS A *HAUNTED* MANSION. AREN'T YOU SCARED?
Eeeeek!
OF THESE THINGS? NO WAY.
BOO!
BOO!
LOOK OUT!

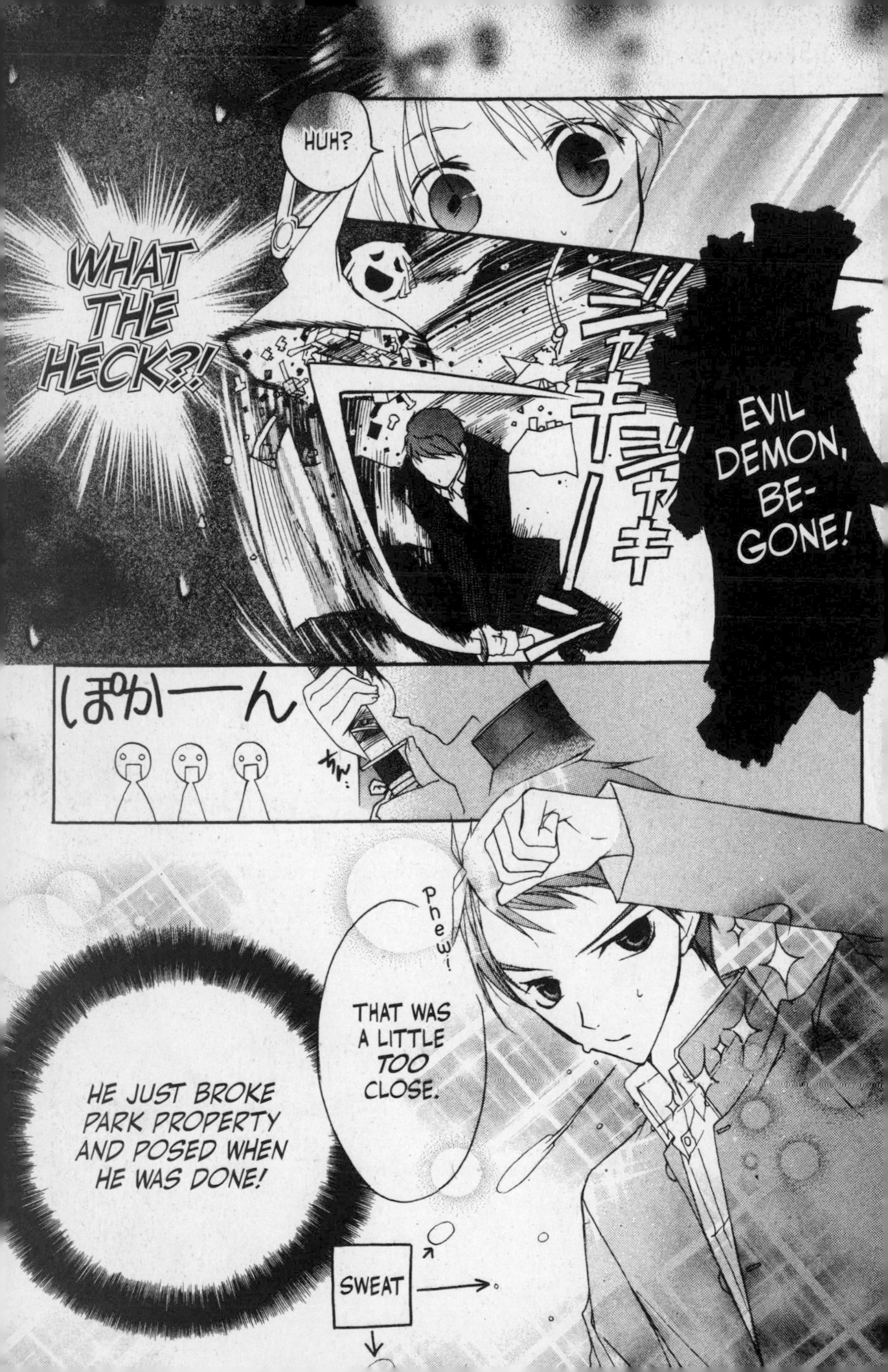
EVIL DEMON, BE-GONE!
HUH?
WHAT THE HECK?!
ぽかーん
Phew!
THAT WAS A LITTLE *TOO* CLOSE.
HE JUST BROKE PARK PROPERTY AND POSED WHEN HE WAS DONE!
SWEAT

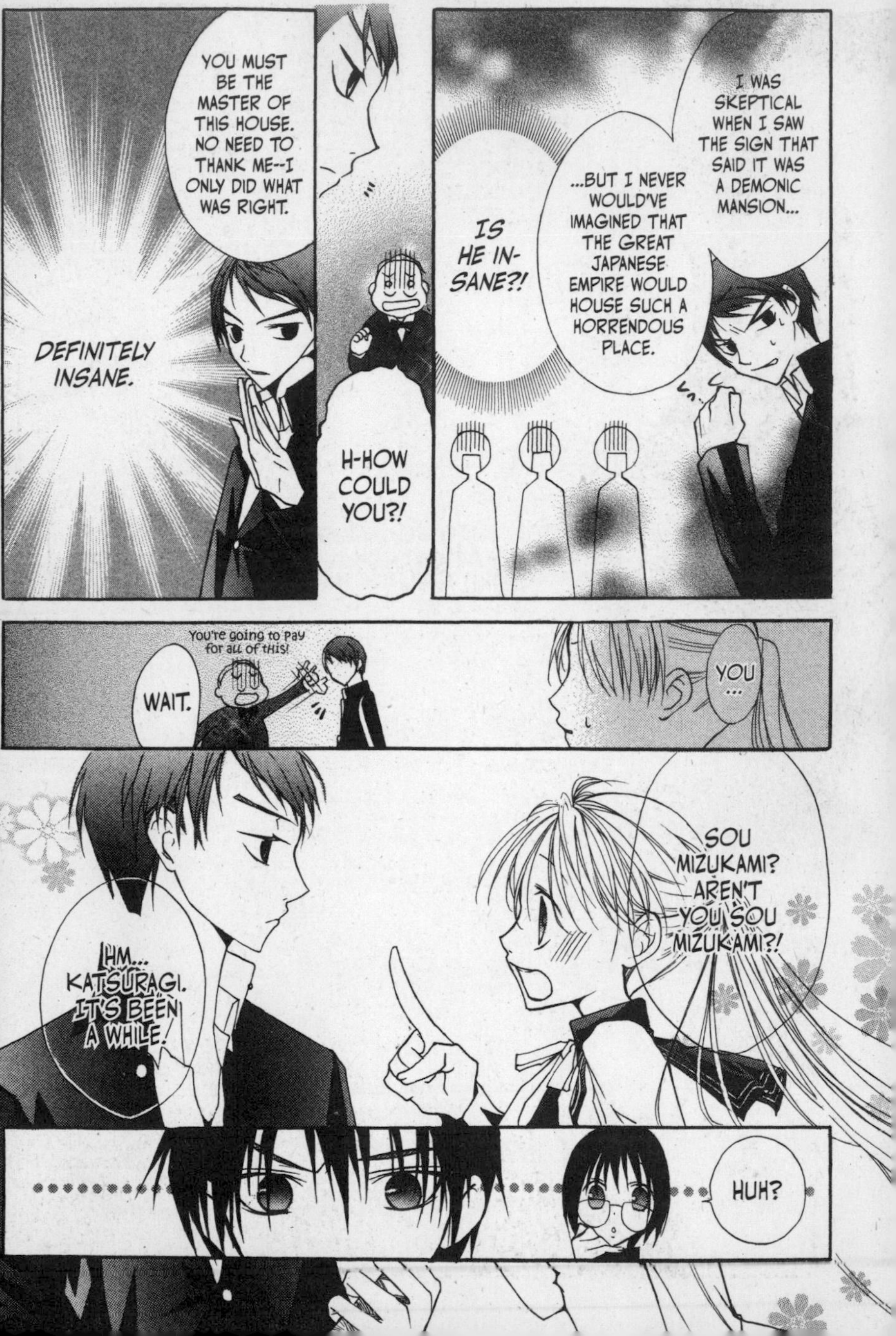
I WAS SKEPTICAL WHEN I SAW THE SIGN THAT SAID IT WAS A DEMONIC MANSION...
...BUT I NEVER WOULD'VE IMAGINED THAT THE GREAT JAPANESE EMPIRE WOULD HOUSE SUCH A HORRENDOUS PLACE.
IS HE IN-SANE?!
H-HOW COULD YOU?!
YOU MUST BE THE MASTER OF THIS HOUSE. NO NEED TO THANK ME--I ONLY DID WHAT WAS RIGHT.
DEFINITELY INSANE.
YOU ...
You're going to pay for all of this!
WAIT.
SOU MIZUKAMI? AREN'T YOU SOU MIZUKAMI?!
HM... KATSURAGI. IT'S BEEN A WHILE.
HUH?
••••••••

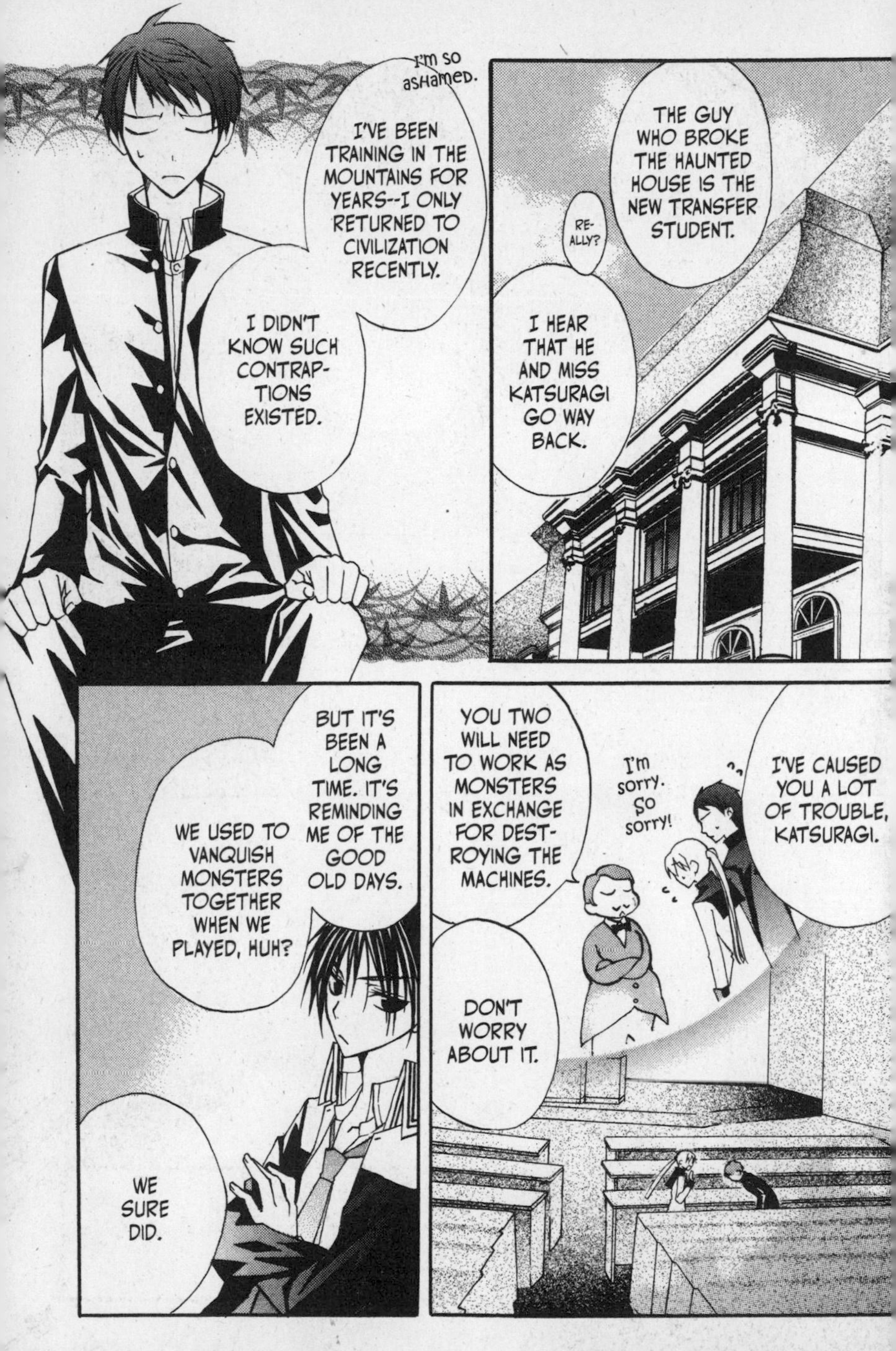
THE GUY WHO BROKE THE HAUNTED HOUSE IS THE NEW TRANSFER STUDENT.
RE-ALLY?
I HEAR THAT HE AND MISS KATSURAGI GO WAY BACK.
I'm so ashamed.
I'VE BEEN TRAINING IN THE MOUNTAINS FOR YEARS--I ONLY RETURNED TO CIVILIZATION RECENTLY.
I DIDN'T KNOW SUCH CONTRAP-TIONS EXISTED.
I'VE CAUSED YOU A LOT OF TROUBLE, KATSURAGI.
I'm sorry. So sorry!
YOU TWO WILL NEED TO WORK AS MONSTERS IN EXCHANGE FOR DEST-ROYING THE MACHINES.
DON'T WORRY ABOUT IT.
BUT IT'S BEEN A LONG TIME. IT'S REMINDING ME OF THE GOOD OLD DAYS.
WE USED TO VANQUISH MONSTERS TOGETHER WHEN WE PLAYED, HUH?
WE SURE DID.

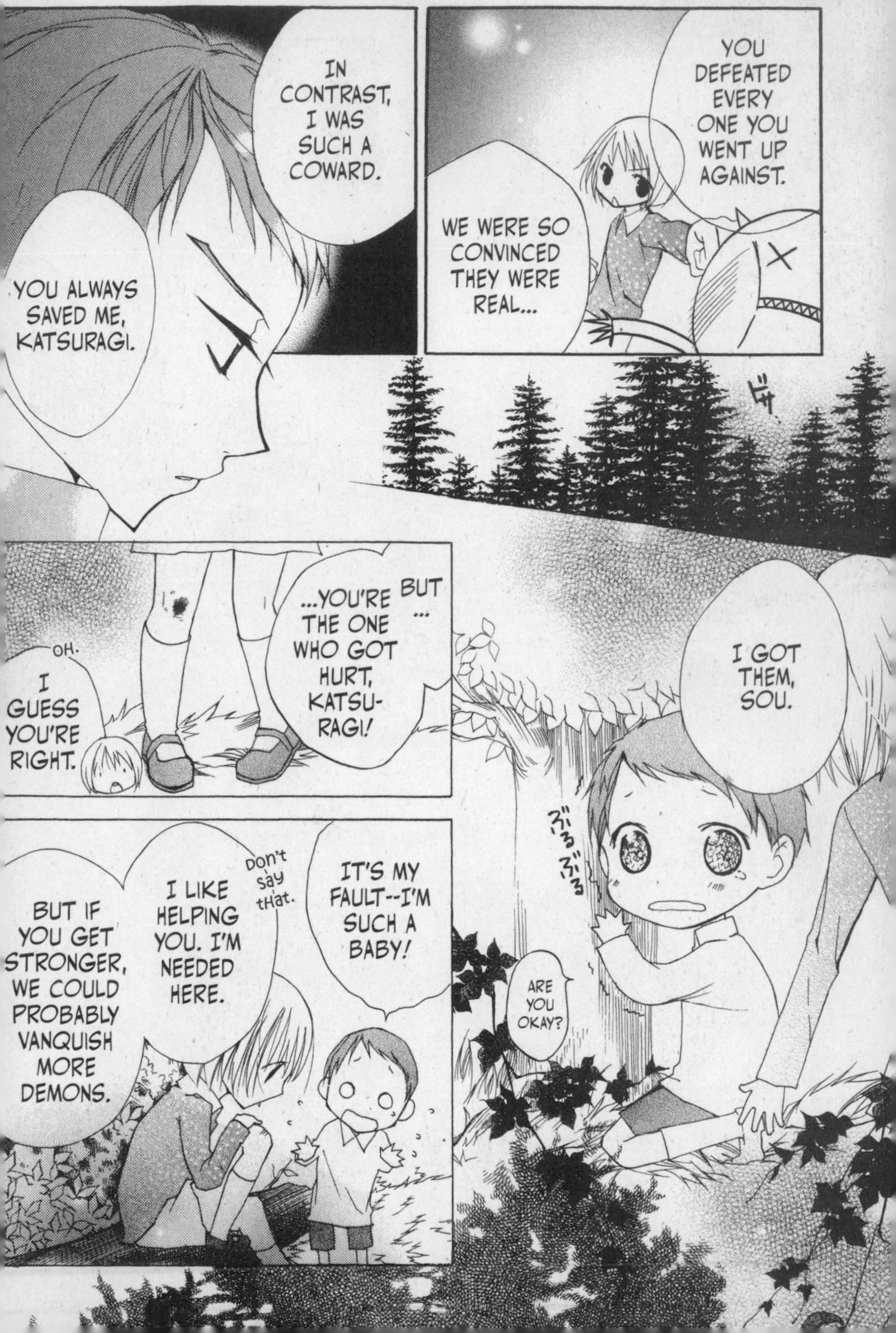
YOU DEFEATED EVERY ONE YOU WENT UP AGAINST.
WE WERE SO CONVINCED THEY WERE REAL...
IN CONTRAST, I WAS SUCH A COWARD.
YOU ALWAYS SAVED ME, KATSURAGI.
ドサ
I GOT THEM, SOU.
ぶるぶる
ARE YOU OKAY?
BUT ...
...YOU'RE THE ONE WHO GOT HURT, KATSURAGI!
OH.
I GUESS YOU'RE RIGHT.
IT'S MY FAULT--I'M SUCH A BABY!
Don't say that.
I LIKE HELPING YOU. I'M NEEDED HERE.
BUT IF YOU GET STRONGER, WE COULD PROBABLY VANQUISH MORE DEMONS.

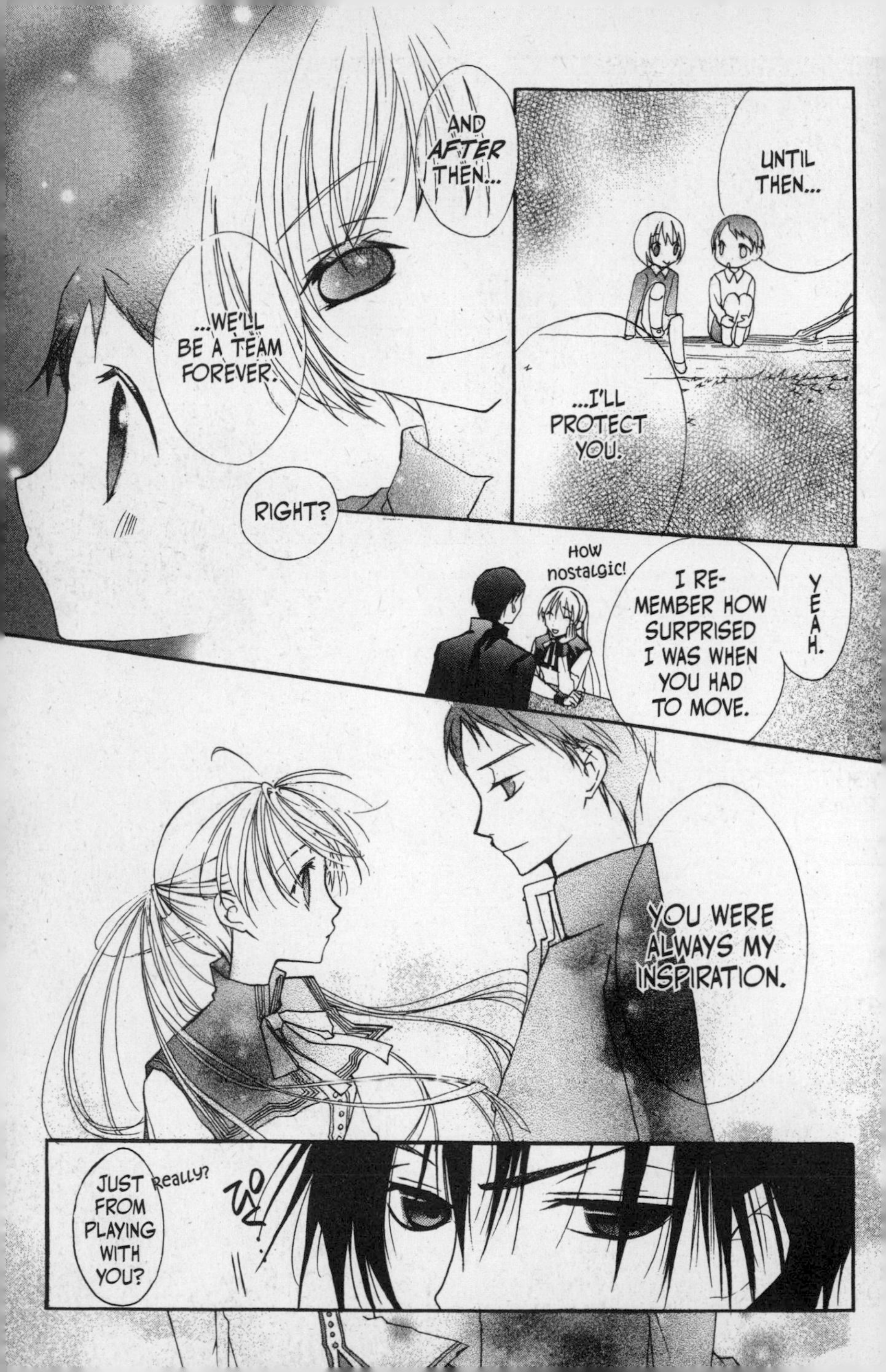
UNTIL THEN...
...I'LL PROTECT YOU.
AND AFTER THEN...
...WE'LL BE A TEAM FOREVER.
RIGHT?
YEAH.
I RE-MEMBER HOW SURPRISED I WAS WHEN YOU HAD TO MOVE.
HOW nostalgic!
YOU WERE ALWAYS MY INSPIRATION.
Really?
JUST FROM PLAYING WITH YOU?

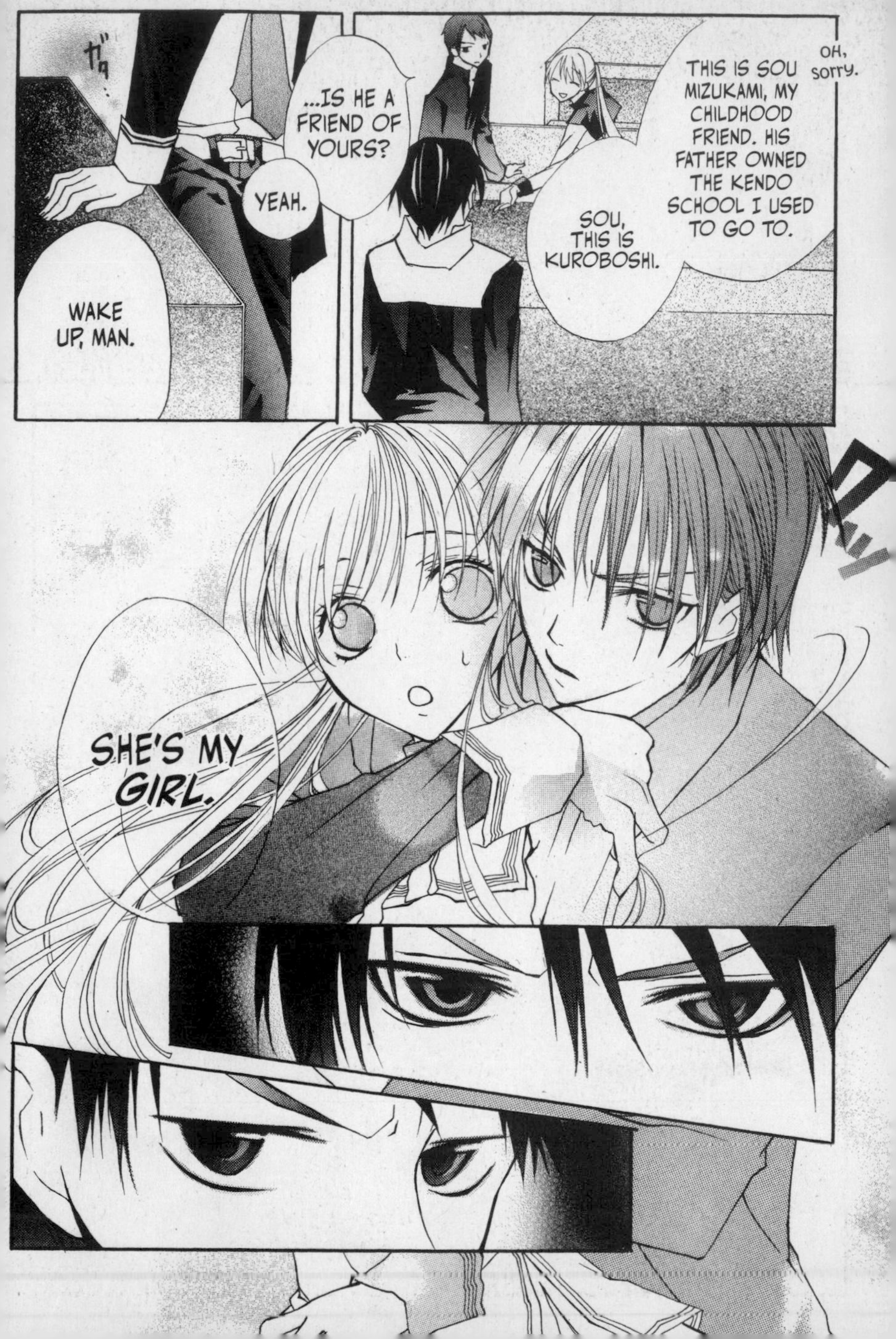
OH, sorry.
THIS IS SOU MIZUKAMI, MY CHILDHOOD FRIEND. HIS FATHER OWNED THE KENDO SCHOOL I USED TO GO TO.
SOU, THIS IS KUROBOSHI.
...IS HE A FRIEND OF YOURS?
YEAH.
WAKE UP, MAN.
SHE'S MY GIRL.

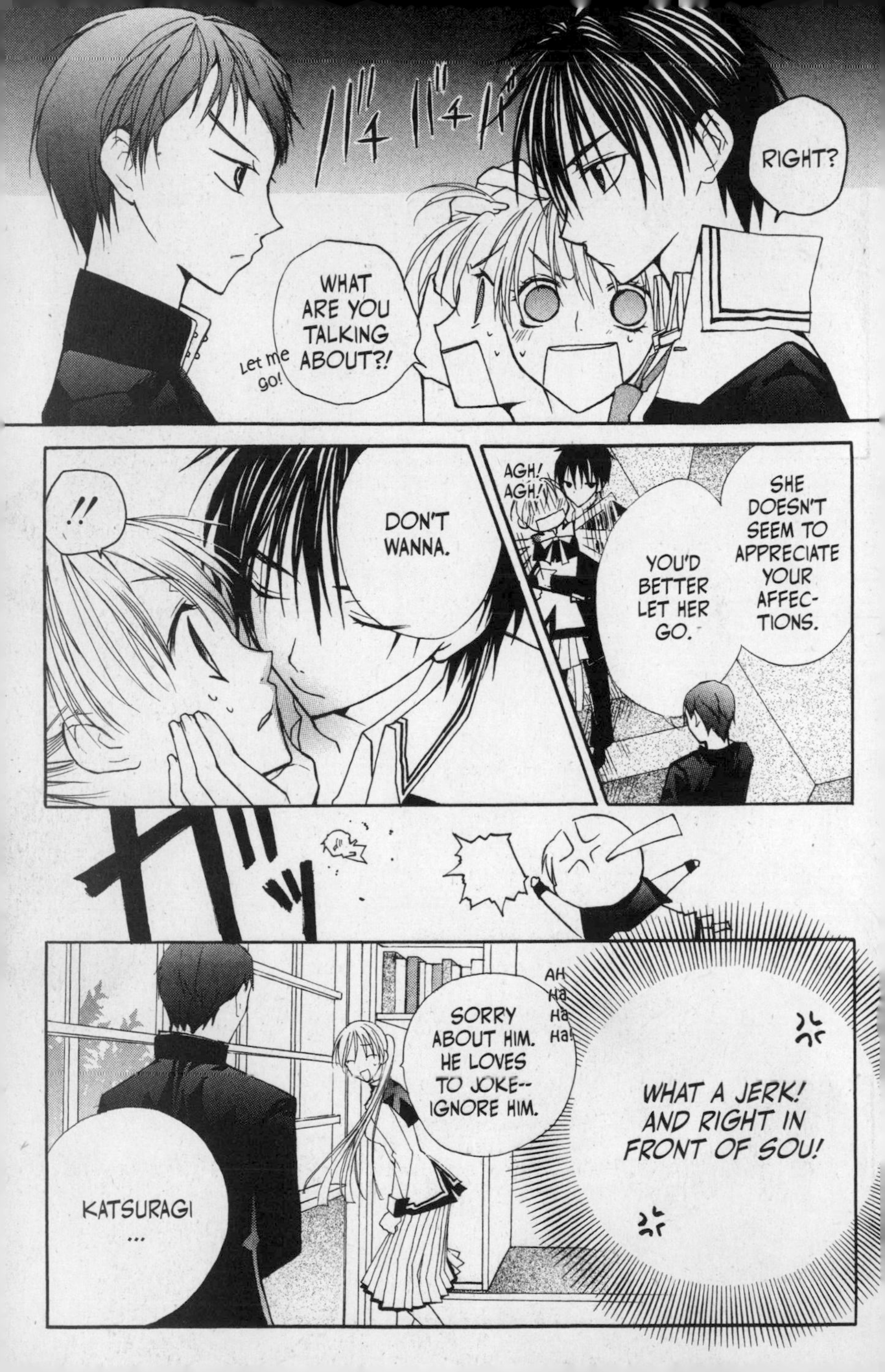
RIGHT?
WHAT ARE YOU TALKING ABOUT?!
Let me go!
SHE DOESN'T SEEM TO APPRECIATE YOUR AFFECTIONS.
YOU'D BETTER LET HER GO.
AGH! AGH!
DON'T WANNA.
!!
WHAT A JERK! AND RIGHT IN FRONT OF SOU!
AH HA HA HA!
SORRY ABOUT HIM. HE LOVES TO JOKE-- IGNORE HIM.
KATSURAGI ...

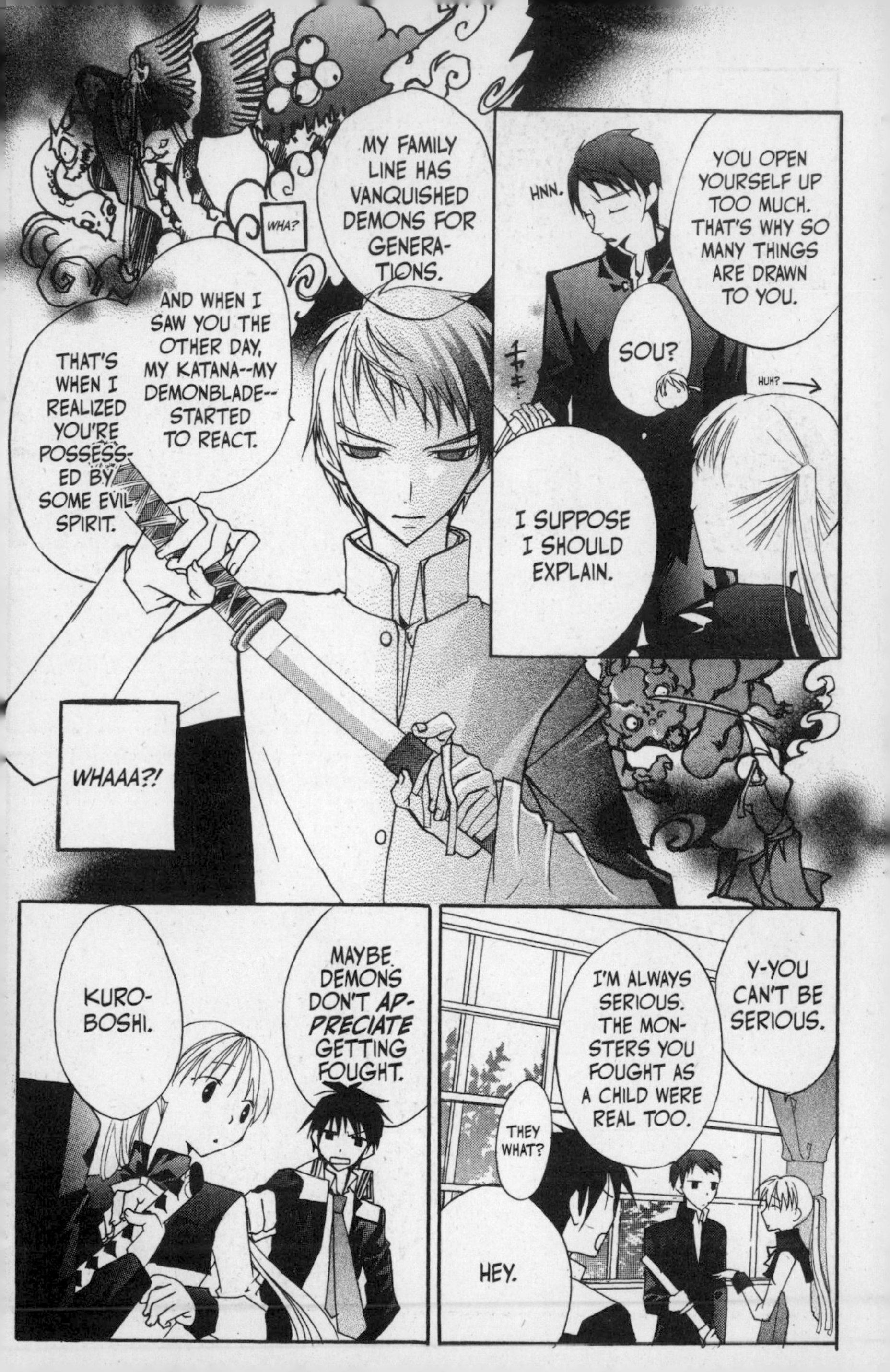

YOU OPEN YOURSELF UP TOO MUCH. THAT'S WHY SO MANY THINGS ARE DRAWN TO YOU.
HNN.
SOU?
HUH?
I SUPPOSE I SHOULD EXPLAIN.
MY FAMILY LINE HAS VANQUISHED DEMONS FOR GENERATIONS.
WHA?
AND WHEN I SAW YOU THE OTHER DAY, MY KATANA--MY DEMONBLADE--STARTED TO REACT.
THAT'S WHEN I REALIZED YOU'RE POSSESSED BY SOME EVIL SPIRIT.
WHAAA?!
Y-YOU CAN'T BE SERIOUS.
I'M ALWAYS SERIOUS. THE MONSTERS YOU FOUGHT AS A CHILD WERE REAL TOO.
THEY WHAT?
HEY.
MAYBE DEMONS DON'T *APPRECIATE* GETTING FOUGHT.
KURO-BOSHI.

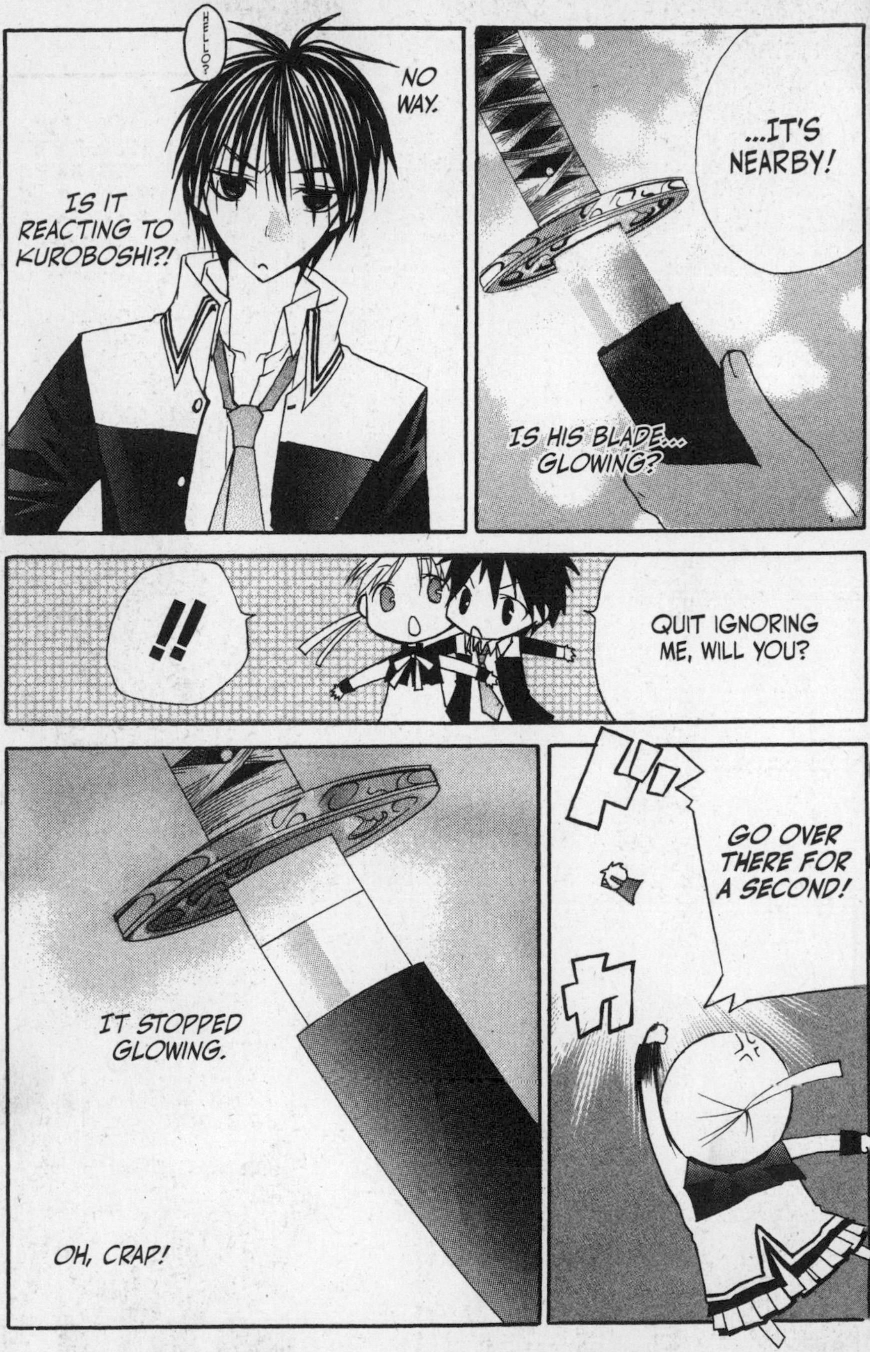
...IT'S NEARBY!
IS HIS BLADE... GLOWING?
NO WAY.
HELLO?
IS IT REACTING TO KUROBOSHI?!
QUIT IGNORING ME, WILL YOU?
!!
GO OVER THERE FOR A SECOND!
IT STOPPED GLOWING.
OH, CRAP!

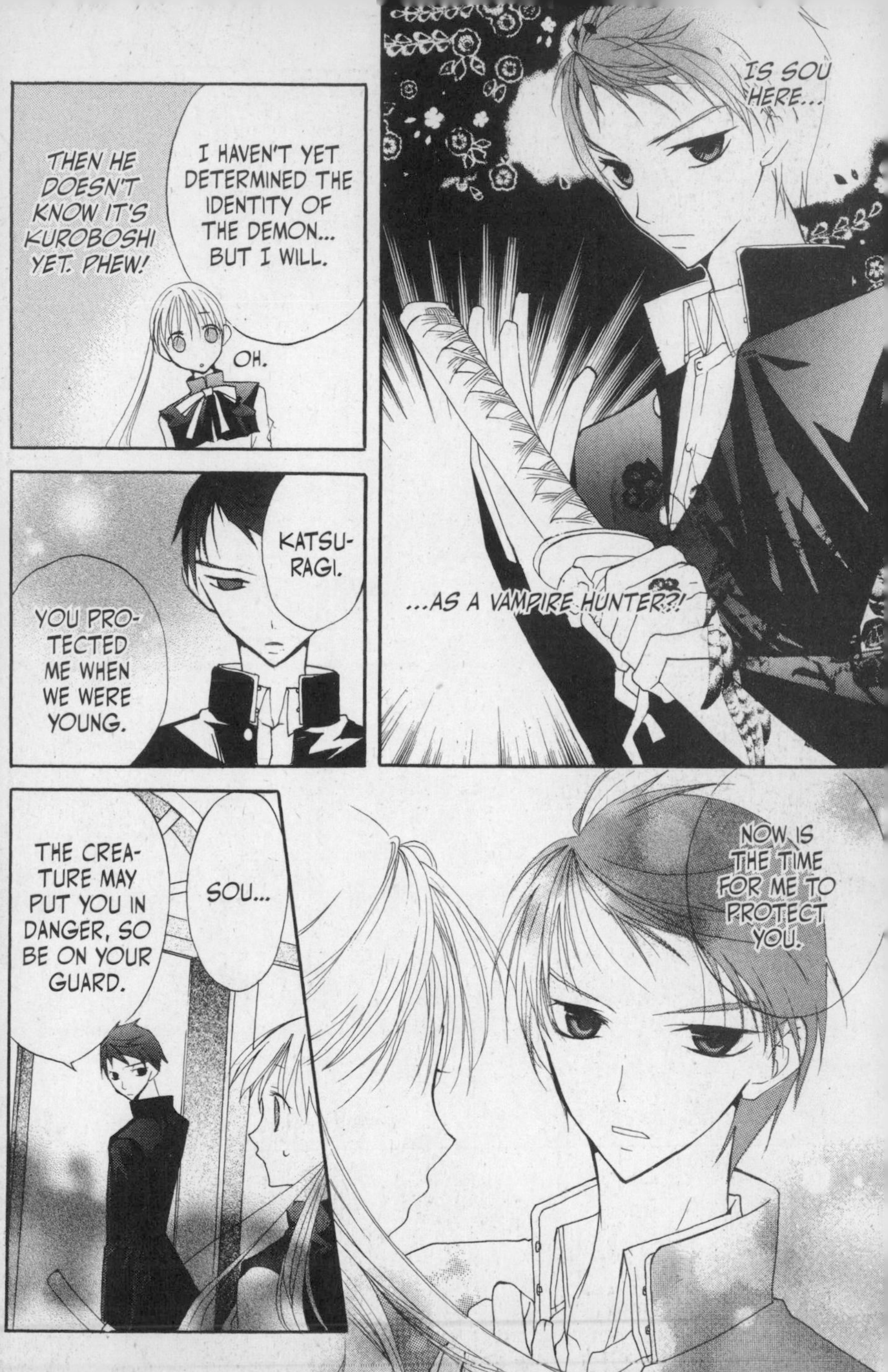
IS SOU HERE...
...AS A VAMPIRE HUNTER?!
I HAVEN'T YET DETERMINED THE IDENTITY OF THE DEMON... BUT I WILL.
THEN HE DOESN'T KNOW IT'S KUROBOSHI YET. PHEW!
OH.
KATSU-RAGI.
YOU PRO-TECTED ME WHEN WE WERE YOUNG.
NOW IS THE TIME FOR ME TO PROTECT YOU.
SOU...
THE CREA-TURE MAY PUT YOU IN DANGER, SO BE ON YOUR GUARD.

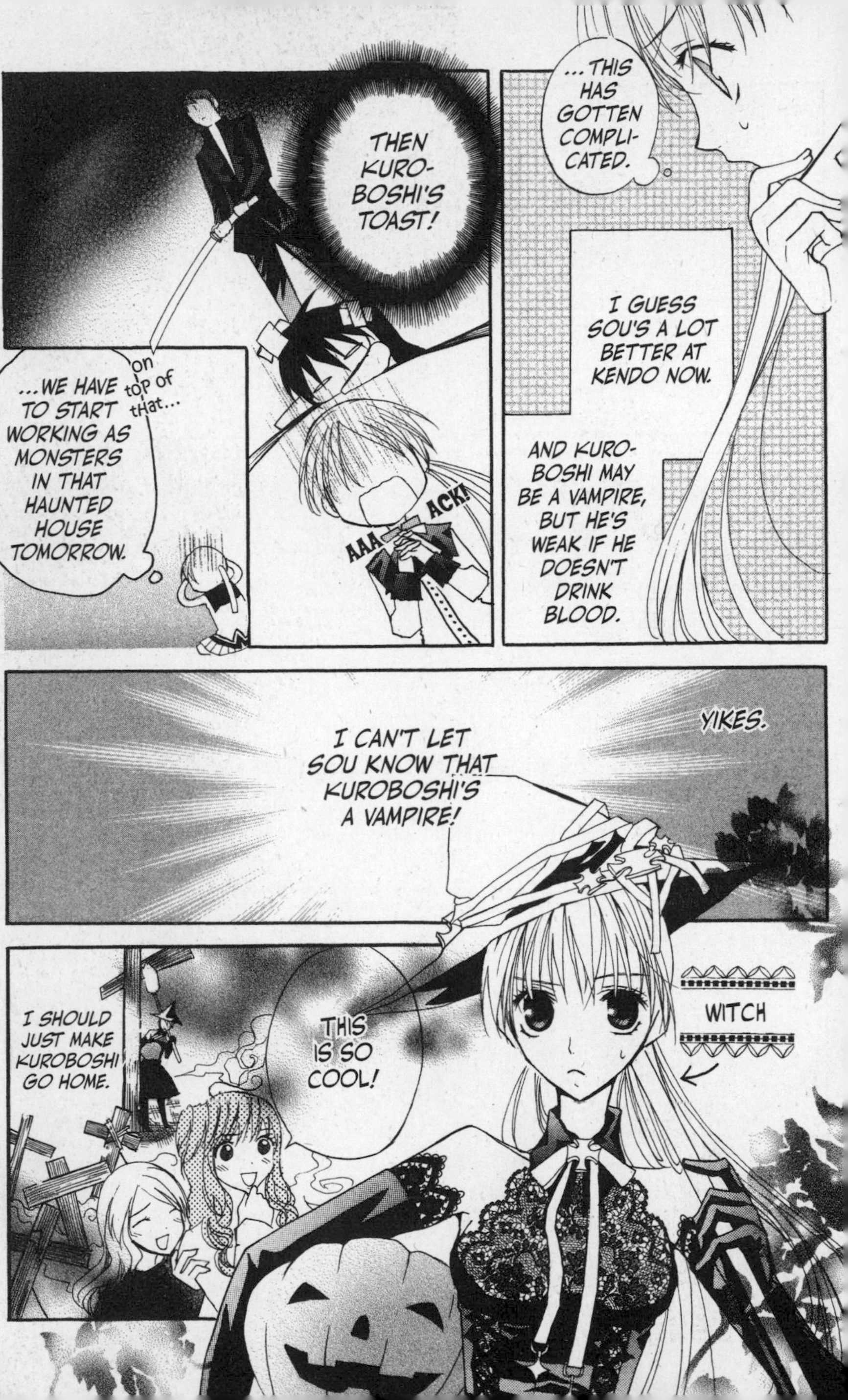
...THIS HAS GOTTEN COMPLICATED.
I GUESS SOU'S A LOT BETTER AT KENDO NOW.
AND KUROBOSHI MAY BE A VAMPIRE, BUT HE'S WEAK IF HE DOESN'T DRINK BLOOD.
THEN KUROBOSHI'S TOAST!
AAAACK!
on top of that...
...WE HAVE TO START WORKING AS MONSTERS IN THAT HAUNTED HOUSE TOMORROW.
YIKES.
I CAN'T LET SOU KNOW THAT KUROBOSHI'S A VAMPIRE!
WITCH
THIS IS SO COOL!
I SHOULD JUST MAKE KUROBOSHI GO HOME.

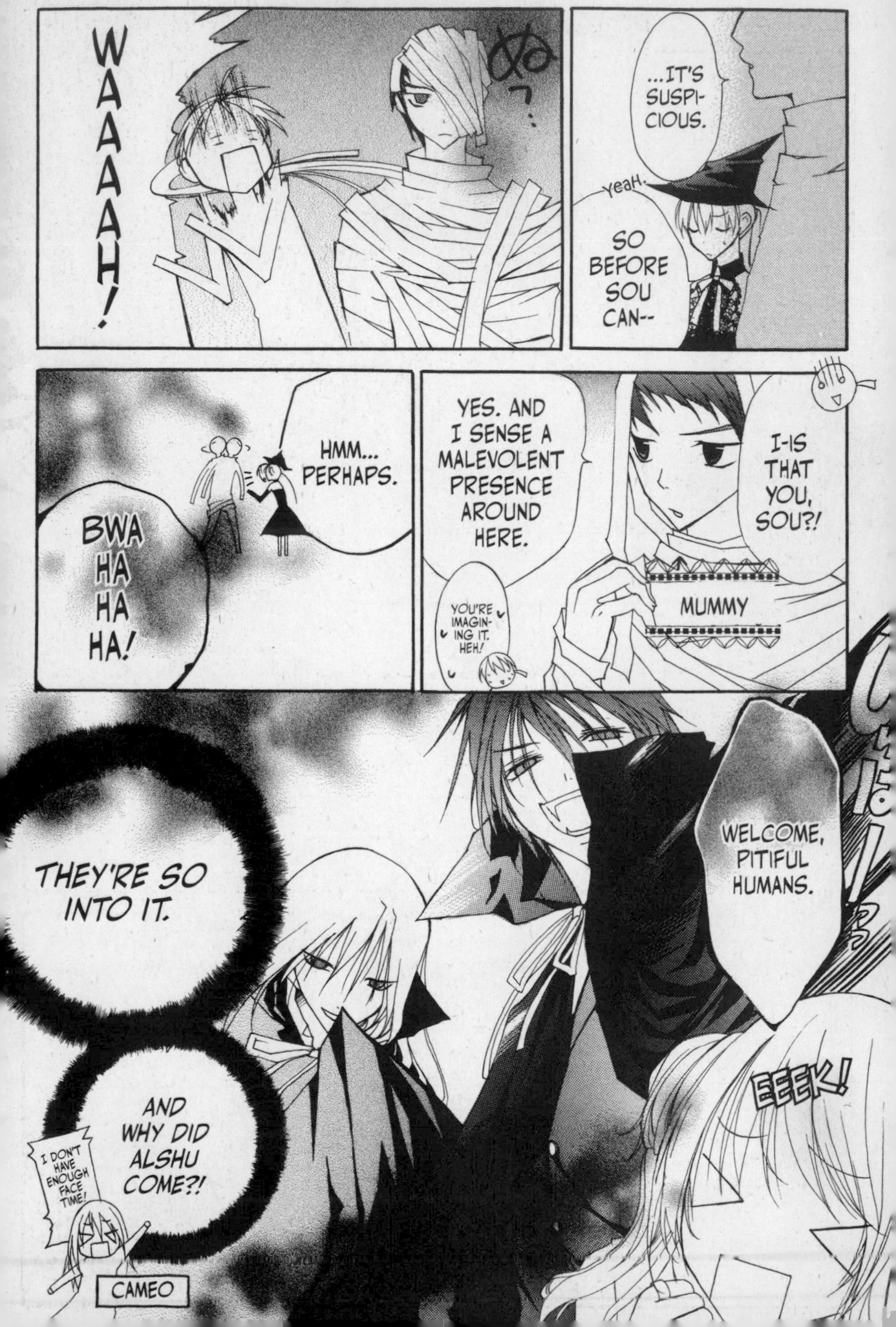
...IT'S SUSPICIOUS.
YeaH.
SO BEFORE SOU CAN--
WAAAAAH!
I-IS THAT YOU, SOU?!
YES. AND I SENSE A MALEVOLENT PRESENCE AROUND HERE.
MUMMY
YOU'RE IMAGINING IT. HEH!
HMM... PERHAPS.
BWA HA HA HA!
EEEK!
WELCOME, PITIFUL HUMANS.
THEY'RE SO INTO IT.
AND WHY DID ALSHU COME?!
I DON'T HAVE ENOUGH FACE TIME!
CAMEO

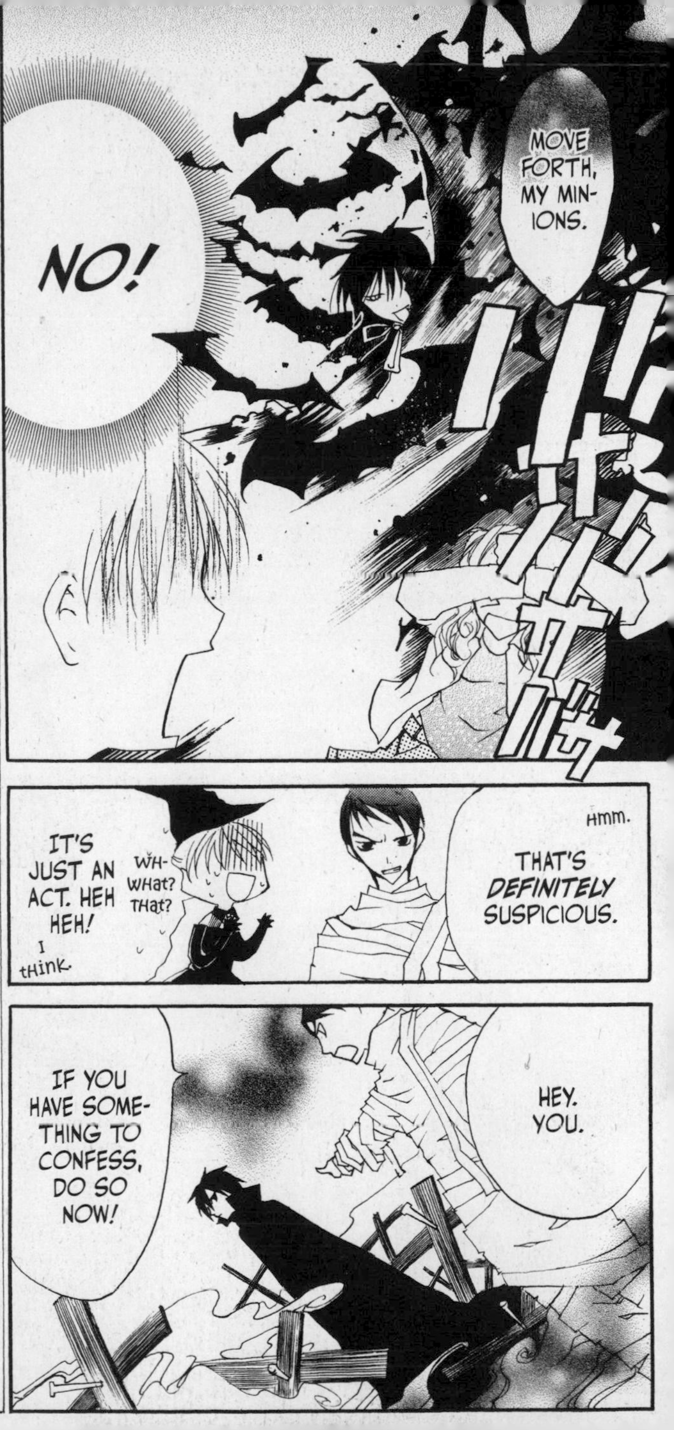
MOVE FORTH, MY MIN-IONS.
NO!
HMM.
THAT'S *DEFINITELY* SUSPICIOUS.
WH-WHAT? THAT?
IT'S JUST AN ACT. HEH HEH!
I THINK.
HEY. YOU.
IF YOU HAVE SOME-THING TO CONFESS, DO SO NOW!

My least favorite parts

Part 2

Nose holes, cleavage and nails.

They're not that bad now, but those three body parts made me miserable when I was a child.

Cleavage is still something I resist drawing...

I'm totally fine now with nose holes and nails, but when I was a kid, I always thought that a particular famous judo anime would've been much more enjoyable if it weren't plagued with nose holes.

I've come to the realization that I probably don't like anything holey.

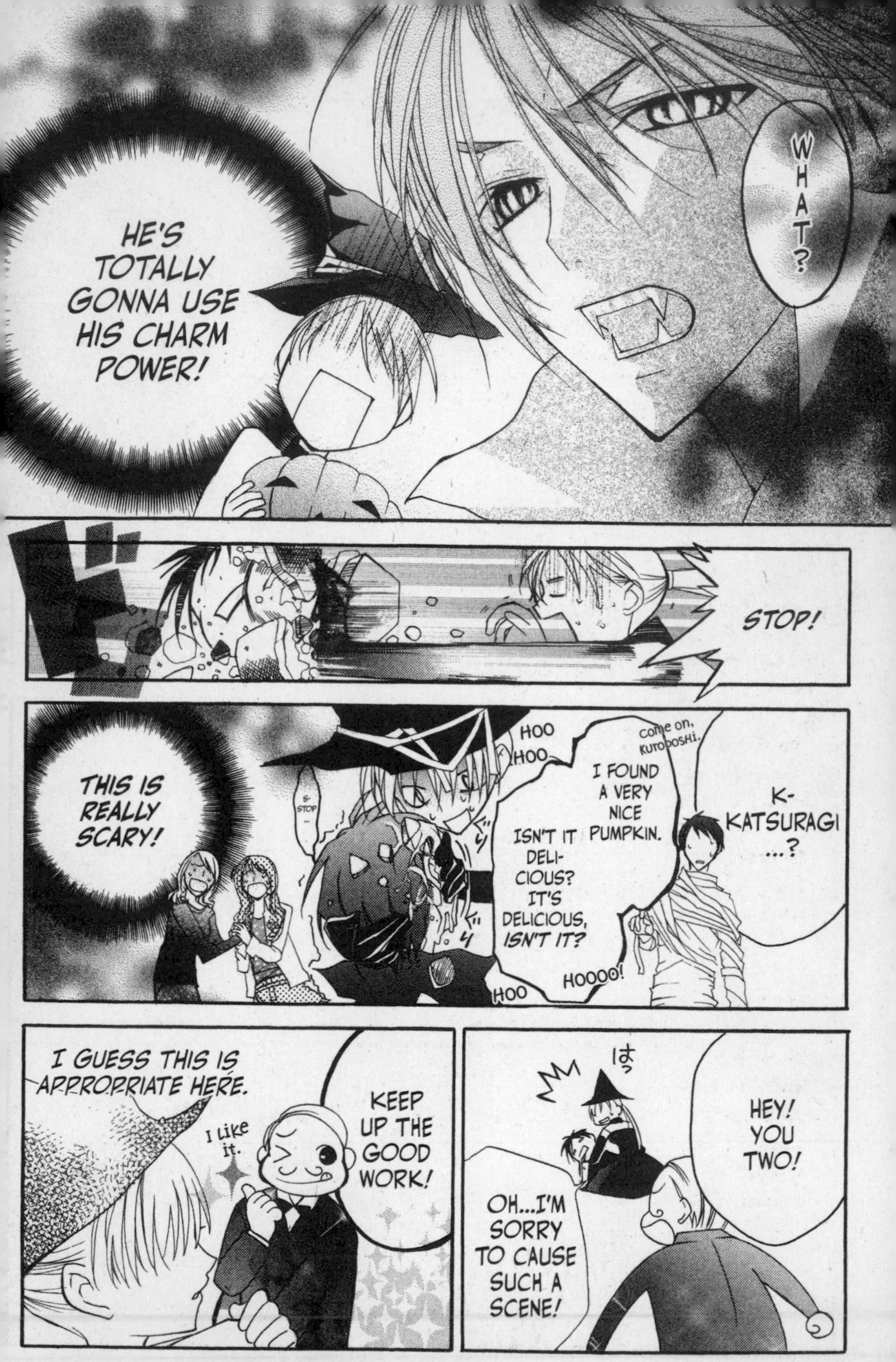
WHAT?
HE'S TOTALLY GONNA USE HIS CHARM POWER!
STOP!
K-KATSURAGI ...?
come on, KUTOBOSHI.
I FOUND A VERY NICE PUMPKIN.
ISN'T IT DELI-CIOUS? IT'S DELICIOUS, ISN'T IT?
HOO HOO
HOO HOOOO!
S-STOP...
THIS IS REALLY SCARY!
HEY! YOU TWO!
はっ
OH...I'M SORRY TO CAUSE SUCH A SCENE!
KEEP UP THE GOOD WORK!
I like it.
I GUESS THIS IS APPROPRIATE HERE.

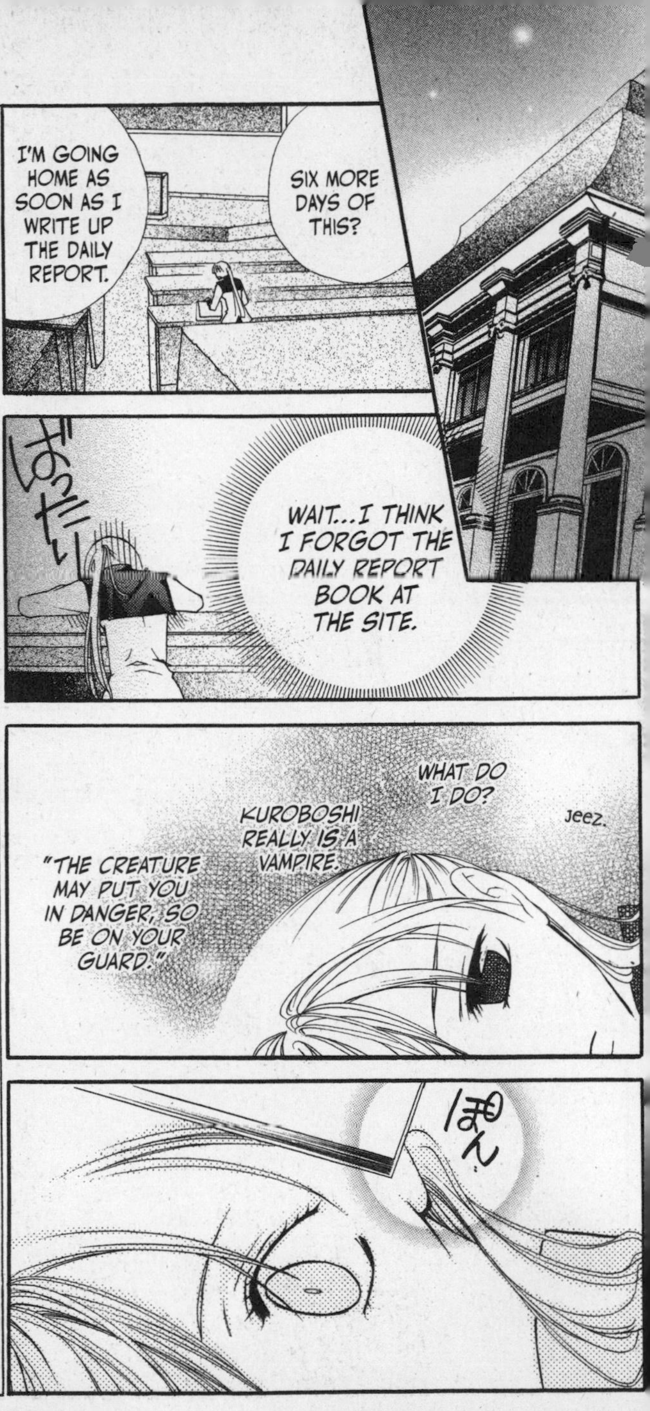
SIX MORE DAYS OF THIS?
I'M GOING HOME AS SOON AS I WRITE UP THE DAILY REPORT.
WAIT...I THINK I FORGOT THE DAILY REPORT BOOK AT THE SITE.
Jeez.
WHAT DO I DO?
KUROBOSHI REALLY IS A VAMPIRE.
"THE CREATURE MAY PUT YOU IN DANGER, SO BE ON YOUR GUARD."
ぽん

My favorite parts.

Part 1

Hands

"I like hands." I bet there are a lot of people out there who think the same thing. People like me. Though it's not to the point of a fetish...

People who play the guitar have beautiful hands.

Beautiful-yet-bulky hands are even more attractive.

I like drawing them, but they're a difficult body part. I only wish I could get better at portraying them.

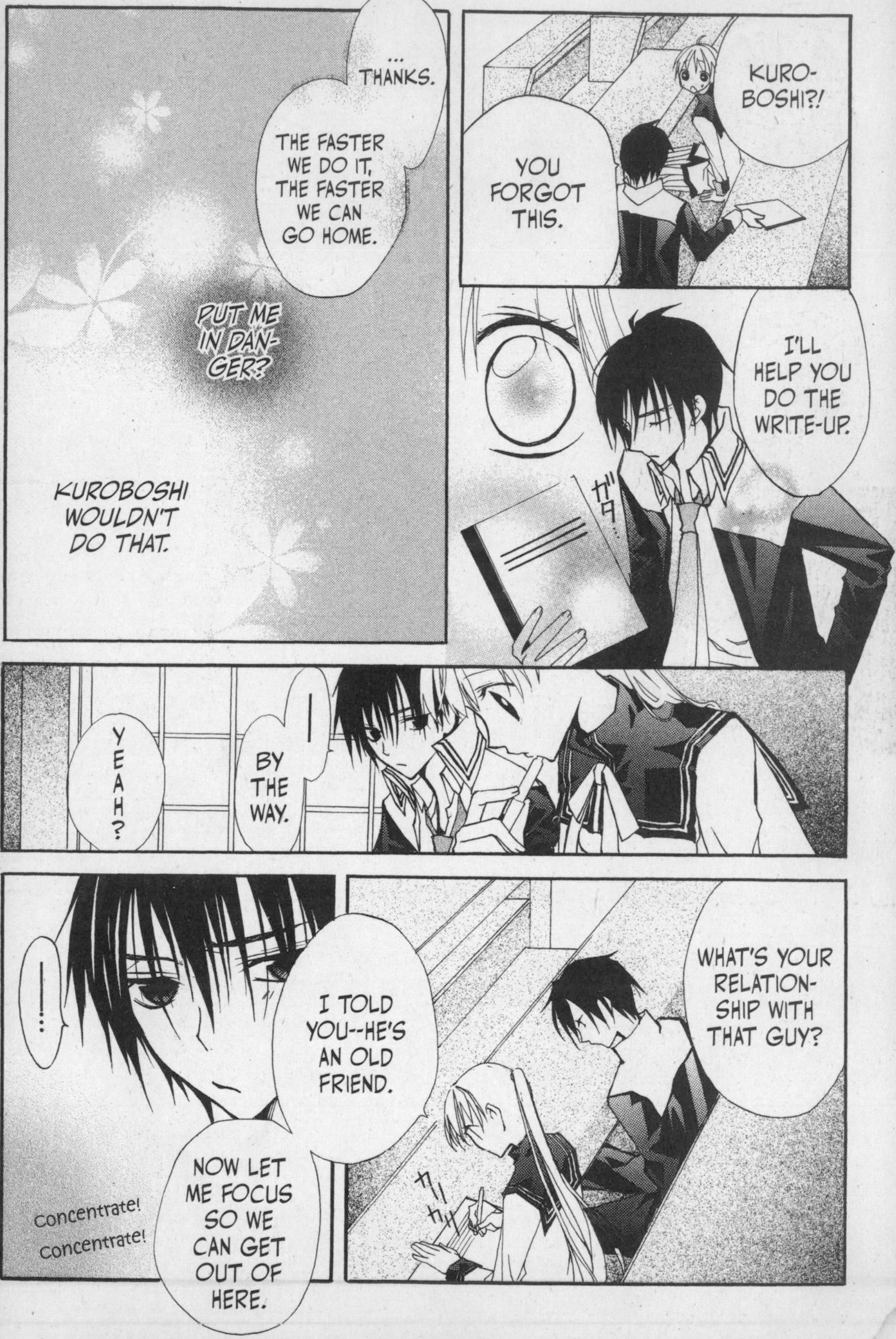
KURO-BOSHI?!
YOU FORGOT THIS.
I'LL HELP YOU DO THE WRITE-UP.
ガタ…
...THANKS.
THE FASTER WE DO IT, THE FASTER WE CAN GO HOME.
PUT ME IN DAN-GER?
KUROBOSHI WOULDN'T DO THAT.
BY THE WAY.
YEAH?
WHAT'S YOUR RELATIONSHIP WITH THAT GUY?
カリカリ
...!!
I TOLD YOU--HE'S AN OLD FRIEND.
NOW LET ME FOCUS SO WE CAN GET OUT OF HERE.
Concentrate!
Concentrate!

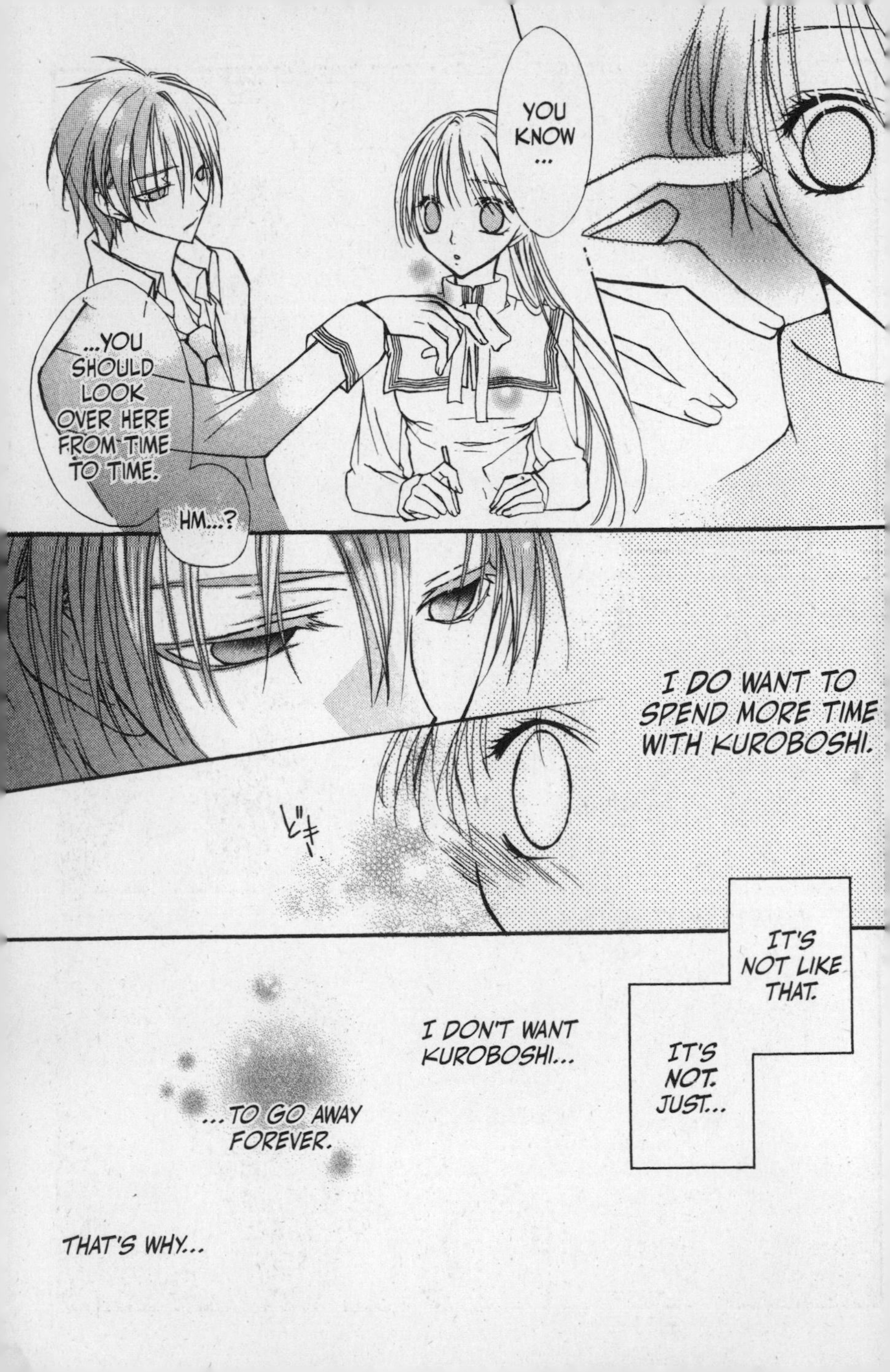
YOU KNOW ...
...YOU SHOULD LOOK OVER HERE FROM TIME TO TIME.
HM...?
I DO WANT TO SPEND MORE TIME WITH KUROBOSHI.
ドキ
IT'S NOT LIKE THAT.
IT'S NOT. JUST...
I DON'T WANT KUROBOSHI...
...TO GO AWAY FOREVER.
THAT'S WHY...

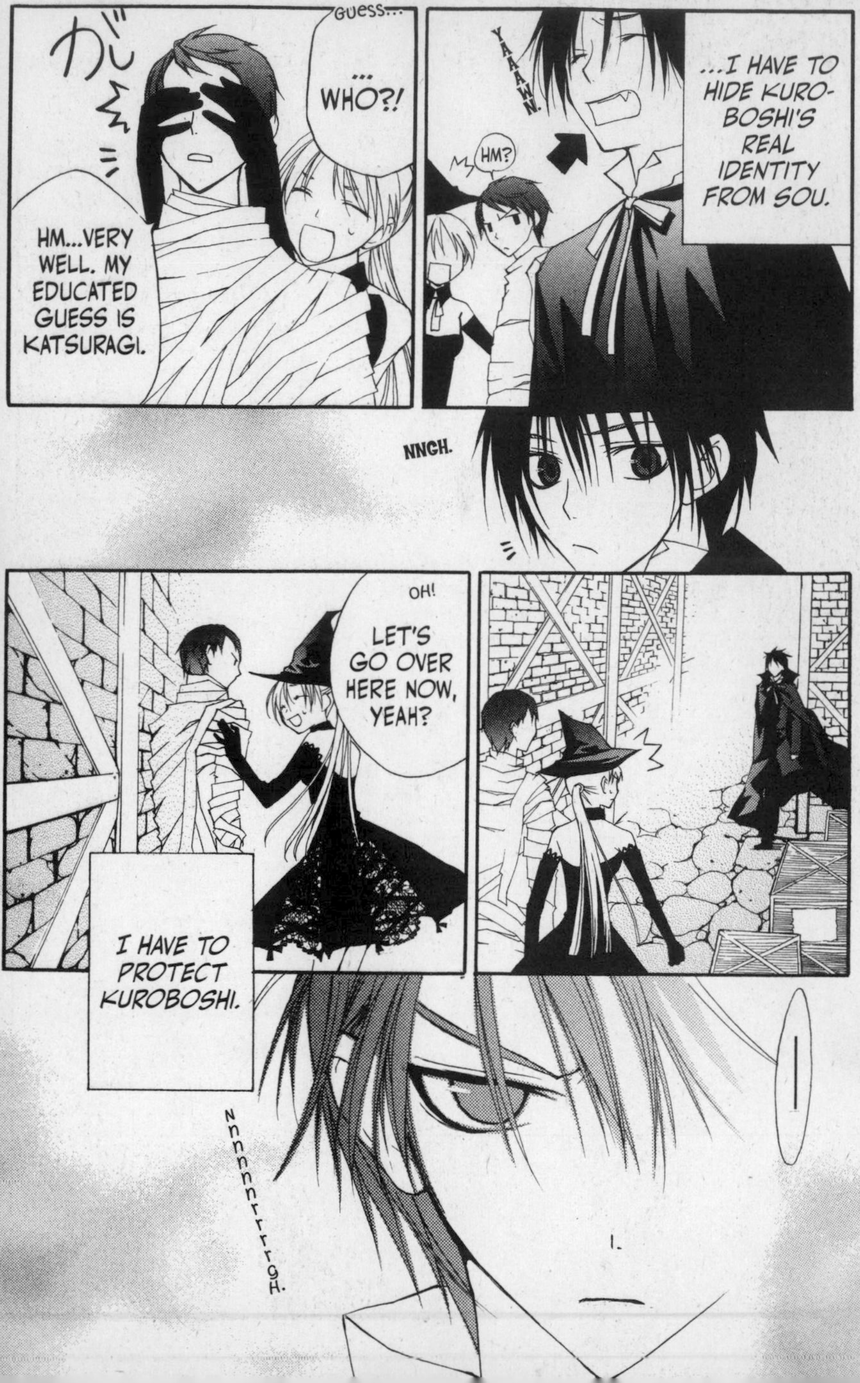
YAAAWN.
HM?
...I HAVE TO HIDE KURO-BOSHI'S REAL IDENTITY FROM SOU.
GUESS...
... WHO?!
HM...VERY WELL. MY EDUCATED GUESS IS KATSURAGI.
NNGH.
OH!
LET'S GO OVER HERE NOW, YEAH?
I HAVE TO PROTECT KUROBOSHI.
!
NnnnnrrrrGH.

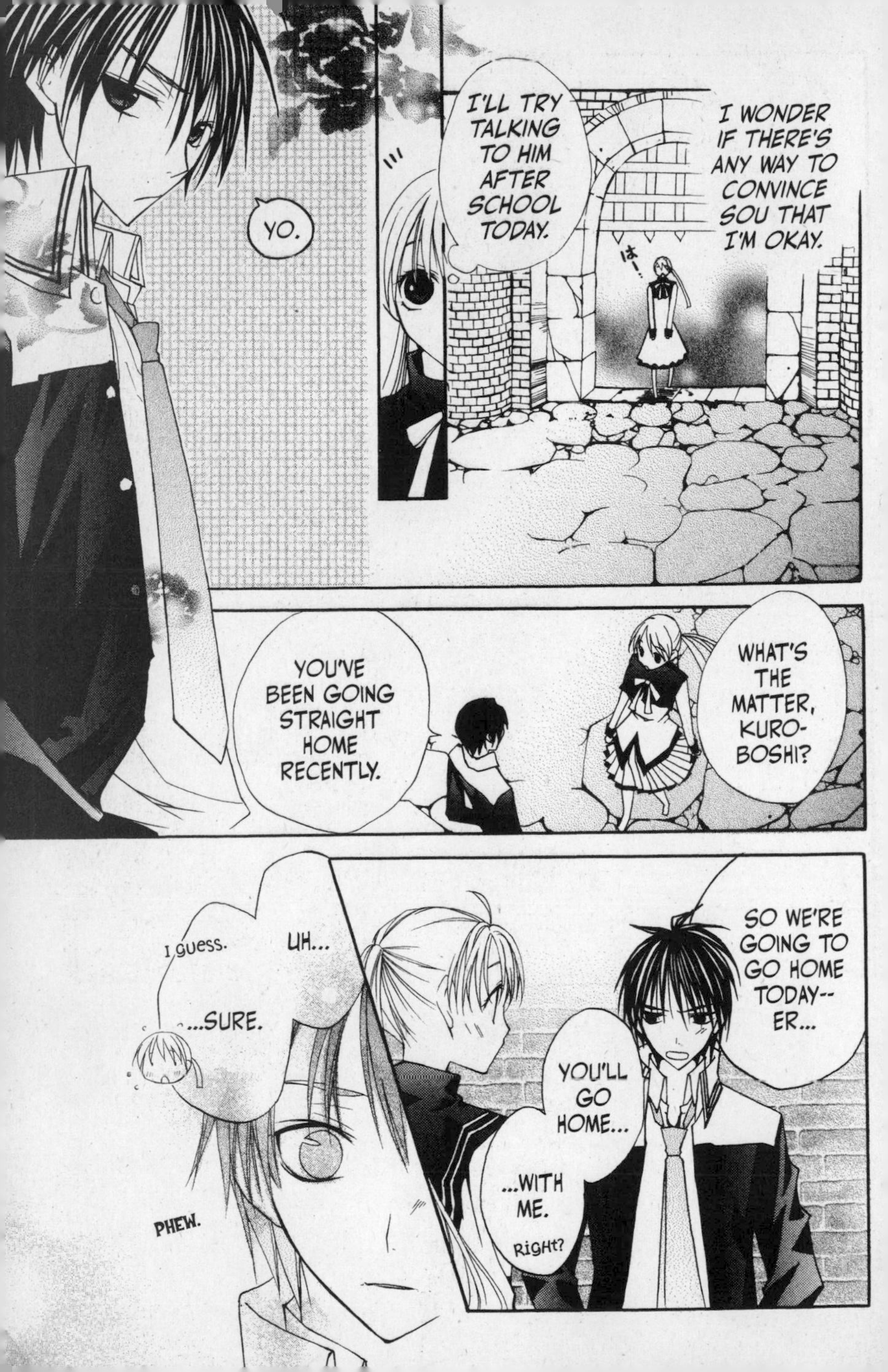
I WONDER IF THERE'S ANY WAY TO CONVINCE SOU THAT I'M OKAY.
は！
I'LL TRY TALKING TO HIM AFTER SCHOOL TODAY.
WHAT'S THE MATTER, KURO-BOSHI?
YOU'VE BEEN GOING STRAIGHT HOME RECENTLY.
YO.
SO WE'RE GOING TO GO HOME TODAY-- ER...
YOU'LL GO HOME...
...WITH ME.
Right?
UH...
...SURE.
I guess.
PHEW.

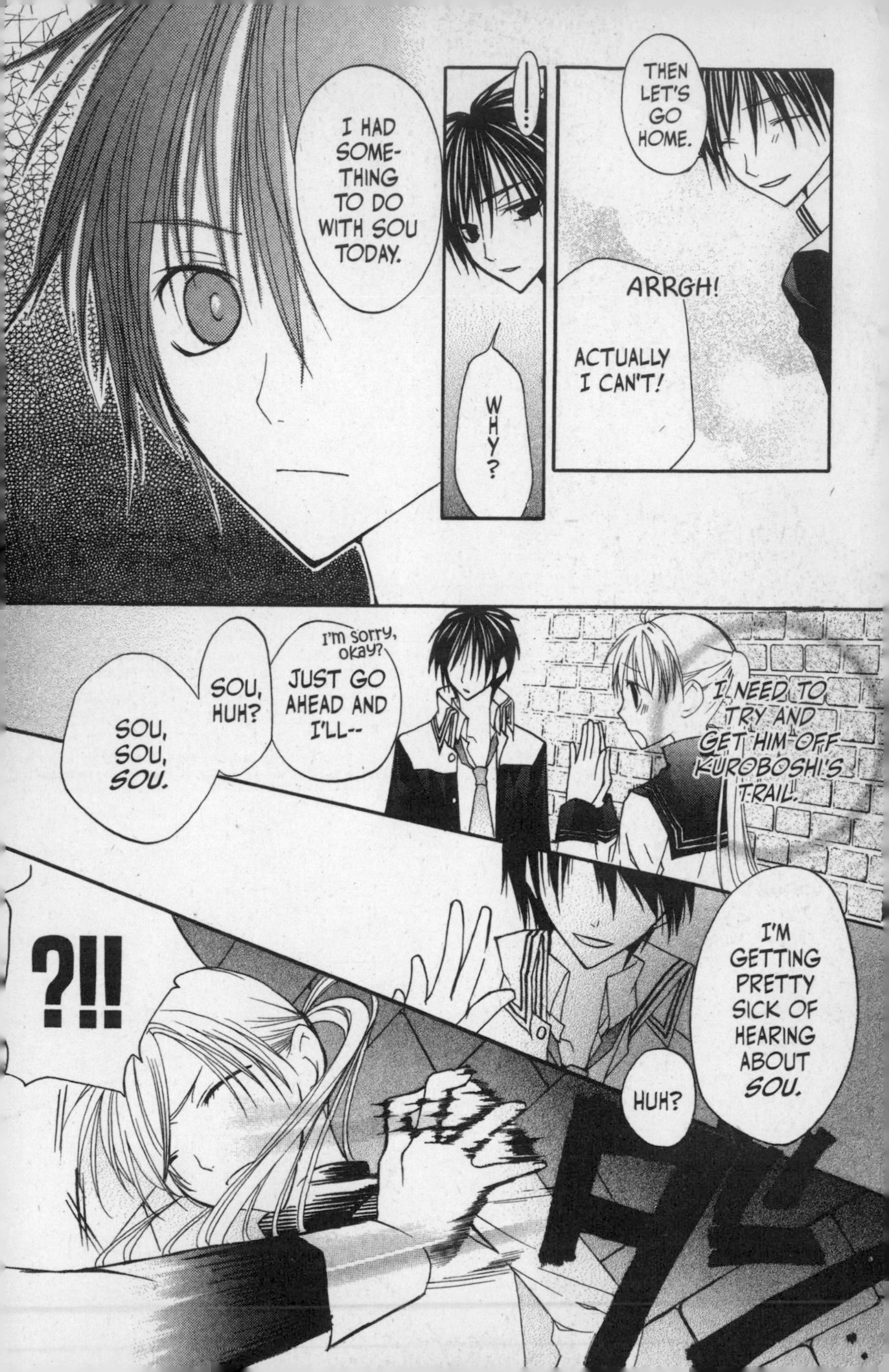
THEN LET'S GO HOME.
ARRGH!
ACTUALLY I CAN'T!
!...
WHY?
I HAD SOME-THING TO DO WITH SOU TODAY.
I NEED TO TRY AND GET HIM OFF KUROBOSHI'S TRAIL.
I'm sorry, okay? JUST GO AHEAD AND I'LL--
SOU, HUH?
SOU, SOU, SOU.
I'M GETTING PRETTY SICK OF HEARING ABOUT SOU.
HUH?
?!!

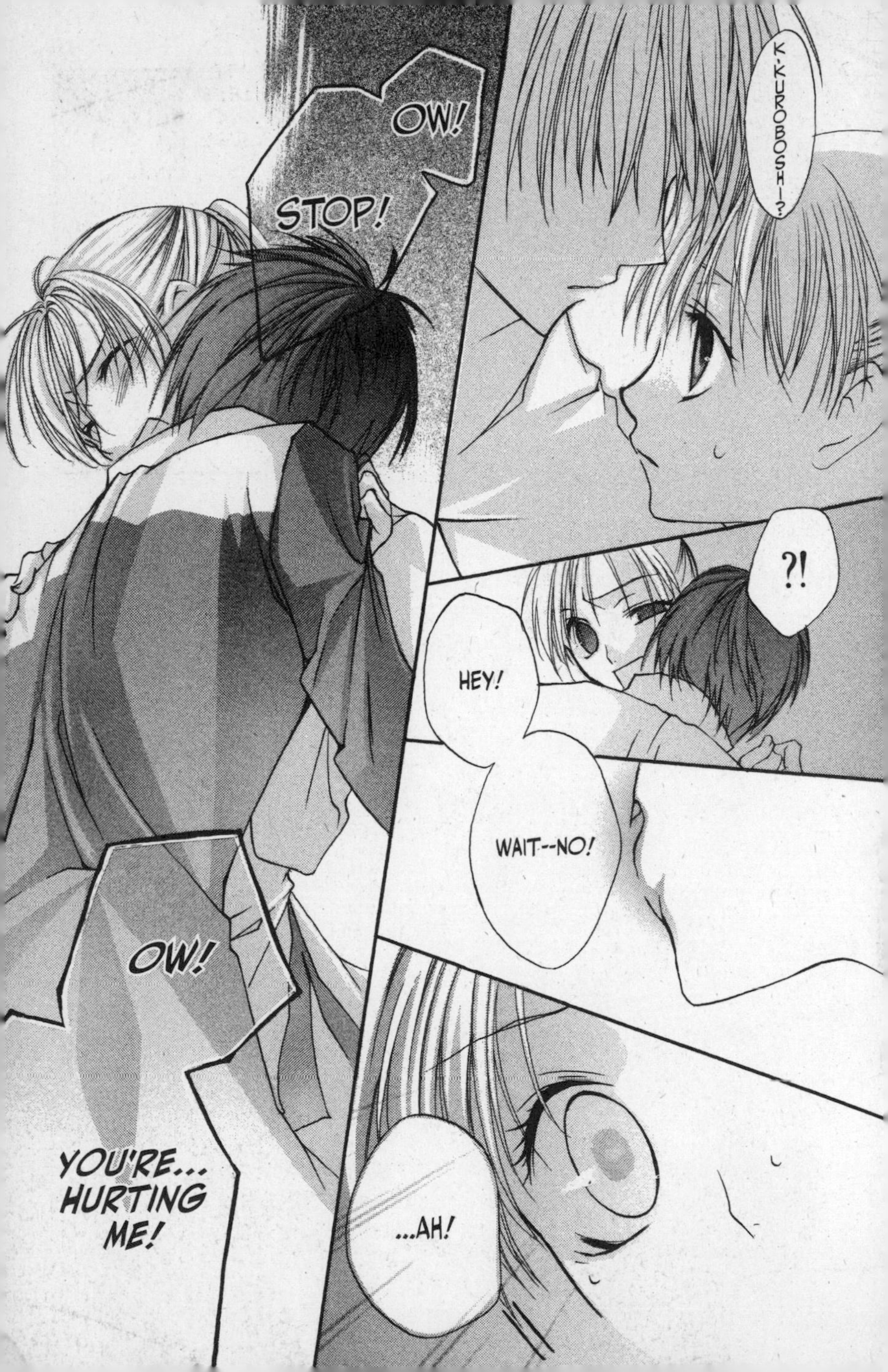
K-KUROBOSHI...?
?!
HEY!
WAIT--NO!
...AH!
OW!
STOP!
OW!
YOU'RE... HURTING ME!

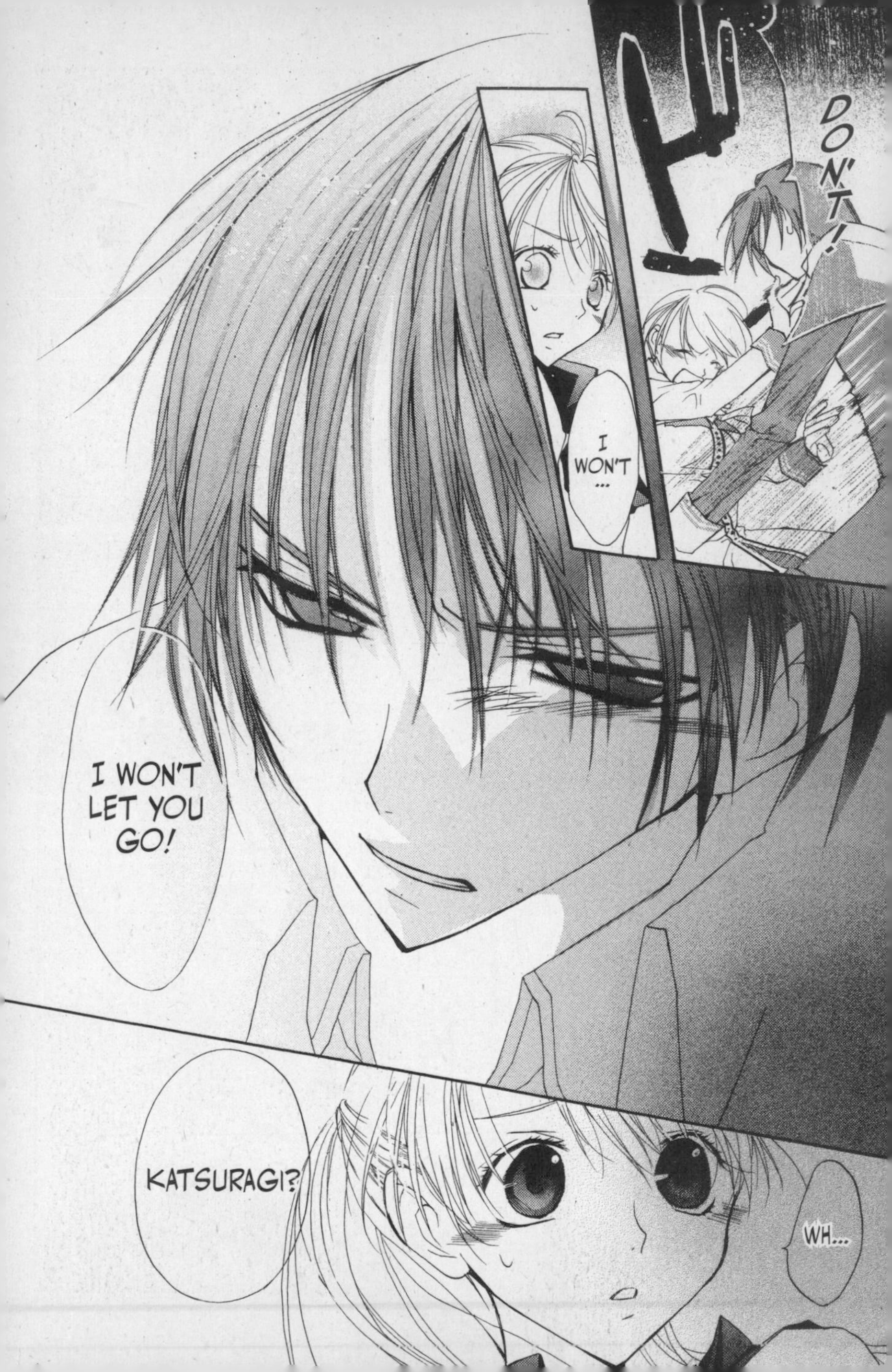
DON'T!
I WON'T ...
I WON'T LET YOU GO!
WH...
KATSURAGI?

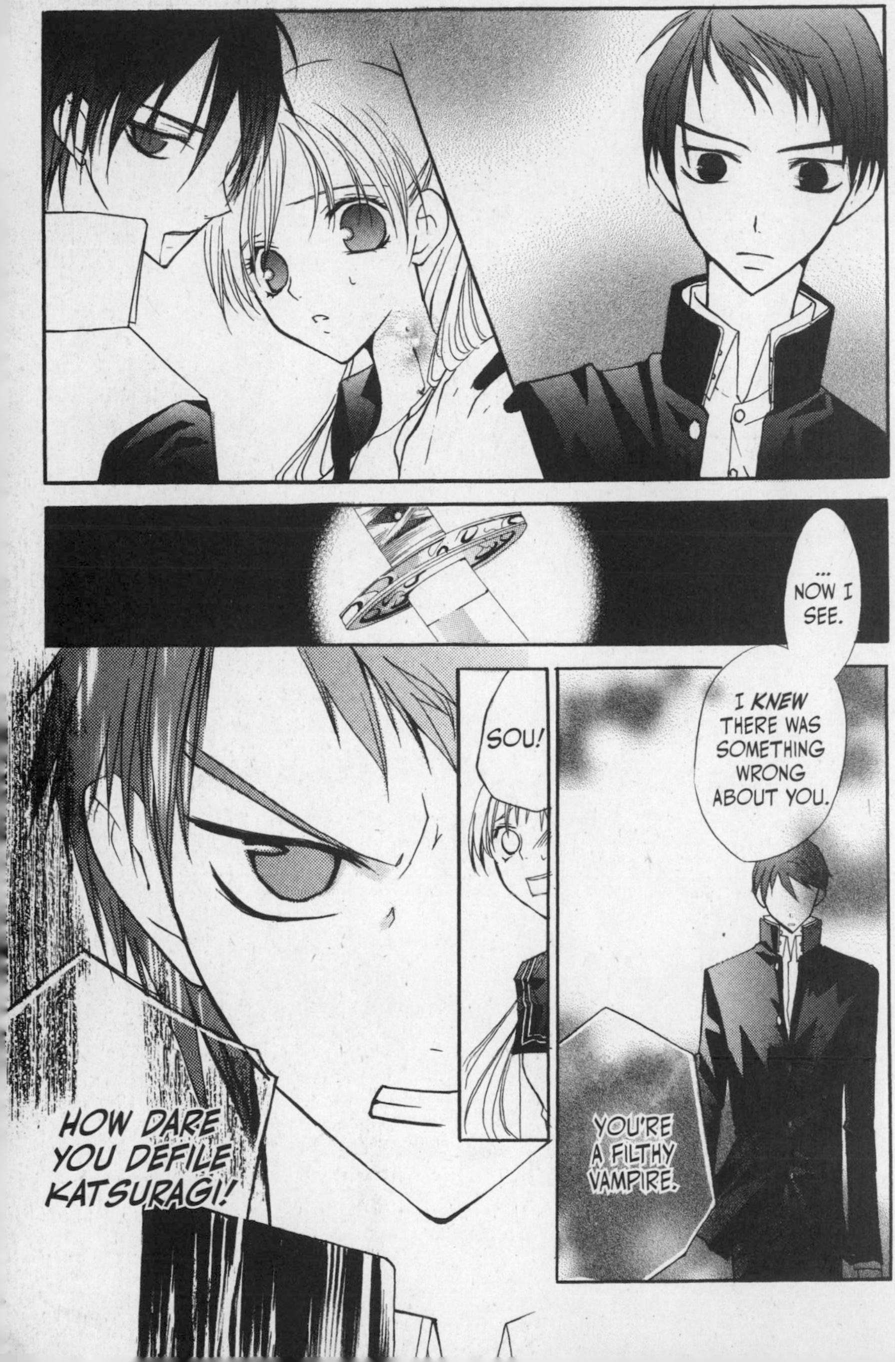
... NOW I SEE.
I KNEW THERE WAS SOMETHING WRONG ABOUT YOU.
YOU'RE A FILTHY VAMPIRE.
SOU!
HOW DARE YOU DEFILE KATSURAGI!

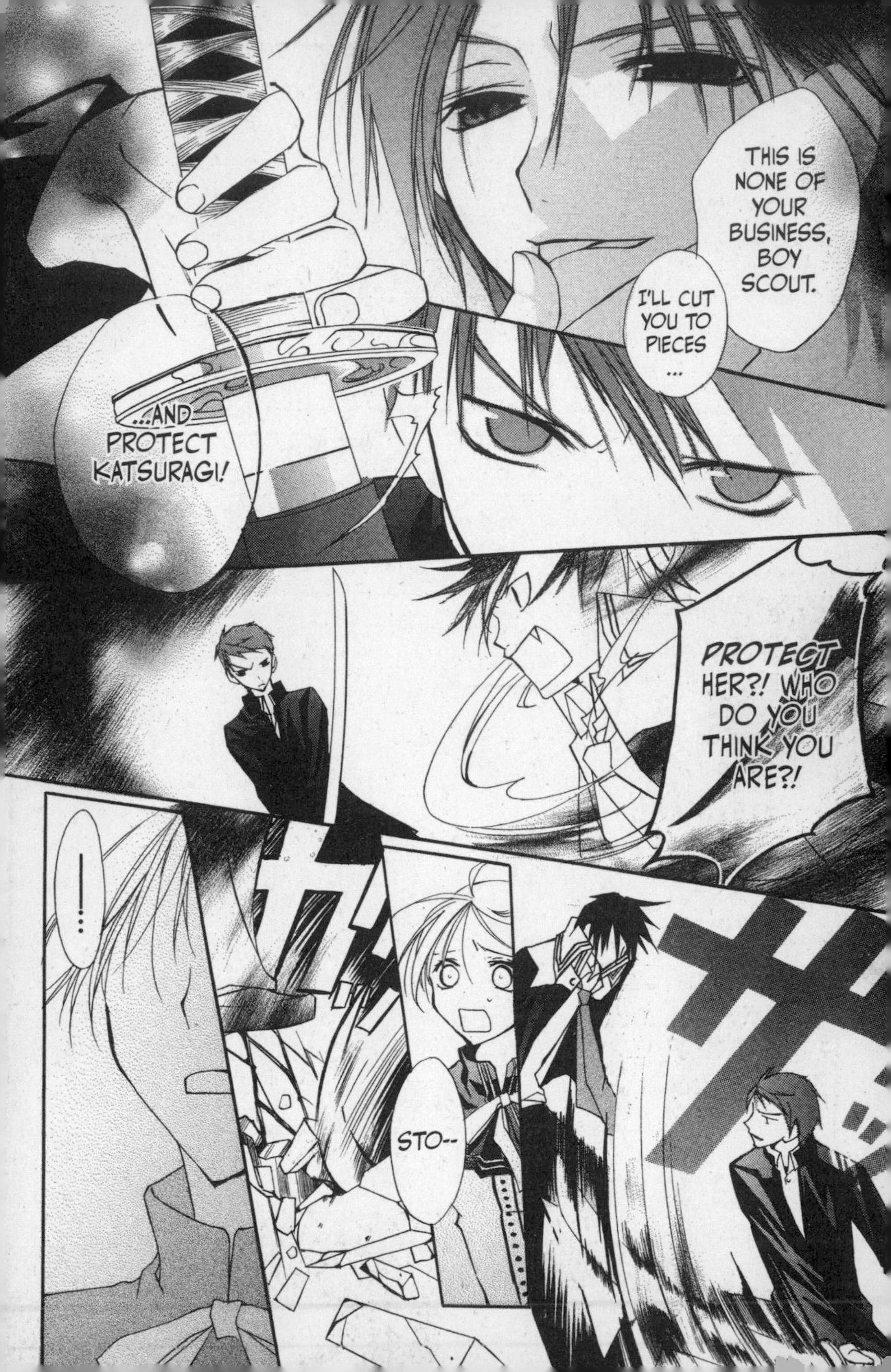
THIS IS NONE OF YOUR BUSINESS, BOY SCOUT.
I'LL CUT YOU TO PIECES ...
...AND PROTECT KATSURAGI!
PROTECT HER?! WHO DO YOU THINK YOU ARE?!
STO--
—!...

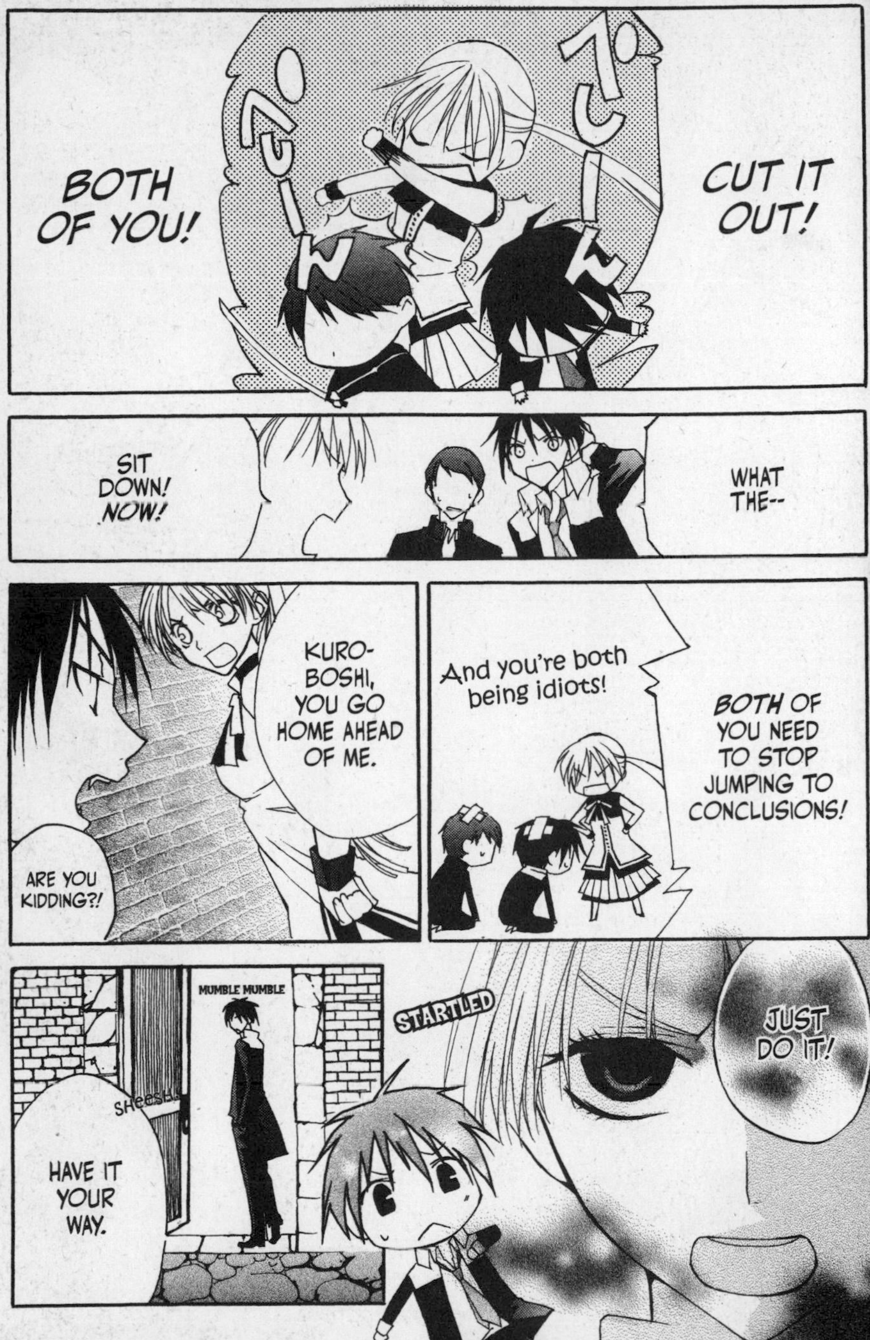
CUT IT OUT!
BOTH OF YOU!
WHAT THE--
SIT DOWN! NOW!
BOTH OF YOU NEED TO STOP JUMPING TO CONCLUSIONS!
And you're both being idiots!
KURO-BOSHI, YOU GO HOME AHEAD OF ME.
ARE YOU KIDDING?!
JUST DO IT!
STARTLED
MUMBLE MUMBLE
SHEESH..
HAVE IT YOUR WAY.

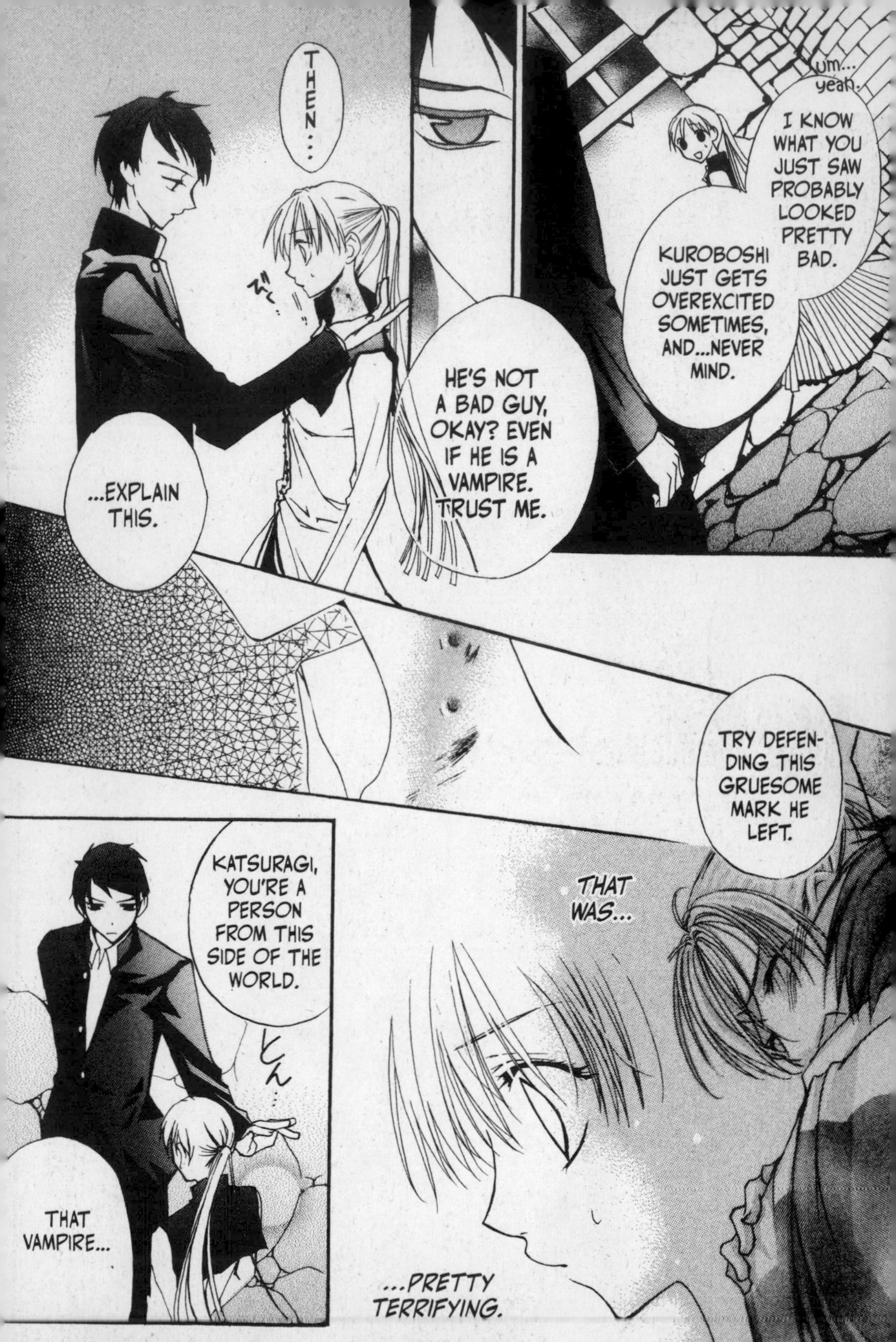
um... yeah.
I KNOW WHAT YOU JUST SAW PROBABLY LOOKED PRETTY BAD.
KUROBOSHI JUST GETS OVEREXCITED SOMETIMES, AND...NEVER MIND.
HE'S NOT A BAD GUY, OKAY? EVEN IF HE IS A VAMPIRE. TRUST ME.
THEN...
ぞく
...EXPLAIN THIS.
TRY DEFENDING THIS GRUESOME MARK HE LEFT.
THAT WAS...
...PRETTY TERRIFYING.
KATSURAGI, YOU'RE A PERSON FROM THIS SIDE OF THE WORLD.
とん...
THAT VAMPIRE...

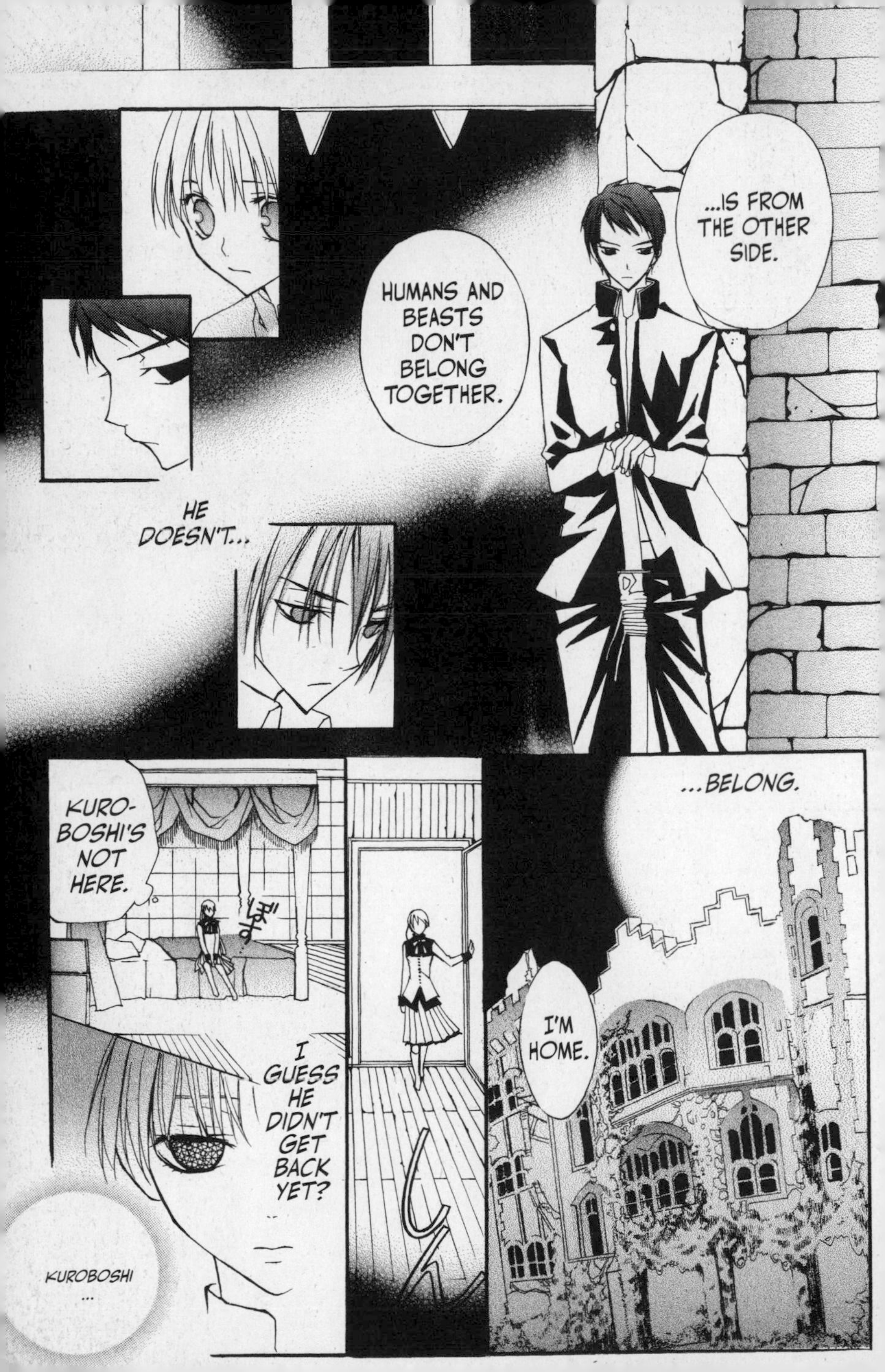

...IS FROM THE OTHER SIDE.
HUMANS AND BEASTS DON'T BELONG TOGETHER.
HE DOESN'T...
...BELONG.
I'M HOME.
KURO-BOSHI'S NOT HERE.
ぼす
I GUESS HE DIDN'T GET BACK YET?
KUROBOSHI ...

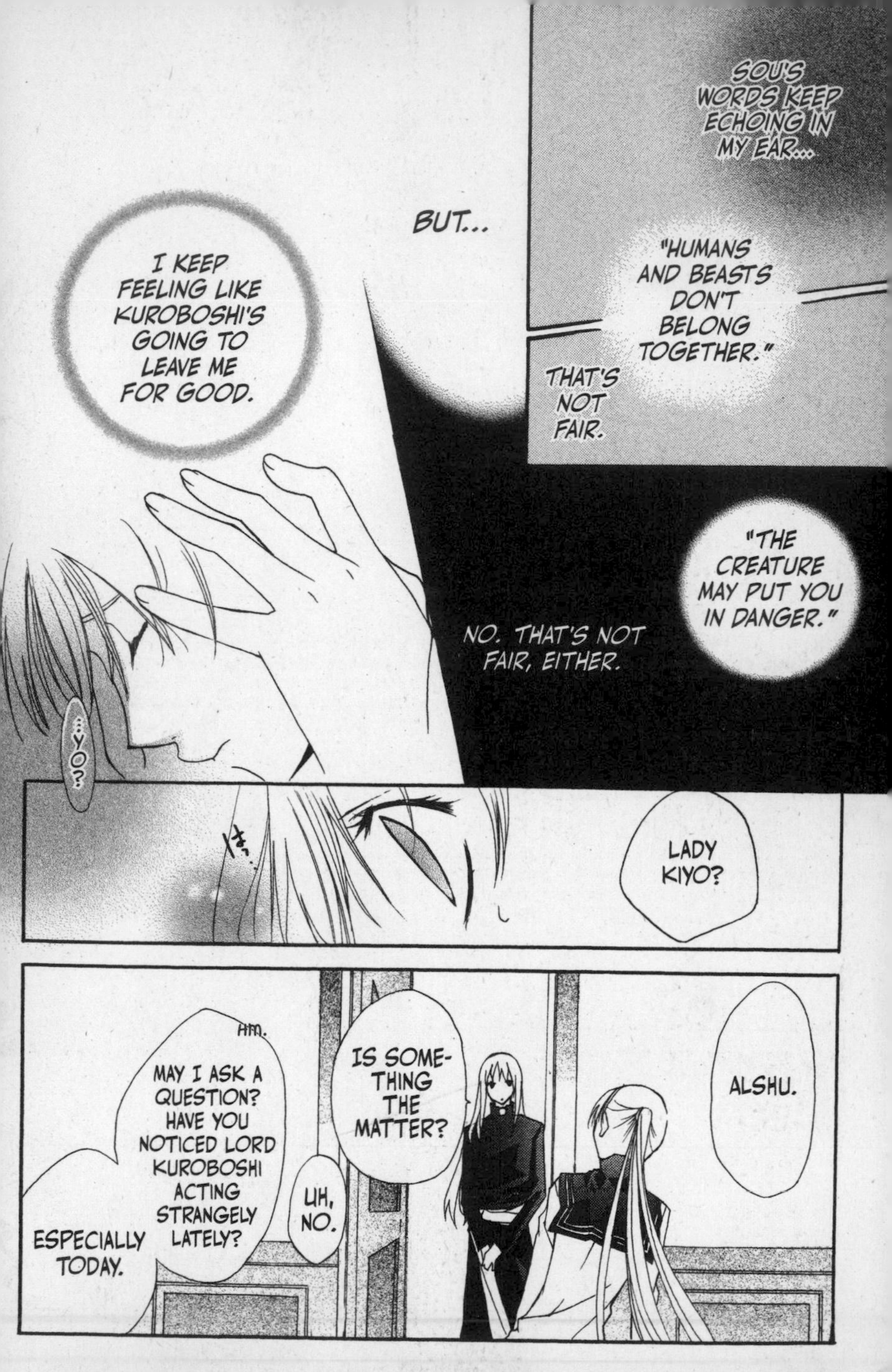
SOU'S WORDS KEEP ECHOING IN MY EAR...
"HUMANS AND BEASTS DON'T BELONG TOGETHER."
THAT'S NOT FAIR.
BUT...
I KEEP FEELING LIKE KUROBOSHI'S GOING TO LEAVE ME FOR GOOD.
"THE CREATURE MAY PUT YOU IN DANGER."
NO. THAT'S NOT FAIR, EITHER.
...YO?
LADY KIYO?
ALSHU.
IS SOME-THING THE MATTER?
UH, NO.
HM.
MAY I ASK A QUESTION? HAVE YOU NOTICED LORD KUROBOSHI ACTING STRANGELY LATELY?
ESPECIALLY TODAY.

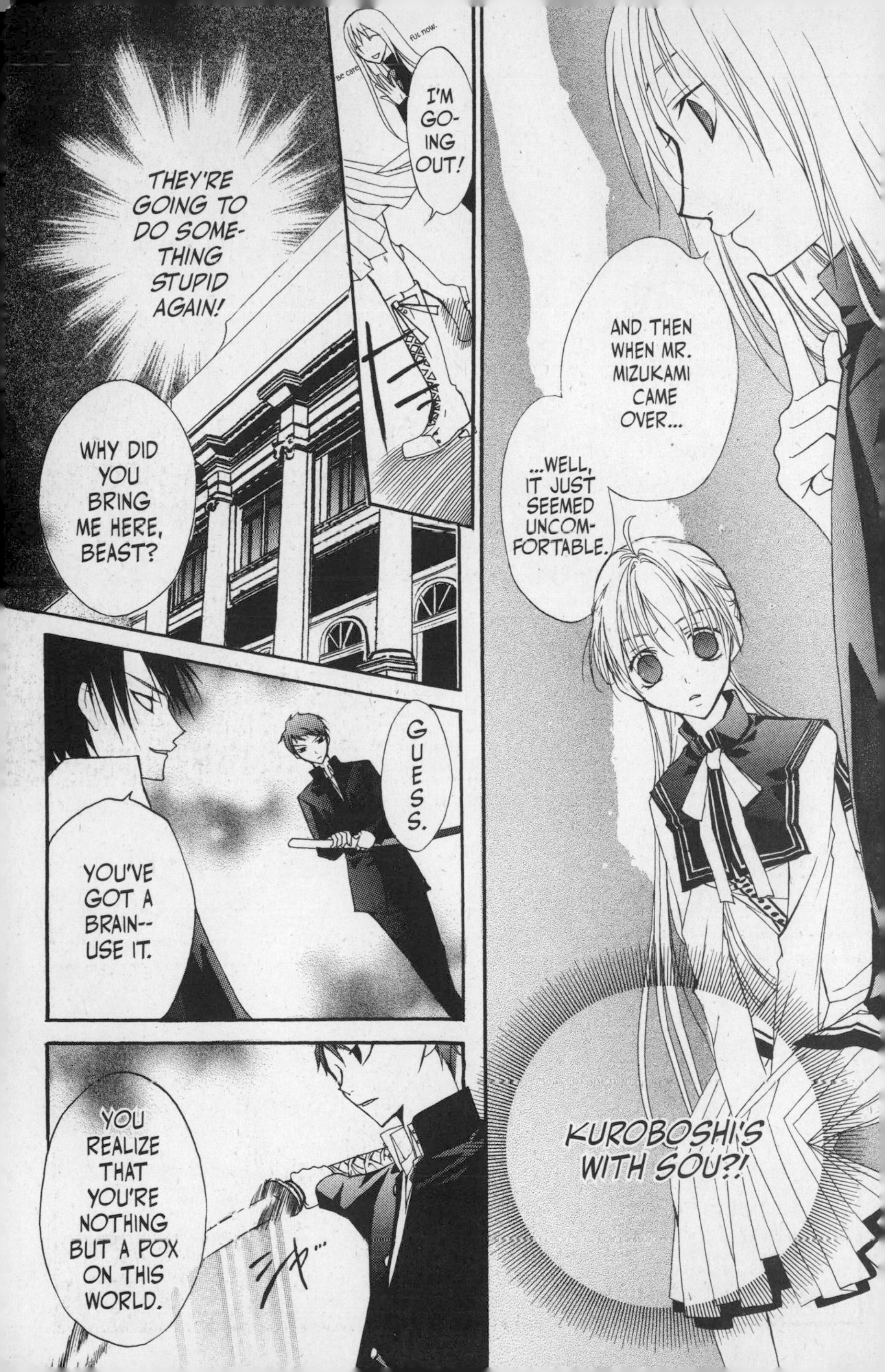
AND THEN WHEN MR. MIZUKAMI CAME OVER...
...WELL, IT JUST SEEMED UNCOMFORTABLE.
KUROBOSHI'S WITH SOU?!
I'M GOING OUT!
Be careful now.
THEY'RE GOING TO DO SOMETHING STUPID AGAIN!
WHY DID YOU BRING ME HERE, BEAST?
GUESS.
YOU'VE GOT A BRAIN--USE IT.
YOU REALIZE THAT YOU'RE NOTHING BUT A POX ON THIS WORLD.
シャ…

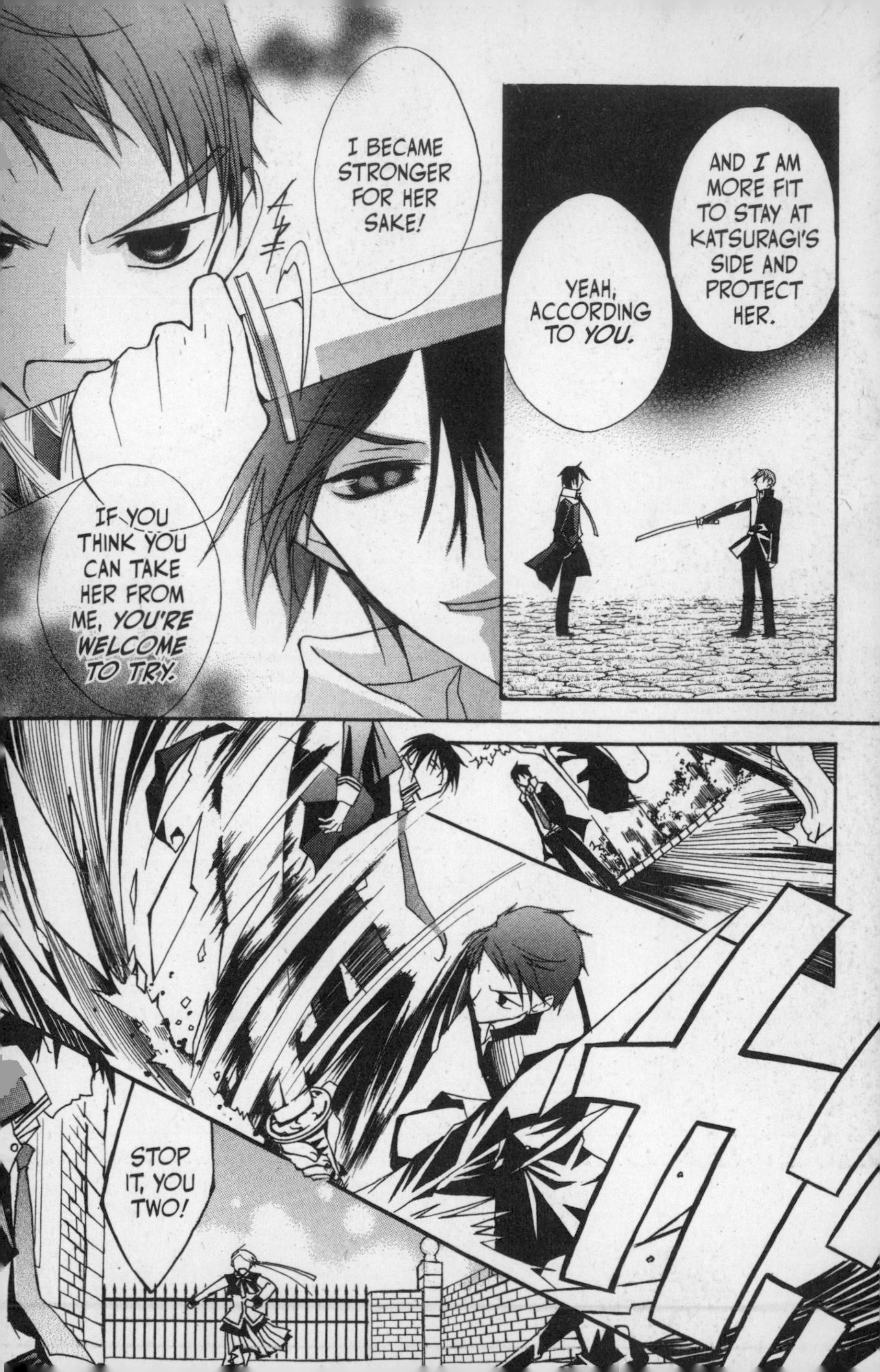
AND *I* AM MORE FIT TO STAY AT KATSURAGI'S SIDE AND PROTECT HER.
YEAH, ACCORDING TO *YOU.*
I BECAME STRONGER FOR HER SAKE!
IF YOU THINK YOU CAN TAKE HER FROM ME, ***YOU'RE WELCOME TO TRY.***
STOP IT, YOU TWO!

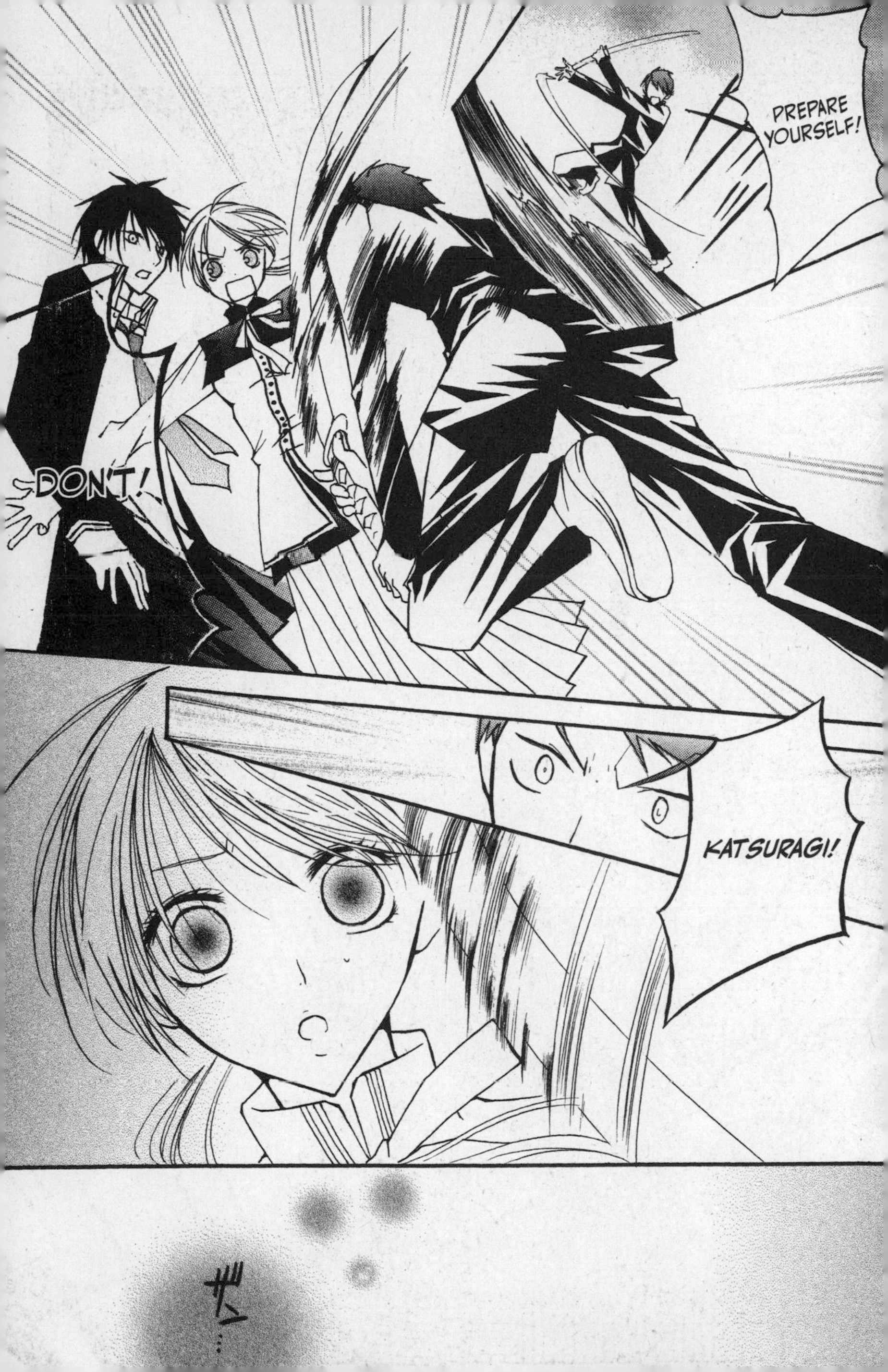
PREPARE YOURSELF!
DON'T!
KATSURAGI!

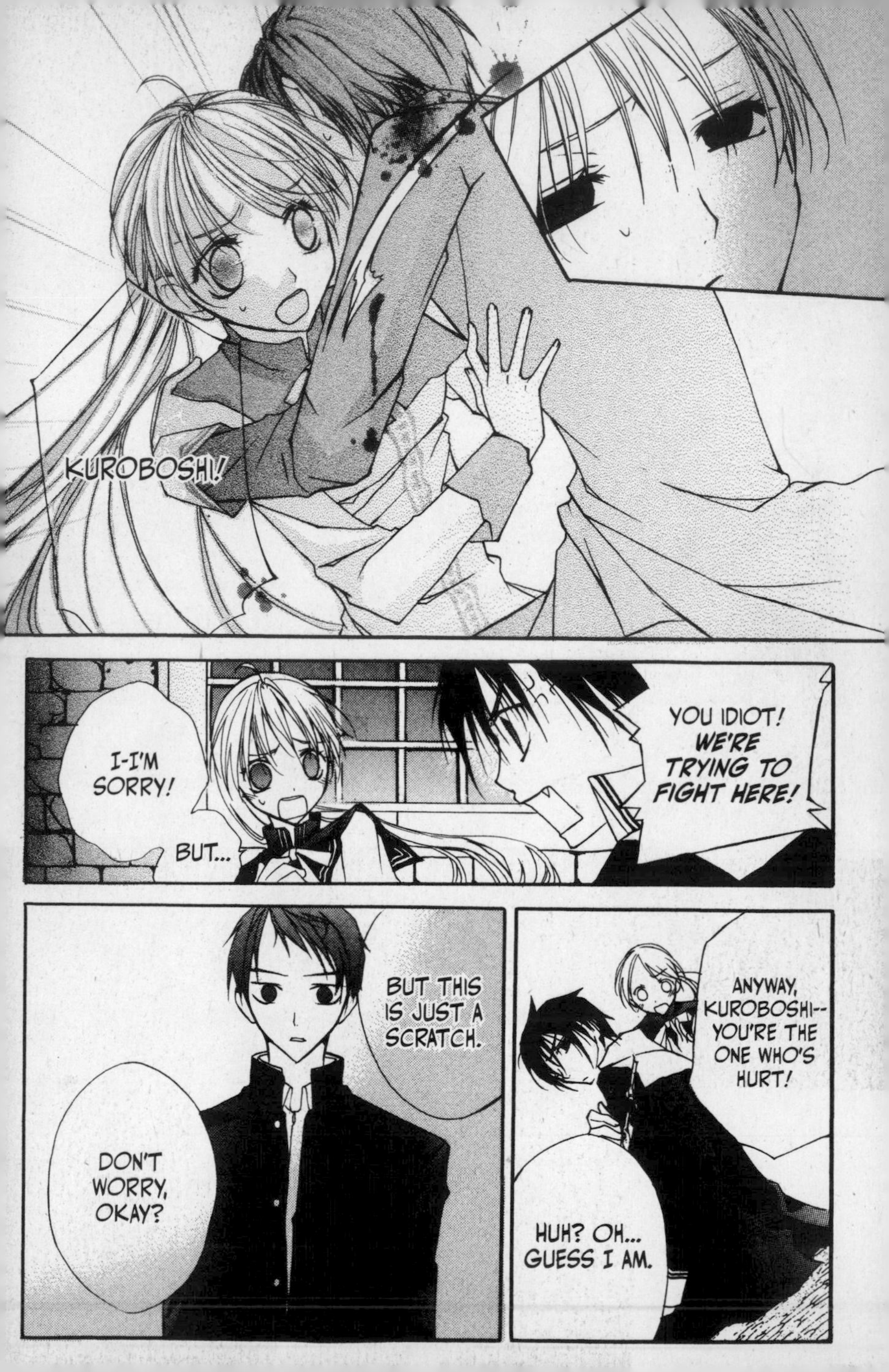
KUROBOSHI!
YOU IDIOT! WE'RE TRYING TO FIGHT HERE!
I-I'M SORRY!
BUT...
ANYWAY, KUROBOSHI-- YOU'RE THE ONE WHO'S HURT!
HUH? OH... GUESS I AM.
BUT THIS IS JUST A SCRATCH.
DON'T WORRY, OKAY?

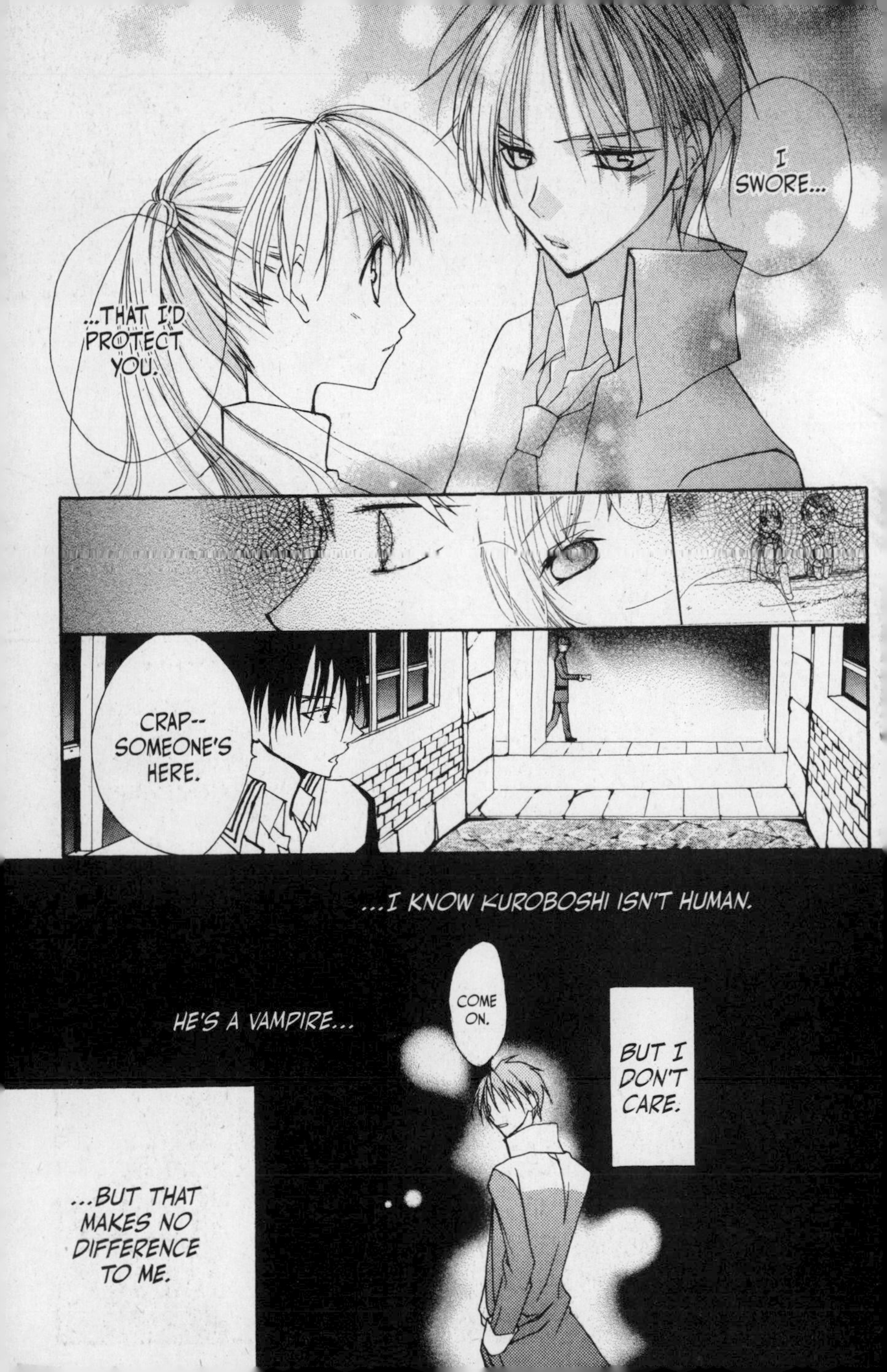
I SWORE...
...THAT I'D PROTECT YOU.
CRAP-- SOMEONE'S HERE.
...I KNOW KUROBOSHI ISN'T HUMAN.
COME ON.
HE'S A VAMPIRE...
BUT I DON'T CARE.
...BUT THAT MAKES NO DIFFERENCE TO ME.

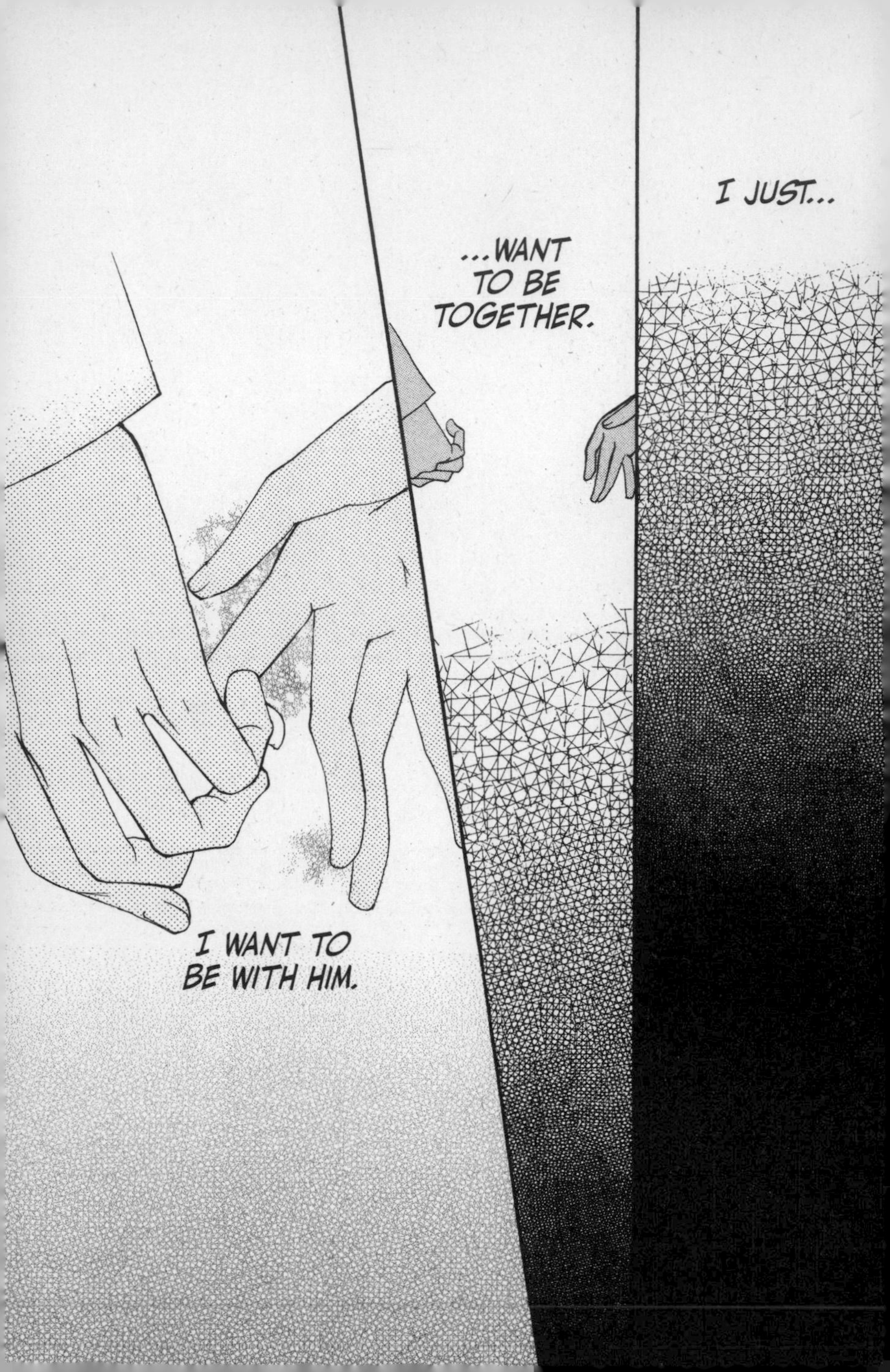
I JUST...
...WANT TO BE TOGETHER.
I WANT TO BE WITH HIM.

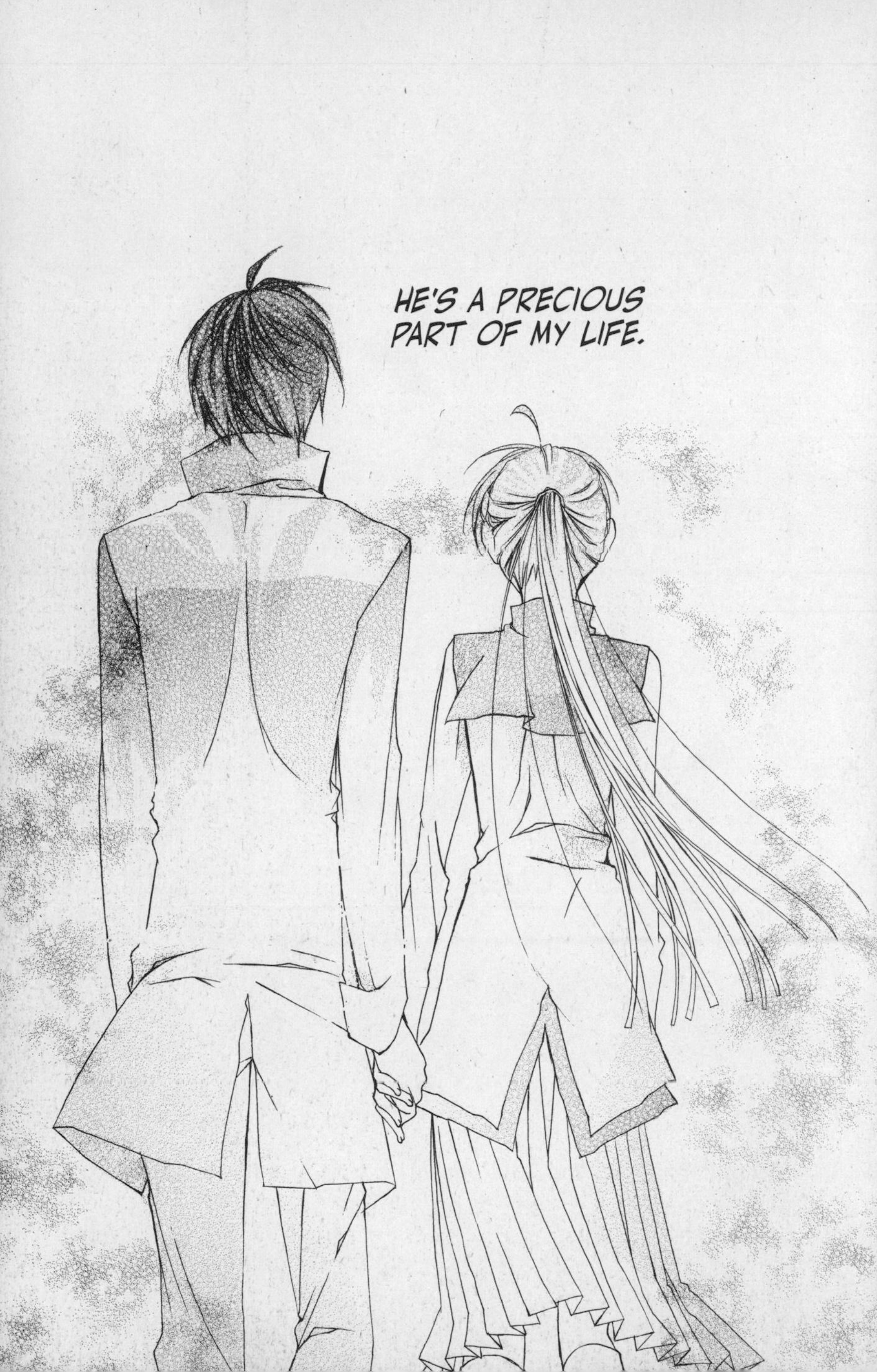
HE'S A PRECIOUS PART OF MY LIFE.

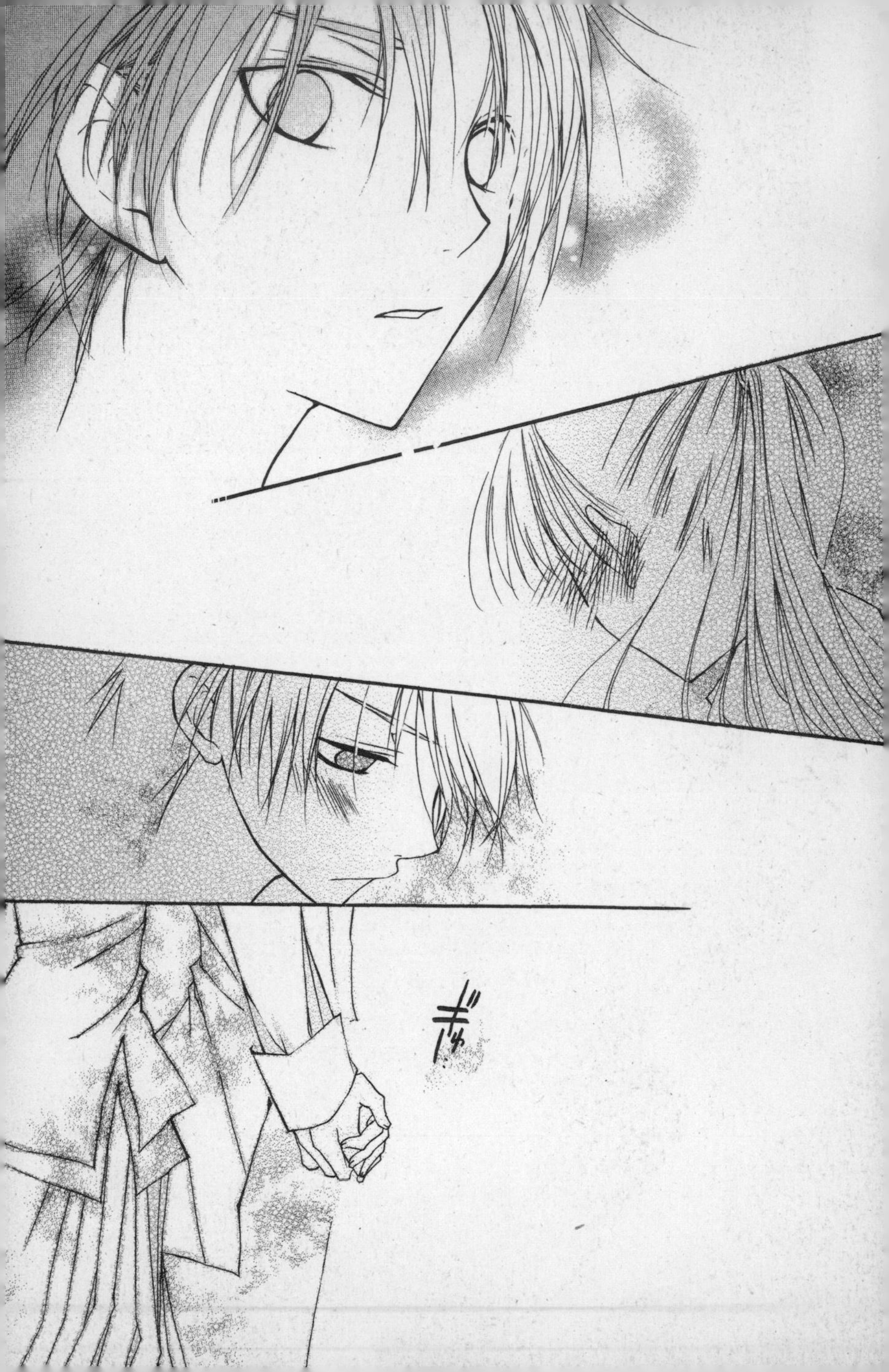
ぎゅ

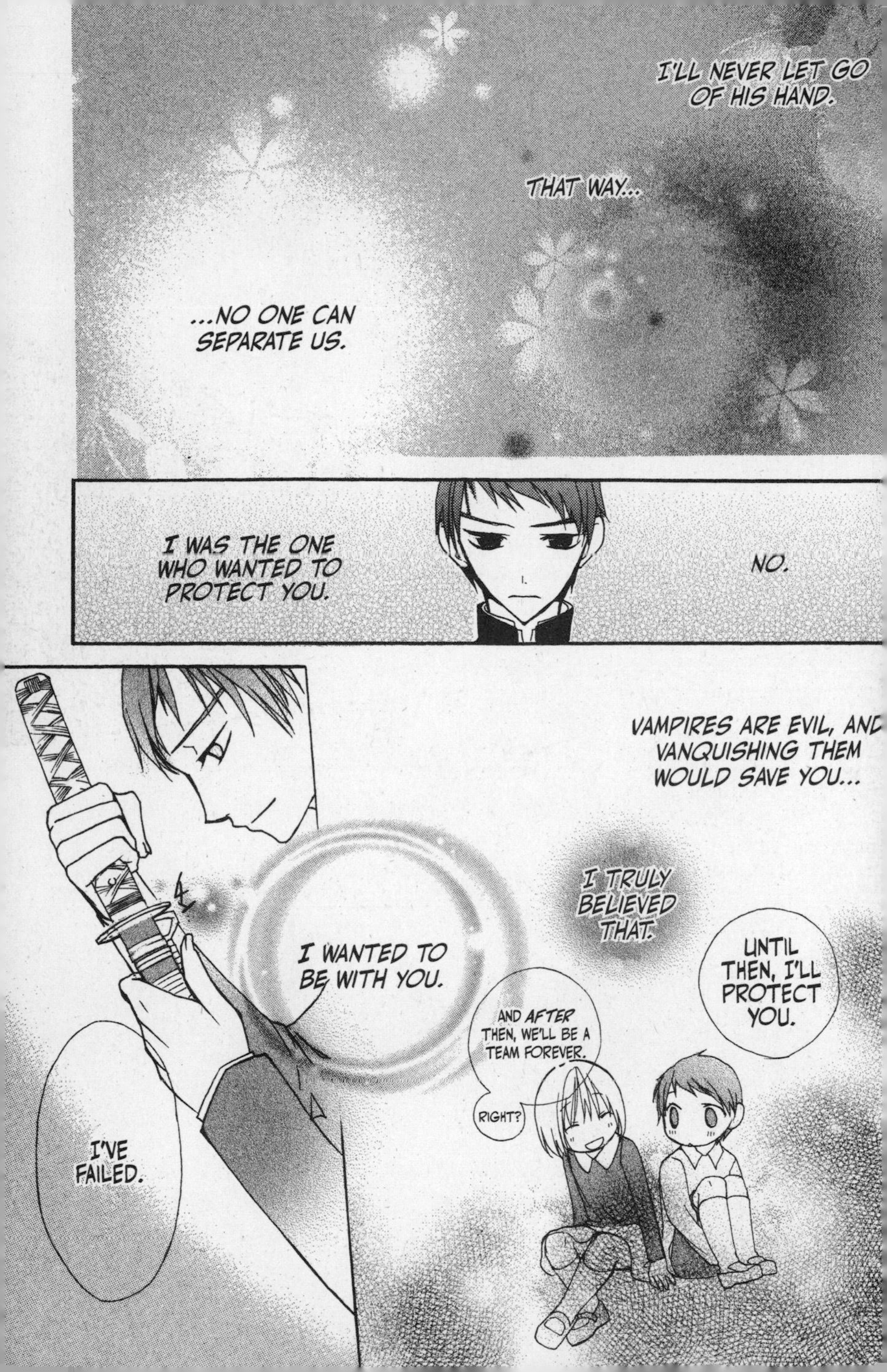
I'LL NEVER LET GO OF HIS HAND.
THAT WAY...
...NO ONE CAN SEPARATE US.
NO.
I WAS THE ONE WHO WANTED TO PROTECT YOU.
VAMPIRES ARE EVIL, AND VANQUISHING THEM WOULD SAVE YOU...
I TRULY BELIEVED THAT.
UNTIL THEN, I'LL PROTECT YOU.
AND AFTER THEN, WE'LL BE A TEAM FOREVER.
RIGHT?
I WANTED TO BE WITH YOU.
I'VE FAILED.

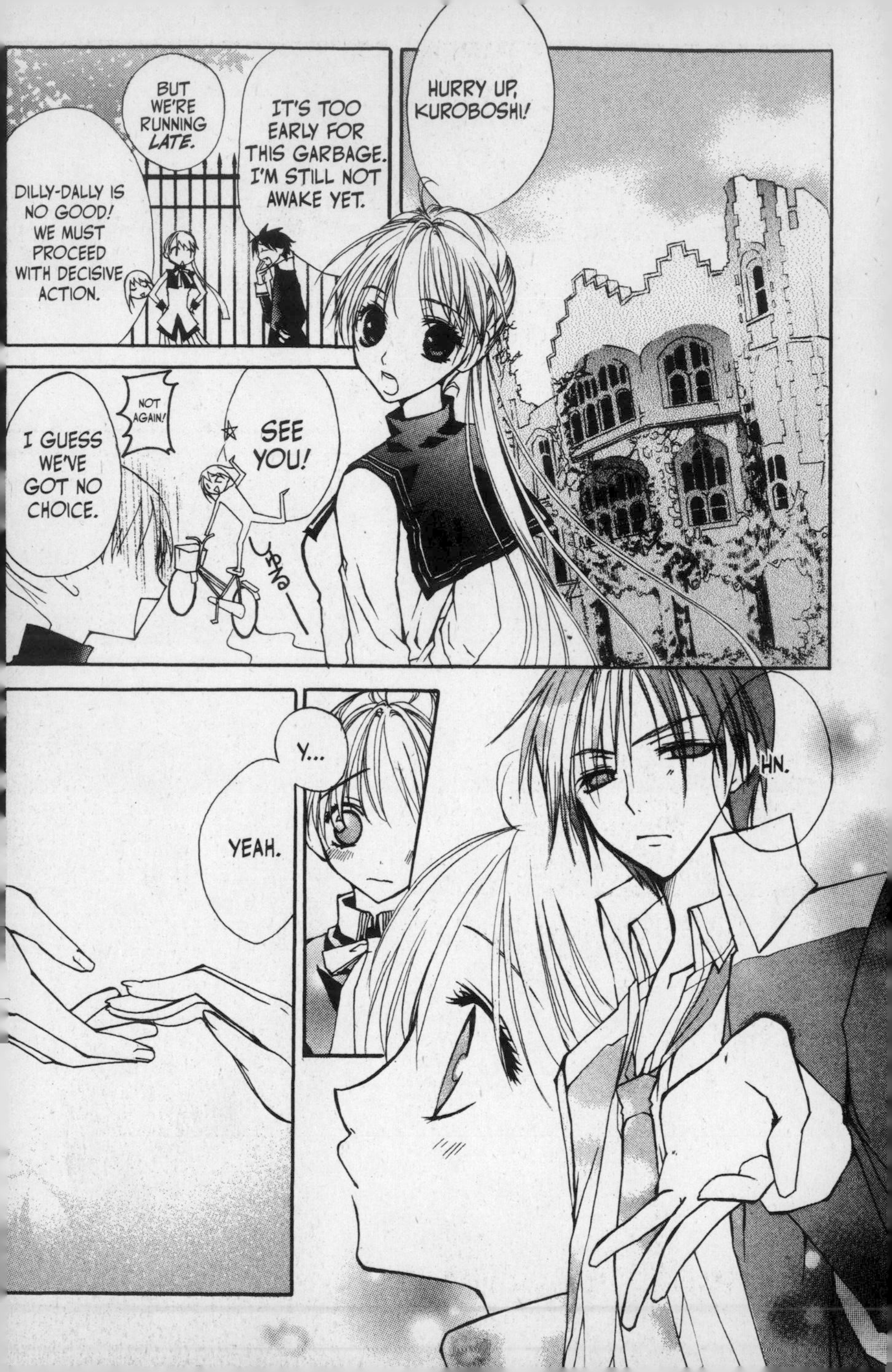
HURRY UP, KUROBOSHI!
IT'S TOO EARLY FOR THIS GARBAGE. I'M STILL NOT AWAKE YET.
BUT WE'RE RUNNING LATE.
DILLY-DALLY IS NO GOOD! WE MUST PROCEED WITH DECISIVE ACTION.
SEE YOU!
NOT AGAIN!
I GUESS WE'VE GOT NO CHOICE.
HN.
Y...
YEAH.

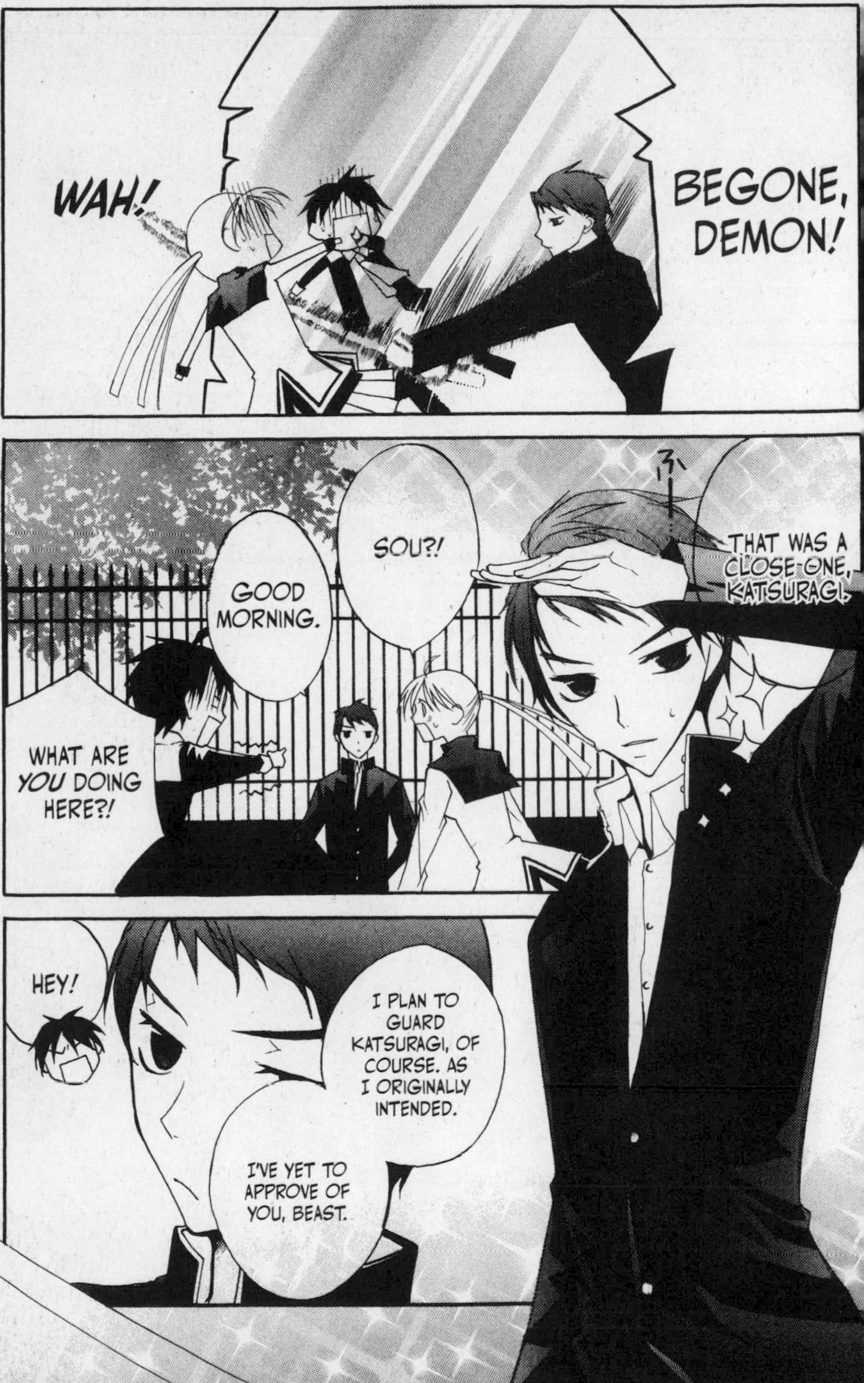
BEGONE, DEMON!
WAH!
THAT WAS A CLOSE ONE, KATSURAGI.
SOU?!
GOOD MORNING.
WHAT ARE YOU DOING HERE?!
I PLAN TO GUARD KATSURAGI, OF COURSE. AS I ORIGINALLY INTENDED.
I'VE YET TO APPROVE OF YOU, BEAST.
HEY!

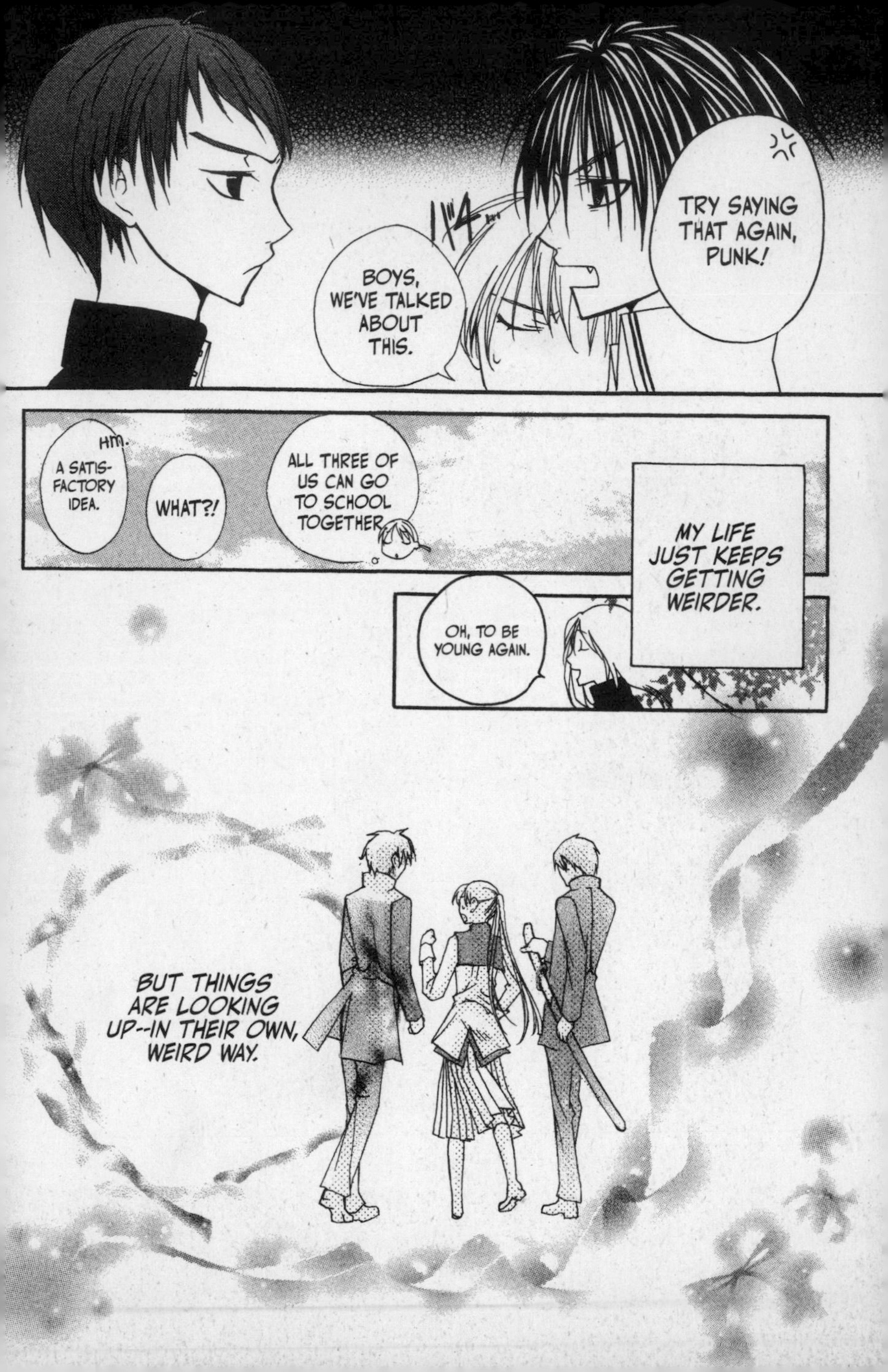
TRY SAYING THAT AGAIN, PUNK!
BOYS, WE'VE TALKED ABOUT THIS.
ALL THREE OF US CAN GO TO SCHOOL TOGETHER.
WHAT?!
HM. A SATIS-FACTORY IDEA.
MY LIFE JUST KEEPS GETTING WEIRDER.
OH, TO BE YOUNG AGAIN.
BUT THINGS ARE LOOKING UP--IN THEIR OWN, WEIRD WAY.

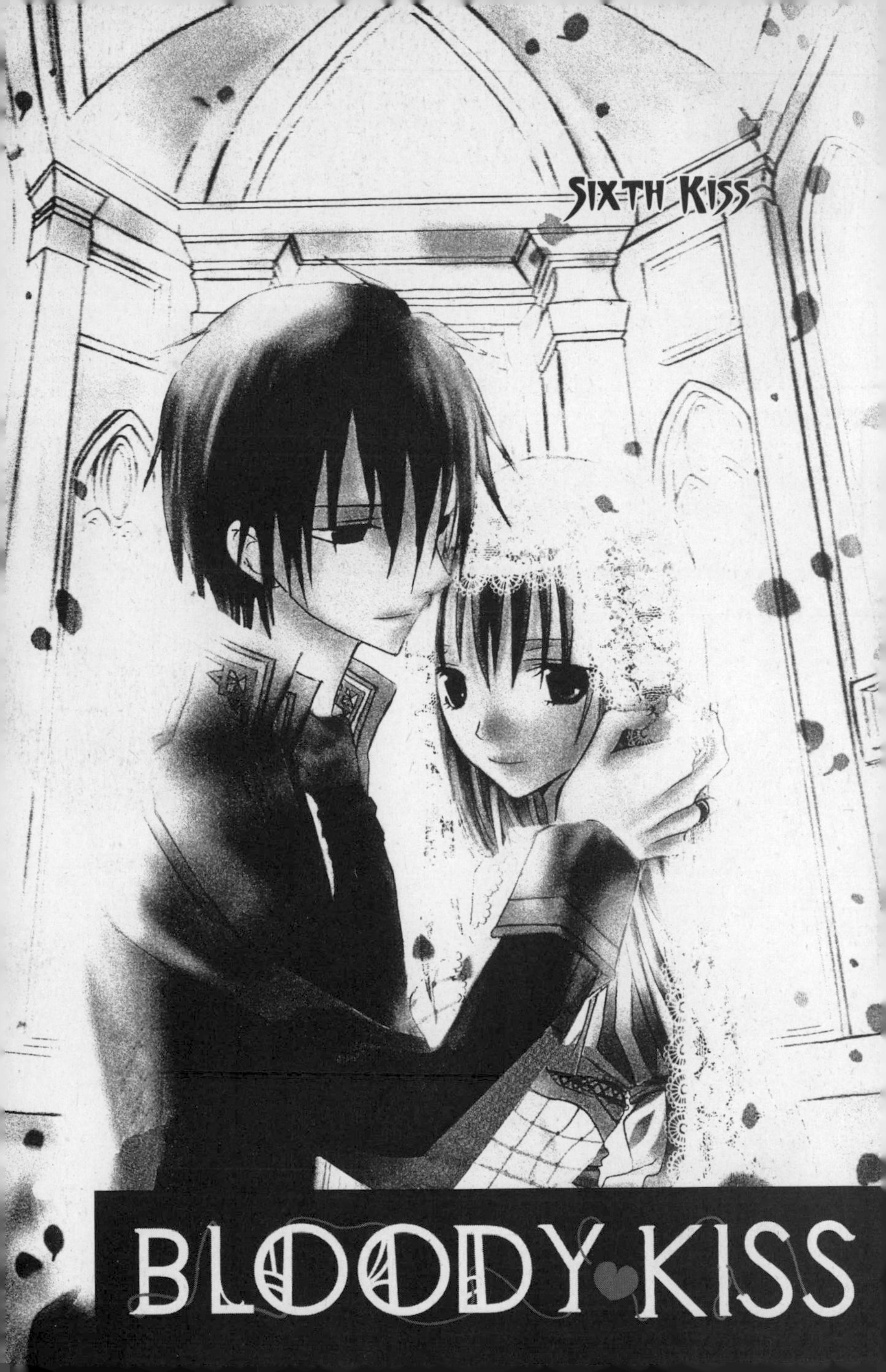
Sixth Kiss
BLOODY KISS

Idiotic Feature

Part 2 Try to draw things as if this were a dating sim.

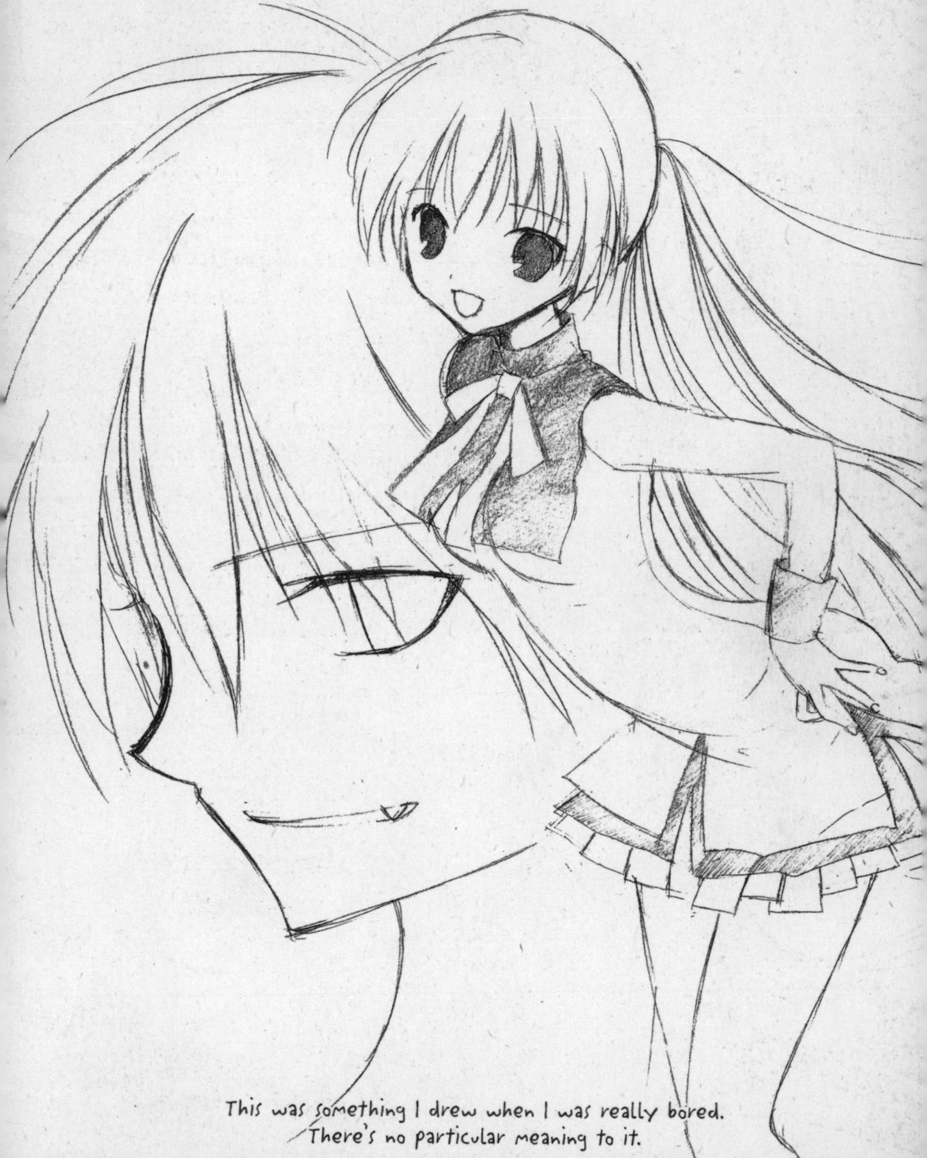

This was something I drew when I was really bored.
There's no particular meaning to it.

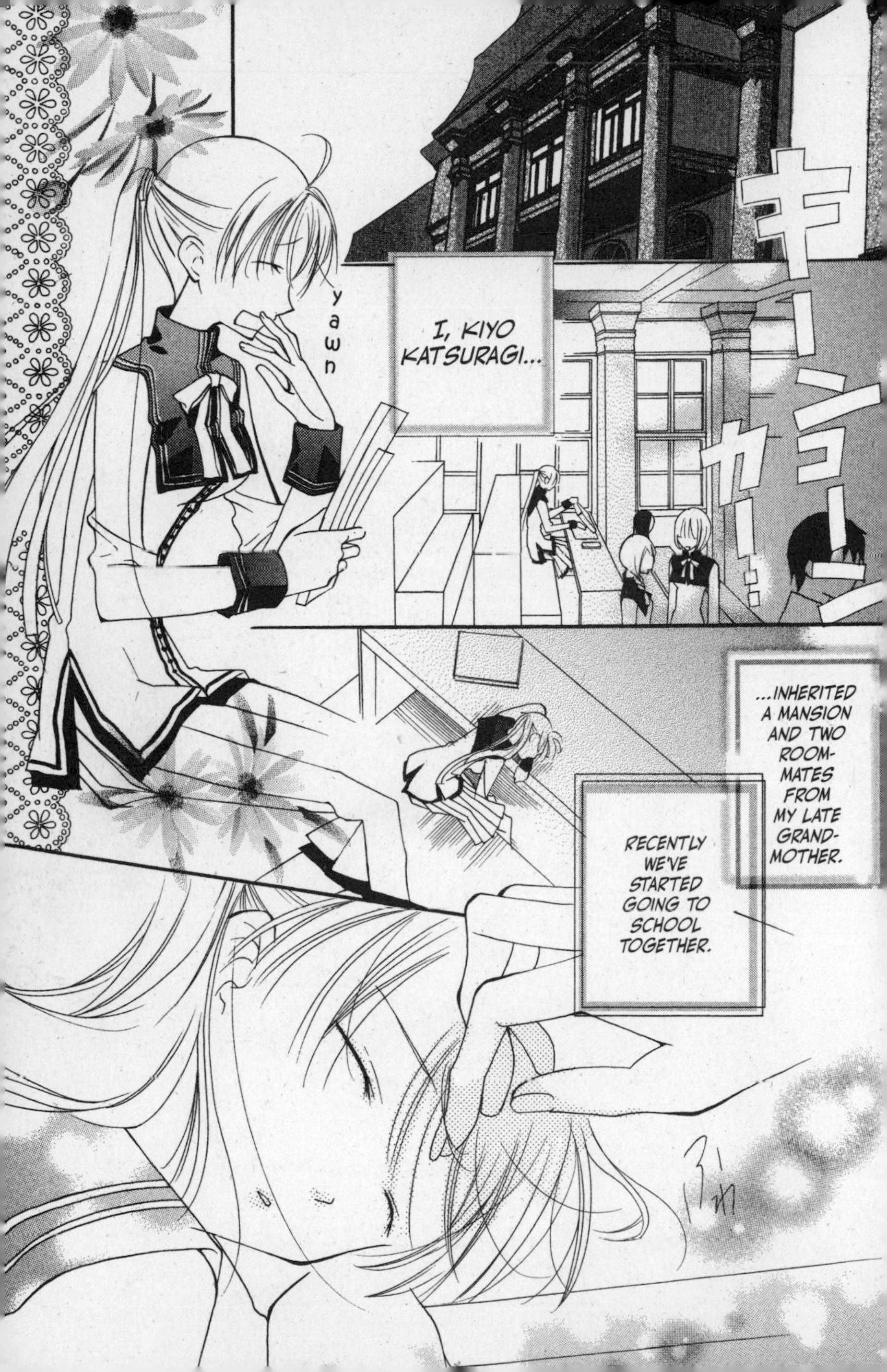
I, KIYO KATSURAGI...
yawn
...INHERITED A MANSION AND TWO ROOM-MATES FROM MY LATE GRAND-MOTHER.
RECENTLY WE'VE STARTED GOING TO SCHOOL TOGETHER.

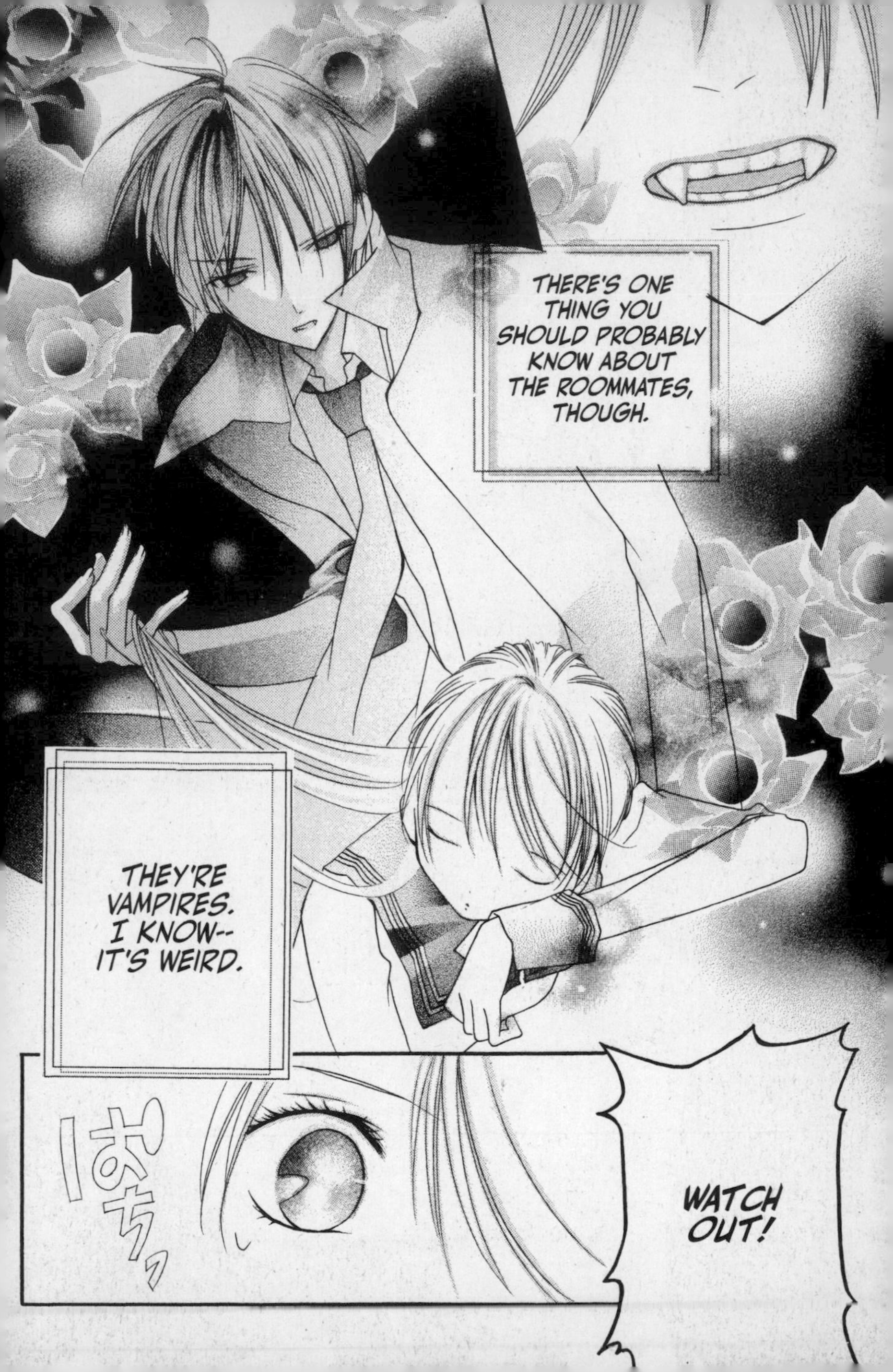
THERE'S ONE THING YOU SHOULD PROBABLY KNOW ABOUT THE ROOMMATES, THOUGH.
THEY'RE VAMPIRES. I KNOW-- IT'S WEIRD.
WATCH OUT!
はちっ

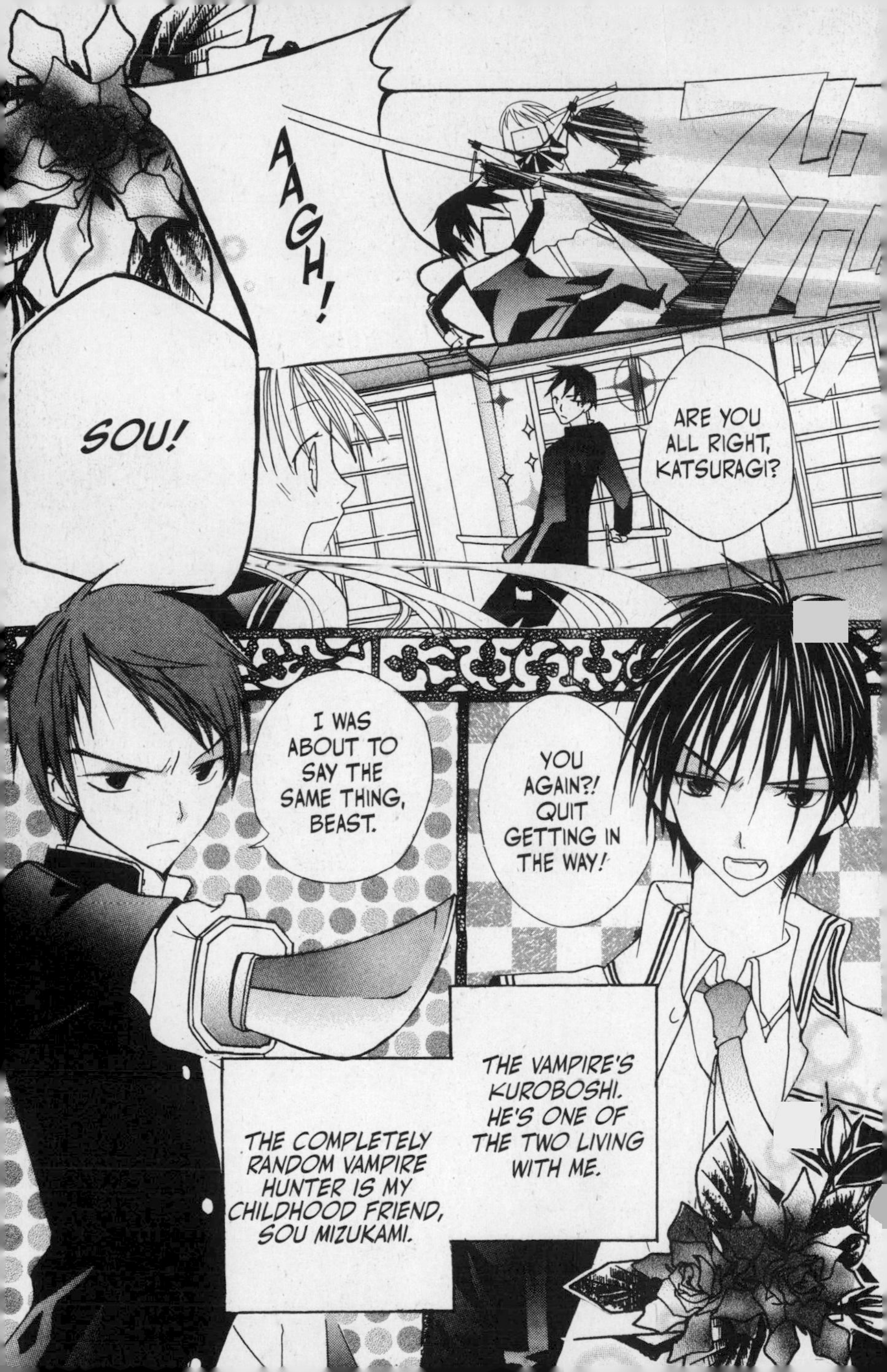
AAGH!
SOU!
ARE YOU ALL RIGHT, KATSURAGI?
YOU AGAIN?! QUIT GETTING IN THE WAY!
I WAS ABOUT TO SAY THE SAME THING, BEAST.
THE VAMPIRE'S KUROBOSHI. HE'S ONE OF THE TWO LIVING WITH ME.
THE COMPLETELY RANDOM VAMPIRE HUNTER IS MY CHILDHOOD FRIEND, SOU MIZUKAMI.

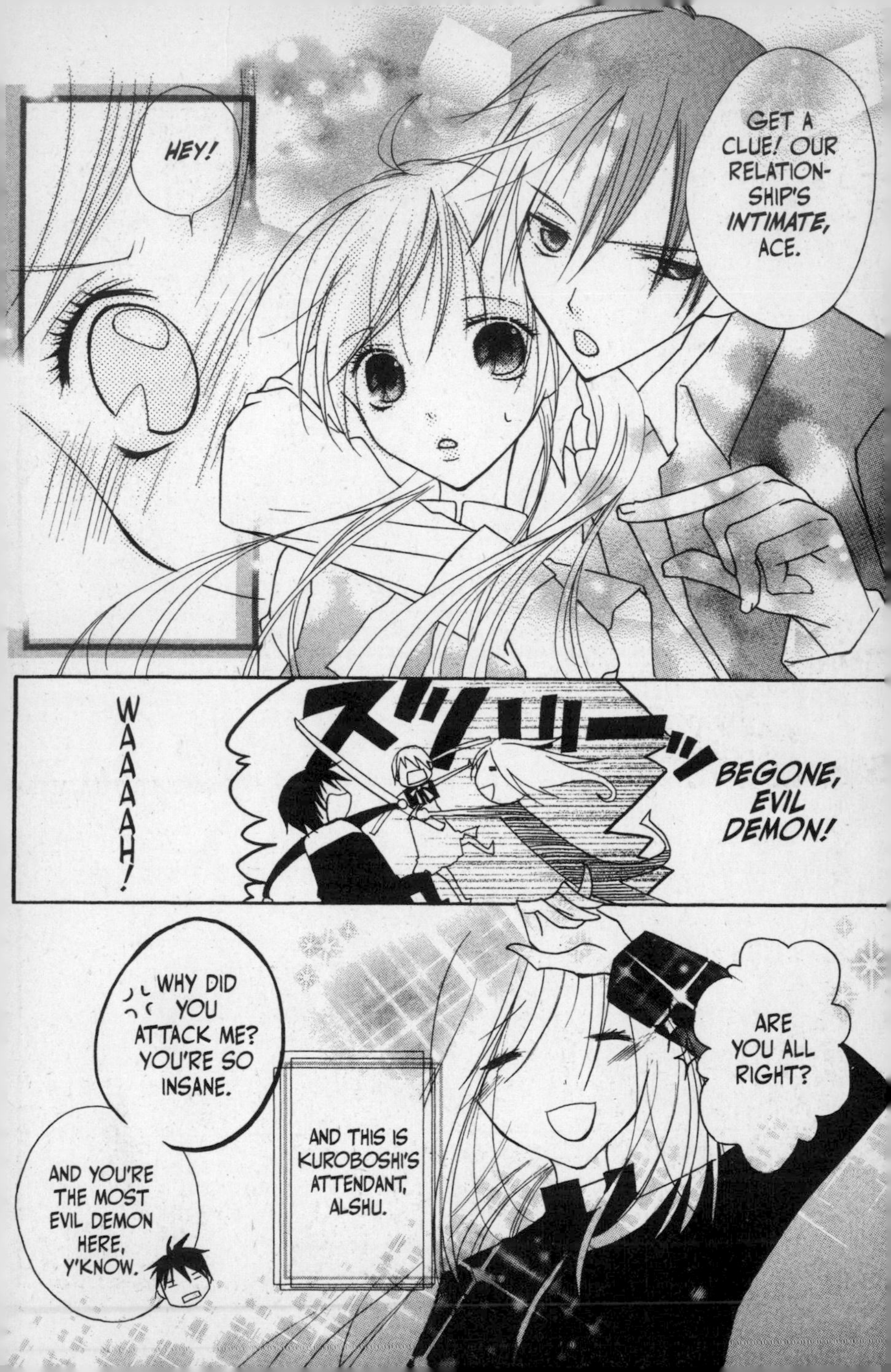
GET A CLUE! OUR RELATION-SHIP'S INTIMATE, ACE.
HEY!
BEGONE, EVIL DEMON!
WAAAAAH!
ARE YOU ALL RIGHT?
AND THIS IS KUROBOSHI'S ATTENDANT, ALSHU.
WHY DID YOU ATTACK ME? YOU'RE SO INSANE.
AND YOU'RE THE MOST EVIL DEMON HERE, Y'KNOW.

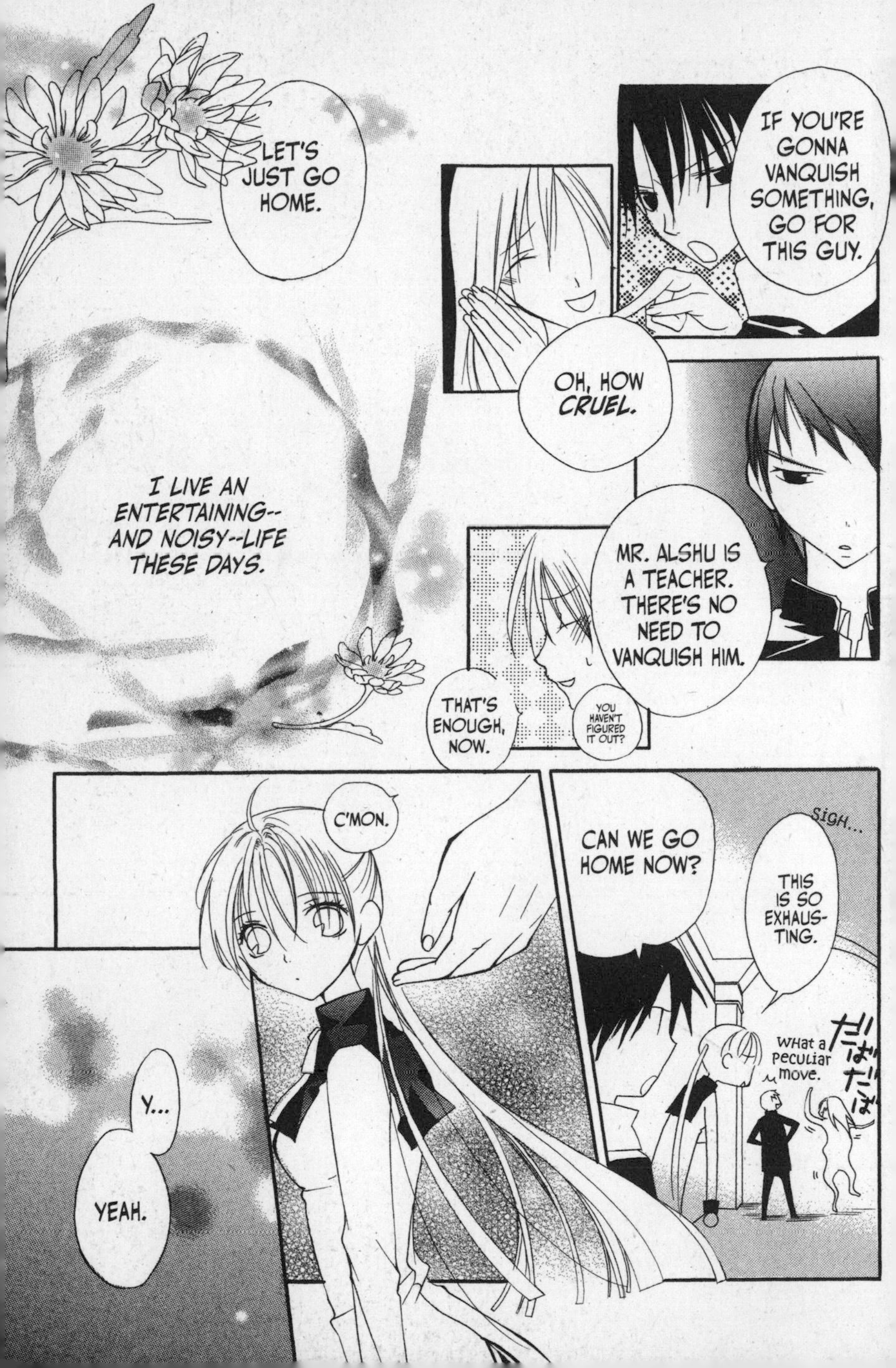
IF YOU'RE GONNA VANQUISH SOMETHING, GO FOR THIS GUY.
OH, HOW CRUEL.
MR. ALSHU IS A TEACHER. THERE'S NO NEED TO VANQUISH HIM.
YOU HAVEN'T FIGURED IT OUT?
THAT'S ENOUGH, NOW.
LET'S JUST GO HOME.
I LIVE AN ENTERTAINING--AND NOISY--LIFE THESE DAYS.
CAN WE GO HOME NOW?
SIGH...
THIS IS SO EXHAUS-TING.
What a peculiar move.
だばだば
C'MON.
Y...
YEAH.

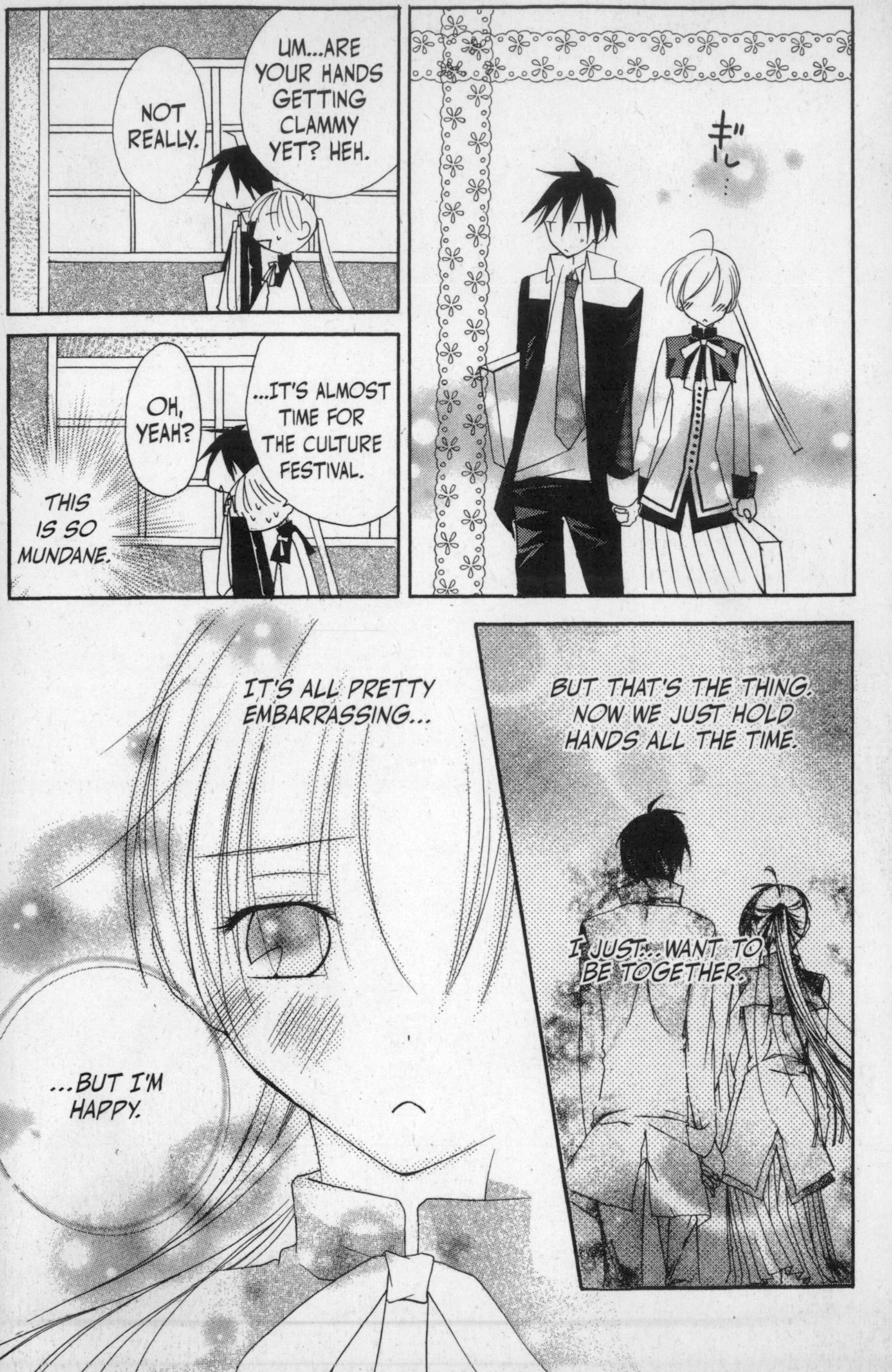
UM...ARE YOUR HANDS GETTING CLAMMY YET? HEH.
NOT REALLY.
...IT'S ALMOST TIME FOR THE CULTURE FESTIVAL.
OH, YEAH?
THIS IS SO MUNDANE.
BUT THAT'S THE THING. NOW WE JUST HOLD HANDS ALL THE TIME.
I JUST... WANT TO BE TOGETHER.
IT'S ALL PRETTY EMBARRASSING...
...BUT I'M HAPPY.

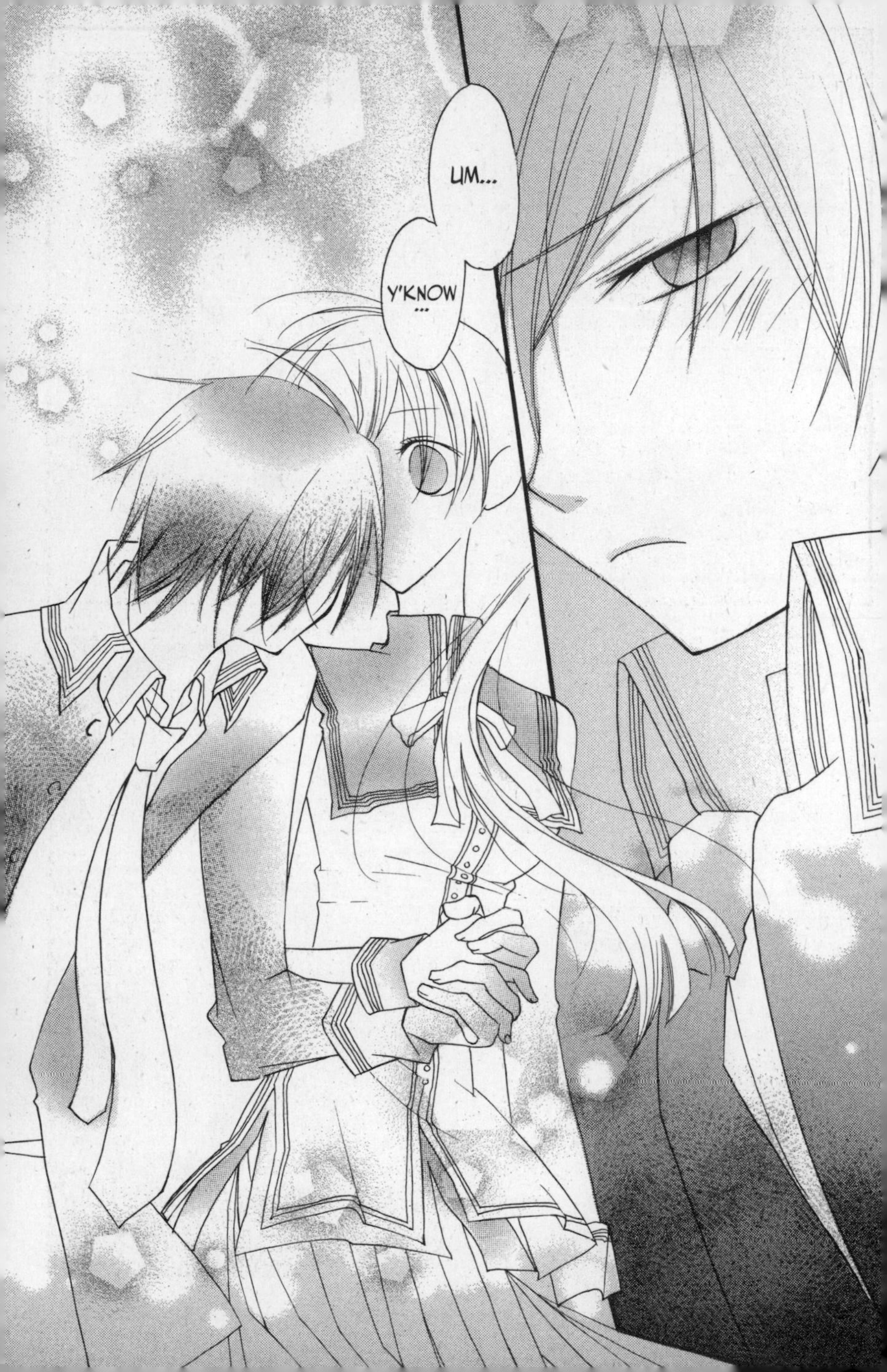
UM...
Y'KNOW ...

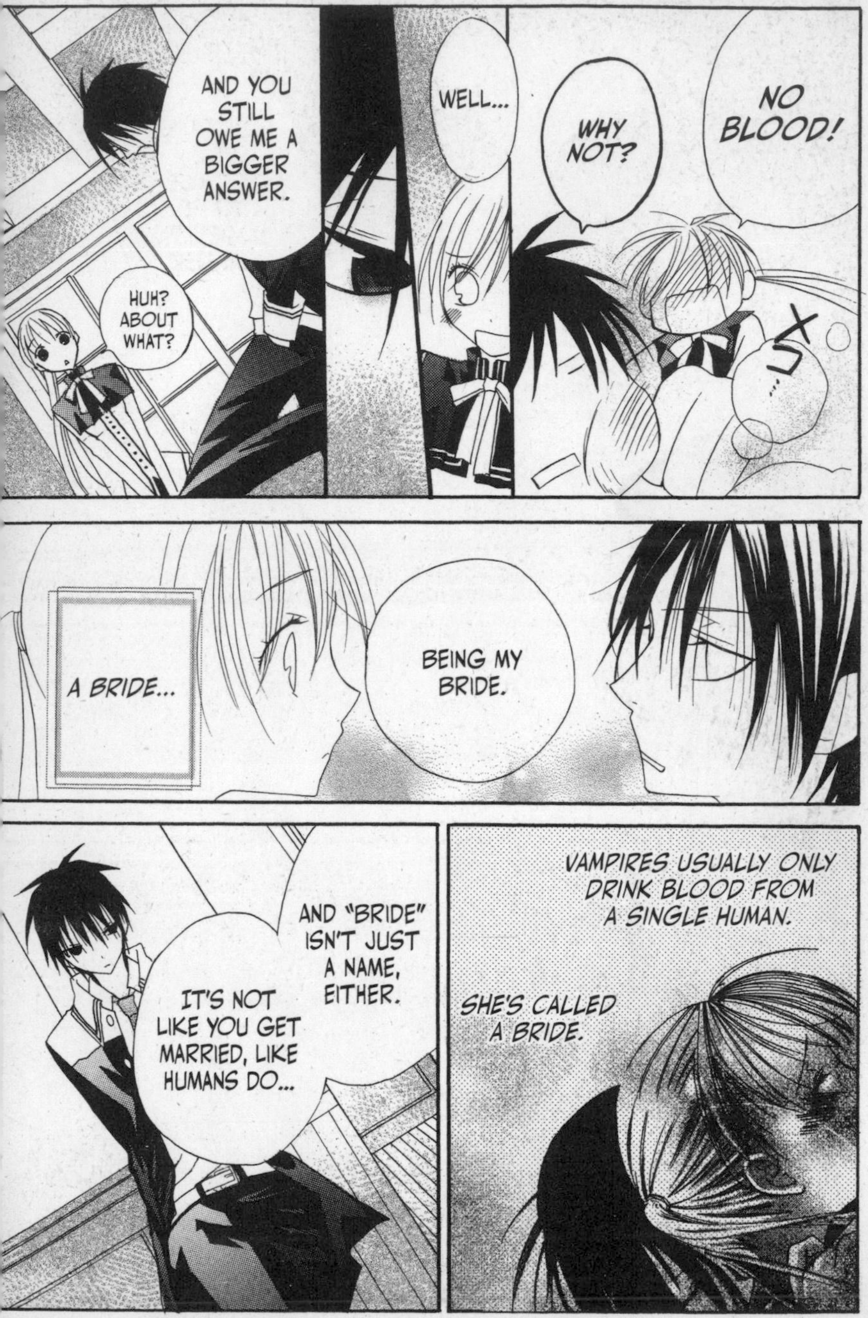
NO BLOOD!
WHY NOT?
WELL...
AND YOU STILL OWE ME A BIGGER ANSWER.
HUH? ABOUT WHAT?
BEING MY BRIDE.
A BRIDE...
VAMPIRES USUALLY ONLY DRINK BLOOD FROM A SINGLE HUMAN.
SHE'S CALLED A BRIDE.
AND "BRIDE" ISN'T JUST A NAME, EITHER.
IT'S NOT LIKE YOU GET MARRIED, LIKE HUMANS DO...

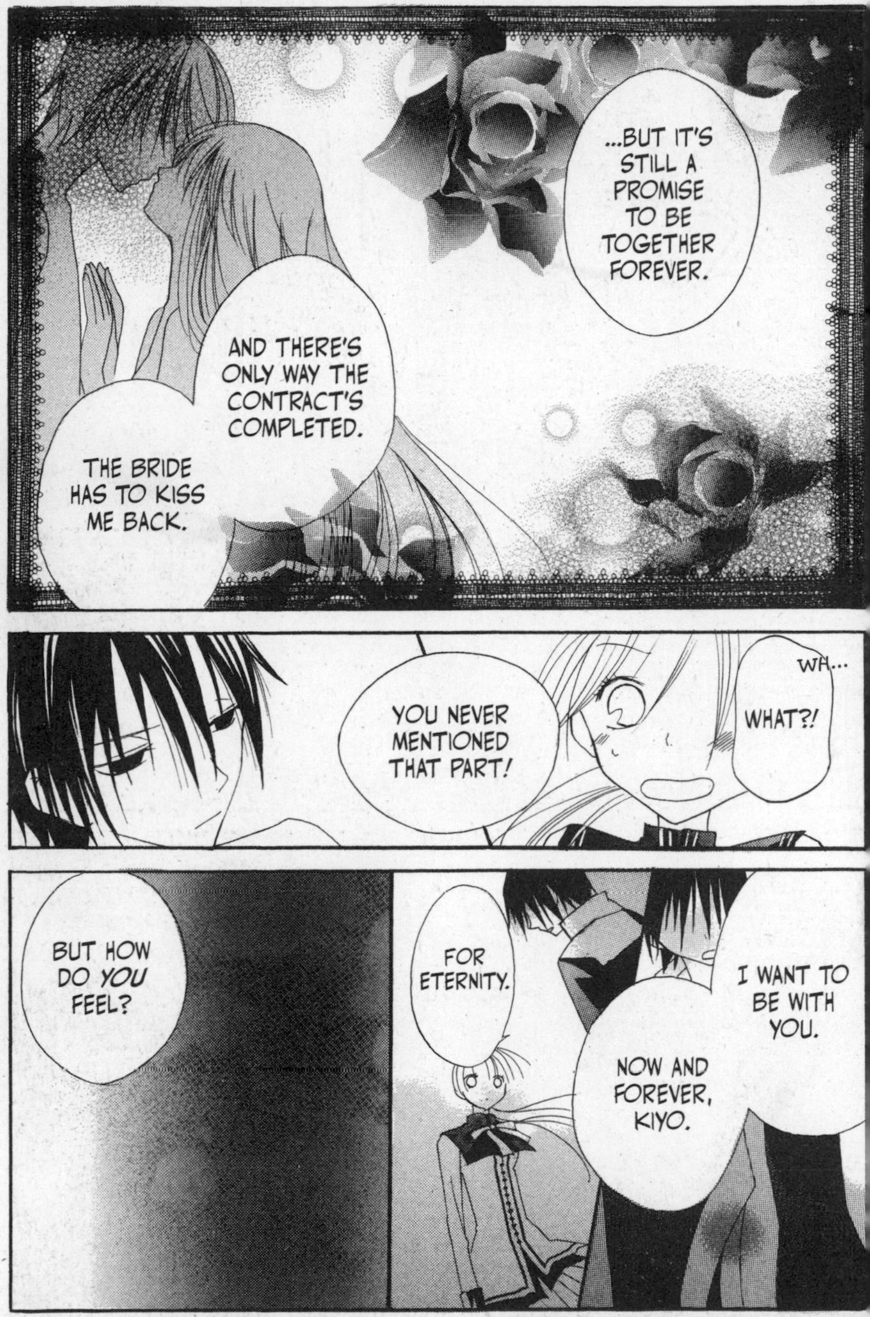
...BUT IT'S STILL A PROMISE TO BE TOGETHER FOREVER.
AND THERE'S ONLY WAY THE CONTRACT'S COMPLETED.
THE BRIDE HAS TO KISS ME BACK.
WH...
WHAT?!
YOU NEVER MENTIONED THAT PART!
I WANT TO BE WITH YOU.
NOW AND FOREVER, KIYO.
FOR ETERNITY.
BUT HOW DO *YOU* FEEL?

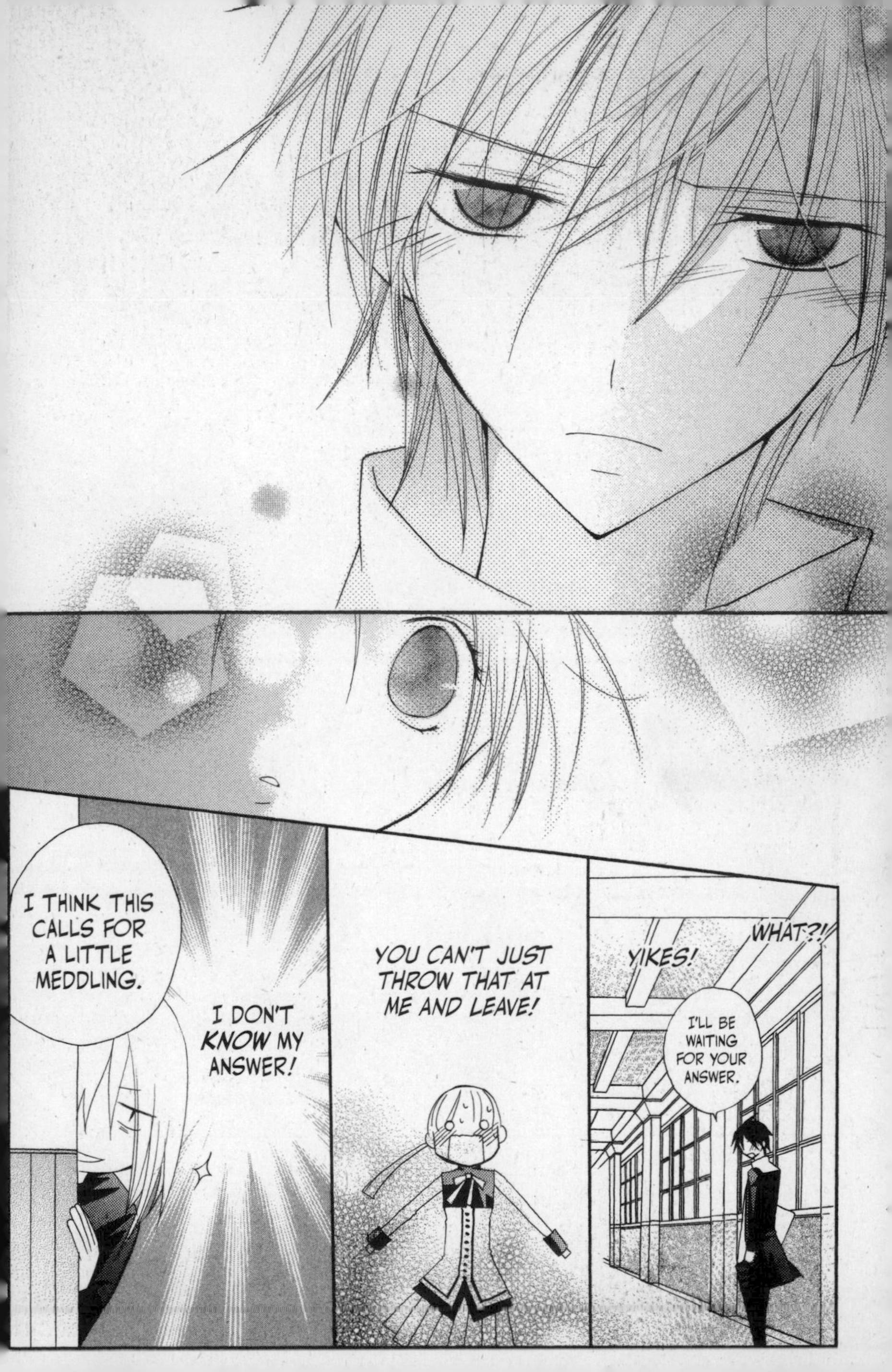
WHAT?!
YIKES!
I'LL BE WAITING FOR YOUR ANSWER.
YOU CAN'T JUST THROW THAT AT ME AND LEAVE!
I DON'T KNOW MY ANSWER!
I THINK THIS CALLS FOR A LITTLE MEDDLING.

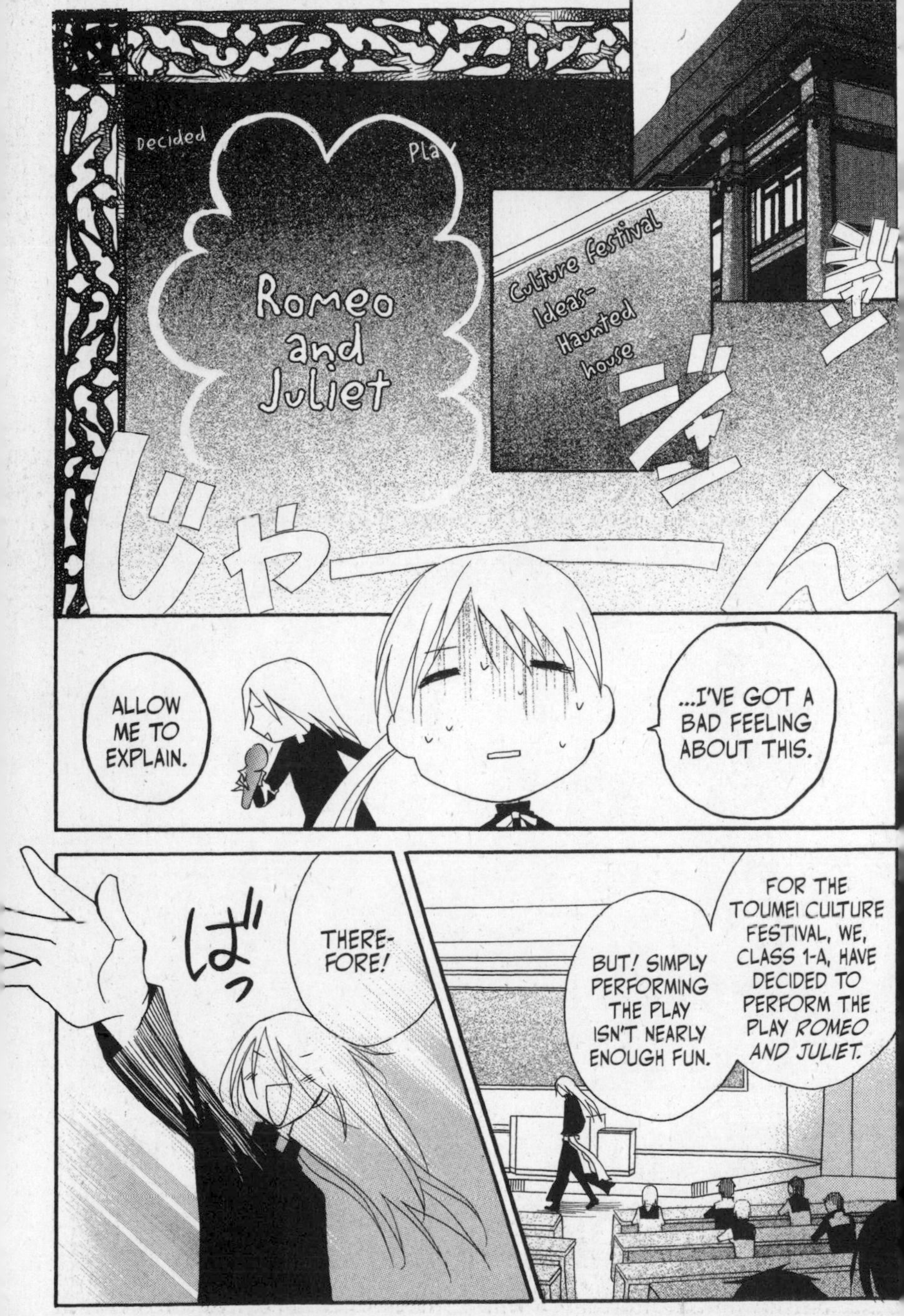

Culture festival Ideas- Haunted house
Decided
Play
Romeo and Juliet
じゃーん
...I'VE GOT A BAD FEELING ABOUT THIS.
ALLOW ME TO EXPLAIN.
FOR THE TOUMEI CULTURE FESTIVAL, WE, CLASS 1-A, HAVE DECIDED TO PERFORM THE PLAY *ROMEO AND JULIET.*
BUT! SIMPLY PERFORMING THE PLAY ISN'T NEARLY ENOUGH FUN.
THERE-FORE!
ばっ

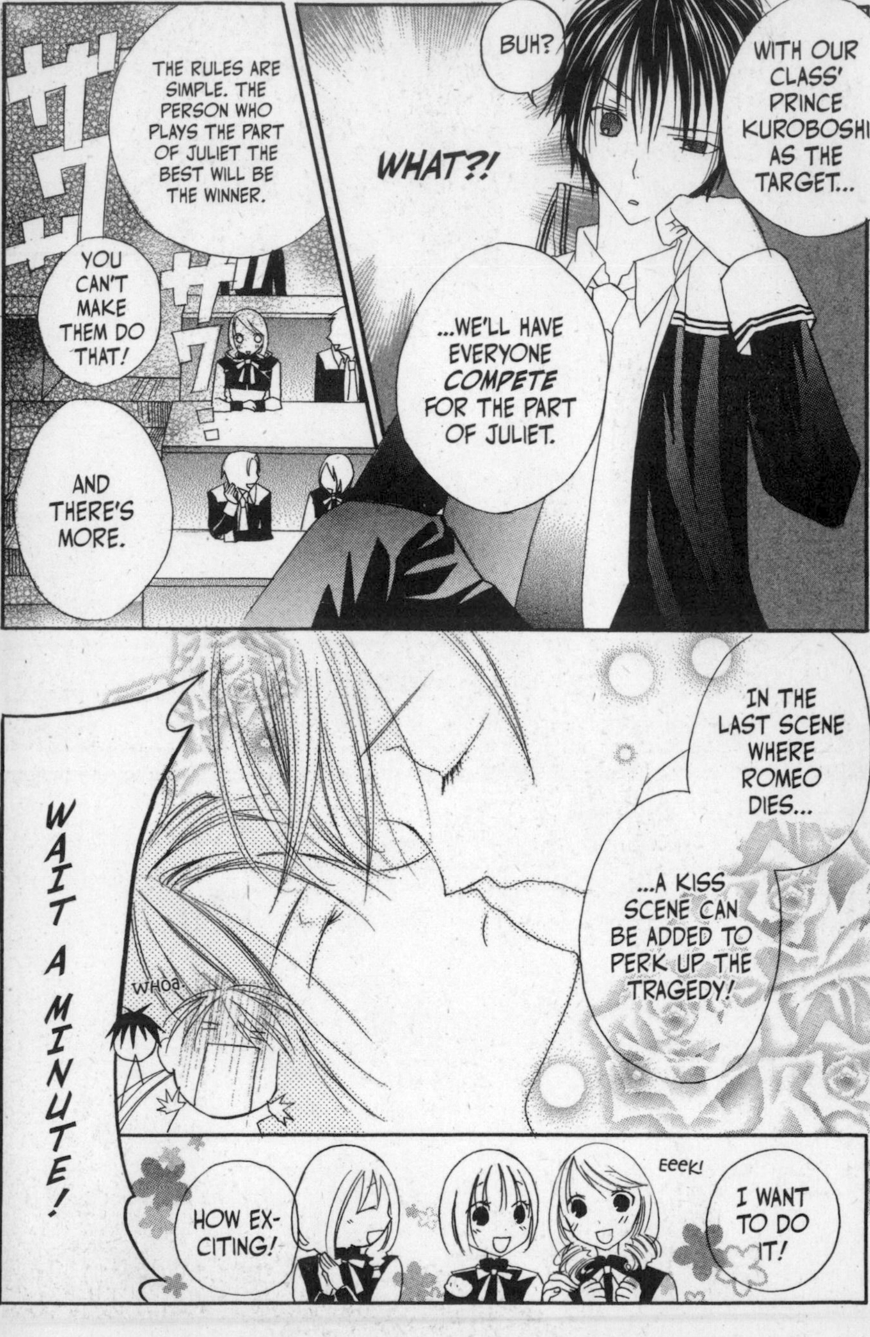
WITH OUR CLASS' PRINCE KUROBOSHI AS THE TARGET...
BUH?
WHAT?!
...WE'LL HAVE EVERYONE COMPETE FOR THE PART OF JULIET.
THE RULES ARE SIMPLE. THE PERSON WHO PLAYS THE PART OF JULIET THE BEST WILL BE THE WINNER.
YOU CAN'T MAKE THEM DO THAT!
AND THERE'S MORE.
IN THE LAST SCENE WHERE ROMEO DIES...
...A KISS SCENE CAN BE ADDED TO PERK UP THE TRAGEDY!
WAIT A MINUTE!
WHOA.
I WANT TO DO IT!
EEEK!
HOW EX-CITING!

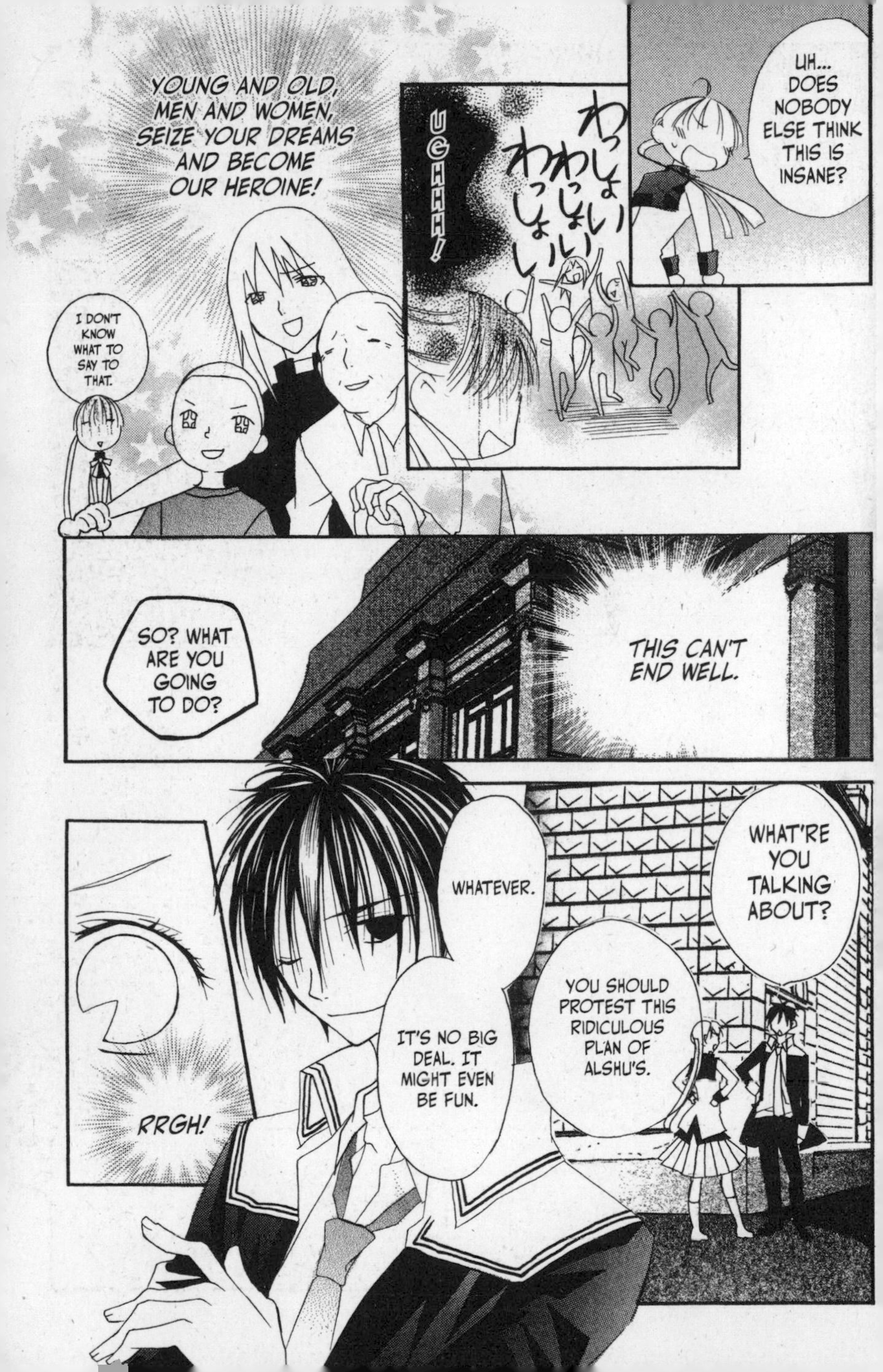
UH... DOES NOBODY ELSE THINK THIS IS INSANE?
わっしょい わっしょい わっしょい
UGHHH!
YOUNG AND OLD, MEN AND WOMEN, SEIZE YOUR DREAMS AND BECOME OUR HEROINE!
I DON'T KNOW WHAT TO SAY TO THAT.
THIS CAN'T END WELL.
SO? WHAT ARE YOU GOING TO DO?
WHAT'RE YOU TALKING ABOUT?
YOU SHOULD PROTEST THIS RIDICULOUS PLAN OF ALSHU'S.
WHATEVER.
IT'S NO BIG DEAL. IT MIGHT EVEN BE FUN.
RRGH!

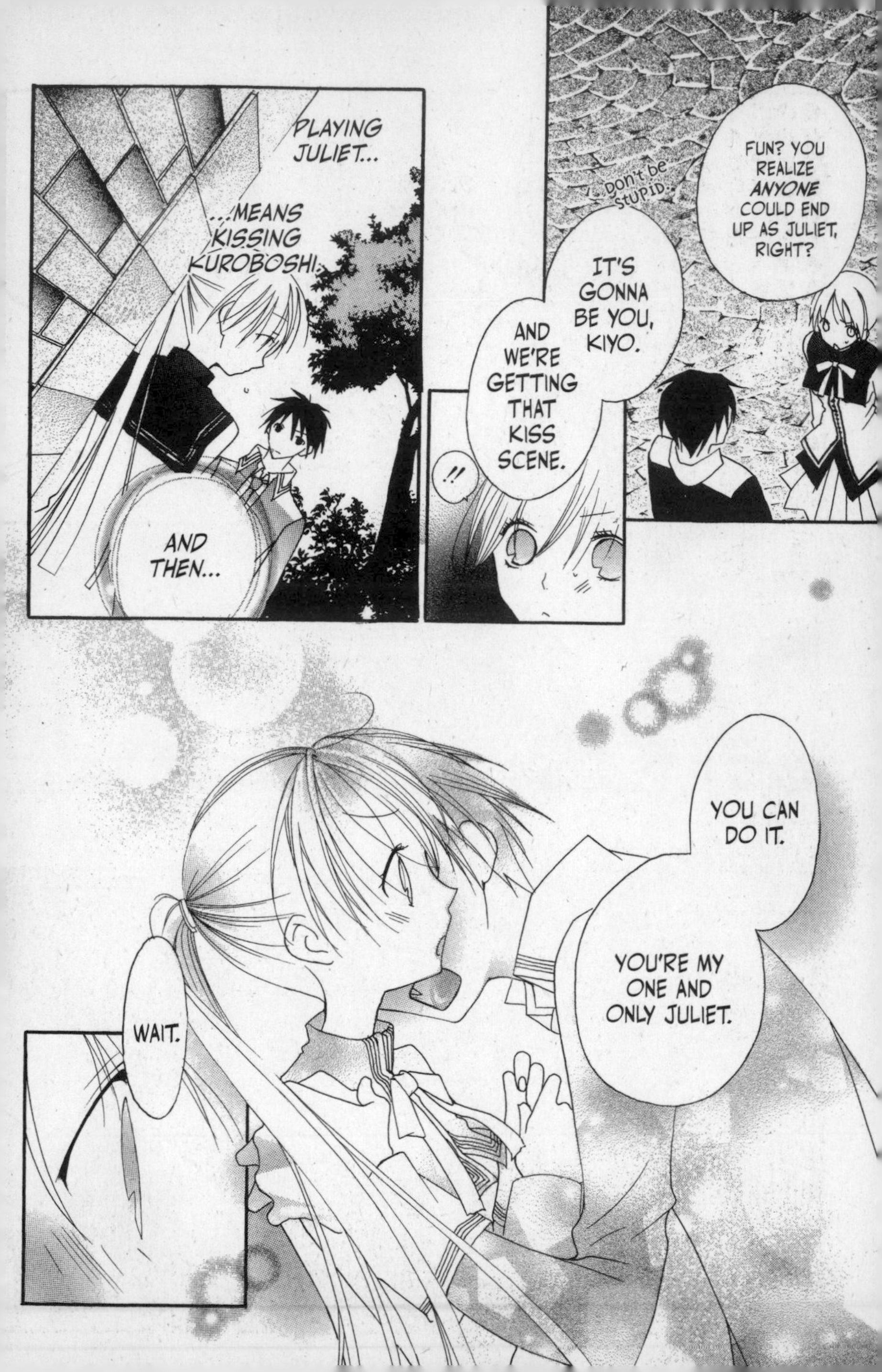
FUN? YOU REALIZE *ANYONE* COULD END UP AS JULIET, RIGHT?
Don't be stupid...
IT'S GONNA BE YOU, KIYO.
AND WE'RE GETTING THAT KISS SCENE.
!!
PLAYING JULIET...
...MEANS KISSING KUROBOSHI.
AND THEN...
YOU CAN DO IT.
YOU'RE MY ONE AND ONLY JULIET.
WAIT.

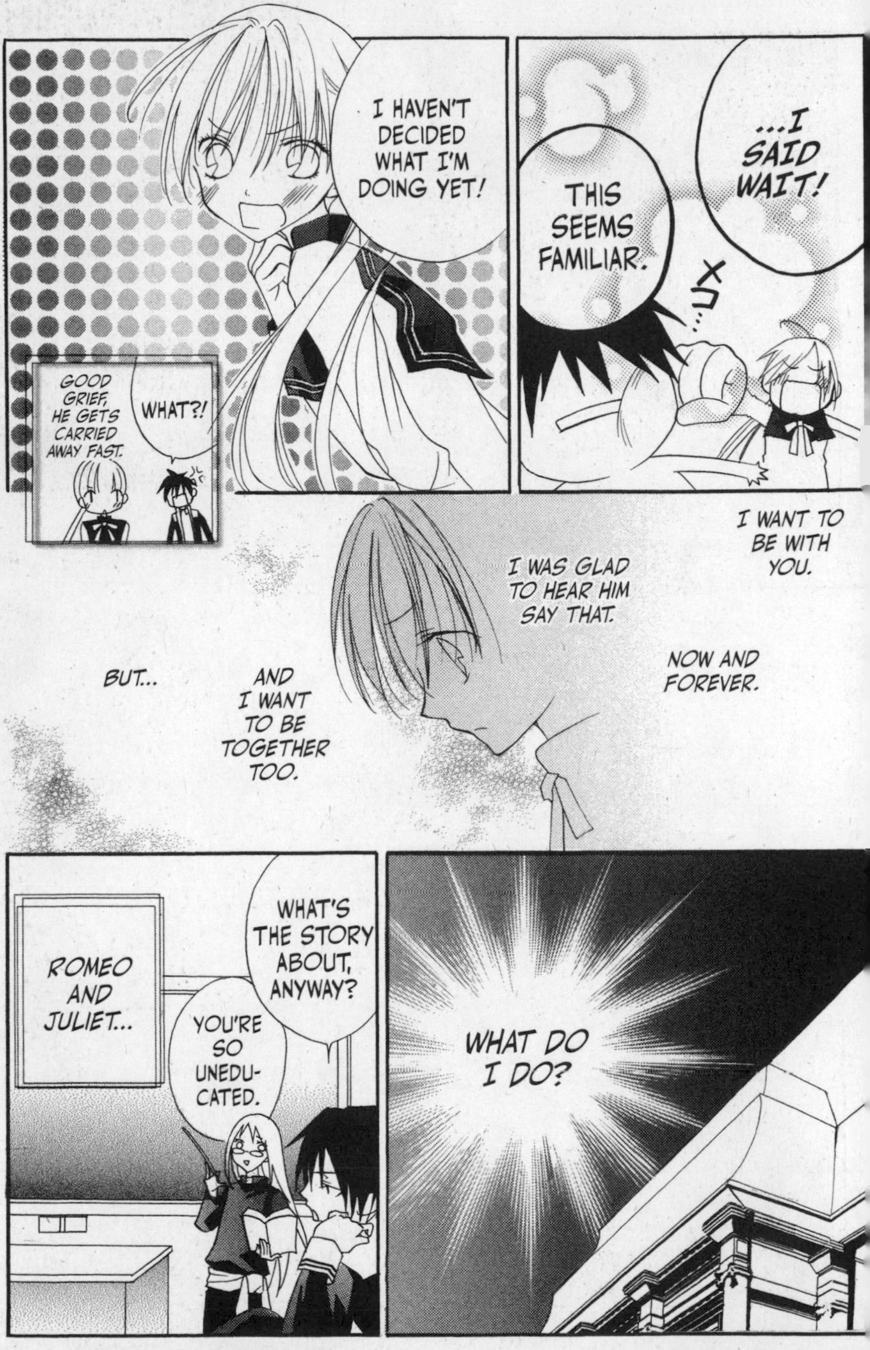
...I SAID WAIT!
THIS SEEMS FAMILIAR.
I HAVEN'T DECIDED WHAT I'M DOING YET!
WHAT?!
GOOD GRIEF, HE GETS CARRIED AWAY FAST.
I WANT TO BE WITH YOU.
NOW AND FOREVER.
I WAS GLAD TO HEAR HIM SAY THAT.
AND I WANT TO BE TOGETHER TOO.
BUT...
WHAT DO I DO?
WHAT'S THE STORY ABOUT, ANYWAY?
YOU'RE SO UNEDUCATED.
ROMEO AND JULIET...

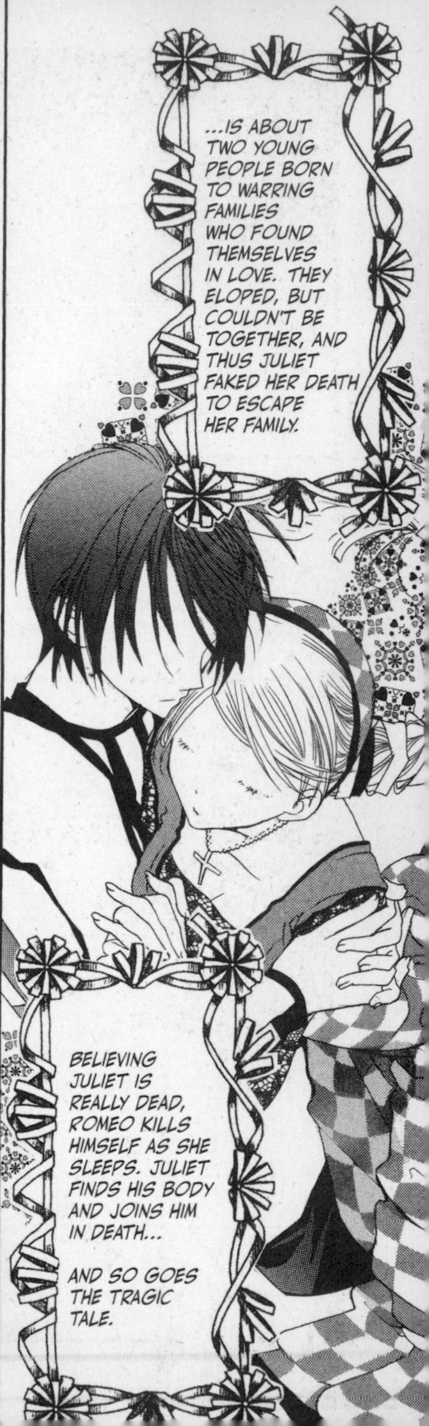
...IS ABOUT TWO YOUNG PEOPLE BORN TO WARRING FAMILIES WHO FOUND THEMSELVES IN LOVE. THEY ELOPED, BUT COULDN'T BE TOGETHER, AND THUS JULIET FAKED HER DEATH TO ESCAPE HER FAMILY.
BELIEVING JULIET IS REALLY DEAD, ROMEO KILLS HIMSELF AS SHE SLEEPS. JULIET FINDS HIS BODY AND JOINS HIM IN DEATH...
AND SO GOES THE TRAGIC TALE.

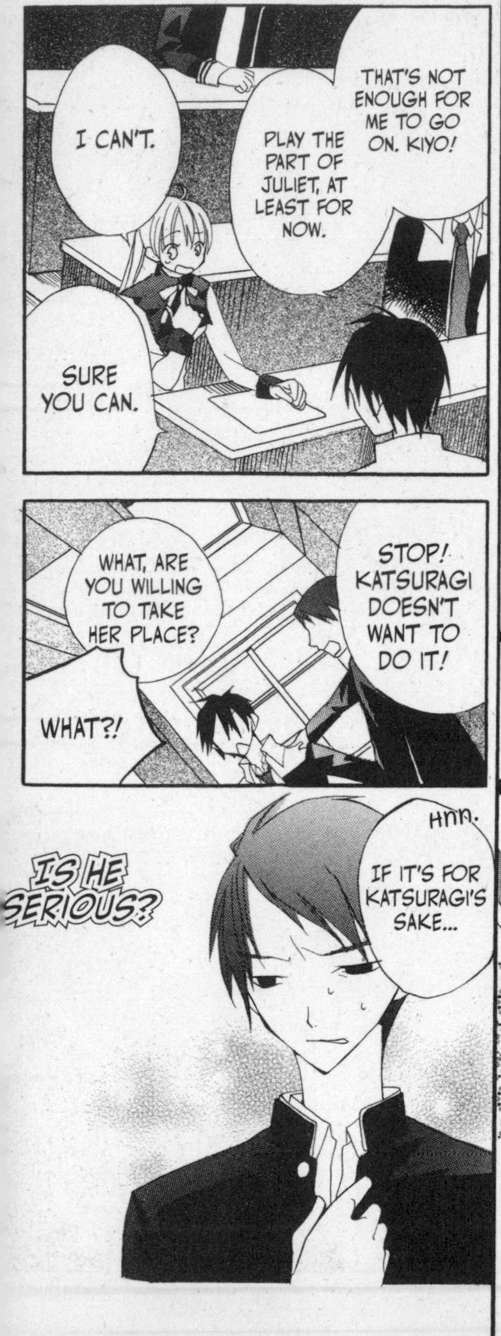
THAT'S NOT ENOUGH FOR ME TO GO ON. KIYO!
PLAY THE PART OF JULIET, AT LEAST FOR NOW.
I CAN'T.
SURE YOU CAN.
STOP! KATSURAGI DOESN'T WANT TO DO IT!
WHAT, ARE YOU WILLING TO TAKE HER PLACE?
WHAT?!
Hnn.
IF IT'S FOR KATSURAGI'S SAKE...
IS HE SERIOUS?

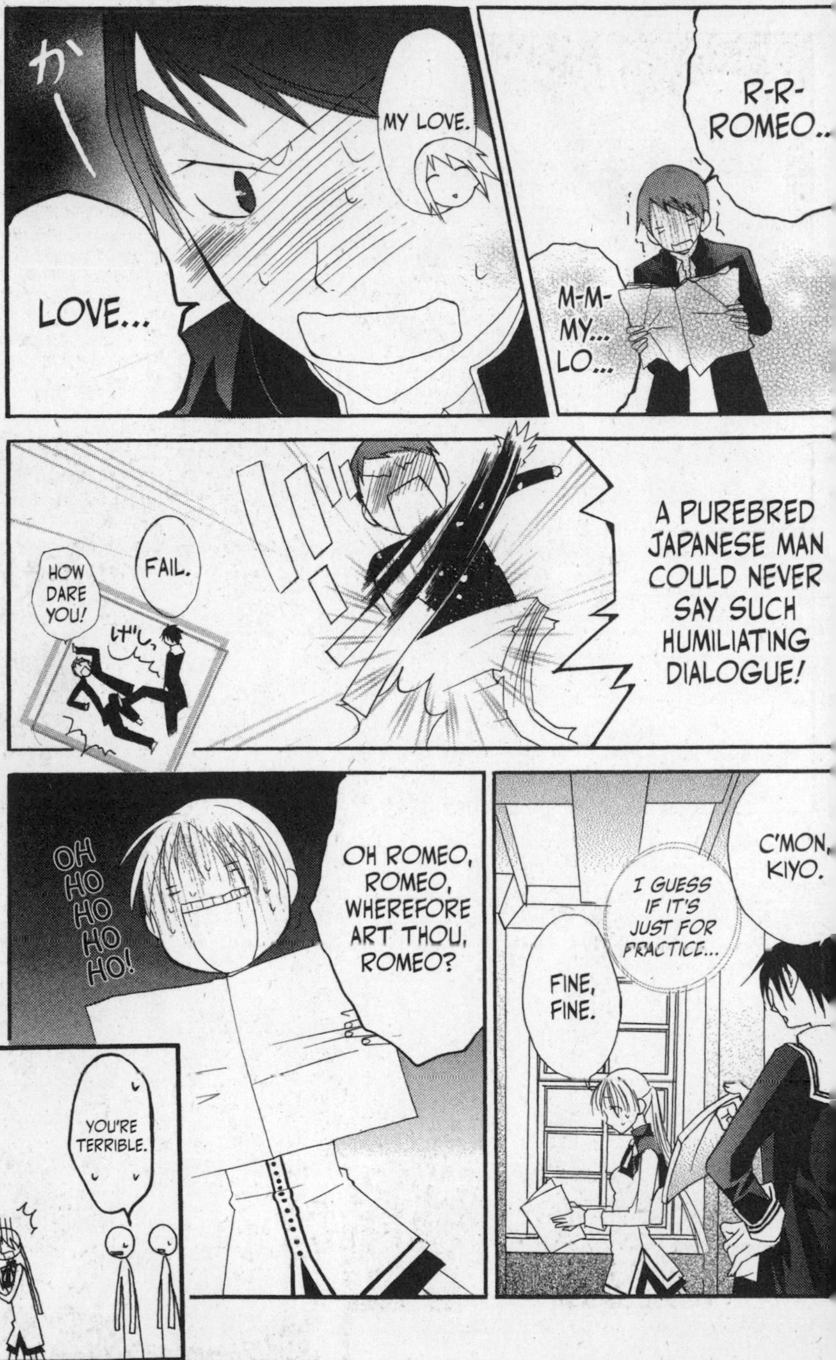
R-R-ROMEO...
M-M-MY... LO...
MY LOVE.
か～
LOVE...
A PUREBRED JAPANESE MAN COULD NEVER SAY SUCH HUMILIATING DIALOGUE!
FAIL.
HOW DARE YOU!
げしっ
C'MON, KIYO.
I GUESS IF IT'S JUST FOR PRACTICE...
FINE, FINE.
OH ROMEO, ROMEO, WHEREFORE ART THOU, ROMEO?
OH HO HO HO HO HO!
YOU'RE TERRIBLE.

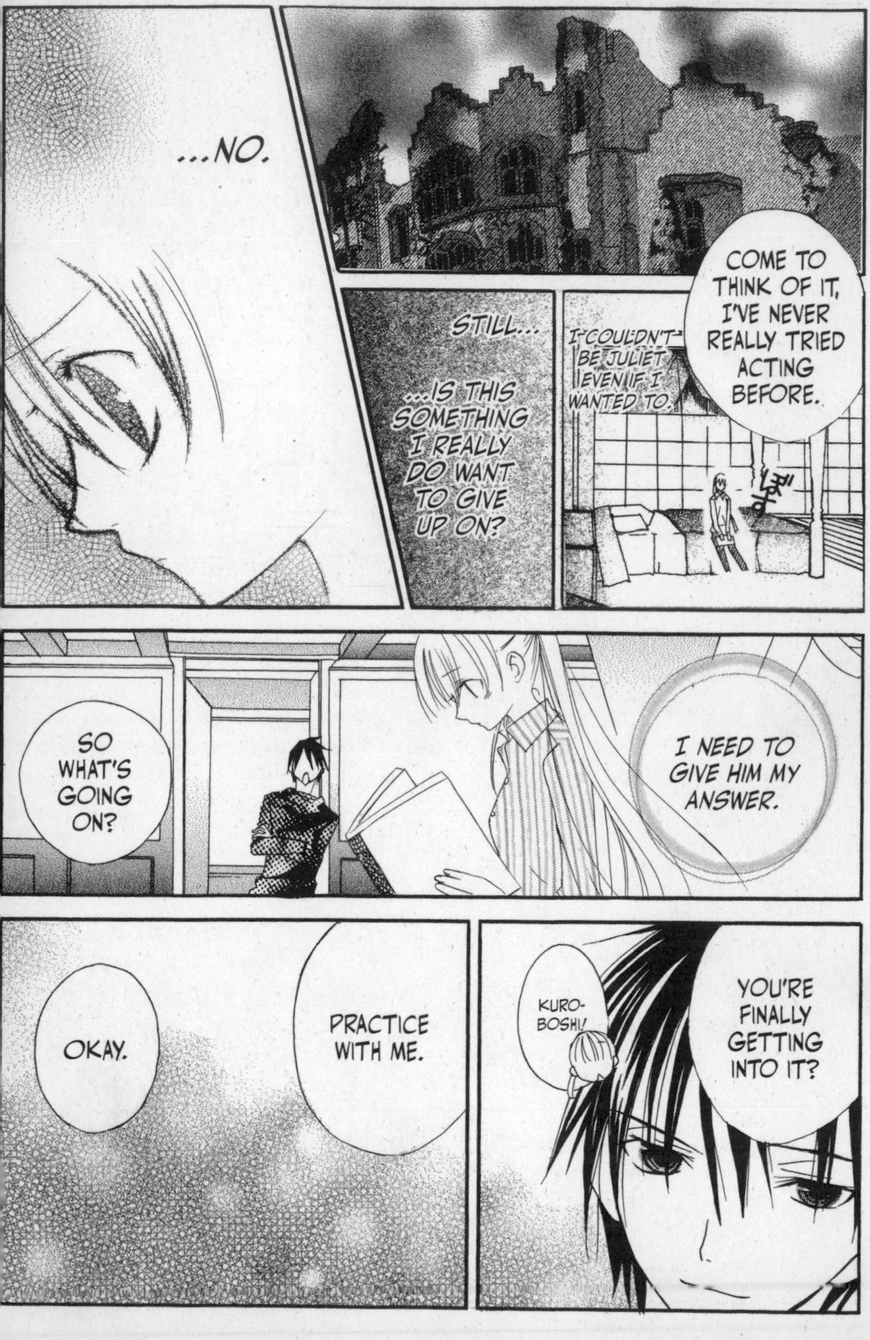
COME TO THINK OF IT, I'VE NEVER REALLY TRIED ACTING BEFORE.
I COULDN'T BE JULIET EVEN IF I WANTED TO.
STILL...
...IS THIS SOMETHING I REALLY DO WANT TO GIVE UP ON?
...NO.
I NEED TO GIVE HIM MY ANSWER.
SO WHAT'S GOING ON?
YOU'RE FINALLY GETTING INTO IT?
KURO-BOSHI!
PRACTICE WITH ME.
OKAY.

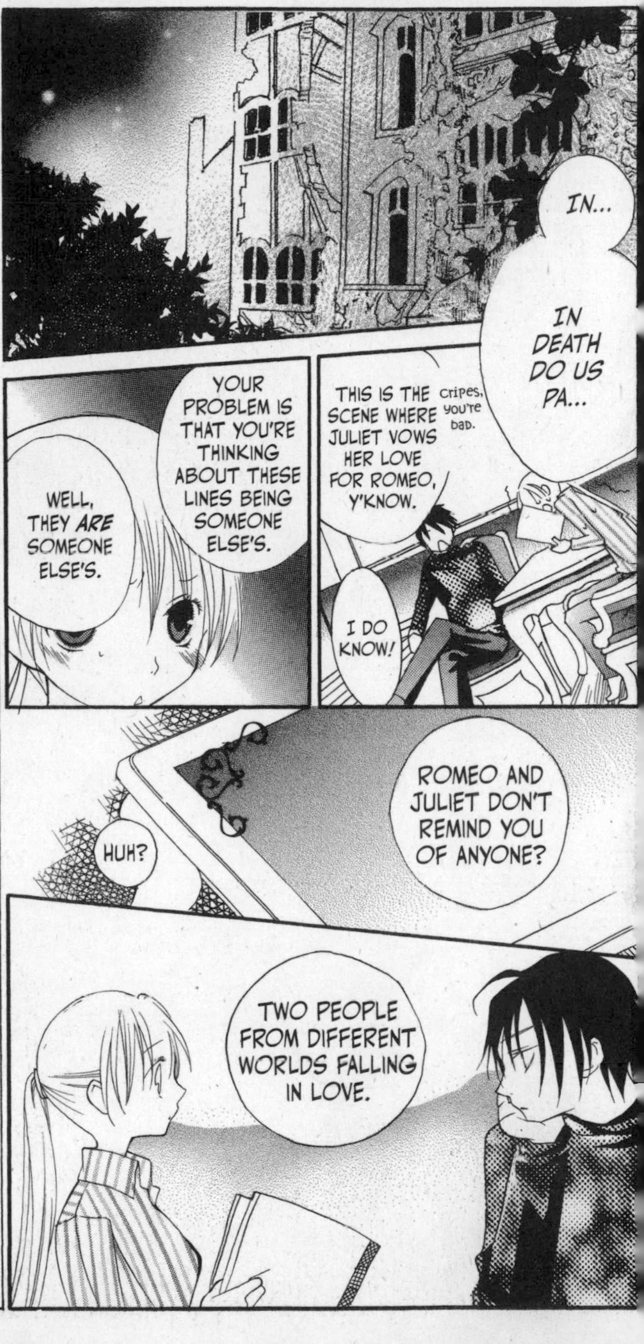
IN...
IN DEATH DO US PA...
THIS IS THE SCENE WHERE JULIET VOWS HER LOVE FOR ROMEO, Y'KNOW.
Cripes, you're bad.
I DO KNOW!
YOUR PROBLEM IS THAT YOU'RE THINKING ABOUT THESE LINES BEING SOMEONE ELSE'S.
WELL, THEY *ARE* SOMEONE ELSE'S.
ROMEO AND JULIET DON'T REMIND YOU OF ANYONE?
HUH?
TWO PEOPLE FROM DIFFERENT WORLDS FALLING IN LOVE.

My Favorite Parts

Part 2
Hair

This part is really "my favorite" to draw.

I like hair, but I'm the most careful with it when I'm drawing something. (I can be careful, believe it or not.)

I save inking it for last. And I redraw it until I'm completely satisfied. Kiyo's hair is a hassle--I always cry a little when working on it. Clear, long hair is very hard to draw.

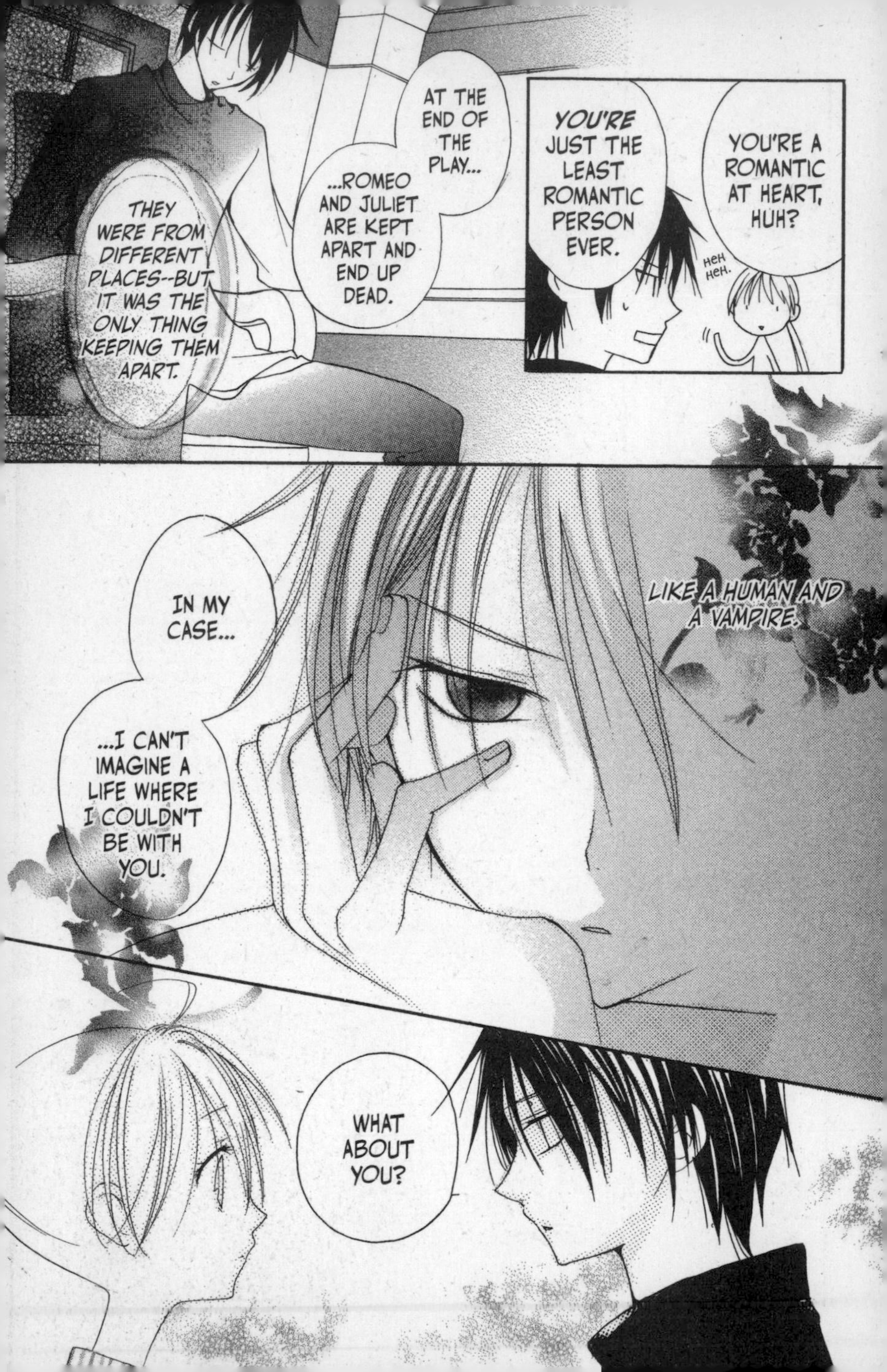
YOU'RE A ROMANTIC AT HEART, HUH?
HEH HEH.
YOU'RE JUST THE LEAST ROMANTIC PERSON EVER.
AT THE END OF THE PLAY...
...ROMEO AND JULIET ARE KEPT APART AND END UP DEAD.
THEY WERE FROM DIFFERENT PLACES--BUT IT WAS THE ONLY THING KEEPING THEM APART.
LIKE A HUMAN AND A VAMPIRE.
IN MY CASE...
...I CAN'T IMAGINE A LIFE WHERE I COULDN'T BE WITH YOU.
WHAT ABOUT YOU?

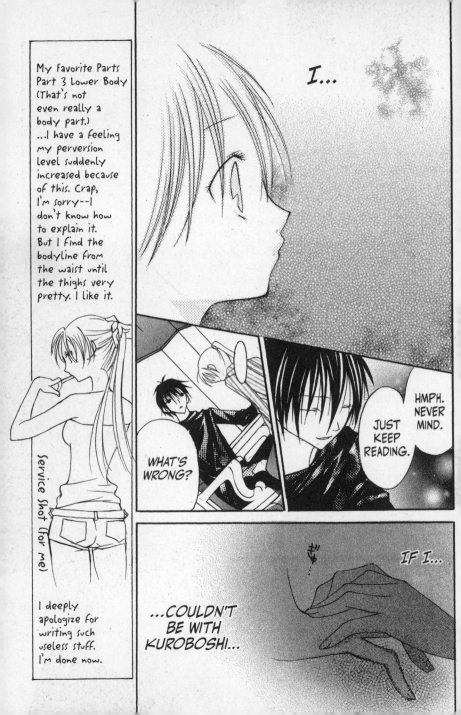

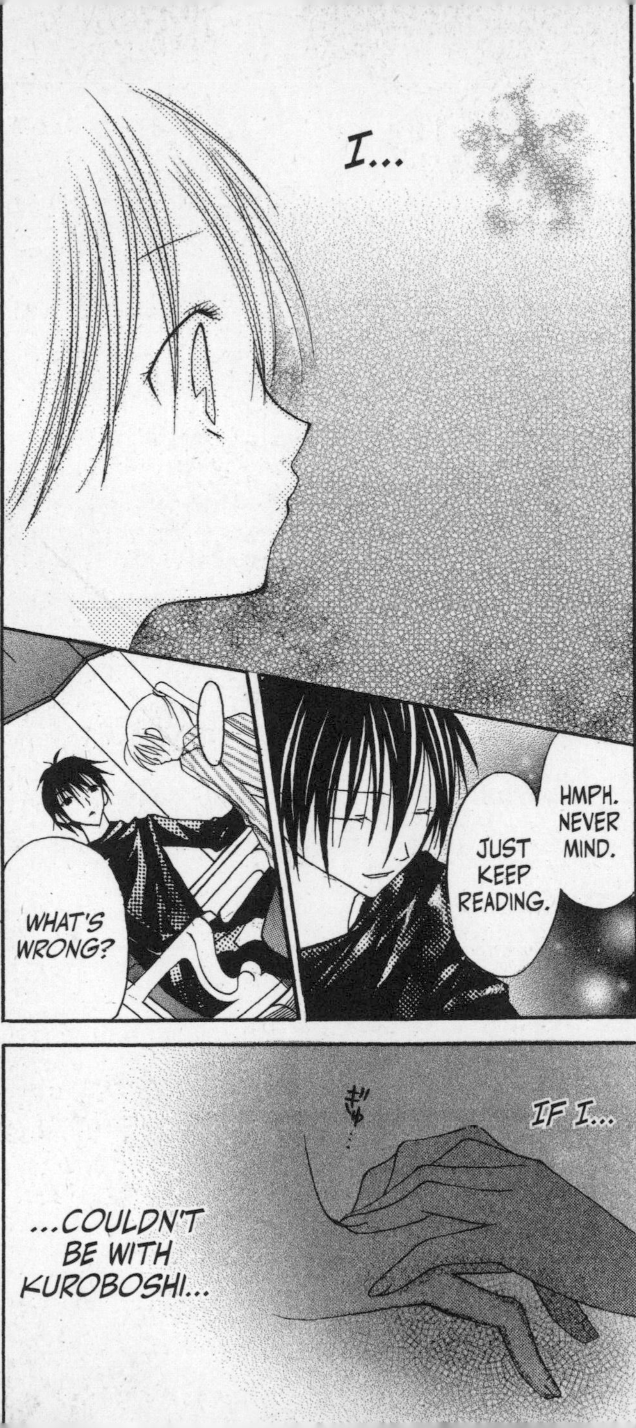
I...
HMPH. NEVER MIND.
JUST KEEP READING.
WHAT'S WRONG?
IF I...
ぎゅ
...COULDN'T BE WITH KUROBOSHI...

My Favorite Parts
Part 3 Lower Body
(That's not even really a body part.)
...I have a feeling my perversion level suddenly increased because of this. Crap, I'm sorry--I don't know how to explain it. But I find the bodyline from the waist until the thighs very pretty. I like it.

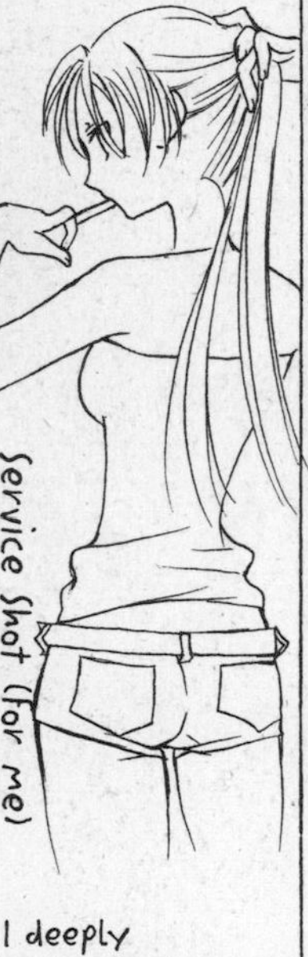
Service Shot (for me)

I deeply apologize for writing such useless stuff. I'm done now.

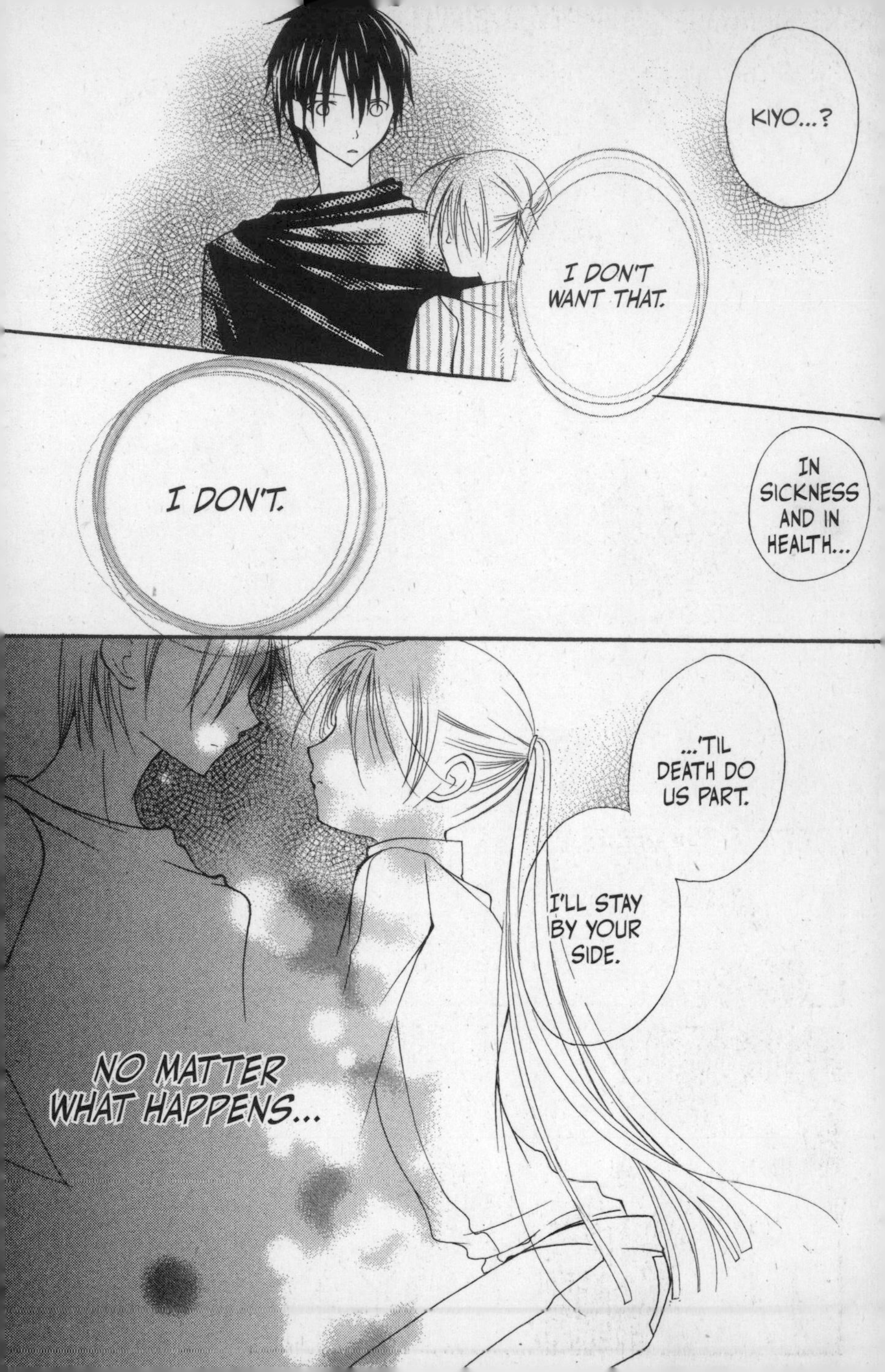
KIYO...?
I DON'T WANT THAT.
IN SICKNESS AND IN HEALTH...
I DON'T.
...'TIL DEATH DO US PART.
I'LL STAY BY YOUR SIDE.
NO MATTER WHAT HAPPENS...

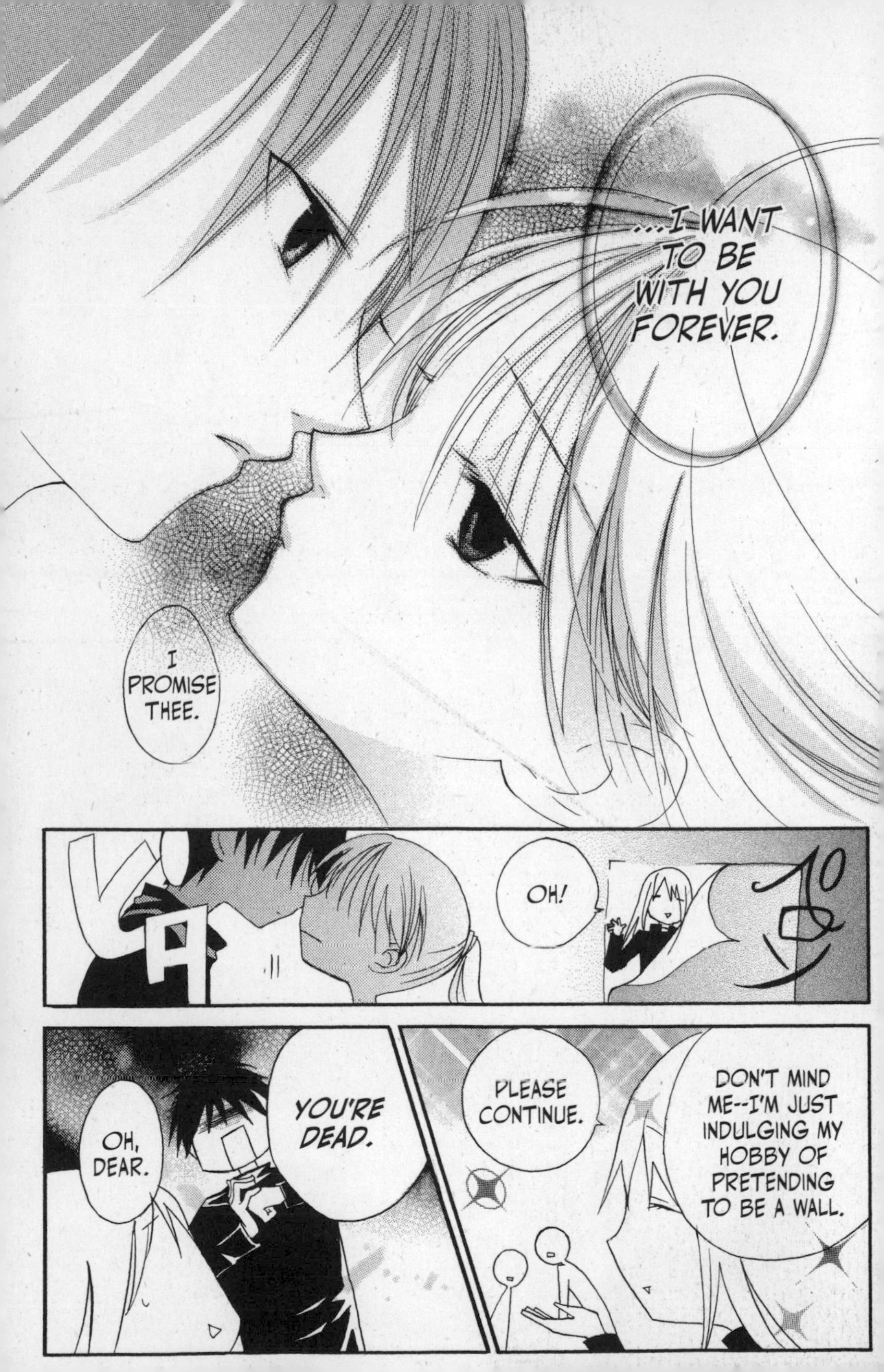
...I WANT TO BE WITH YOU FOREVER.
I PROMISE THEE.
OH!
DON'T MIND ME--I'M JUST INDULGING MY HOBBY OF PRETENDING TO BE A WALL.
PLEASE CONTINUE.
YOU'RE DEAD.
OH, DEAR.

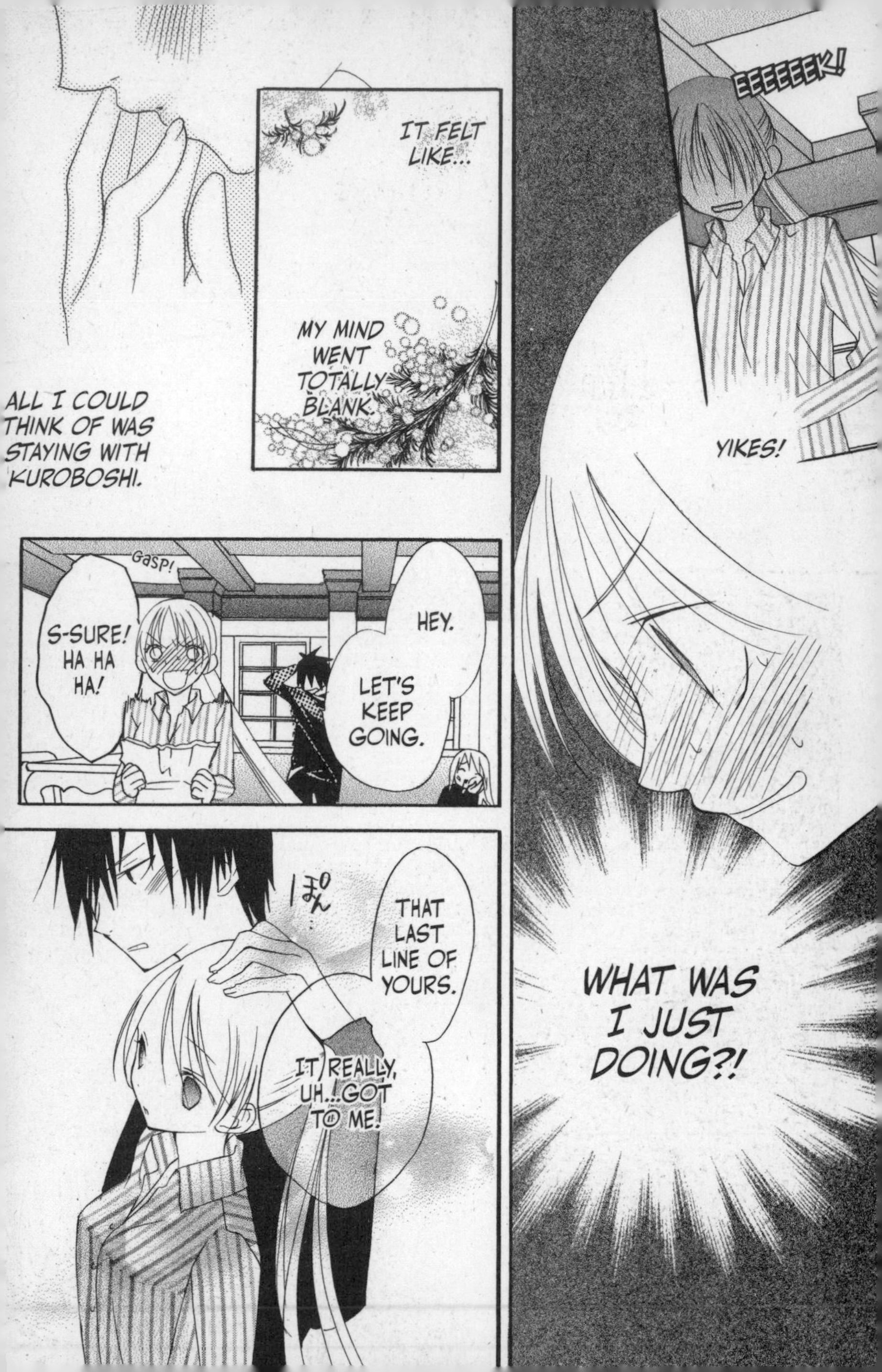
EEEEEEK!!
YIKES!
WHAT WAS I JUST DOING?!
IT FELT LIKE...
MY MIND WENT TOTALLY BLANK.
ALL I COULD THINK OF WAS STAYING WITH KUROBOSHI.
HEY.
LET'S KEEP GOING.
GASP!
S-SURE! HA HA HA!
ぽん
THAT LAST LINE OF YOURS.
IT REALLY, UH...GOT TO ME.

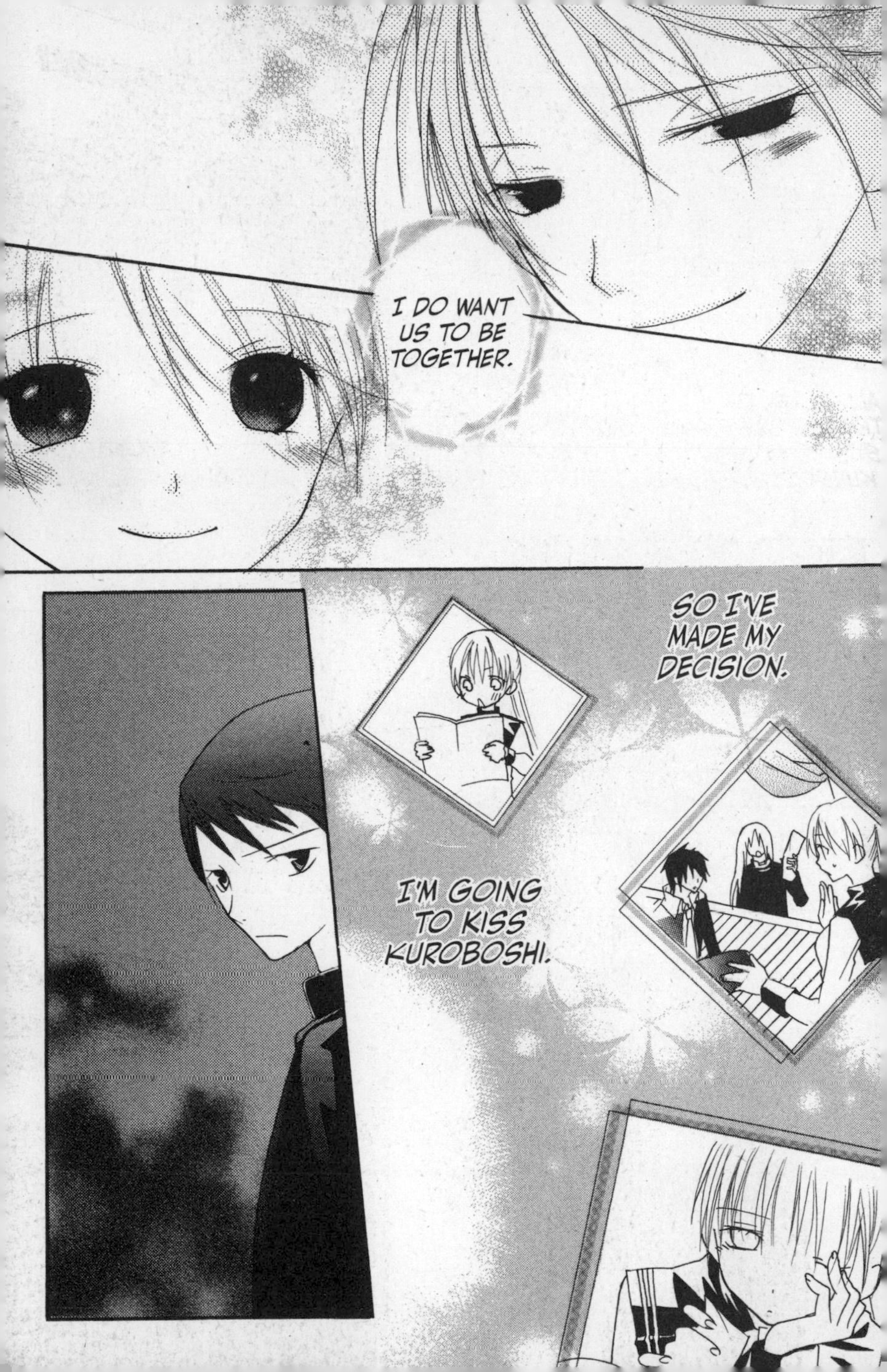
I DO WANT US TO BE TOGETHER.
SO I'VE MADE MY DECISION.
I'M GOING TO KISS KUROBOSHI.

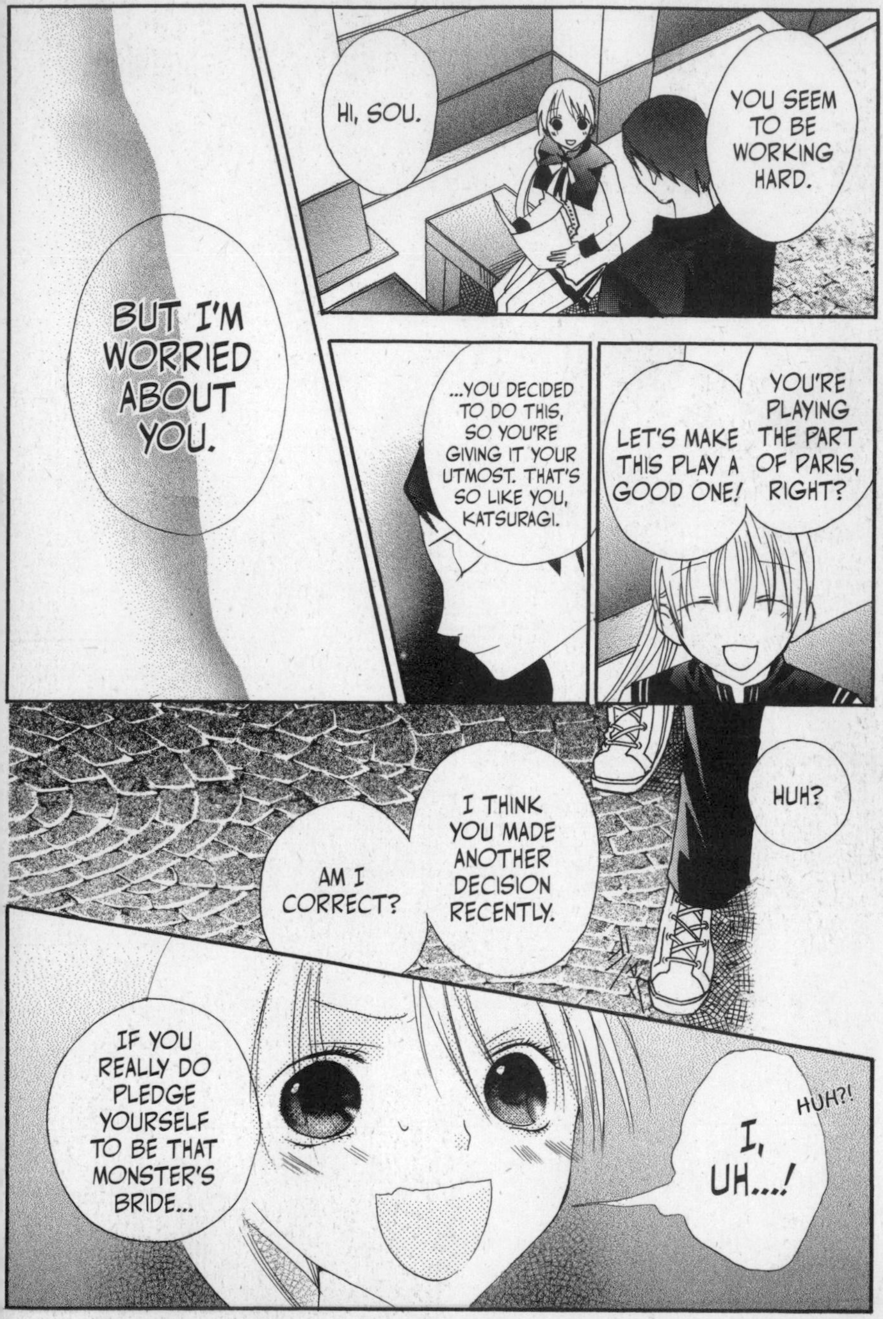
YOU SEEM TO BE WORKING HARD.
HI, SOU.
YOU'RE PLAYING THE PART OF PARIS, RIGHT?
LET'S MAKE THIS PLAY A GOOD ONE!
...YOU DECIDED TO DO THIS, SO YOU'RE GIVING IT YOUR UTMOST. THAT'S SO LIKE YOU, KATSURAGI.
BUT I'M WORRIED ABOUT YOU.
HUH?
I THINK YOU MADE ANOTHER DECISION RECENTLY.
AM I CORRECT?
HUH?!
I, UH...!
IF YOU REALLY DO PLEDGE YOURSELF TO BE THAT MONSTER'S BRIDE...

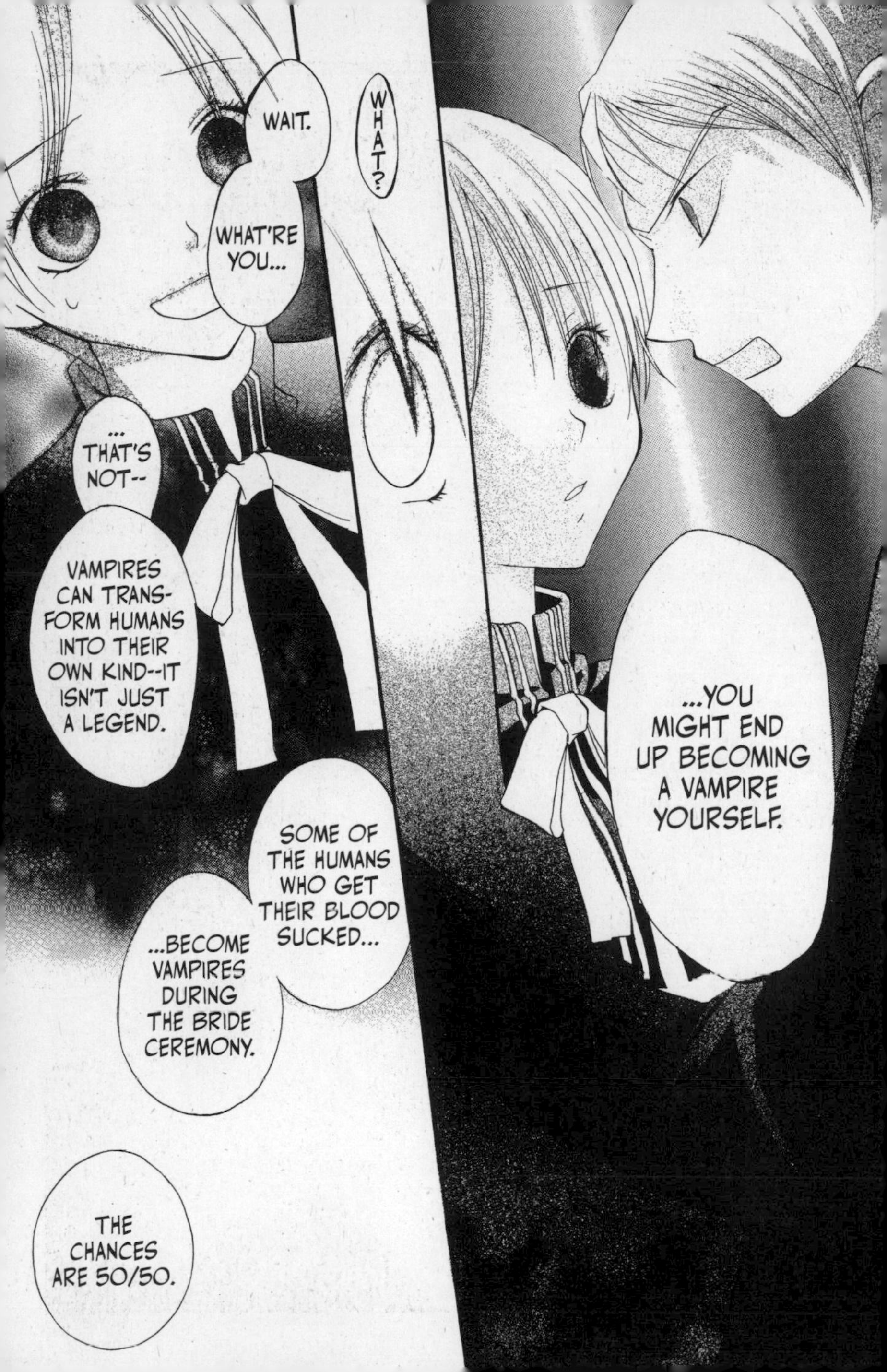
...YOU MIGHT END UP BECOMING A VAMPIRE YOURSELF.
WHAT?
WAIT.
WHAT'RE YOU...
... THAT'S NOT--
VAMPIRES CAN TRANS-FORM HUMANS INTO THEIR OWN KIND--IT ISN'T JUST A LEGEND.
SOME OF THE HUMANS WHO GET THEIR BLOOD SUCKED...
...BECOME VAMPIRES DURING THE BRIDE CEREMONY.
THE CHANCES ARE 50/50.

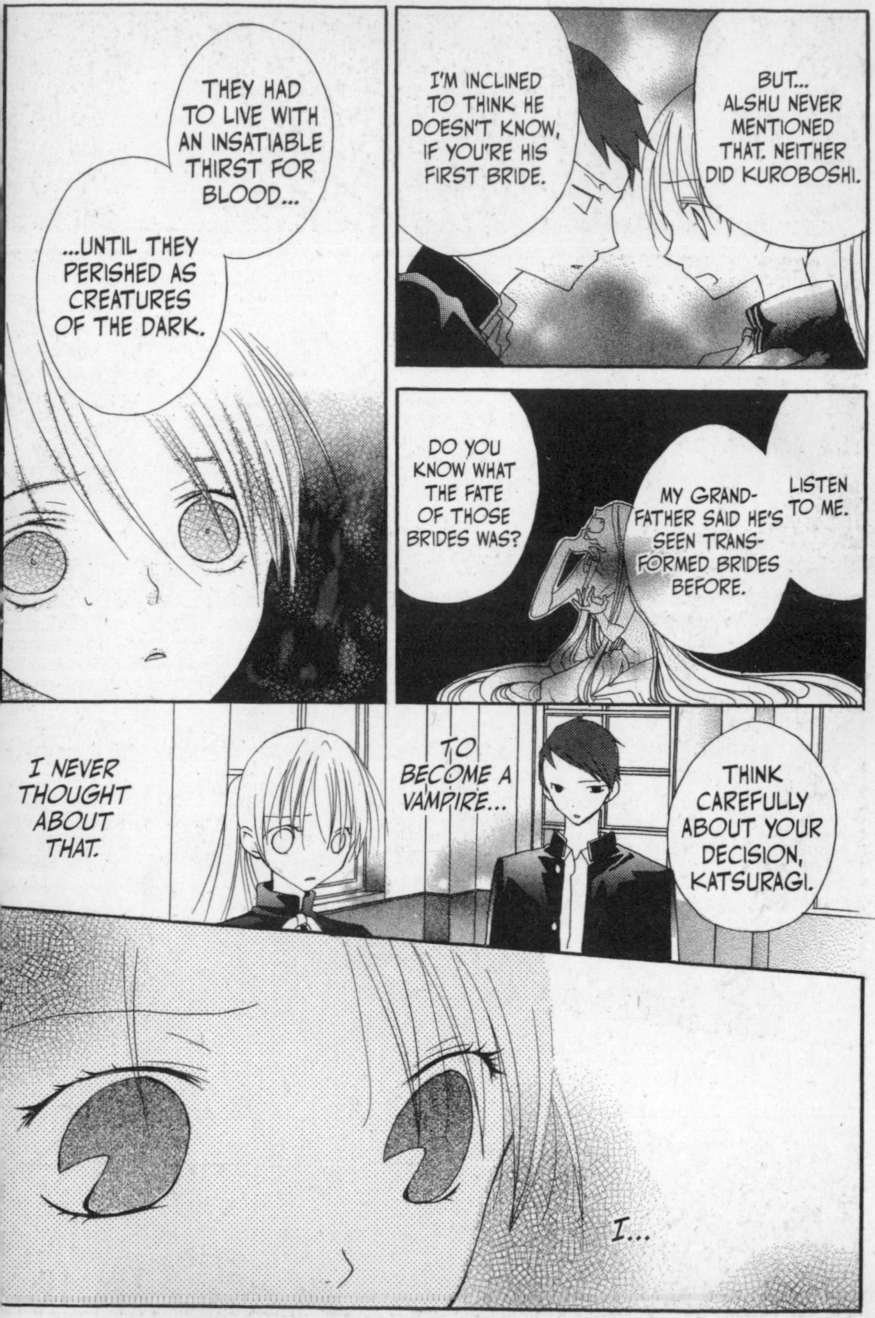
BUT... ALSHU NEVER MENTIONED THAT. NEITHER DID KUROBOSHI.
I'M INCLINED TO THINK HE DOESN'T KNOW, IF YOU'RE HIS FIRST BRIDE.
LISTEN TO ME.
MY GRAND-FATHER SAID HE'S SEEN TRANS-FORMED BRIDES BEFORE.
DO YOU KNOW WHAT THE FATE OF THOSE BRIDES WAS?
THEY HAD TO LIVE WITH AN INSATIABLE THIRST FOR BLOOD...
...UNTIL THEY PERISHED AS CREATURES OF THE DARK.
THINK CAREFULLY ABOUT YOUR DECISION, KATSURAGI.
TO BECOME A VAMPIRE...
I NEVER THOUGHT ABOUT THAT.
I...

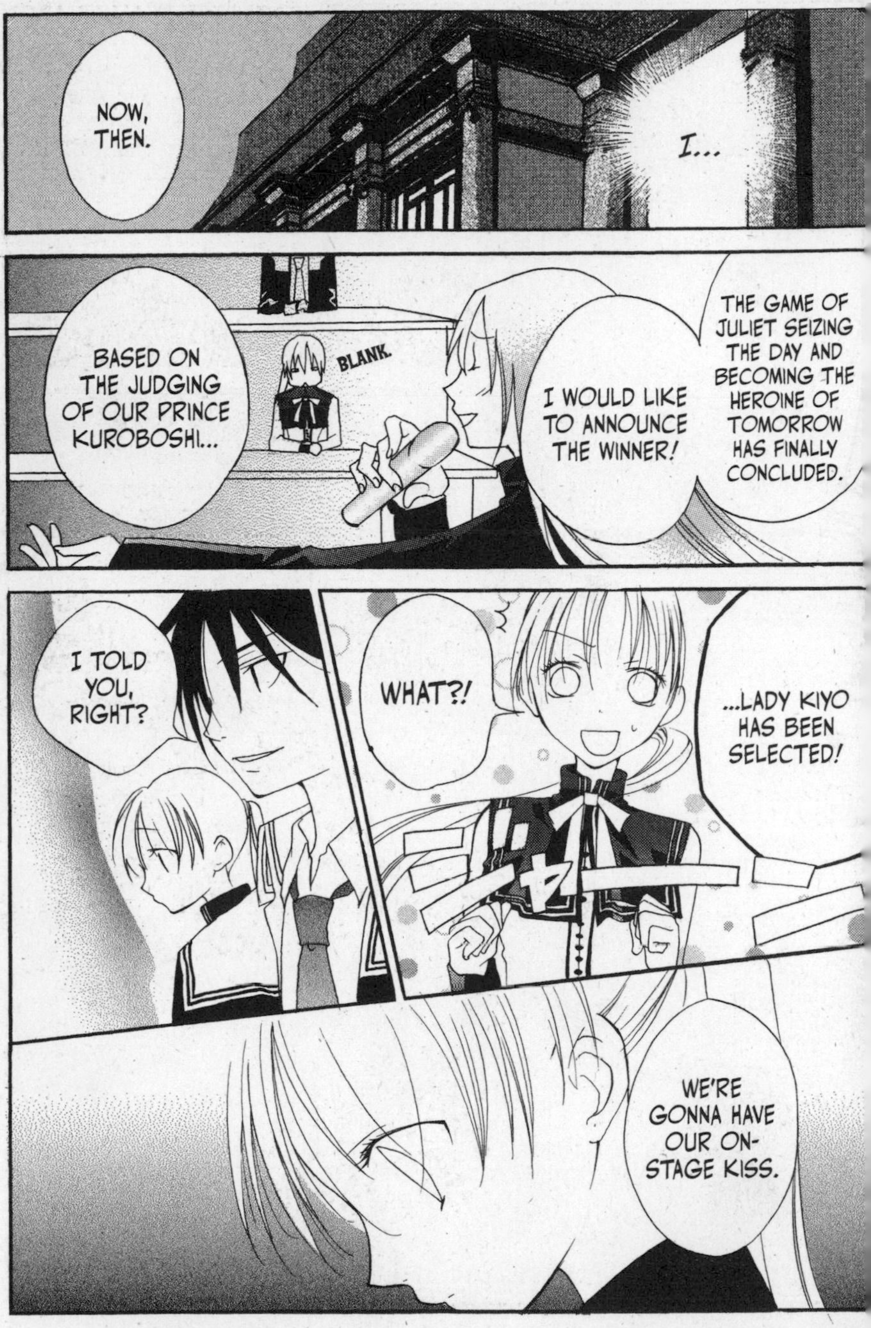
I...
NOW, THEN.
THE GAME OF JULIET SEIZING THE DAY AND BECOMING THE HEROINE OF TOMORROW HAS FINALLY CONCLUDED.
I WOULD LIKE TO ANNOUNCE THE WINNER!
BLANK.
BASED ON THE JUDGING OF OUR PRINCE KUROBOSHI...
...LADY KIYO HAS BEEN SELECTED!
WHAT?!
I TOLD YOU, RIGHT?
WE'RE GONNA HAVE OUR ON-STAGE KISS.

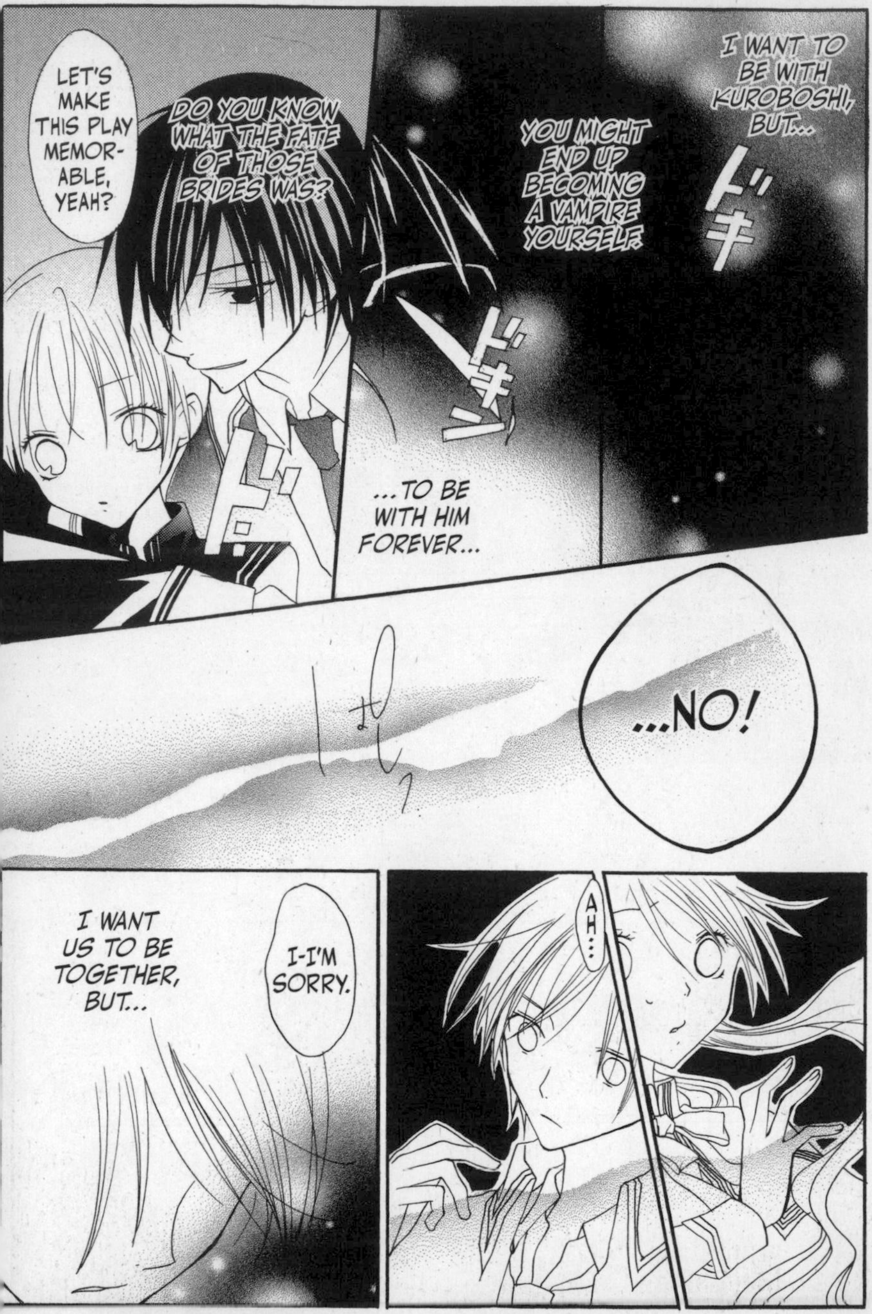
I WANT TO BE WITH KUROBOSHI, BUT...
ドキ
YOU MIGHT END UP BECOMING A VAMPIRE YOURSELF.
ドキン
...TO BE WITH HIM FOREVER...
DO YOU KNOW WHAT THE FATE OF THOSE BRIDES WAS?
LET'S MAKE THIS PLAY MEMORABLE, YEAH?
ドド
...NO!
AH...
I-I'M SORRY.
I WANT US TO BE TOGETHER, BUT...

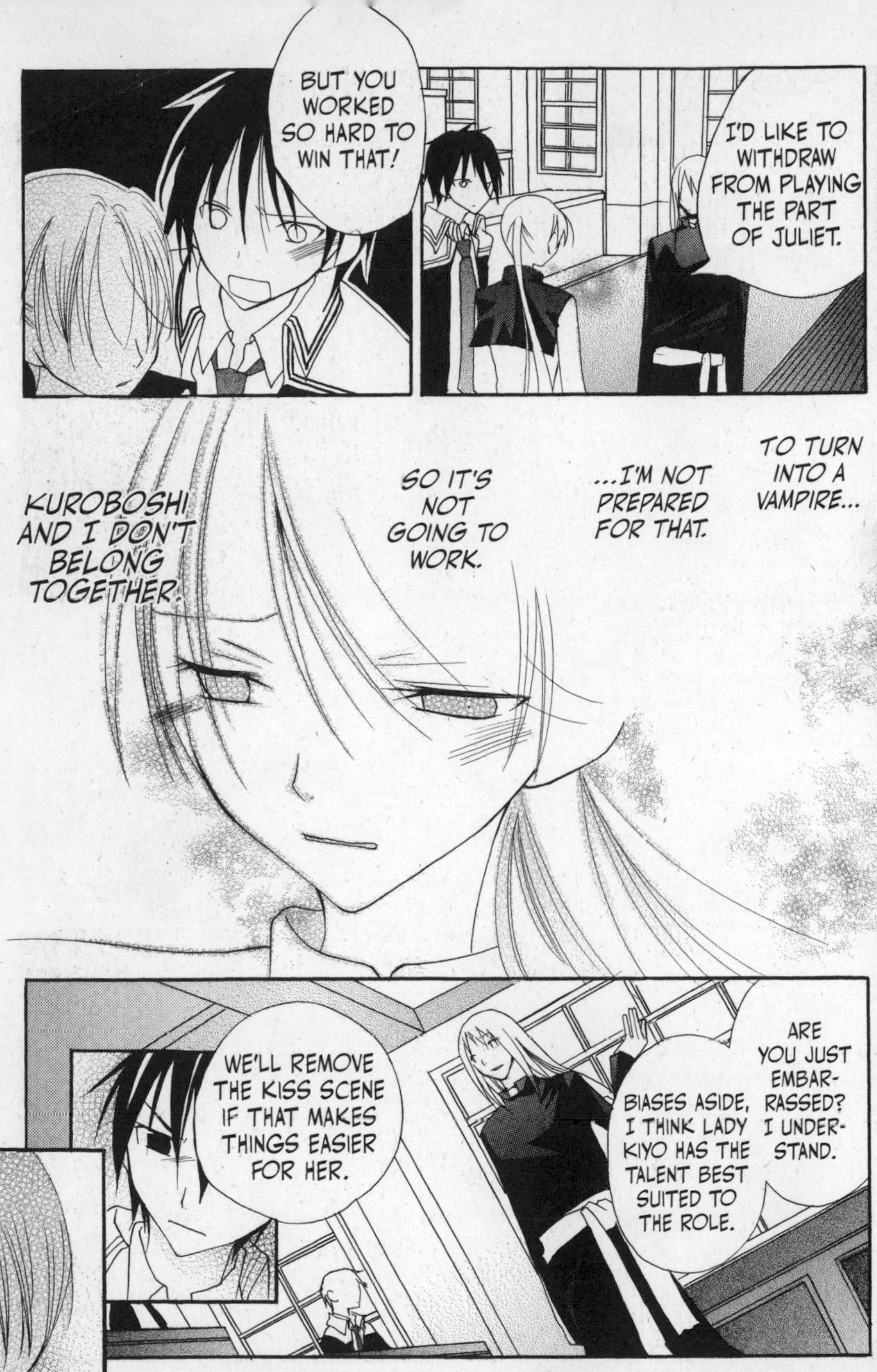
I'D LIKE TO WITHDRAW FROM PLAYING THE PART OF JULIET.
BUT YOU WORKED SO HARD TO WIN THAT!
TO TURN INTO A VAMPIRE...
...I'M NOT PREPARED FOR THAT.
SO IT'S NOT GOING TO WORK.
KUROBOSHI AND I DON'T BELONG TOGETHER.
ARE YOU JUST EMBAR-RASSED? I UNDER-STAND.
BIASES ASIDE, I THINK LADY KIYO HAS THE TALENT BEST SUITED TO THE ROLE.
WE'LL REMOVE THE KISS SCENE IF THAT MAKES THINGS EASIER FOR HER.

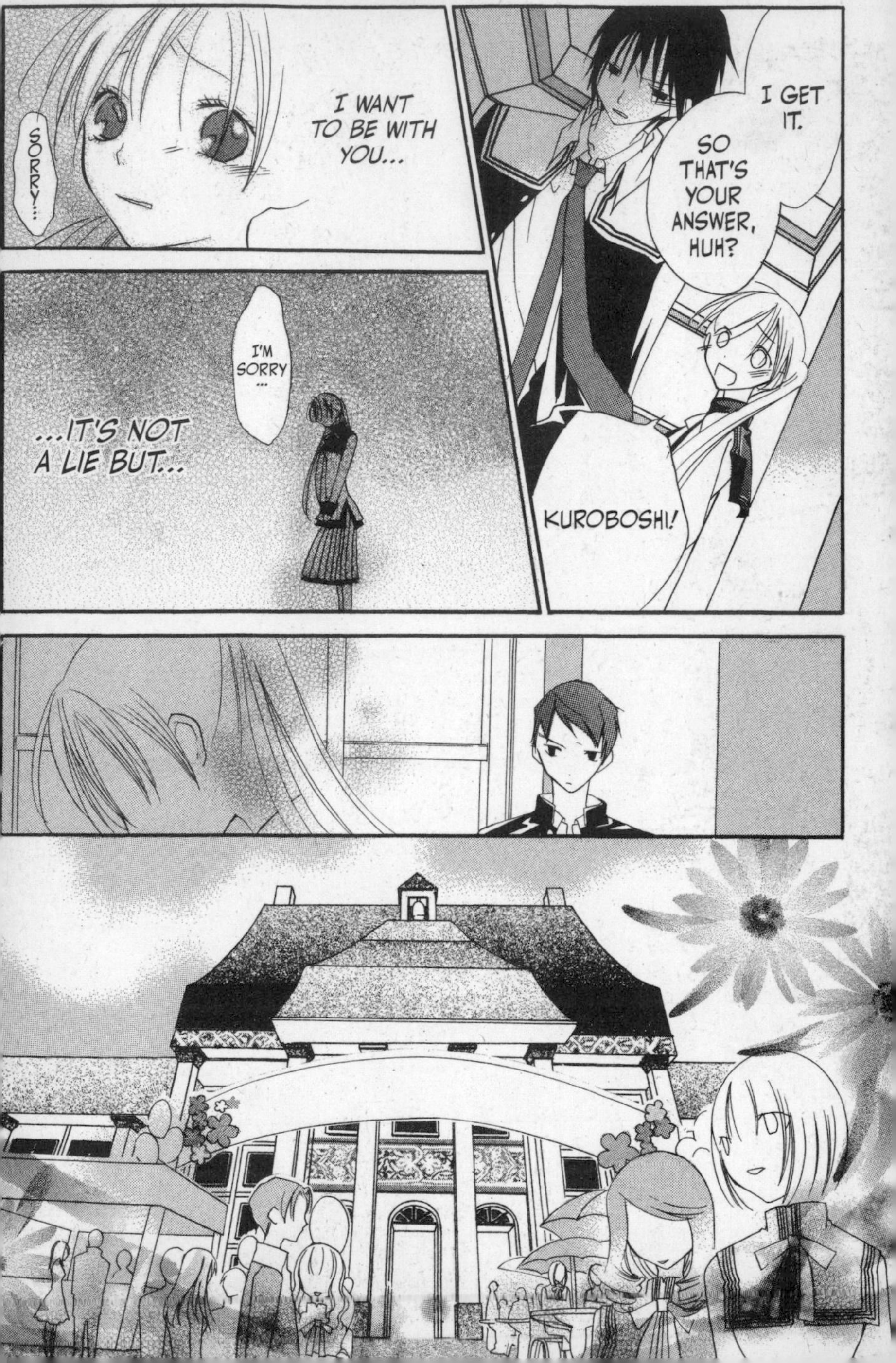
I GET IT.
SO THAT'S YOUR ANSWER, HUH?
KUROBOSHI!
I WANT TO BE WITH YOU...
SORRY...
I'M SORRY ...
...IT'S NOT A LIE BUT...

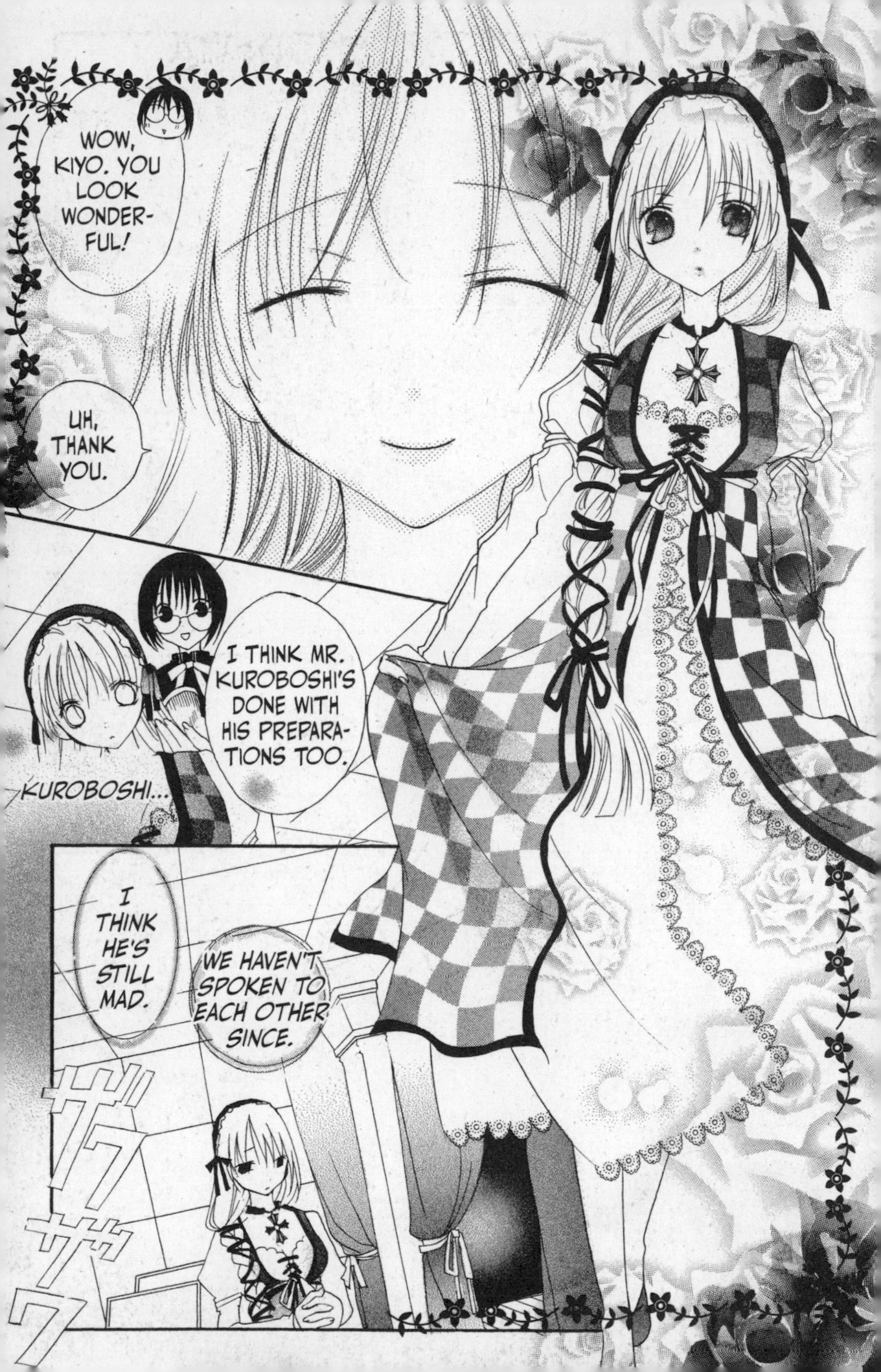
WOW, KIYO. YOU LOOK WONDER-FUL!
UH, THANK YOU.
I THINK MR. KUROBOSHI'S DONE WITH HIS PREPARA-TIONS TOO.
KUROBOSHI...
I THINK HE'S STILL MAD.
WE HAVEN'T SPOKEN TO EACH OTHER SINCE.
ザワザワ

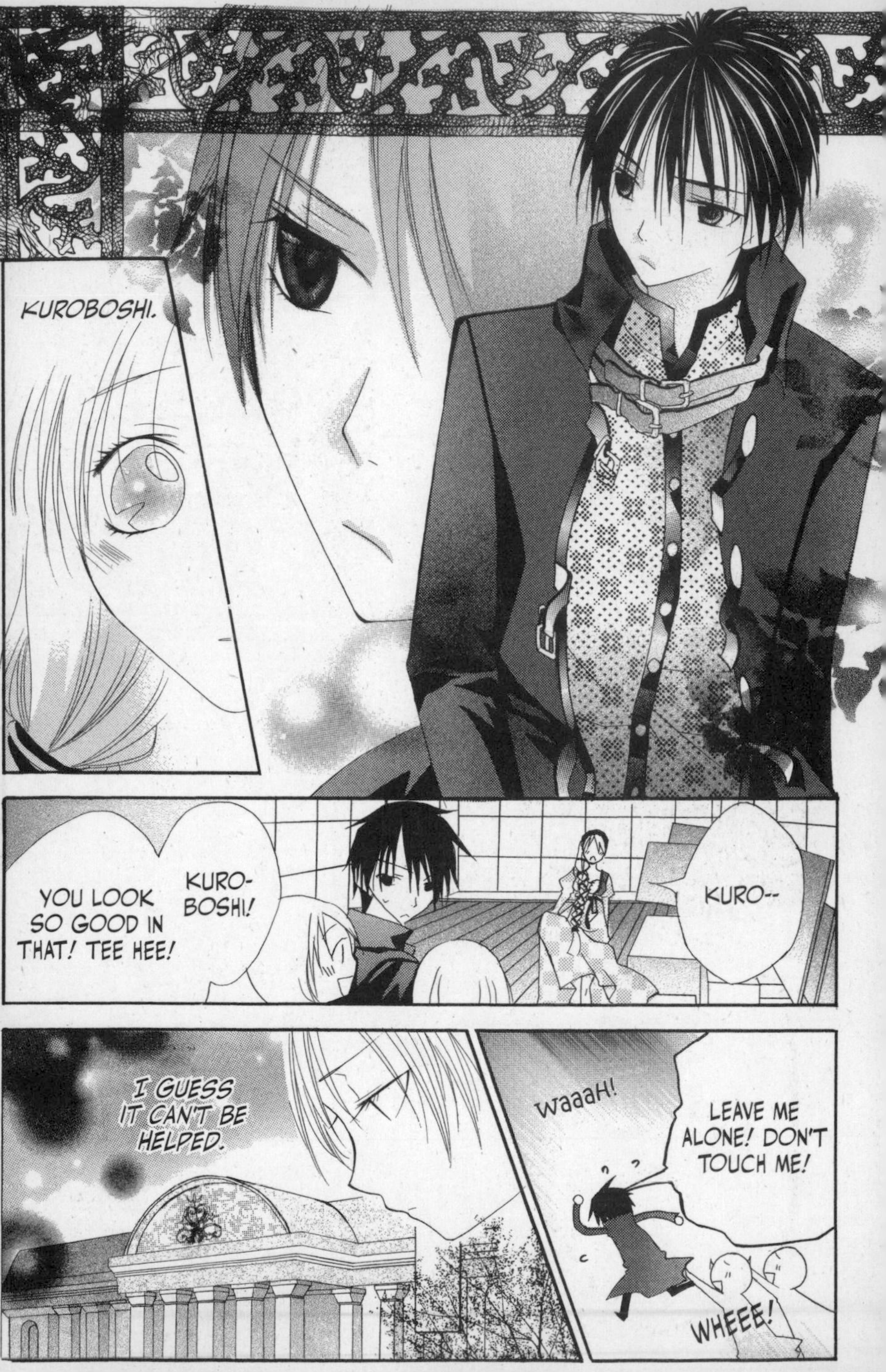
KUROBOSHI.
KURO--
KURO-BOSHI!
YOU LOOK SO GOOD IN THAT! TEE HEE!
LEAVE ME ALONE! DON'T TOUCH ME!
WaaaH!
WHEEE!
I GUESS IT CAN'T BE HELPED.

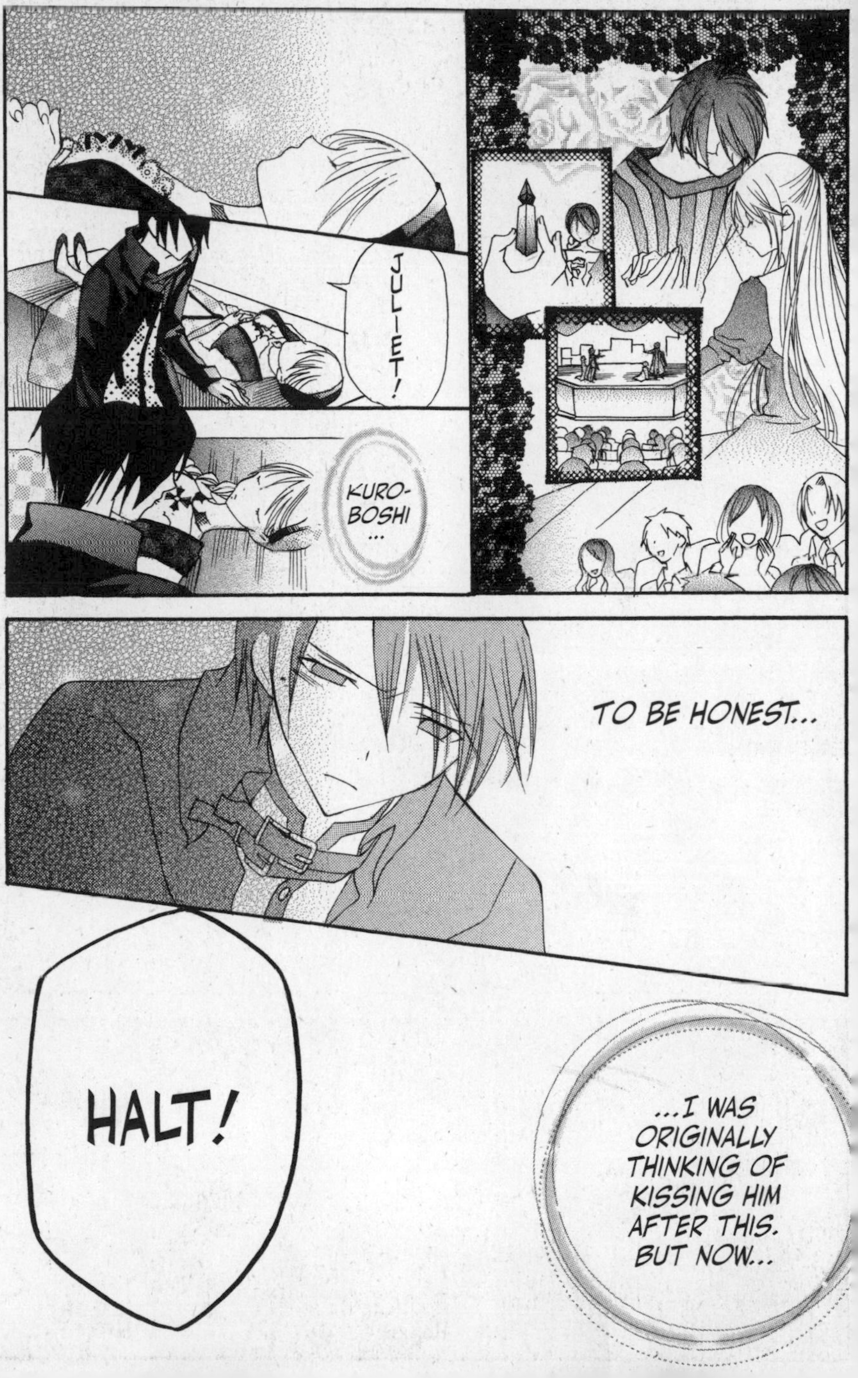
JULIET!
KURO-BOSHI...
TO BE HONEST...
...I WAS ORIGINALLY THINKING OF KISSING HIM AFTER THIS. BUT NOW...
HALT!

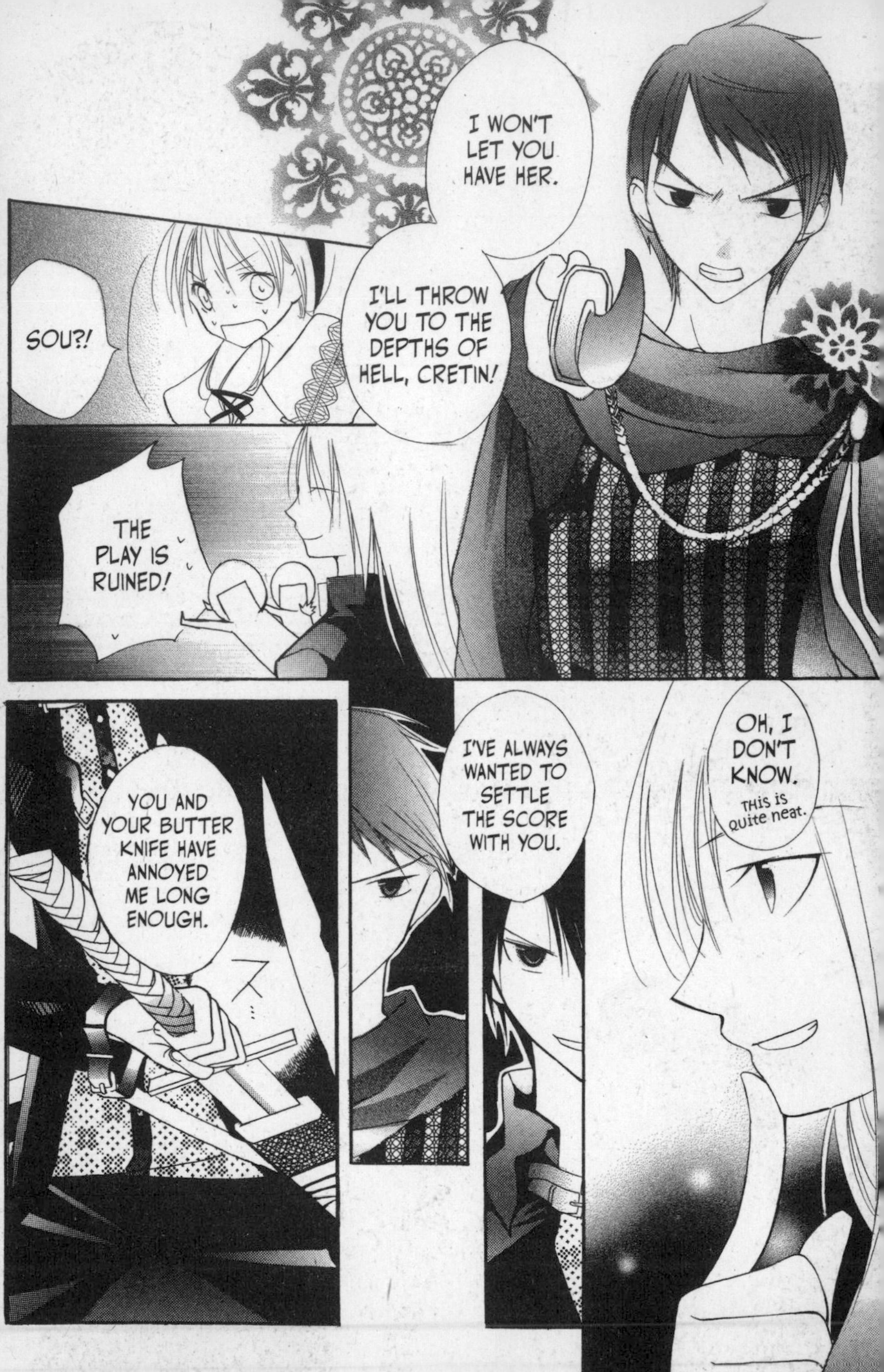
I WON'T LET YOU HAVE HER.
I'LL THROW YOU TO THE DEPTHS OF HELL, CRETIN!
SOU?!
THE PLAY IS RUINED!
OH, I DON'T KNOW.
THIS is quite neat.
I'VE ALWAYS WANTED TO SETTLE THE SCORE WITH YOU.
YOU AND YOUR BUTTER KNIFE HAVE ANNOYED ME LONG ENOUGH.

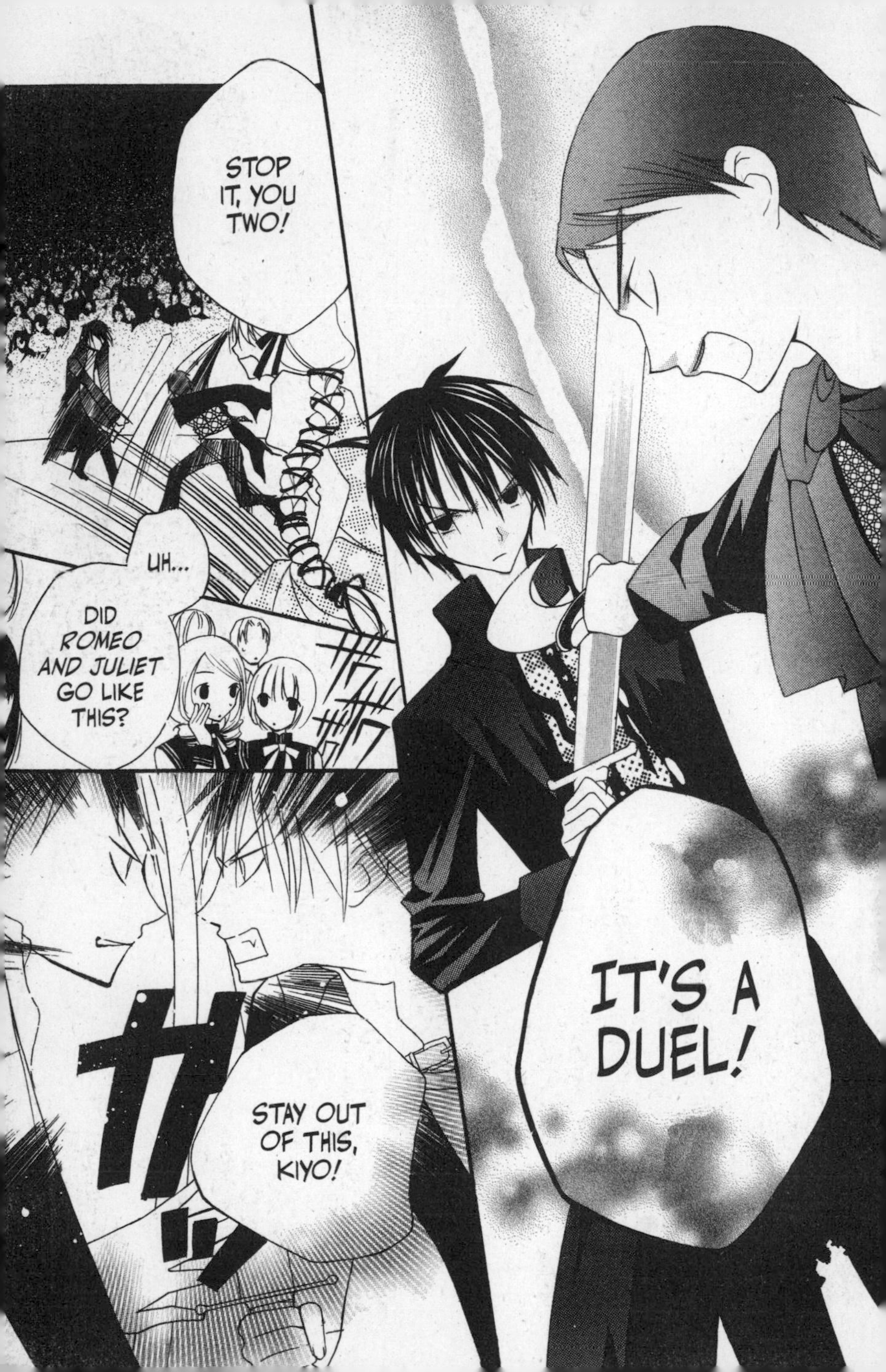
IT'S A DUEL!
STOP IT, YOU TWO!
UH...
DID ROMEO AND JULIET GO LIKE THIS?
STAY OUT OF THIS, KIYO!

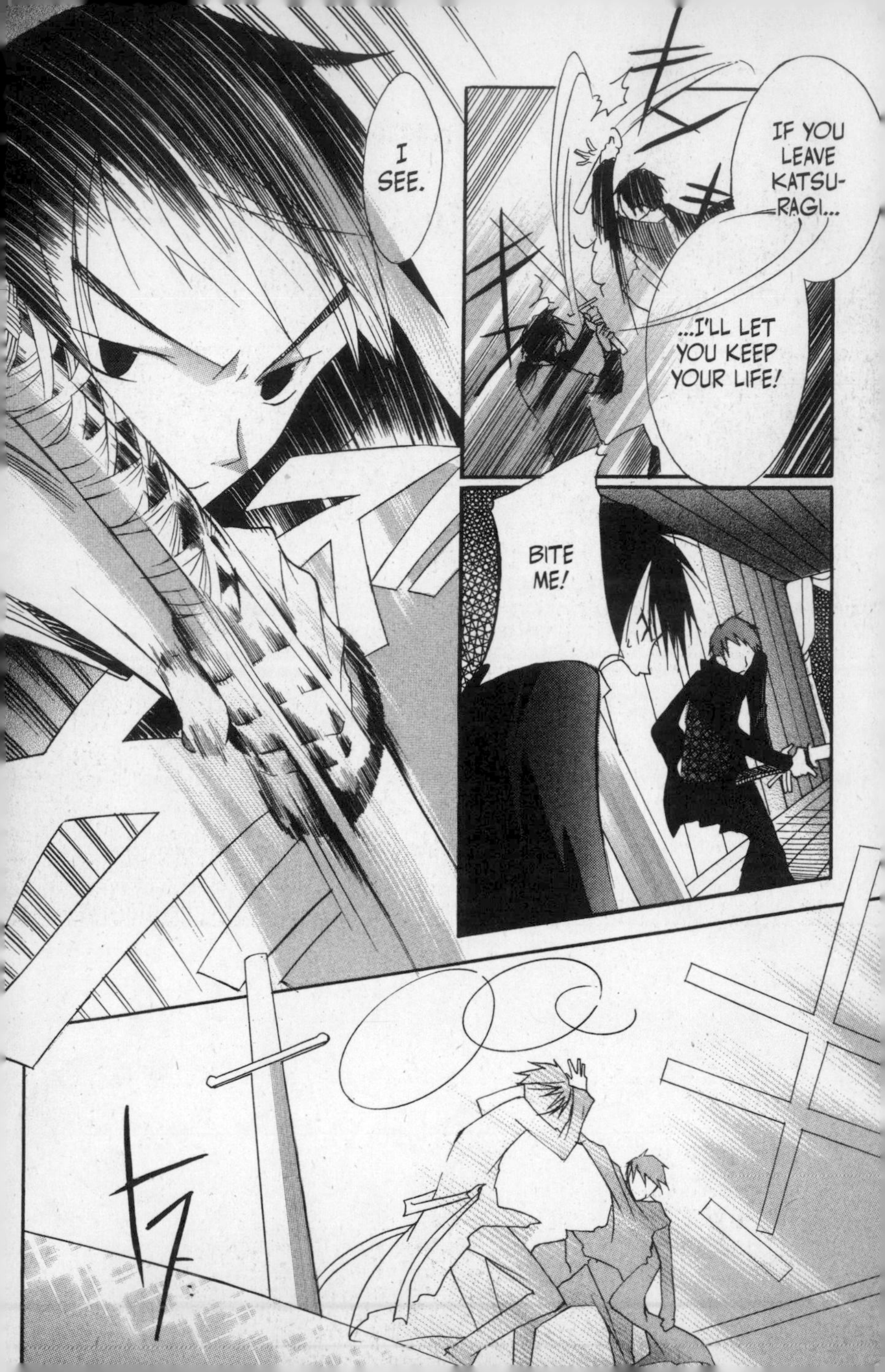
IF YOU LEAVE KATSU-RAGI...
...I'LL LET YOU KEEP YOUR LIFE!
BITE ME!
I SEE.

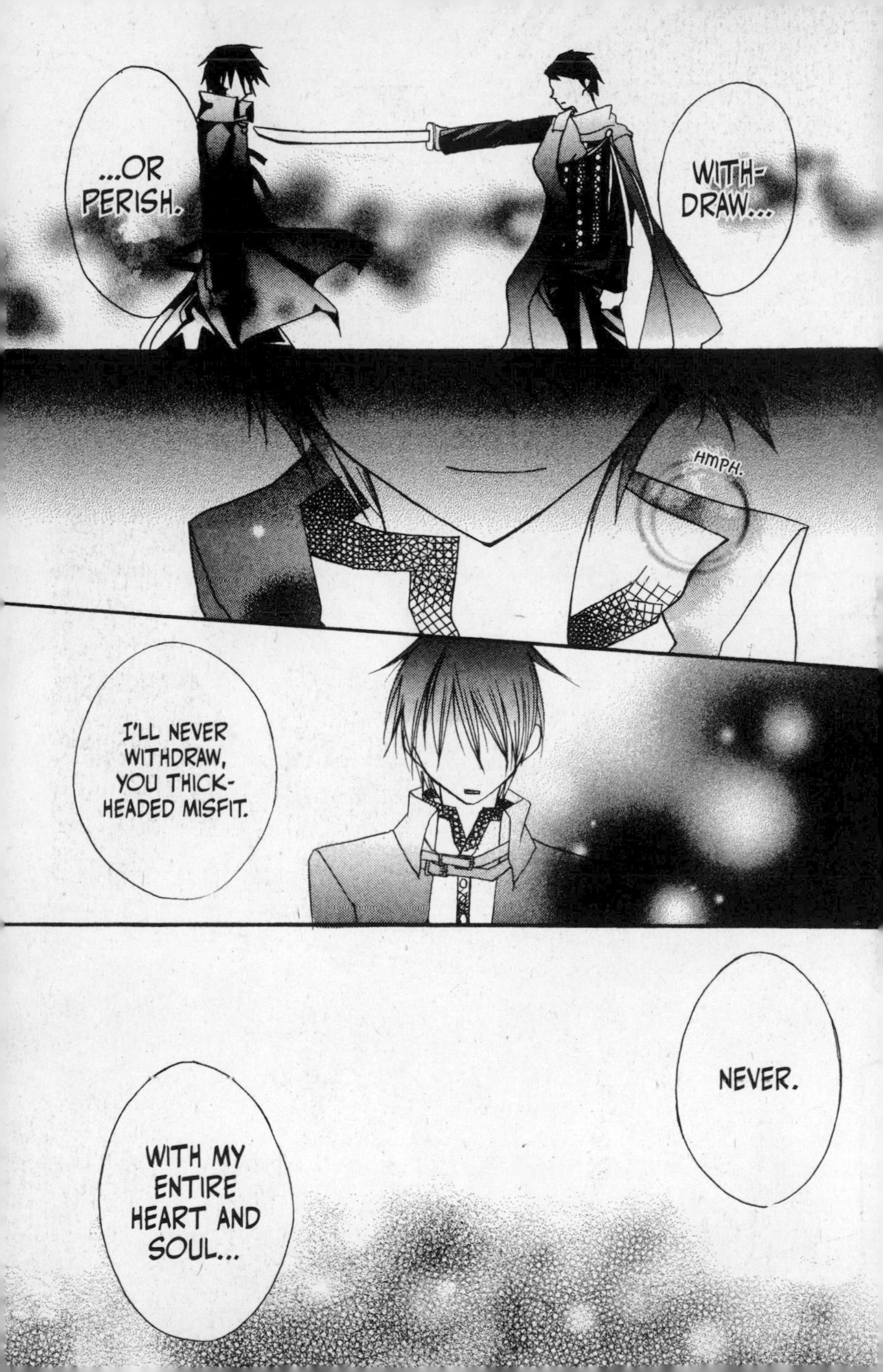
WITH-DRAW...
...OR PERISH.
HMPH.
I'LL NEVER WITHDRAW, YOU THICK-HEADED MISFIT.
NEVER.
WITH MY ENTIRE HEART AND SOUL...

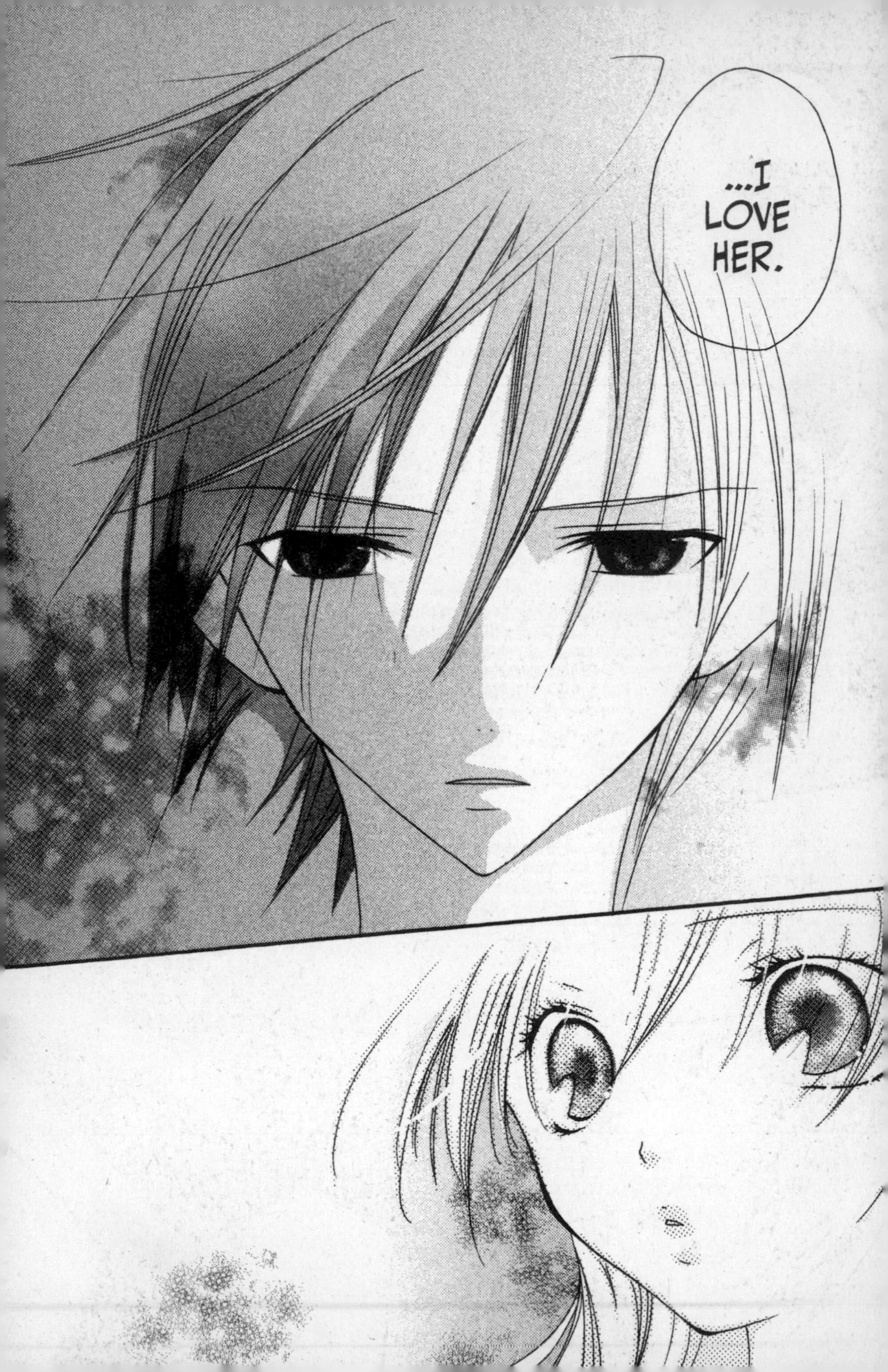
...I LOVE HER.

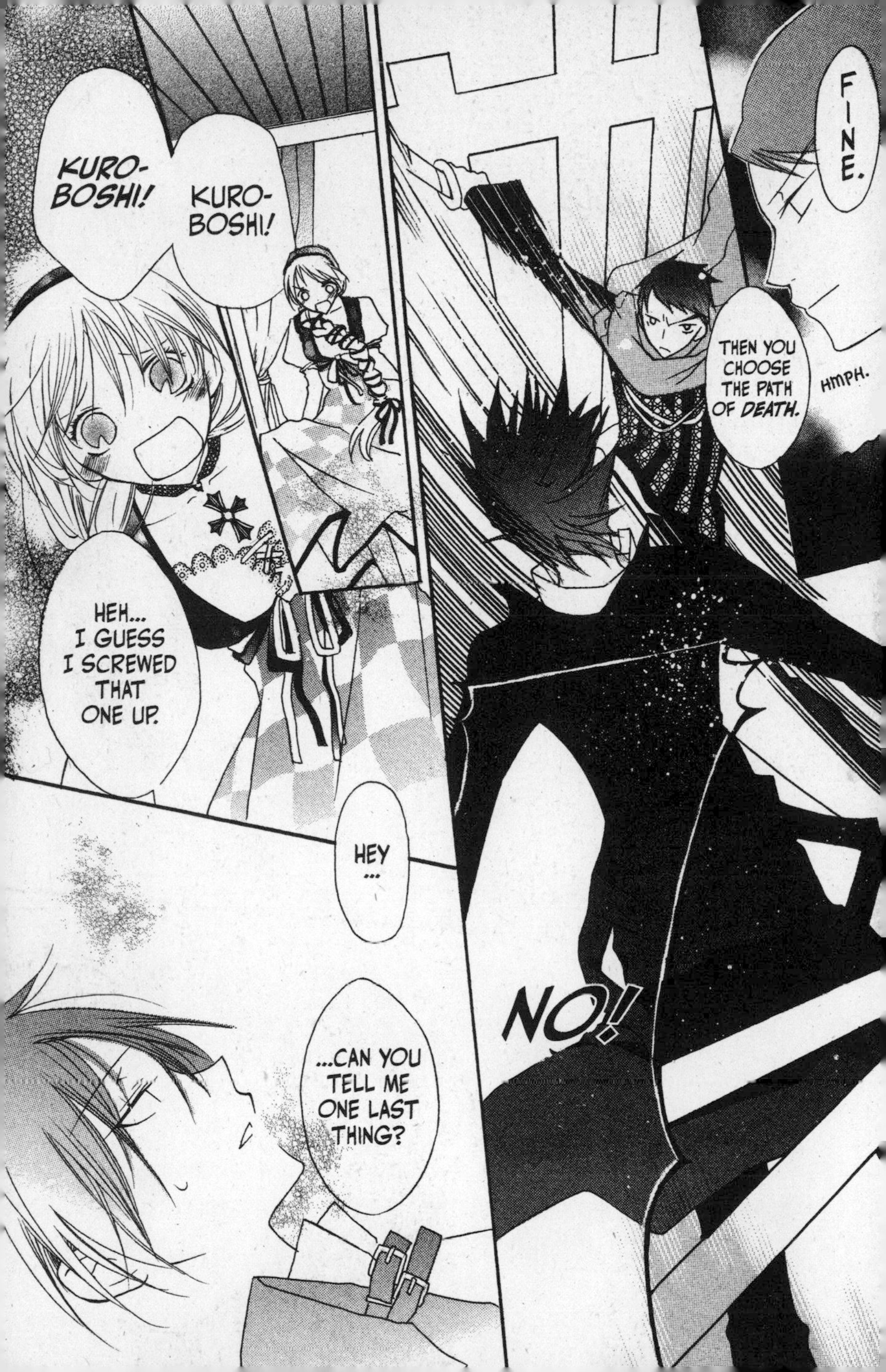
FINE.
HMPH.
THEN YOU CHOOSE THE PATH OF DEATH.
NO!
KURO-BOSHI!
KURO-BOSHI!
HEH... I GUESS I SCREWED THAT ONE UP.
HEY ...
...CAN YOU TELL ME ONE LAST THING?

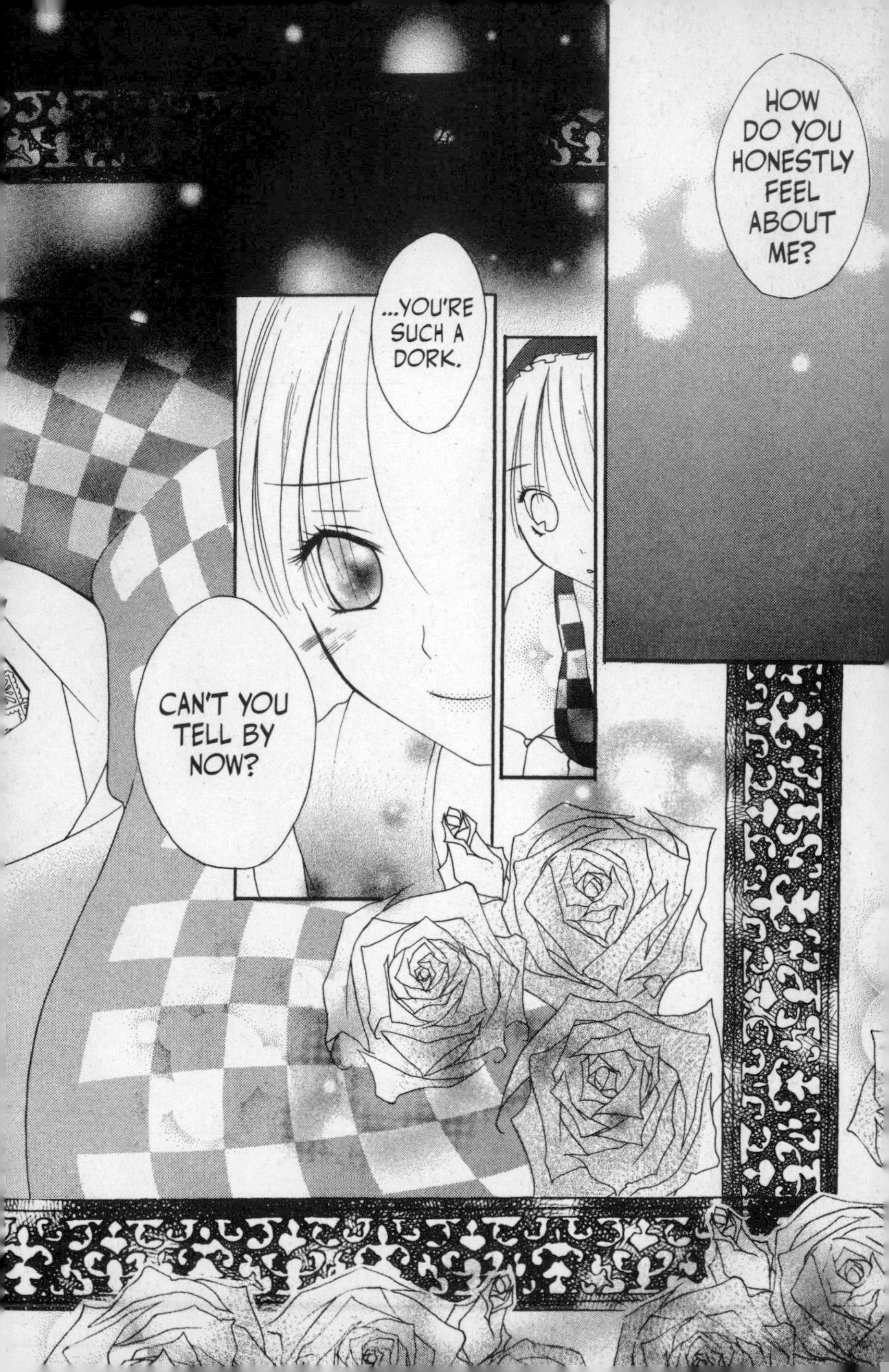
HOW DO YOU HONESTLY FEEL ABOUT ME?
...YOU'RE SUCH A DORK.
CAN'T YOU TELL BY NOW?

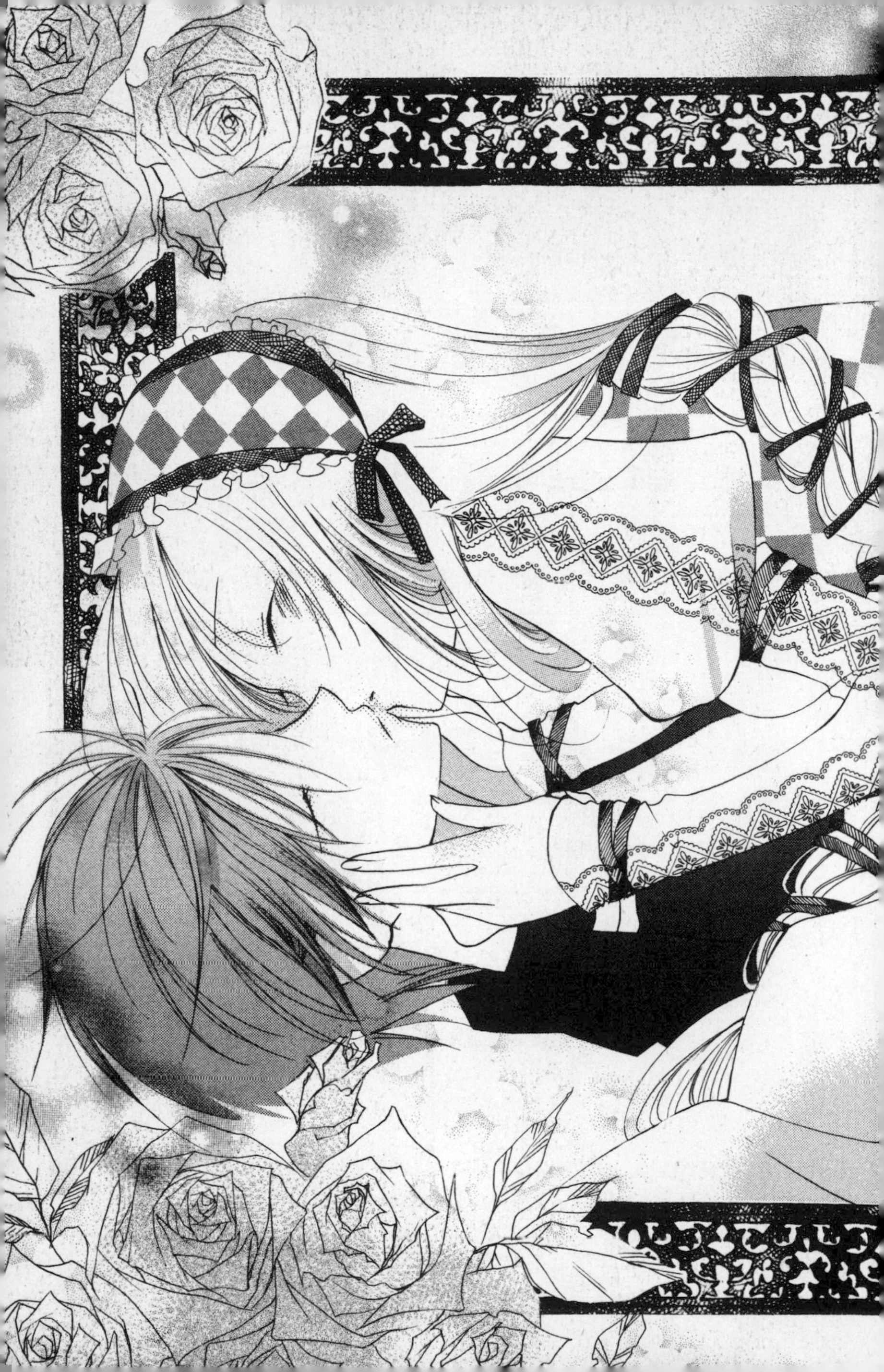

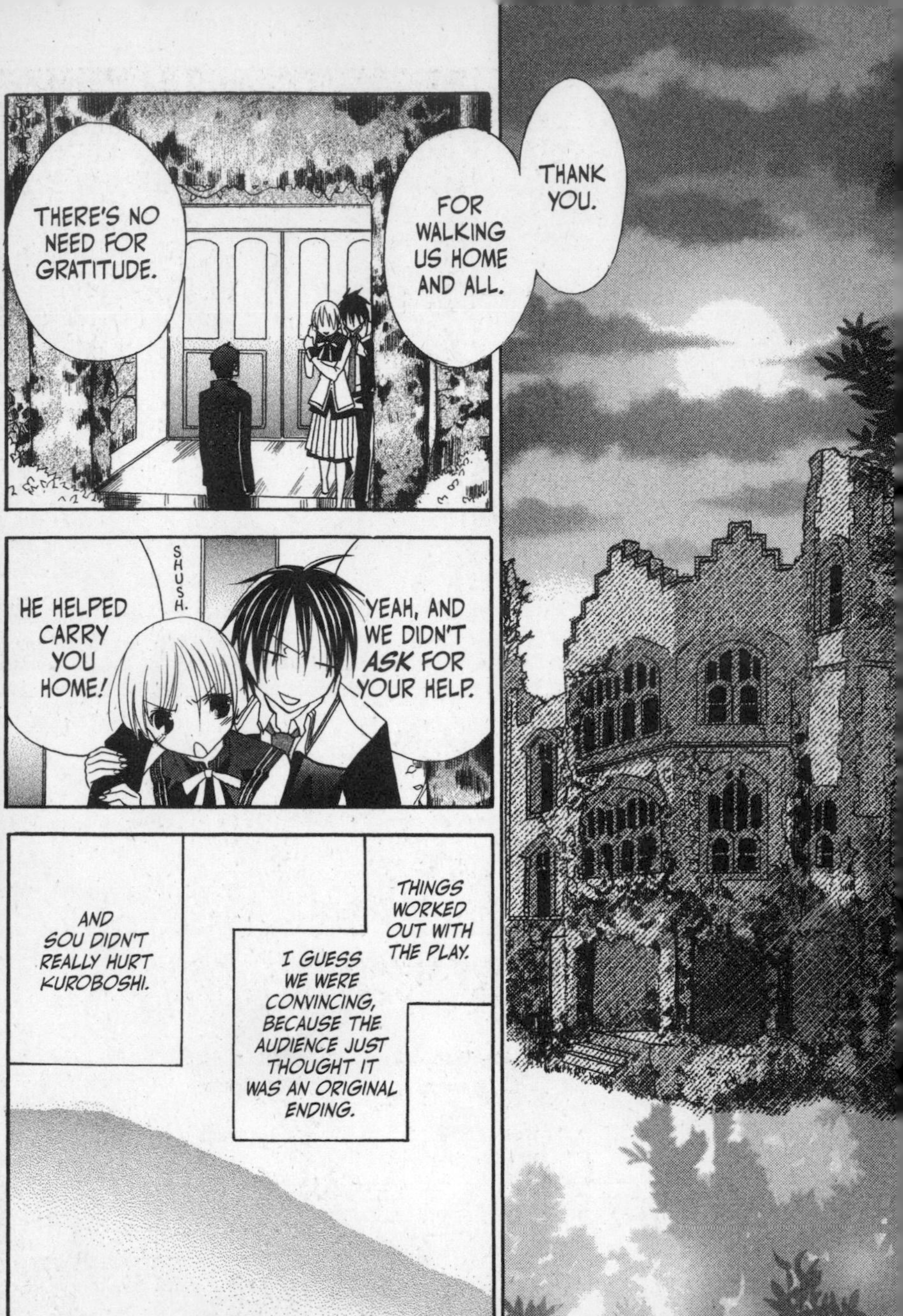
THANK YOU.
FOR WALKING US HOME AND ALL.
THERE'S NO NEED FOR GRATITUDE.
YEAH, AND WE DIDN'T *ASK* FOR YOUR HELP.
SHUSH.
HE HELPED CARRY YOU HOME!
THINGS WORKED OUT WITH THE PLAY.
I GUESS WE WERE CONVINCING, BECAUSE THE AUDIENCE JUST THOUGHT IT WAS AN ORIGINAL ENDING.
AND SOU DIDN'T REALLY HURT KUROBOSHI.

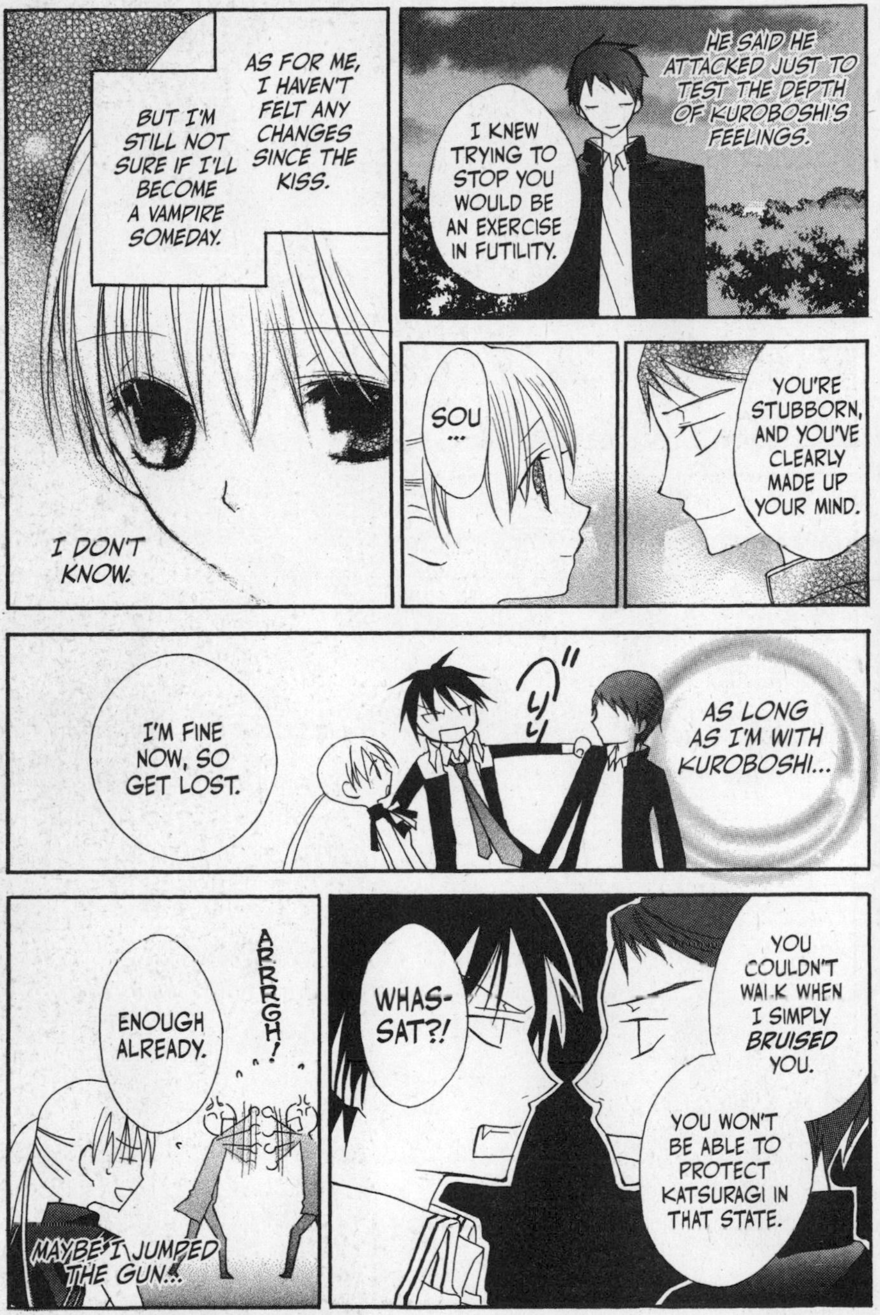
HE SAID HE ATTACKED JUST TO TEST THE DEPTH OF KUROBOSHI'S FEELINGS.
I KNEW TRYING TO STOP YOU WOULD BE AN EXERCISE IN FUTILITY.
YOU'RE STUBBORN, AND YOU'VE CLEARLY MADE UP YOUR MIND.
SOU...
AS FOR ME, I HAVEN'T FELT ANY CHANGES SINCE THE KISS.
BUT I'M STILL NOT SURE IF I'LL BECOME A VAMPIRE SOMEDAY.
I DON'T KNOW.
AS LONG AS I'M WITH KUROBOSHI...
I'M FINE NOW, SO GET LOST.
YOU COULDN'T WALK WHEN I SIMPLY BRUISED YOU.
YOU WON'T BE ABLE TO PROTECT KATSURAGI IN THAT STATE.
WHAS-SAT?!
ARRRGH!
ENOUGH ALREADY.
MAYBE I JUMPED THE GUN...

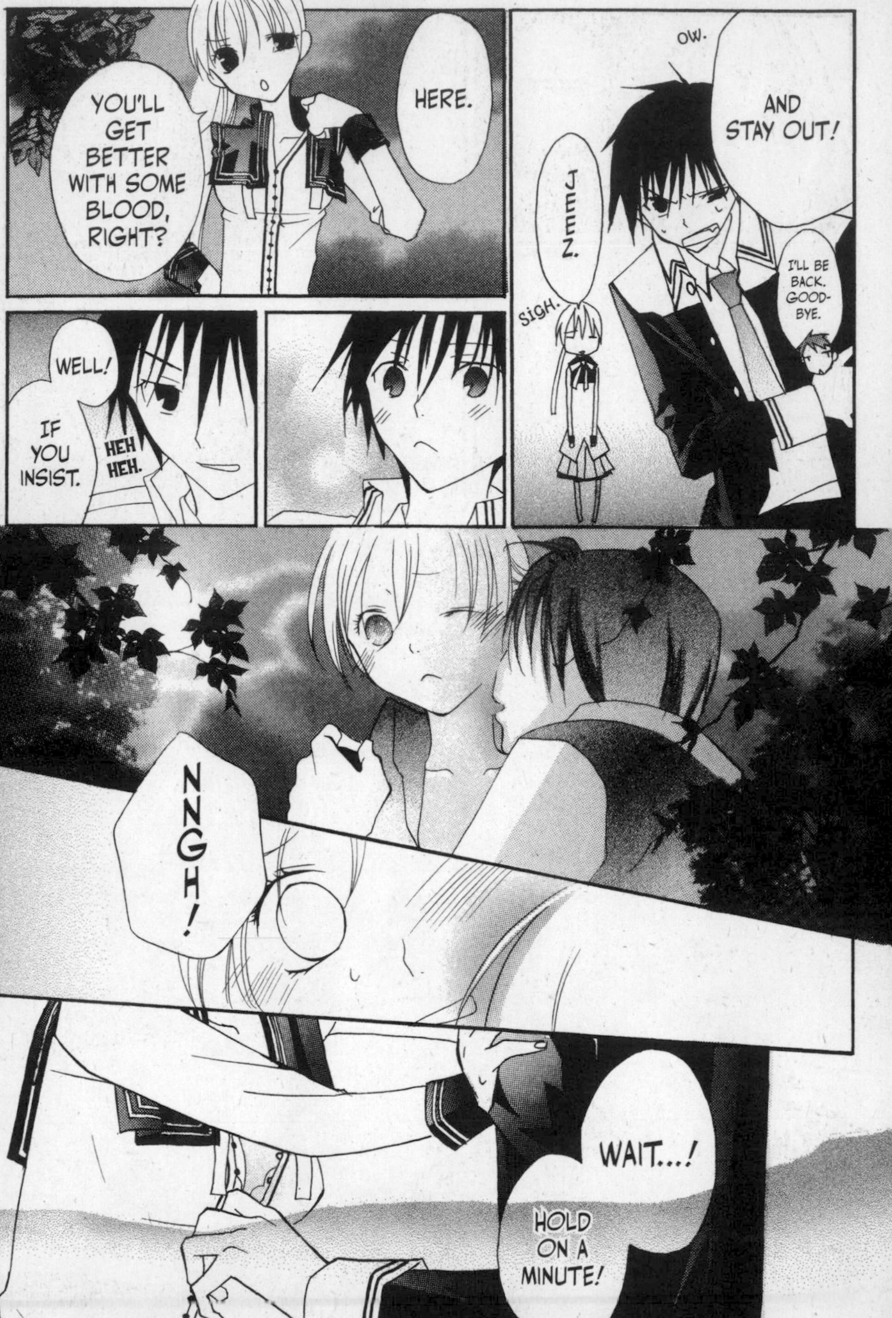
OW.
AND STAY OUT!
I'LL BE BACK. GOOD-BYE.
JEEZ.
SIGH.
HERE.
YOU'LL GET BETTER WITH SOME BLOOD, RIGHT?
WELL!
IF YOU INSIST.
HEH HEH.
NNGH!
WAIT...!
HOLD ON A MINUTE!

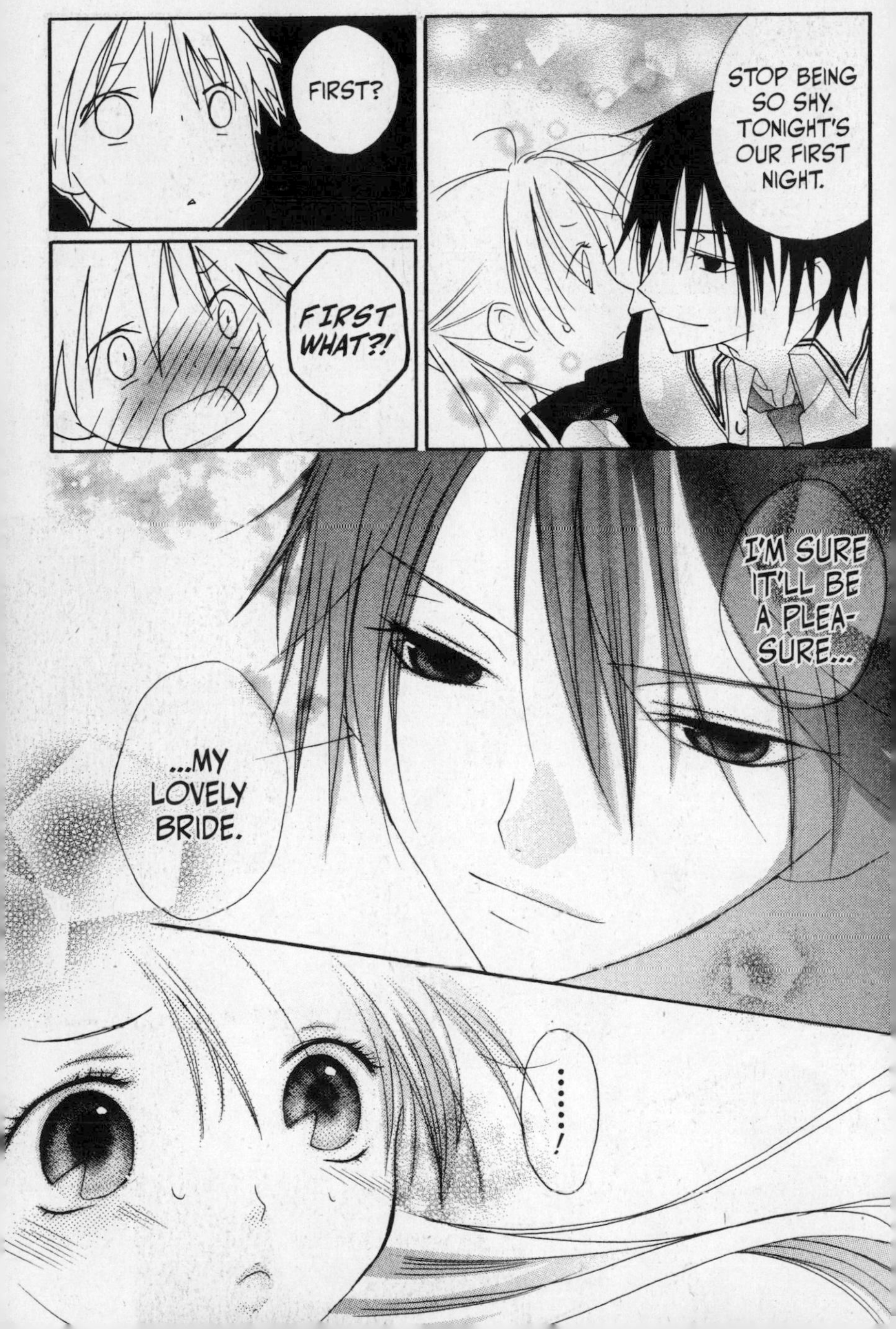
STOP BEING SO SHY. TONIGHT'S OUR FIRST NIGHT.
FIRST?
FIRST WHAT?!
I'M SURE IT'LL BE A PLEA-SURE...
...MY LOVELY BRIDE.
......!

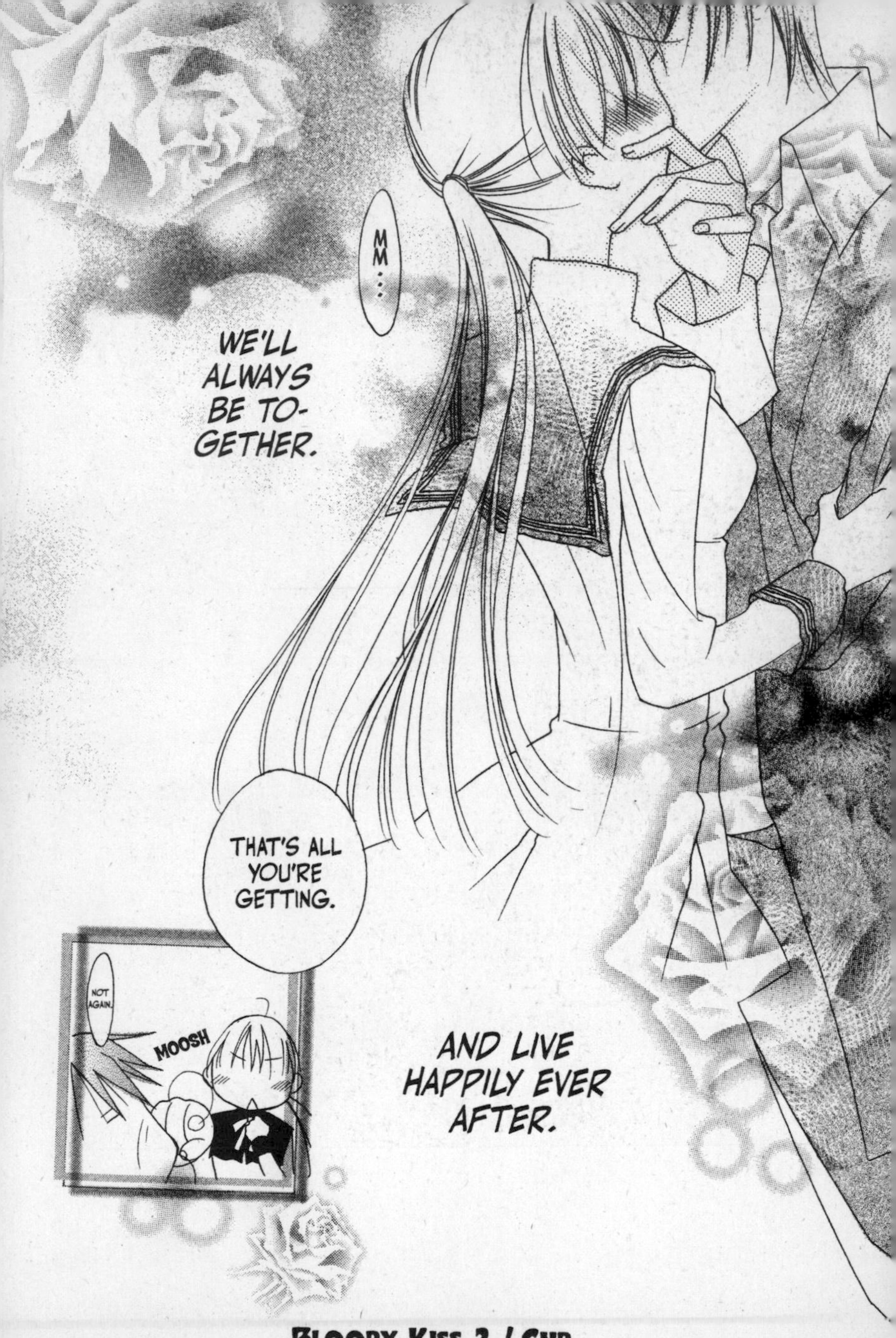
MM...
WE'LL ALWAYS BE TOGETHER.
THAT'S ALL YOU'RE GETTING.
AND LIVE HAPPILY EVER AFTER.
NOT AGAIN.
MOOSH

Bloody Kiss 2 / End

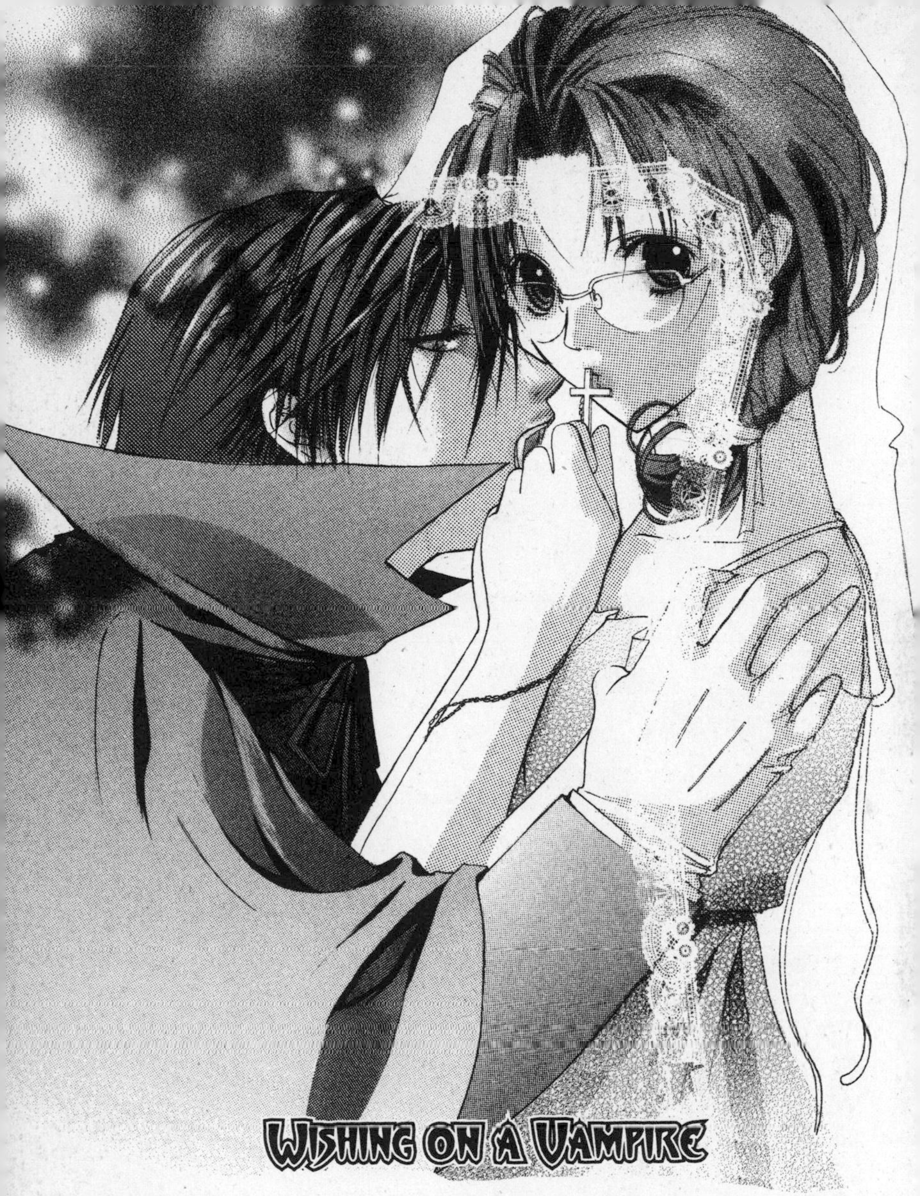
WISHING ON A VAMPIRE

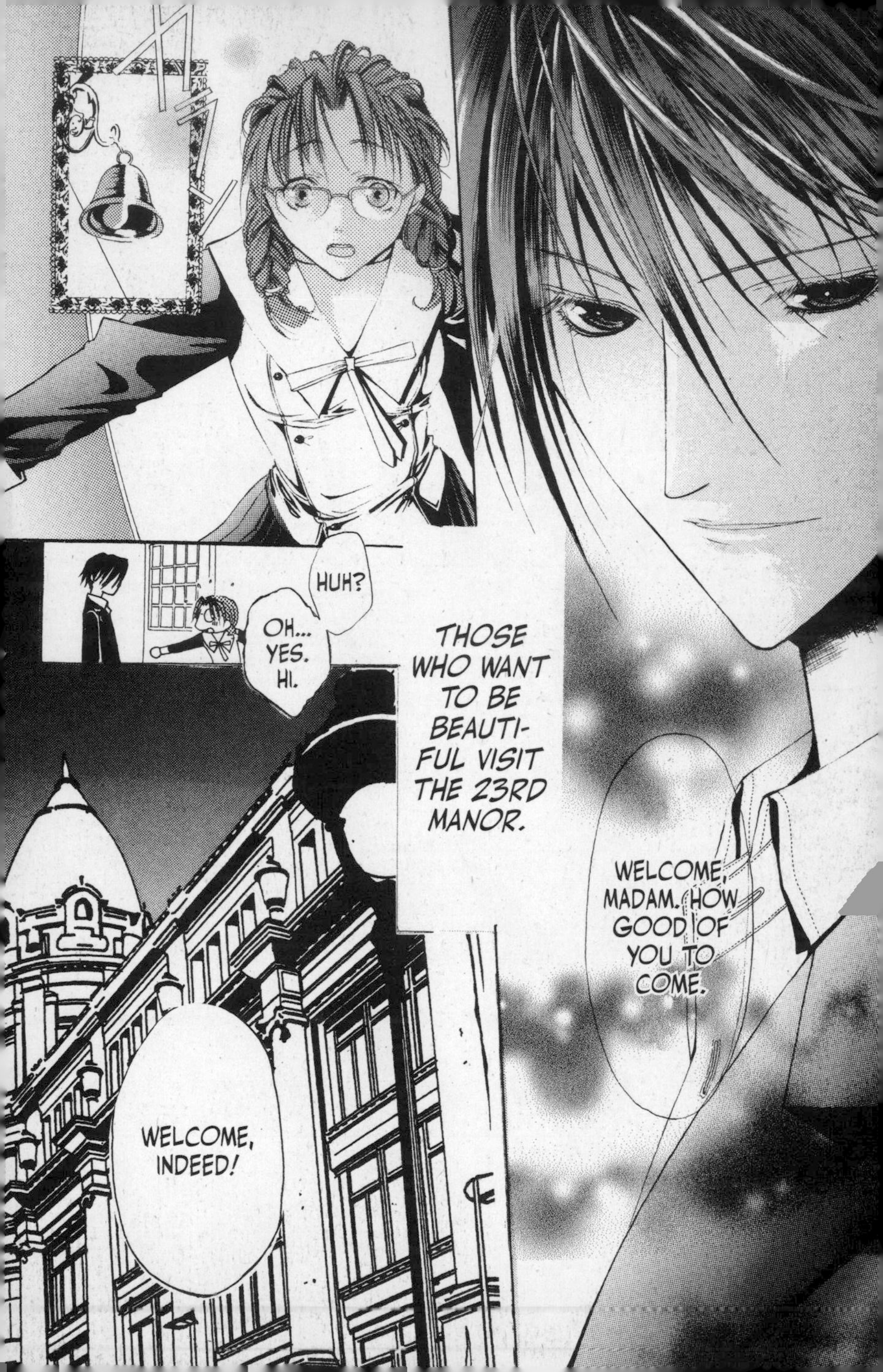
WELCOME, MADAM. HOW GOOD OF YOU TO COME.
HUH?
OH... YES. HI.
THOSE WHO WANT TO BE BEAUTIFUL VISIT THE 23RD MANOR.
WELCOME, INDEED!

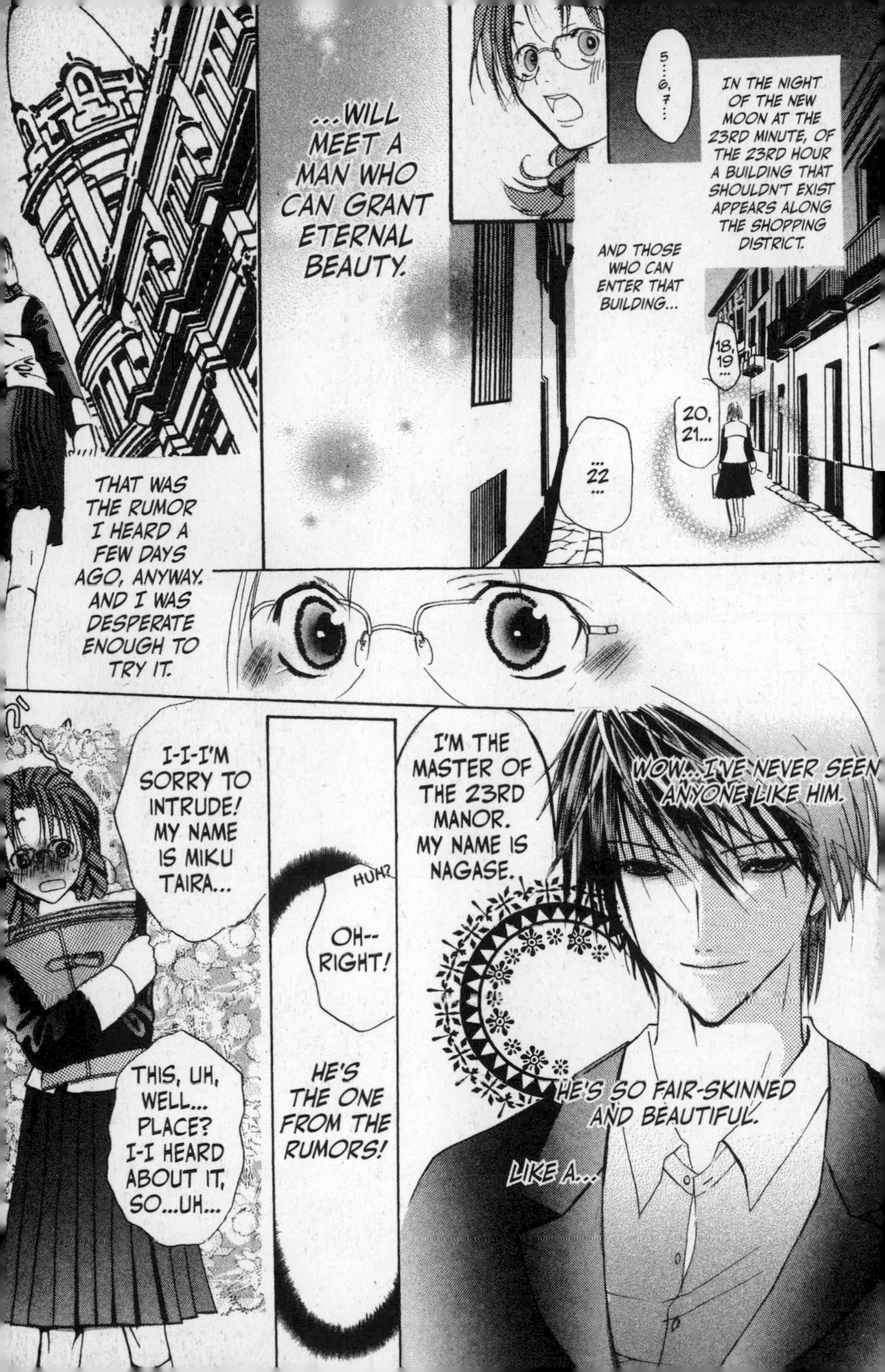
IN THE NIGHT OF THE NEW MOON AT THE 23RD MINUTE, OF THE 23RD HOUR A BUILDING THAT SHOULDN'T EXIST APPEARS ALONG THE SHOPPING DISTRICT.
5...6, 7...
AND THOSE WHO CAN ENTER THAT BUILDING...
18, 19...
20, 21...
...22...
...WILL MEET A MAN WHO CAN GRANT ETERNAL BEAUTY.
THAT WAS THE RUMOR I HEARD A FEW DAYS AGO, ANYWAY. AND I WAS DESPERATE ENOUGH TO TRY IT.
WOW...I'VE NEVER SEEN ANYONE LIKE HIM.
I'M THE MASTER OF THE 23RD MANOR. MY NAME IS NAGASE.
HE'S SO FAIR-SKINNED AND BEAUTIFUL.
LIKE A...
HUH?
OH--RIGHT!
HE'S THE ONE FROM THE RUMORS!
I-I-I'M SORRY TO INTRUDE! MY NAME IS MIKU TAIRA...
THIS, UH, WELL... PLACE? I-I HEARD ABOUT IT, SO...UH...

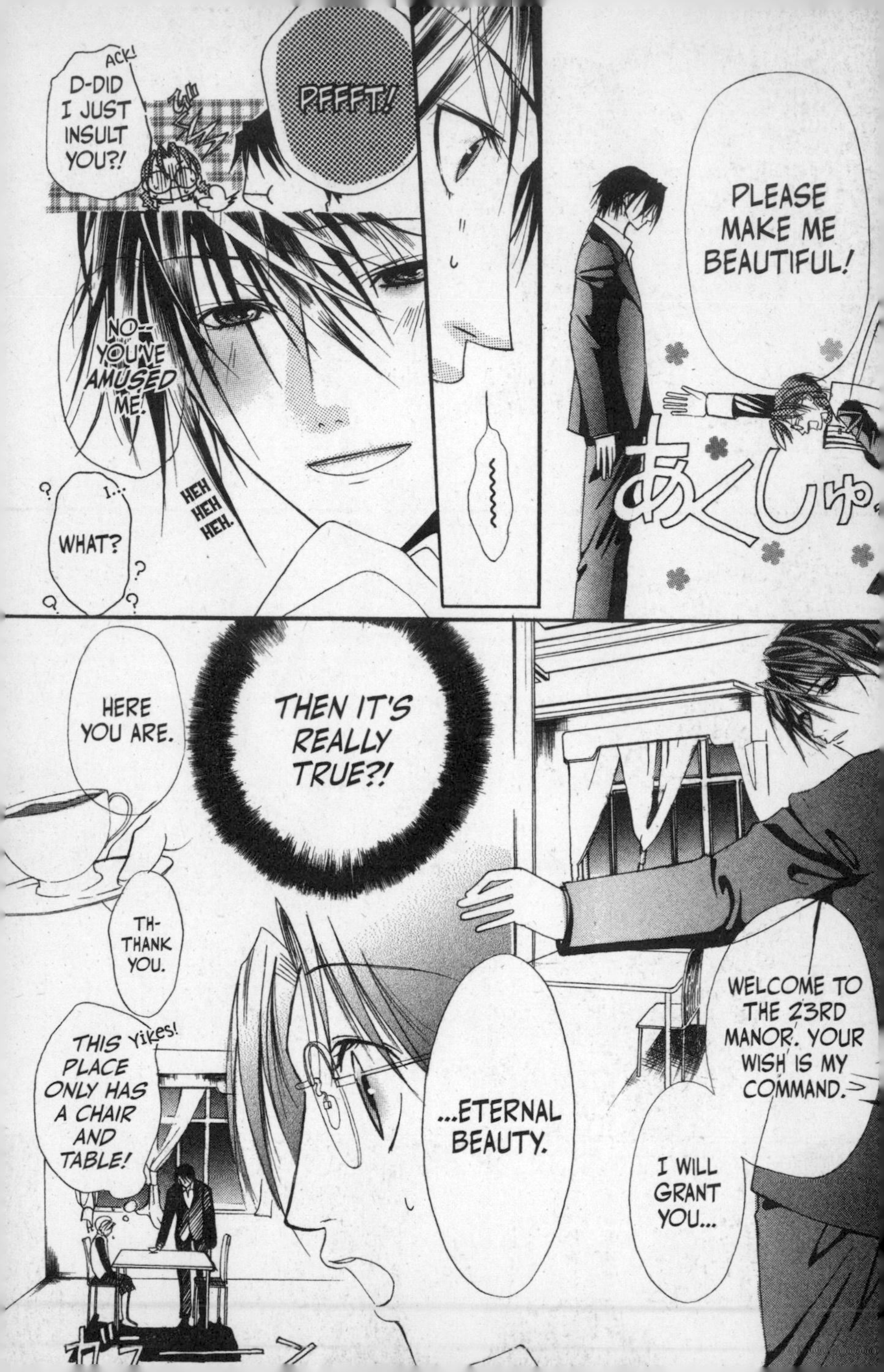
PLEASE MAKE ME BEAUTIFUL!
あくしゅ
PFFFT!
ACK!
D-DID I JUST INSULT YOU?!
NO-- YOU'VE AMUSED ME.
HEH HEH HEH.
I... WHAT?
WELCOME TO THE 23RD MANOR. YOUR WISH IS MY COMMAND.
I WILL GRANT YOU...
...ETERNAL BEAUTY.
THEN IT'S REALLY TRUE?!
HERE YOU ARE.
TH-THANK YOU.
Yikes!
THIS PLACE ONLY HAS A CHAIR AND TABLE!

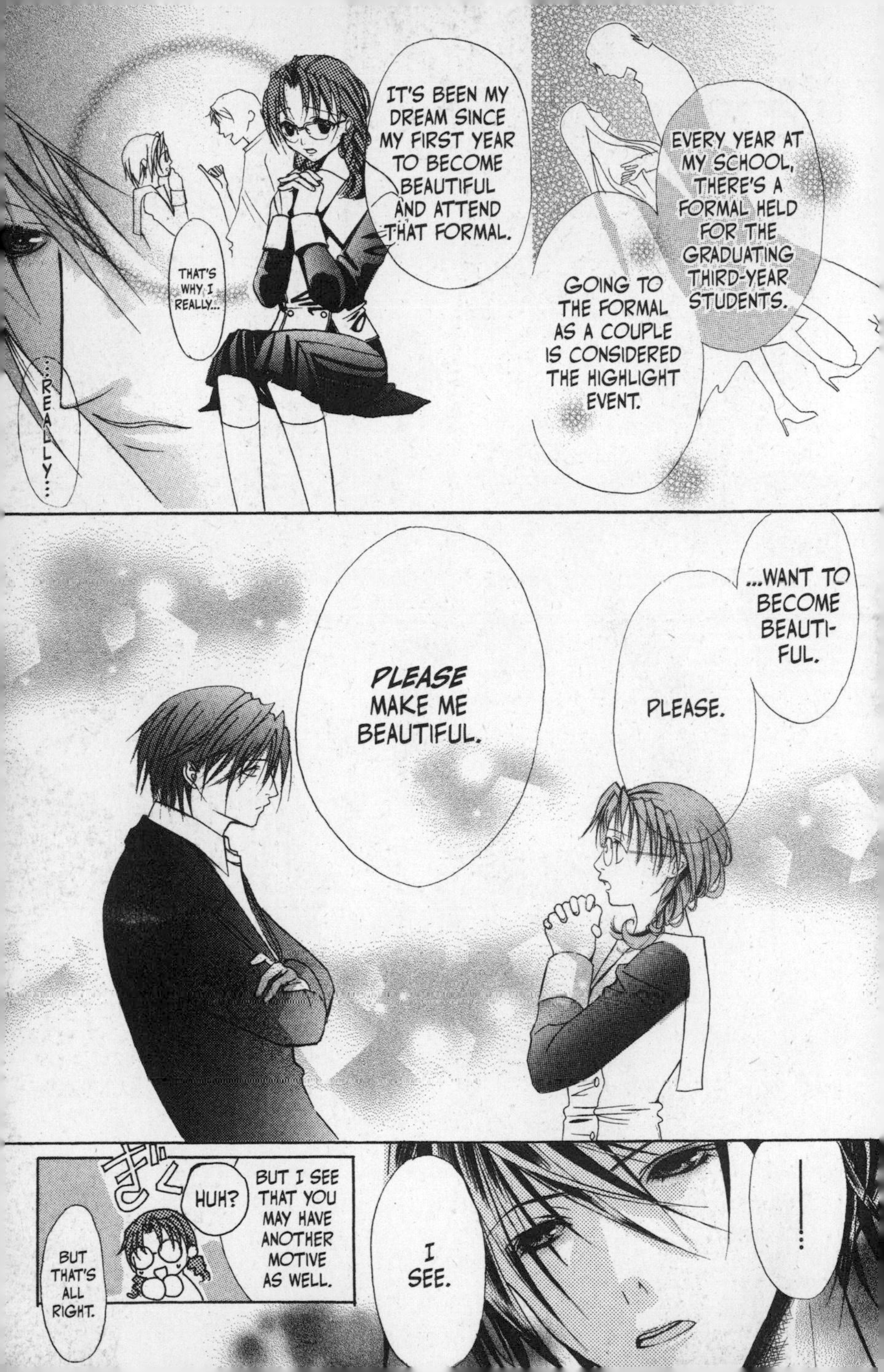
EVERY YEAR AT MY SCHOOL, THERE'S A FORMAL HELD FOR THE GRADUATING THIRD-YEAR STUDENTS.
GOING TO THE FORMAL AS A COUPLE IS CONSIDERED THE HIGHLIGHT EVENT.
IT'S BEEN MY DREAM SINCE MY FIRST YEAR TO BECOME BEAUTIFUL AND ATTEND THAT FORMAL.
THAT'S WHY I REALLY...
...REALLY...
...WANT TO BECOME BEAUTI-FUL.
PLEASE.
PLEASE MAKE ME BEAUTIFUL.
......
I SEE.
BUT I SEE THAT YOU MAY HAVE ANOTHER MOTIVE AS WELL.
HUH?
ぎく
BUT THAT'S ALL RIGHT.

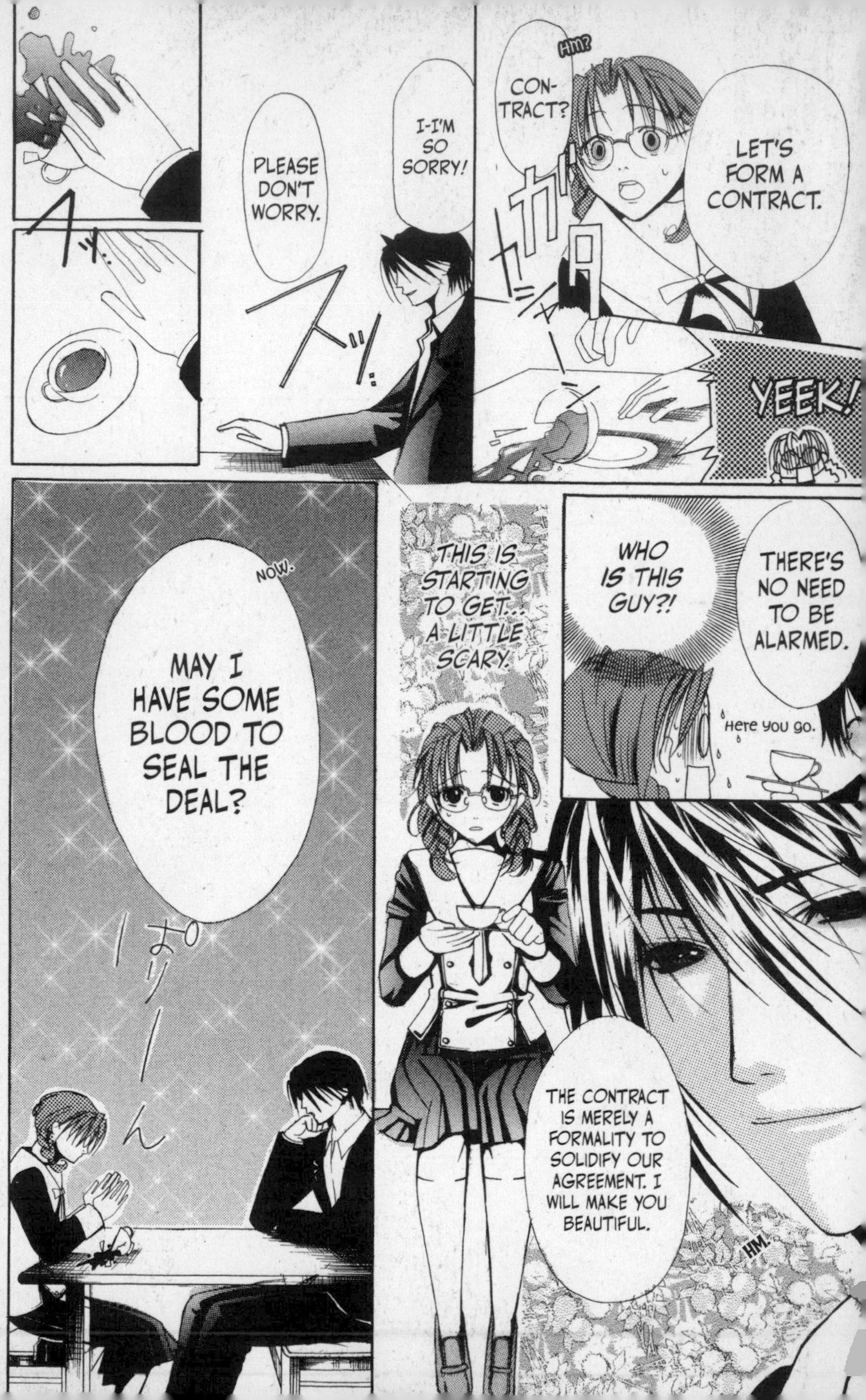
LET'S FORM A CONTRACT.
Hm?
CON-TRACT?
YEEK!
I-I'M SO SORRY!
PLEASE DON'T WORRY.
THERE'S NO NEED TO BE ALARMED.
WHO IS THIS GUY?!
Here you go.
HM.
THE CONTRACT IS MERELY A FORMALITY TO SOLIDIFY OUR AGREEMENT. I WILL MAKE YOU BEAUTIFUL.
THIS IS STARTING TO GET... A LITTLE SCARY.
NOW.
MAY I HAVE SOME BLOOD TO SEAL THE DEAL?

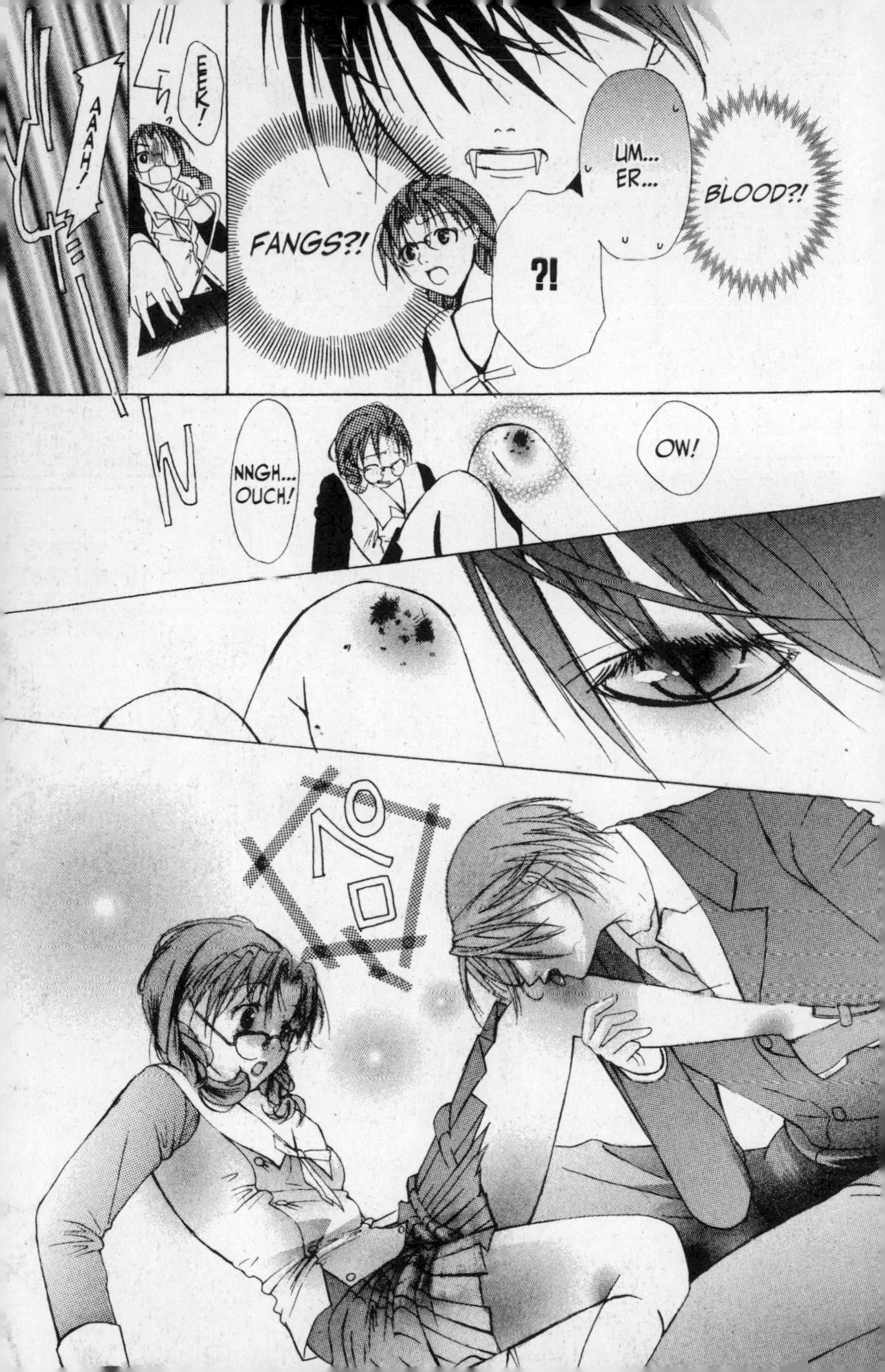

UM...
ER...
BLOOD?!
?!
FANGS?!
EEK!
AAAH!
OW!
NNGH... OUCH!

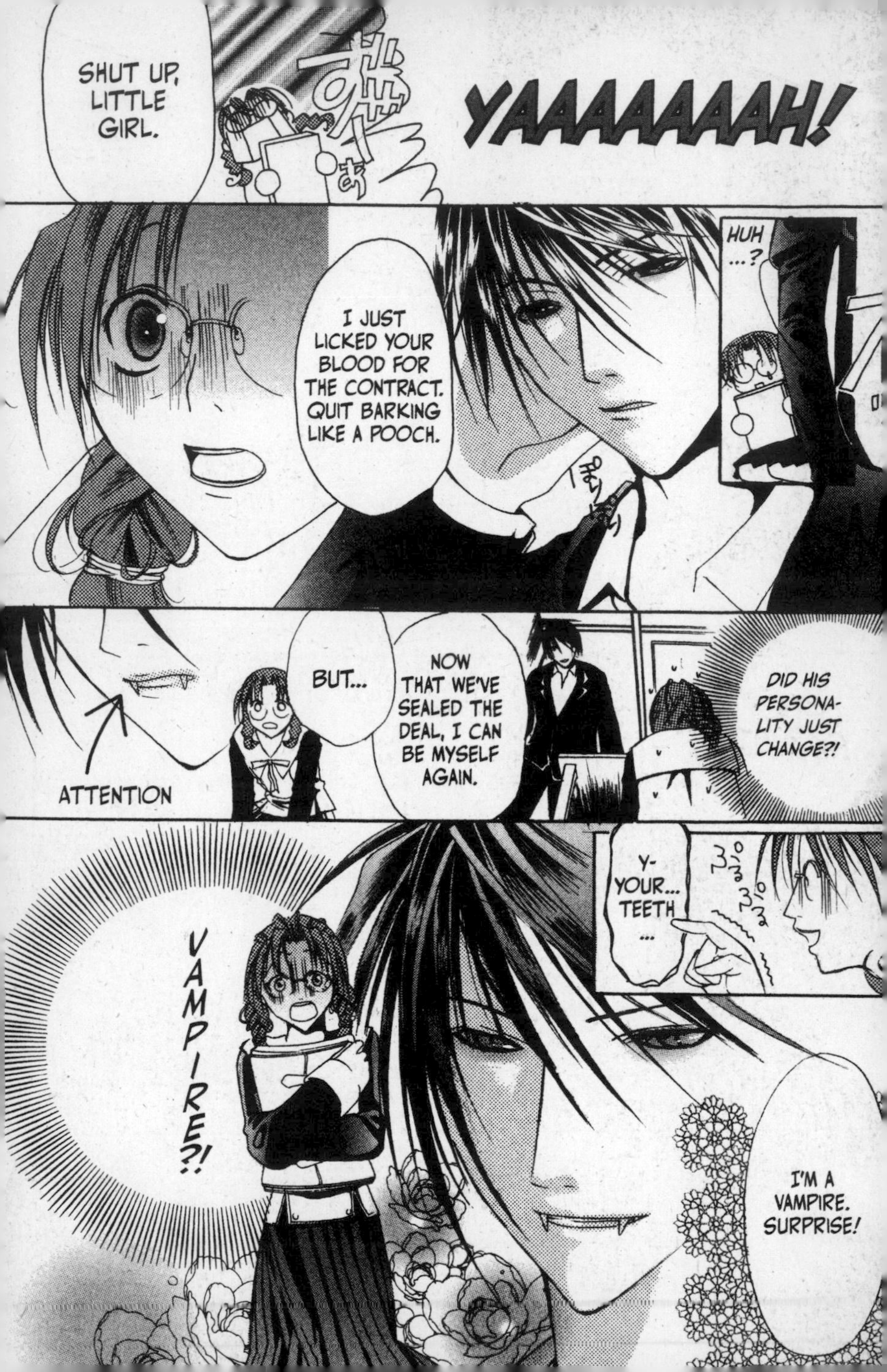
YAAAAAAAH!
SHUT UP, LITTLE GIRL.
HUH ...?
I JUST LICKED YOUR BLOOD FOR THE CONTRACT. QUIT BARKING LIKE A POOCH.
DID HIS PERSONALITY JUST CHANGE?!
NOW THAT WE'VE SEALED THE DEAL, I CAN BE MYSELF AGAIN.
BUT...
ATTENTION
Y-YOUR... TEETH ...
I'M A VAMPIRE. SURPRISE!
VAMPIRE?!

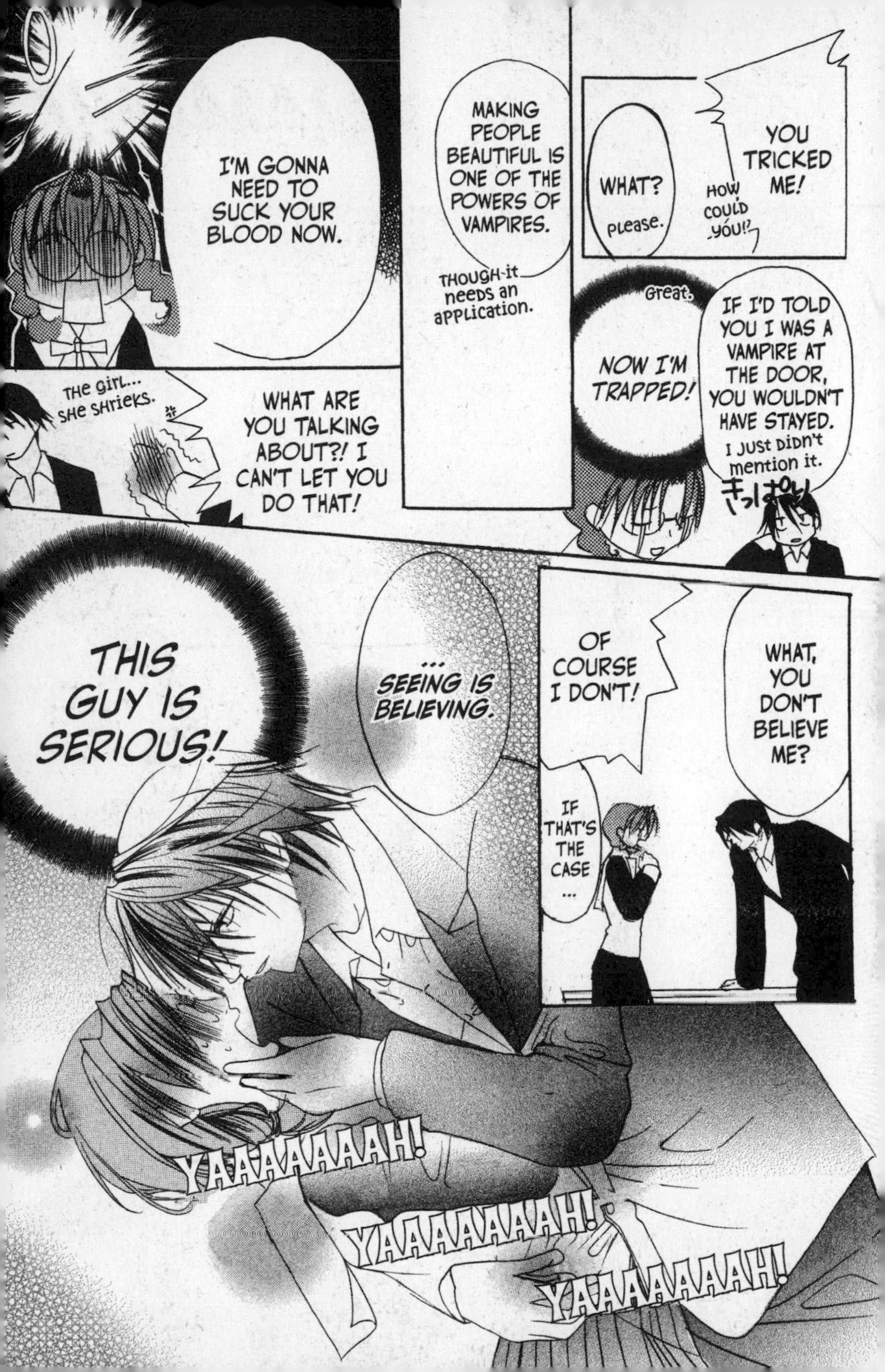
YOU TRICKED ME!
HOW COULD YOU!?
WHAT?
Please.
Great.
IF I'D TOLD YOU I WAS A VAMPIRE AT THE DOOR, YOU WOULDN'T HAVE STAYED.
I JUST DIDN'T mention it.
NOW I'M TRAPPED!
MAKING PEOPLE BEAUTIFUL IS ONE OF THE POWERS OF VAMPIRES.
THOUGH it needs an application.
I'M GONNA NEED TO SUCK YOUR BLOOD NOW.
WHAT ARE YOU TALKING ABOUT?! I CAN'T LET YOU DO THAT!
The girl... she shrieks.
WHAT, YOU DON'T BELIEVE ME?
OF COURSE I DON'T!
IF THAT'S THE CASE ...
... SEEING IS BELIEVING.
THIS GUY IS SERIOUS!
YAAAAAAAH!
YAAAAAAAAH!
YAAAAAAAAH!

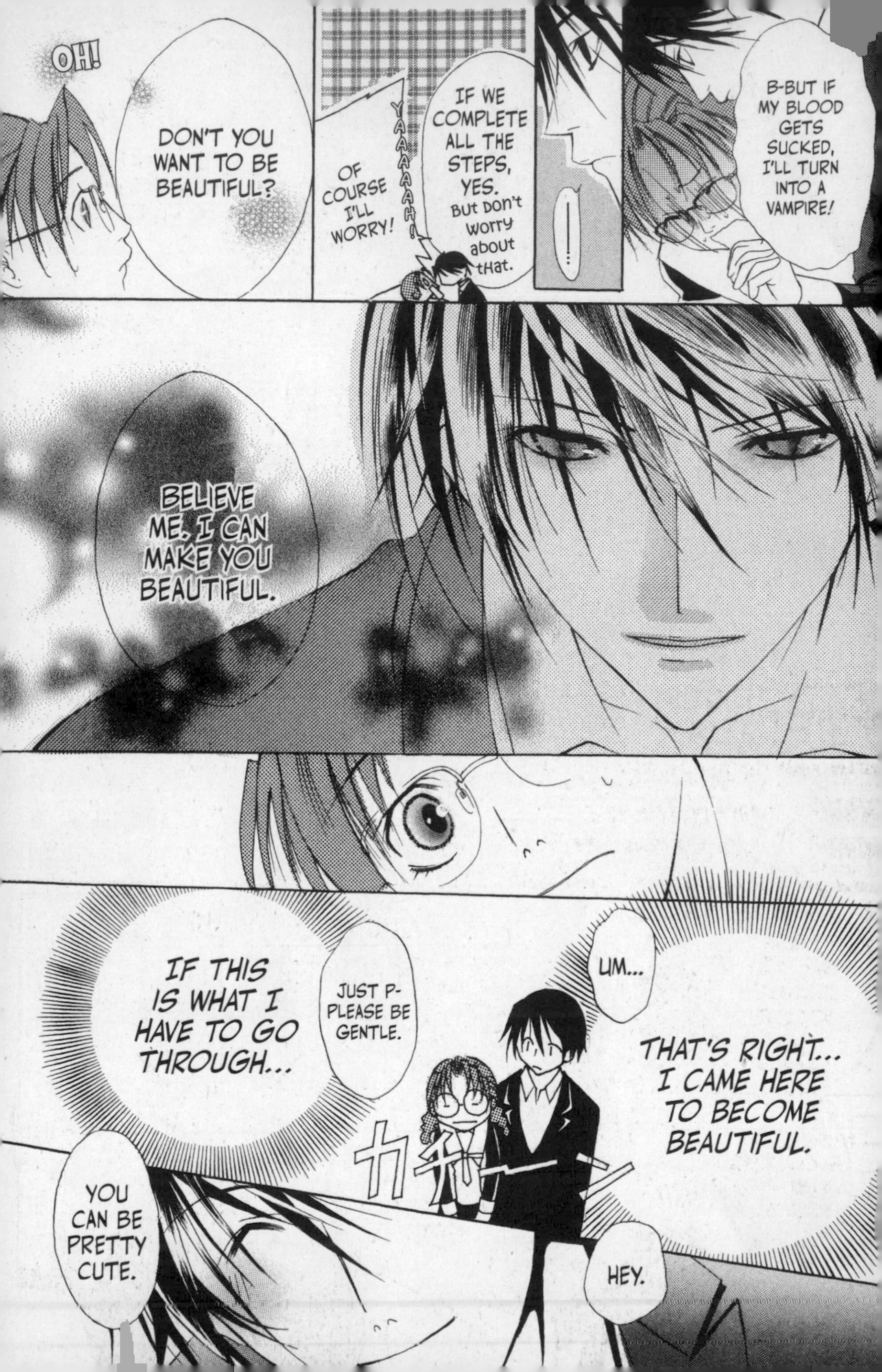
B-BUT IF MY BLOOD GETS SUCKED, I'LL TURN INTO A VAMPIRE!
!......
IF WE COMPLETE ALL THE STEPS, YES. But Don't worry about that.
YAAAAAAAH!
OF COURSE I'LL WORRY!
OH!
DON'T YOU WANT TO BE BEAUTIFUL?
BELIEVE ME, I CAN MAKE YOU BEAUTIFUL.
UM...
THAT'S RIGHT... I CAME HERE TO BECOME BEAUTIFUL.
JUST P-PLEASE BE GENTLE.
IF THIS IS WHAT I HAVE TO GO THROUGH...
カチ
HEY.
YOU CAN BE PRETTY CUTE.

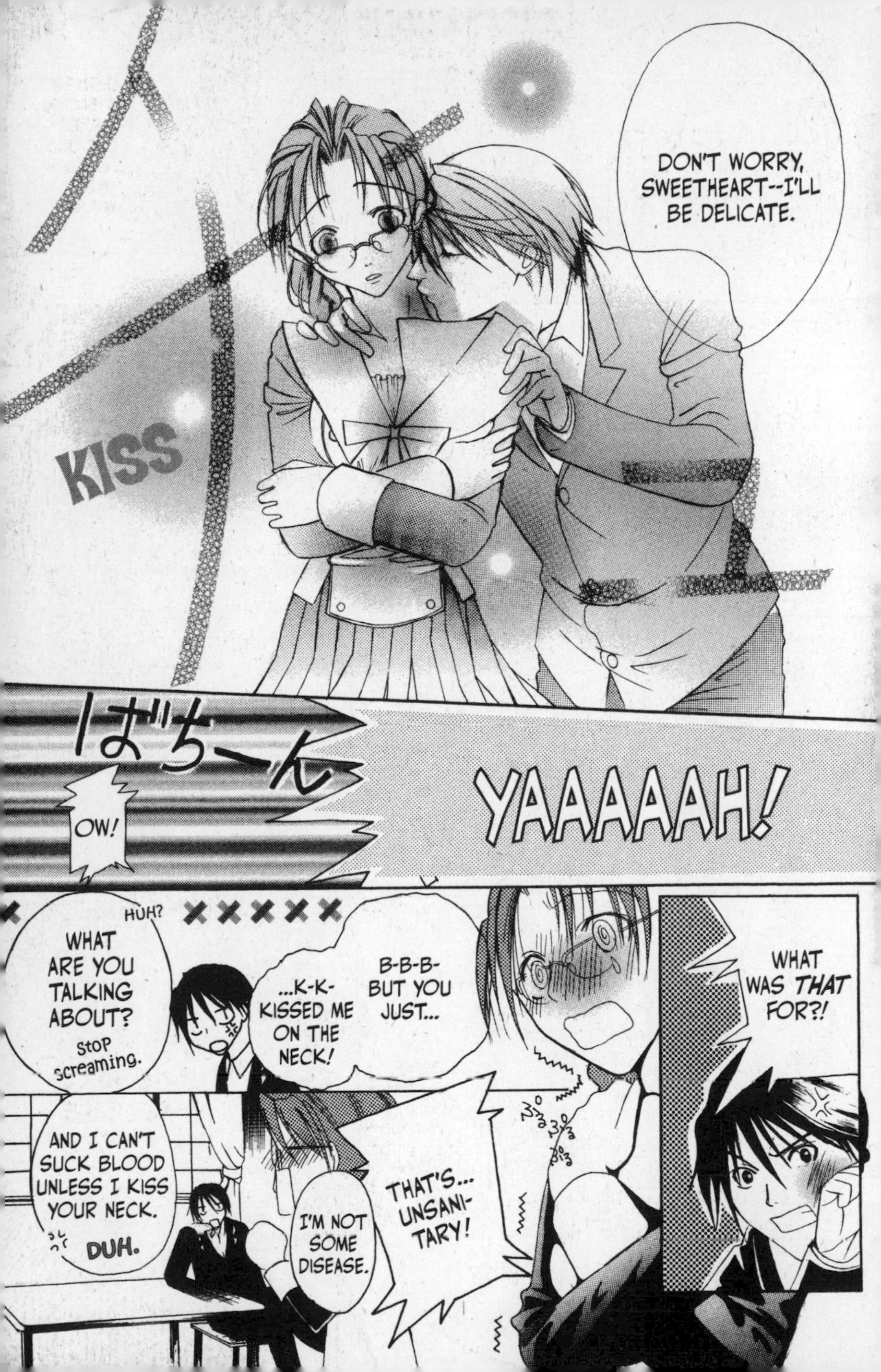
DON'T WORRY, SWEETHEART--I'LL BE DELICATE.
KISS
YAAAAAH!
ばち～ん
OW!
WHAT WAS *THAT* FOR?!
B-B-B-BUT YOU JUST...
...K-K-KISSED ME ON THE NECK!
HUH?
WHAT ARE YOU TALKING ABOUT? Stop screaming.
THAT'S... UNSANITARY!
I'M NOT SOME DISEASE.
AND I CAN'T SUCK BLOOD UNLESS I KISS YOUR NECK.
DUH.

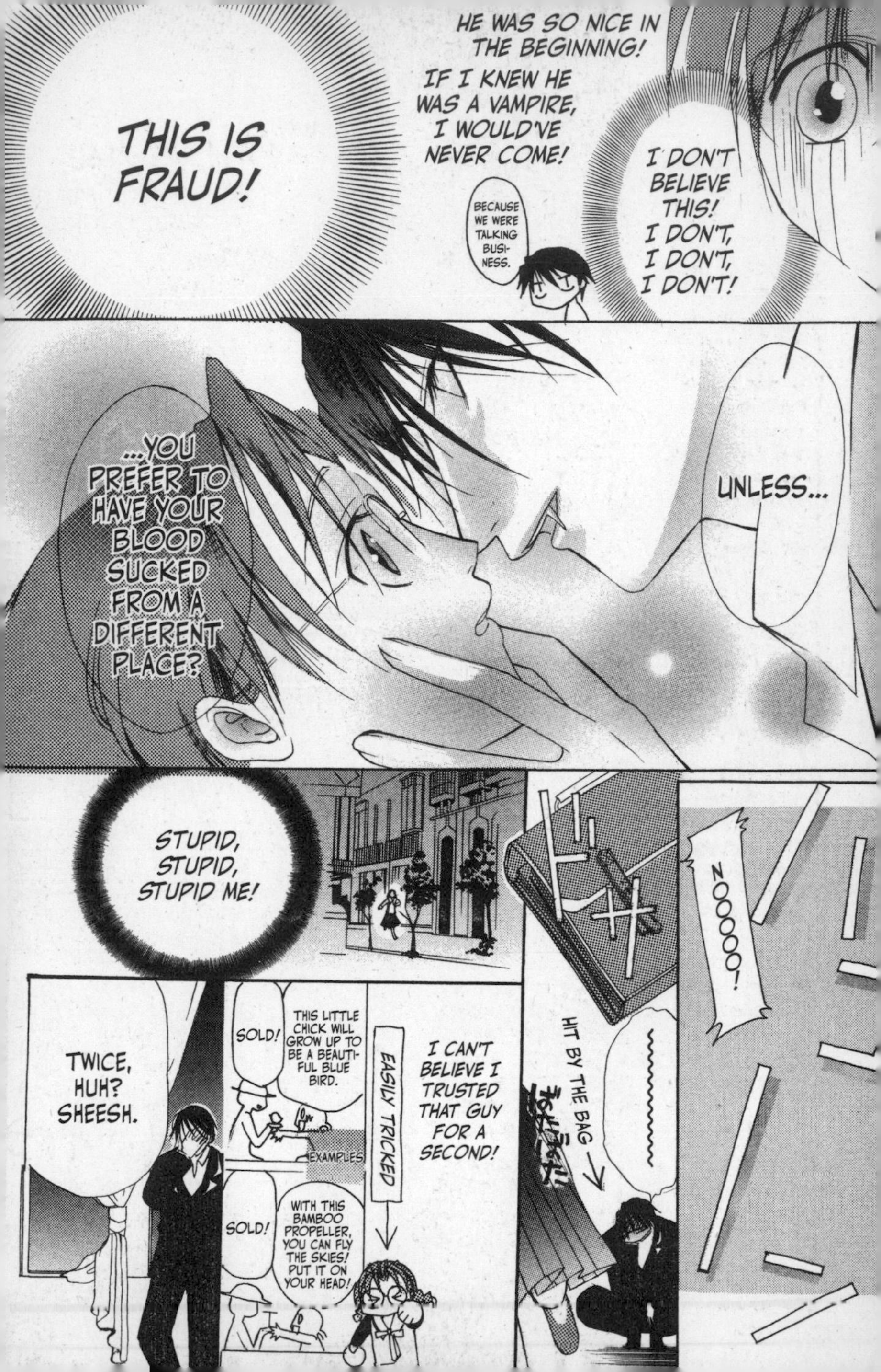
I DON'T BELIEVE THIS! I DON'T, I DON'T, I DON'T!
HE WAS SO NICE IN THE BEGINNING!
IF I KNEW HE WAS A VAMPIRE, I WOULD'VE NEVER COME!
BECAUSE WE WERE TALKING BUSI-NESS.
THIS IS FRAUD!
UNLESS...
...YOU PREFER TO HAVE YOUR BLOOD SUCKED FROM A DIFFERENT PLACE?
NOOOOO!
HIT BY THE BAG
~~~~~~
STUPID, STUPID, STUPID ME!
I CAN'T BELIEVE I TRUSTED THAT GUY FOR A SECOND!
EASILY TRICKED
THIS LITTLE CHICK WILL GROW UP TO BE A BEAUTI-FUL BLUE BIRD.
SOLD!
EXAMPLES
WITH THIS BAMBOO PROPELLER, YOU CAN FLY THE SKIES! PUT IT ON YOUR HEAD!
SOLD!
TWICE, HUH? SHEESH.
~~~~~~

Yes, this is my debut work. Coincidently, it's about a vampire, so I had it put in this volume. I did it about 5 years ago, and the original manuscript is extremely yellow. After not seeing it for a long time, my comments:

- oThe drawings are skewed. (Though things aren't that different now.)
- oThe guy looks old. (Well, the drawings themselves are old...)
- oThe comments are too enthusiastic and it seems like an eyesore.
- oBut I did work hard on it...

That is all.

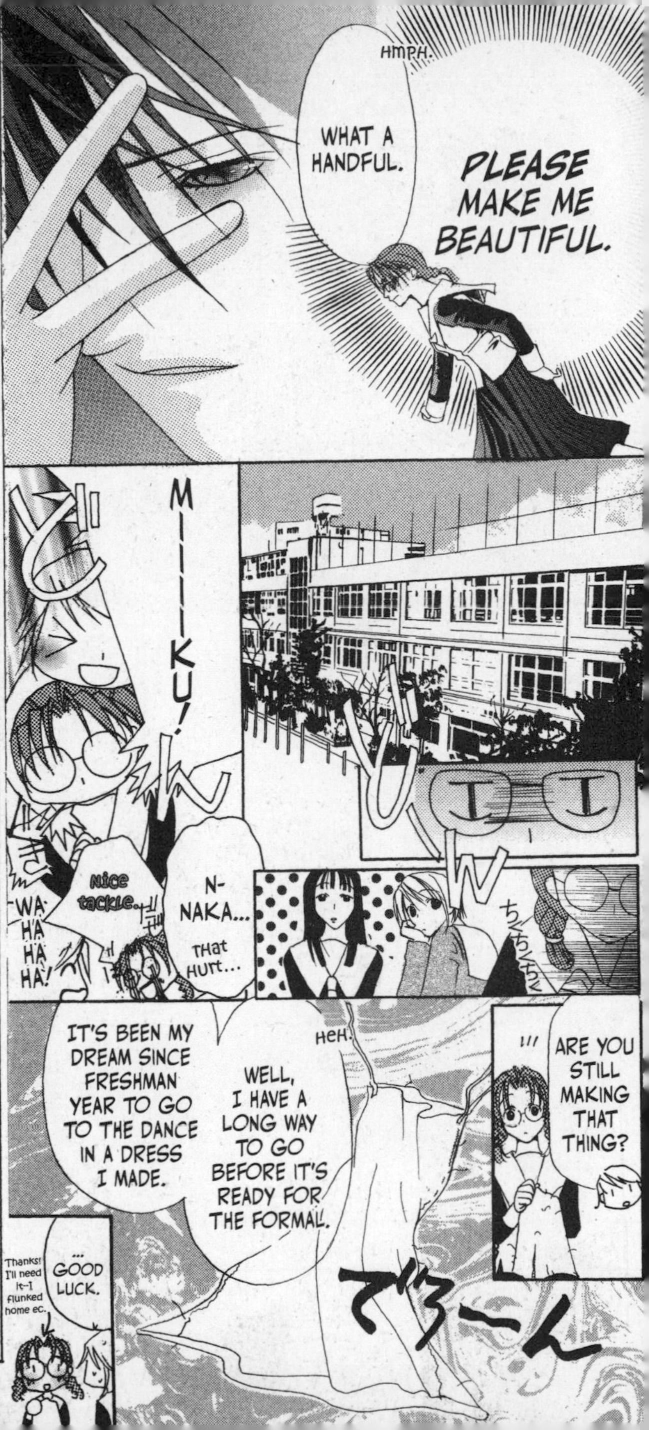
PLEASE MAKE ME BEAUTIFUL.
HMPH.
WHAT A HANDFUL.
MIIIKU!
W
ちくちくちく
Nice tackle.
N-NAKA...
That Hurt...
WA HA HA HA HA!
ARE YOU STILL MAKING THAT THING?
HEH.
IT'S BEEN MY DREAM SINCE FRESHMAN YEAR TO GO TO THE DANCE IN A DRESS I MADE.
WELL, I HAVE A LONG WAY TO GO BEFORE IT'S READY FOR THE FORMAL.
でろ〜ん
... GOOD LUCK.
Thanks! I'll need it--I flunked home ec.

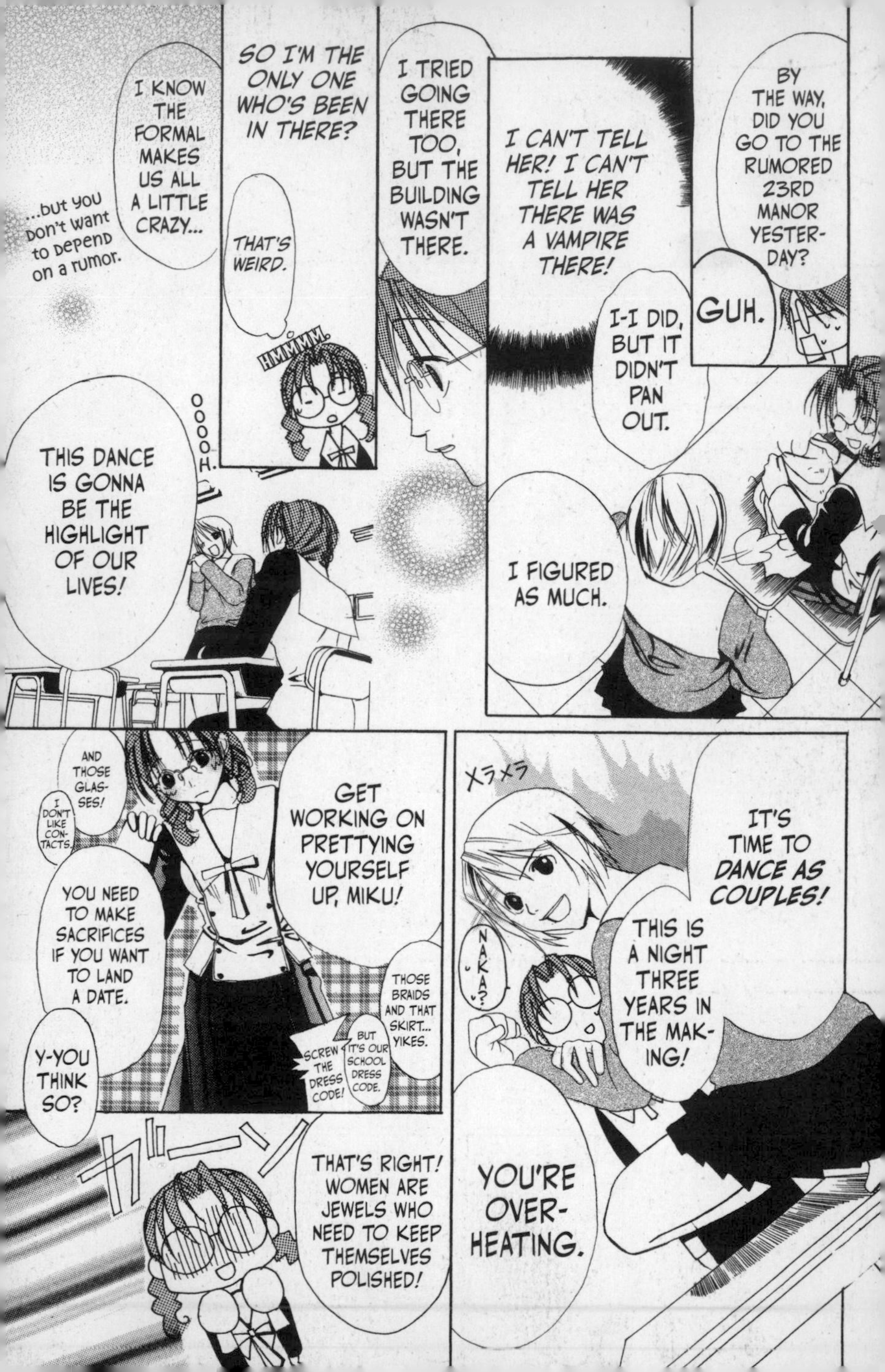
BY THE WAY, DID YOU GO TO THE RUMORED 23RD MANOR YESTERDAY?
GUH.
I CAN'T TELL HER! I CAN'T TELL HER THERE WAS A VAMPIRE THERE!
I-I DID, BUT IT DIDN'T PAN OUT.
I FIGURED AS MUCH.
I TRIED GOING THERE TOO, BUT THE BUILDING WASN'T THERE.
SO I'M THE ONLY ONE WHO'S BEEN IN THERE?
THAT'S WEIRD.
HMMMM.
I KNOW THE FORMAL MAKES US ALL A LITTLE CRAZY...
...but you don't want to depend on a rumor.
OOOOH.
THIS DANCE IS GONNA BE THE HIGHLIGHT OF OUR LIVES!
メラメラ
IT'S TIME TO DANCE AS COUPLES!
THIS IS A NIGHT THREE YEARS IN THE MAKING!
NAKA...?
YOU'RE OVERHEATING.
GET WORKING ON PRETTYING YOURSELF UP, MIKU!
AND THOSE GLASSES!
I DON'T LIKE CONTACTS.
THOSE BRAIDS AND THAT SKIRT... YIKES.
BUT IT'S OUR SCHOOL DRESS CODE.
SCREW THE DRESS CODE!
YOU NEED TO MAKE SACRIFICES IF YOU WANT TO LAND A DATE.
Y-YOU THINK SO?
カーー
THAT'S RIGHT! WOMEN ARE JEWELS WHO NEED TO KEEP THEMSELVES POLISHED!

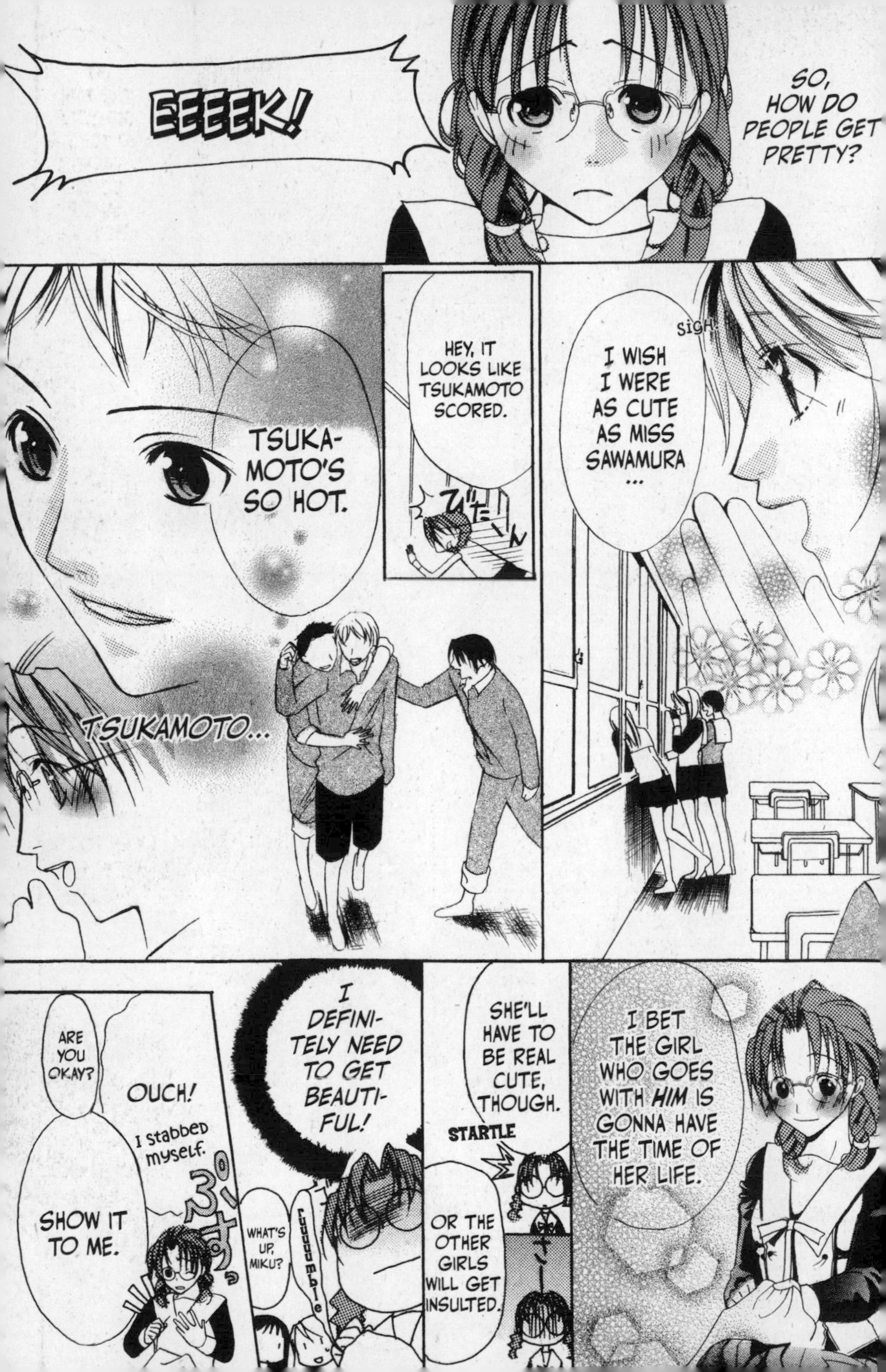
SO, HOW DO PEOPLE GET PRETTY?
EEEEK!
SIGH!
I WISH I WERE AS CUTE AS MISS SAWAMURA...
HEY, IT LOOKS LIKE TSUKAMOTO SCORED.
TSUKA-MOTO'S SO HOT.
TSUKAMOTO...
I BET THE GIRL WHO GOES WITH HIM IS GONNA HAVE THE TIME OF HER LIFE.
SHE'LL HAVE TO BE REAL CUTE, THOUGH.
STARTLE
OR THE OTHER GIRLS WILL GET INSULTED.
I DEFINITELY NEED TO GET BEAUTIFUL!
ruuuumble
WHAT'S UP, MIKU?
ARE YOU OKAY?
OUCH!
I stabbed myself.
SHOW IT TO ME.

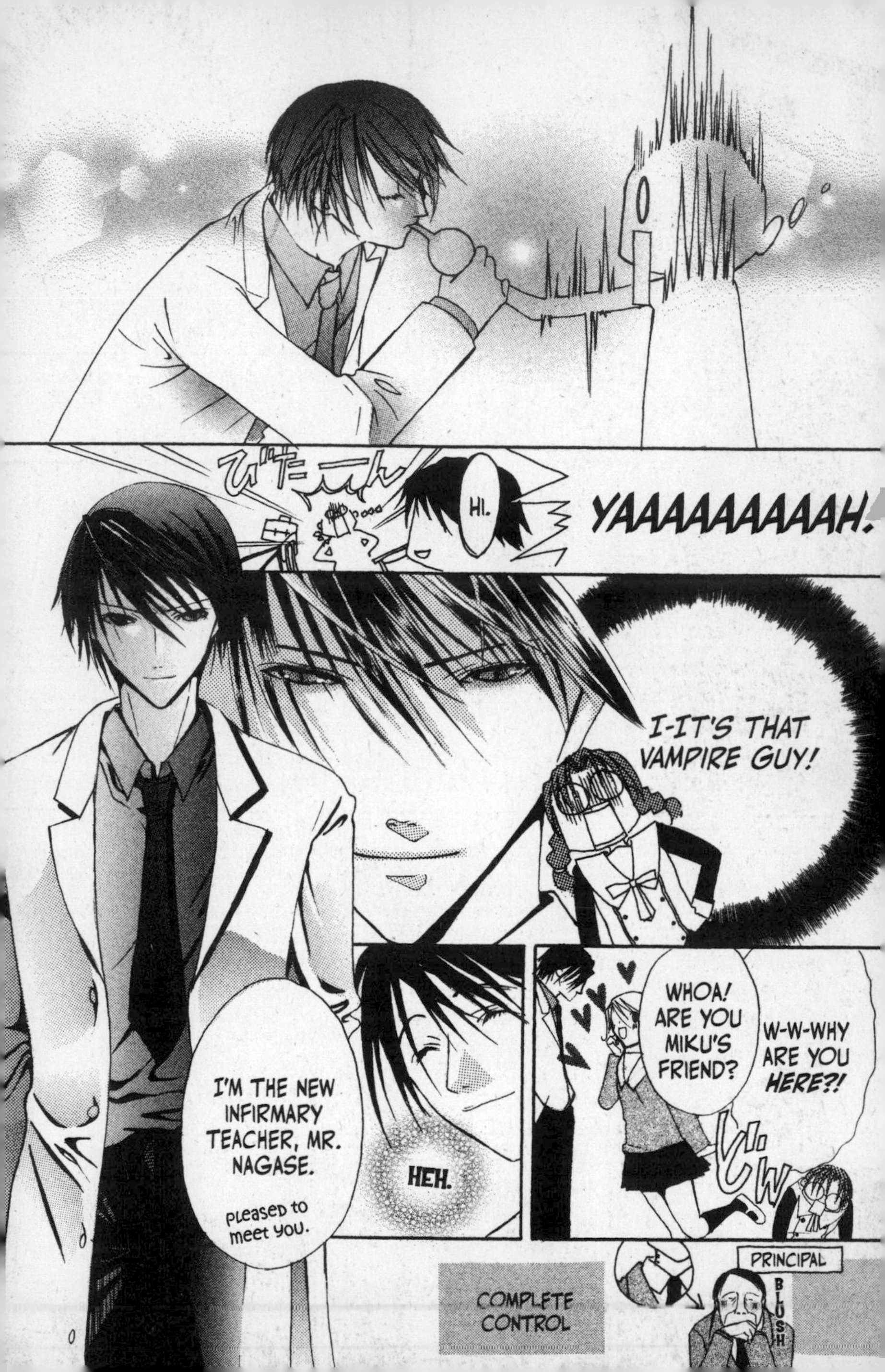

びたーん
HI.
YAAAAAAAAAH.
I-IT'S THAT VAMPIRE GUY!
W-W-WHY ARE YOU HERE?!
WHOA! ARE YOU MIKU'S FRIEND?
HEH.
I'M THE NEW INFIRMARY TEACHER, MR. NAGASE.
pleased to meet you.
PRINCIPAL
BLUSH
COMPLETE CONTROL

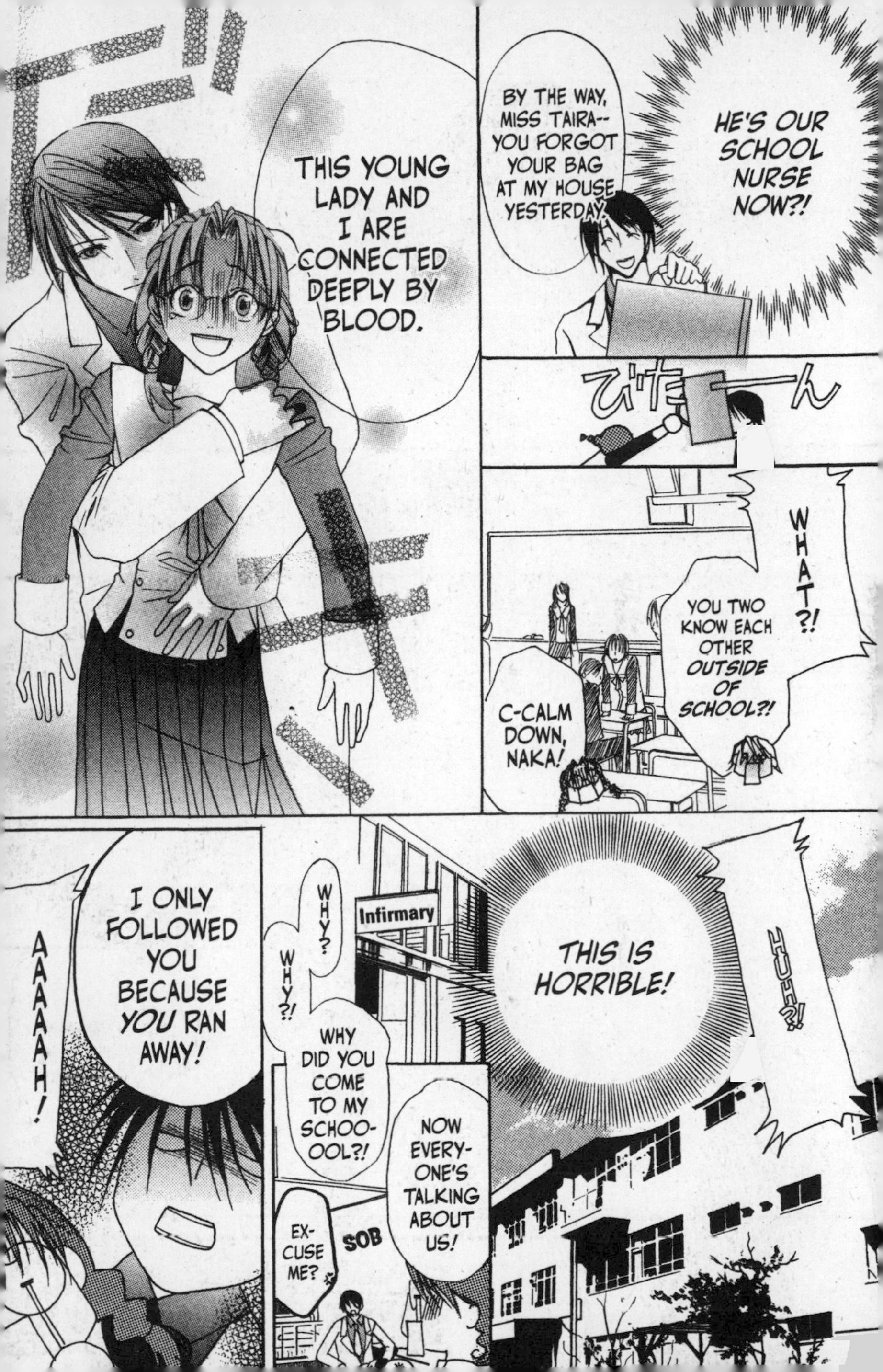
HE'S OUR SCHOOL NURSE NOW?!
BY THE WAY, MISS TAIRA-- YOU FORGOT YOUR BAG AT MY HOUSE YESTERDAY.
WHAT?!
YOU TWO KNOW EACH OTHER OUTSIDE OF SCHOOL?!
C-CALM DOWN, NAKA!
THIS YOUNG LADY AND I ARE CONNECTED DEEPLY BY BLOOD.
HUH?!
THIS IS HORRIBLE!
Infirmary
WHY?
WHY?!
WHY DID YOU COME TO MY SCHOOOOL?!
NOW EVERYONE'S TALKING ABOUT US!
SOB
EXCUSE ME?
I ONLY FOLLOWED YOU BECAUSE YOU RAN AWAY!
AAAAAH!

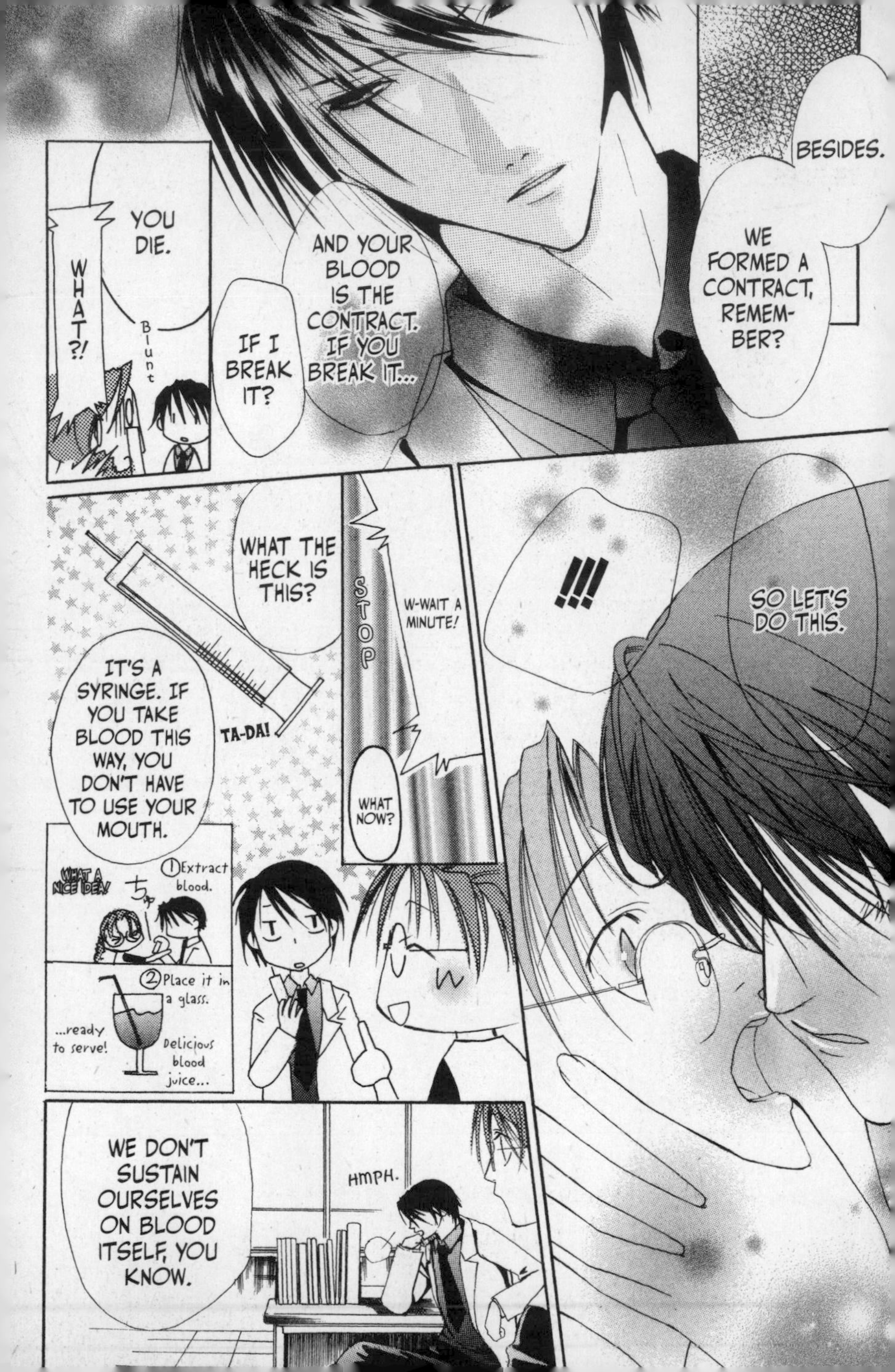
BESIDES.
WE FORMED A CONTRACT, REMEMBER?
AND YOUR BLOOD IS THE CONTRACT. IF YOU BREAK IT...
IF I BREAK IT?
YOU DIE.
Blunt
WHAT?!
!!!
SO LET'S DO THIS.
STOP
W-WAIT A MINUTE!
WHAT NOW?
WHAT THE HECK IS THIS?
TA-DA!
IT'S A SYRINGE. IF YOU TAKE BLOOD THIS WAY, YOU DON'T HAVE TO USE YOUR MOUTH.
WHAT A NICE IDEA!
①Extract blood.
②Place it in a glass.
...ready to serve!
Delicious blood juice...
HMPH.
WE DON'T SUSTAIN OURSELVES ON BLOOD ITSELF, YOU KNOW.

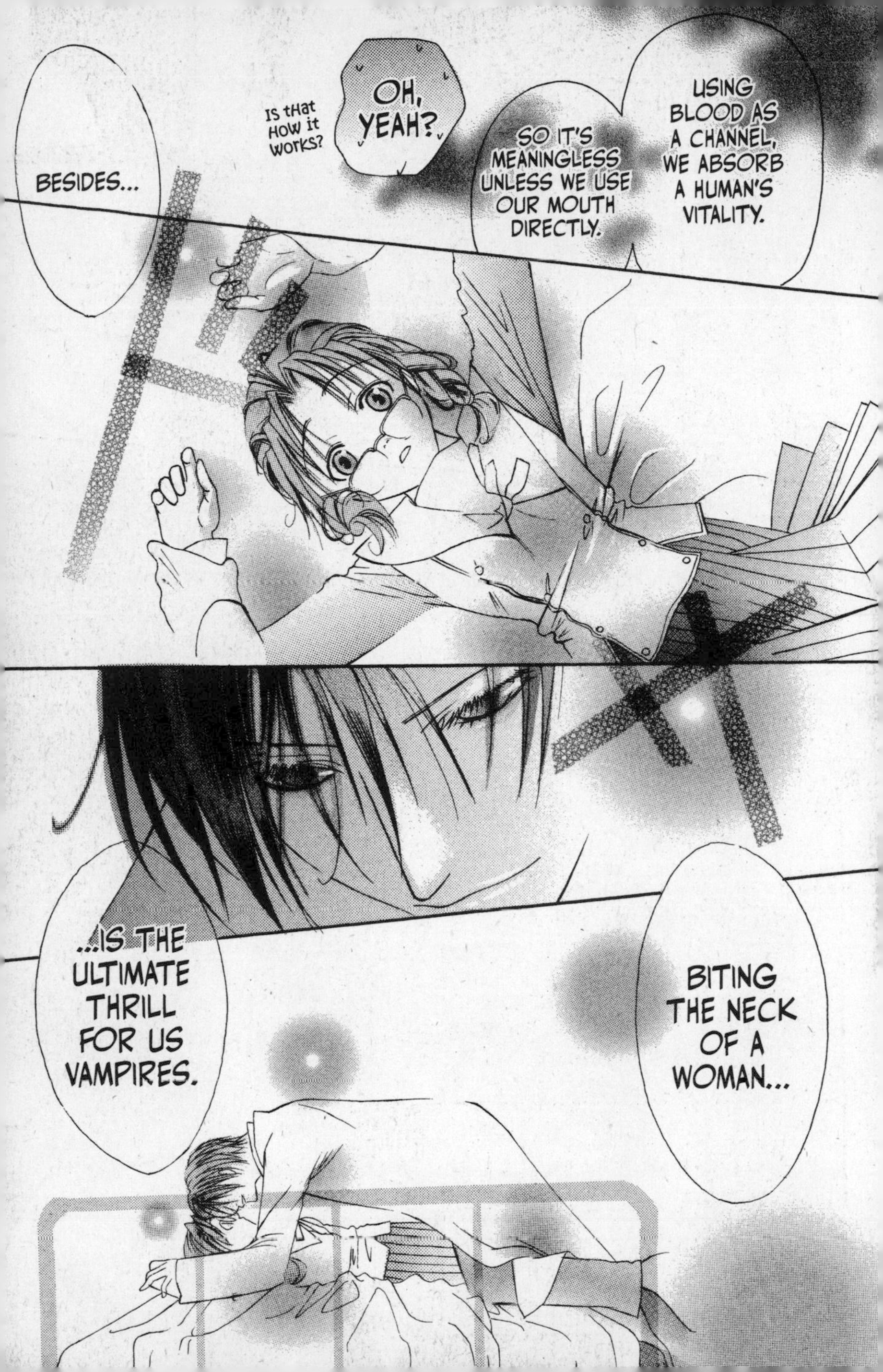
USING BLOOD AS A CHANNEL, WE ABSORB A HUMAN'S VITALITY.
SO IT'S MEANINGLESS UNLESS WE USE OUR MOUTH DIRECTLY.
OH, YEAH?
Is that How it works?
BESIDES...
BITING THE NECK OF A WOMAN...
...IS THE ULTIMATE THRILL FOR US VAMPIRES.

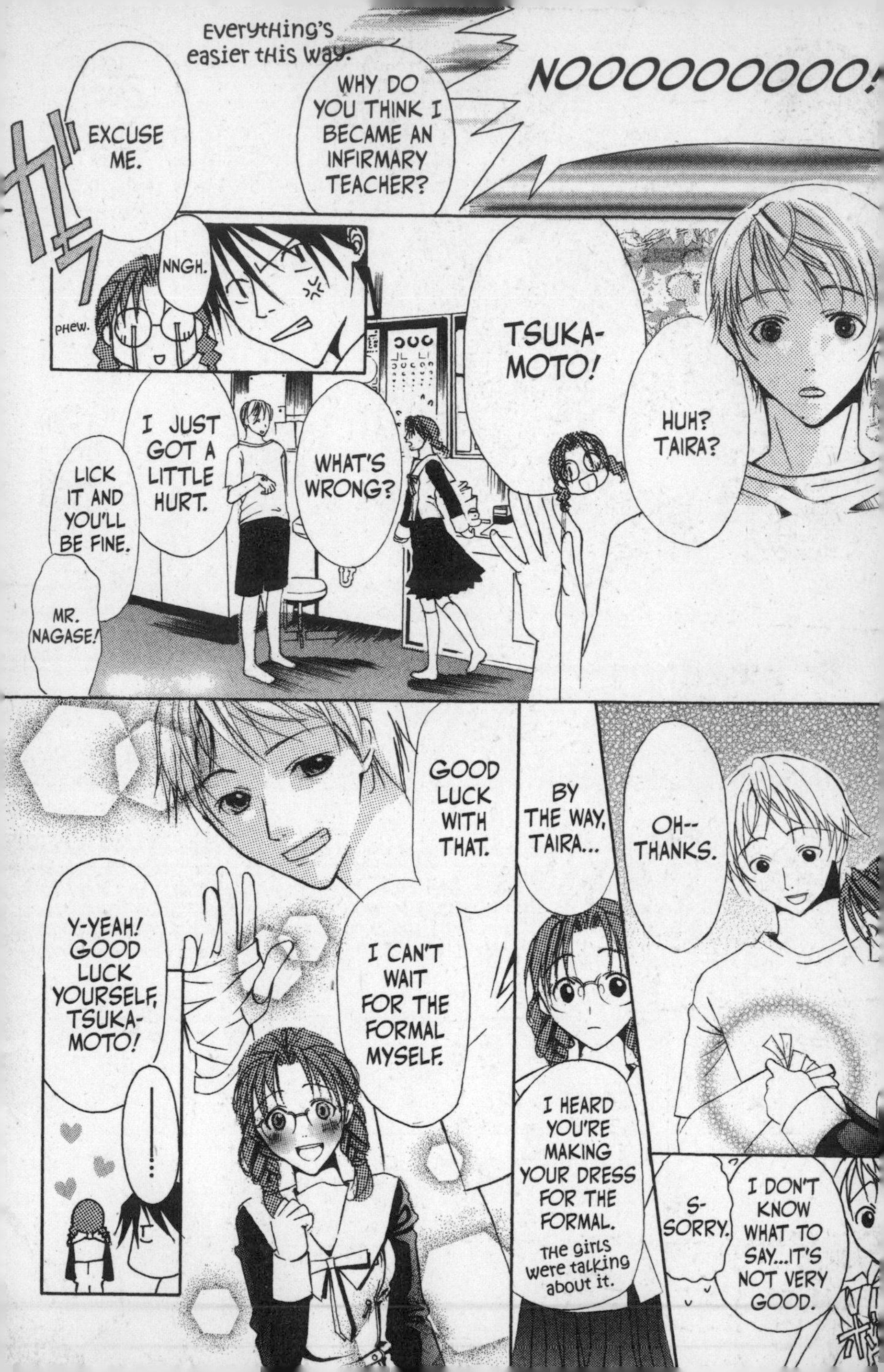
NOOOOOOOOO!
WHY DO YOU THINK I BECAME AN INFIRMARY TEACHER?
Everything's easier this way.
EXCUSE ME.
NNGH.
PHEW.
HUH? TAIRA?
TSUKA-MOTO!
WHAT'S WRONG?
I JUST GOT A LITTLE HURT.
LICK IT AND YOU'LL BE FINE.
MR. NAGASE!
OH-- THANKS.
BY THE WAY, TAIRA...
I HEARD YOU'RE MAKING YOUR DRESS FOR THE FORMAL.
The girls were talking about it.
I DON'T KNOW WHAT TO SAY...IT'S NOT VERY GOOD.
S-SORRY.
GOOD LUCK WITH THAT.
I CAN'T WAIT FOR THE FORMAL MYSELF.
Y-YEAH! GOOD LUCK YOURSELF, TSUKA-MOTO!
......!

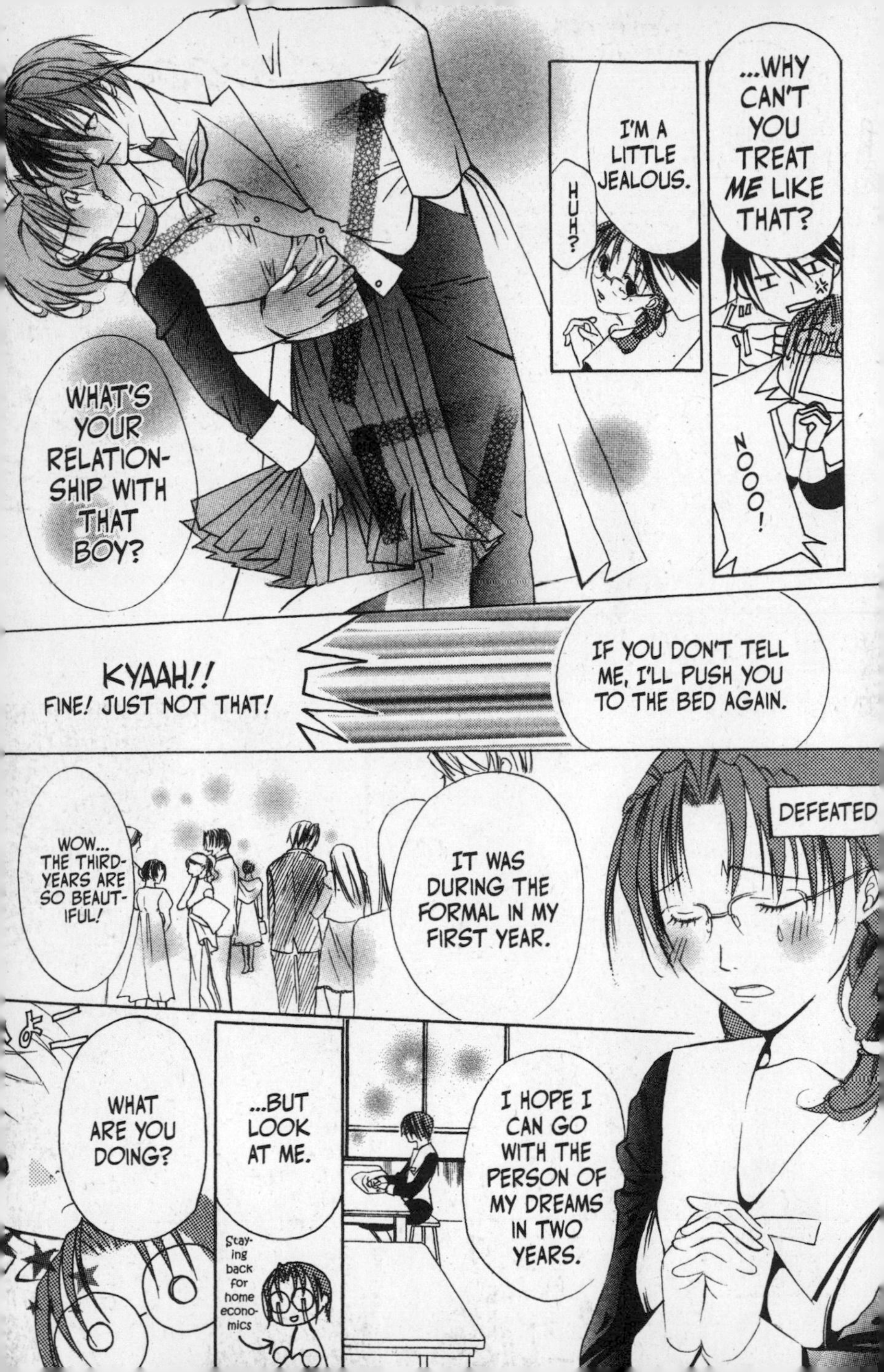
...WHY CAN'T YOU TREAT ME LIKE THAT?
NOOO!
I'M A LITTLE JEALOUS.
HUH?
WHAT'S YOUR RELATIONSHIP WITH THAT BOY?
IF YOU DON'T TELL ME, I'LL PUSH YOU TO THE BED AGAIN.
KYAAH!! FINE! JUST NOT THAT!
DEFEATED
IT WAS DURING THE FORMAL IN MY FIRST YEAR.
WOW... THE THIRD-YEARS ARE SO BEAUTIFUL!
I HOPE I CAN GO WITH THE PERSON OF MY DREAMS IN TWO YEARS.
...BUT LOOK AT ME.
Staying back for home economics
WHAT ARE YOU DOING?

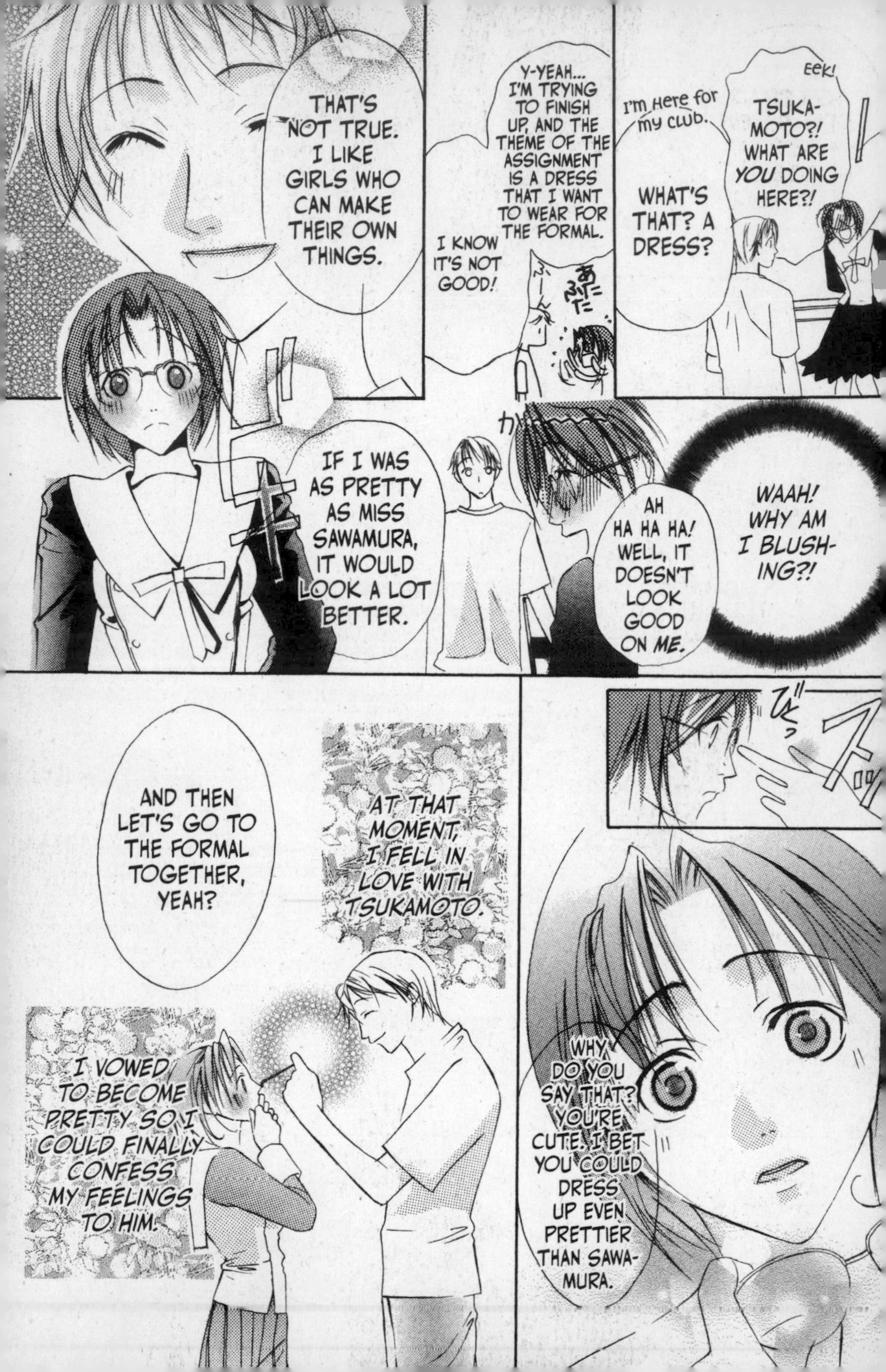
EEK!
TSUKAMOTO?! WHAT ARE YOU DOING HERE?!
I'm here for my club.
WHAT'S THAT? A DRESS?
Y-YEAH... I'M TRYING TO FINISH UP, AND THE THEME OF THE ASSIGNMENT IS A DRESS THAT I WANT TO WEAR FOR THE FORMAL.
あたふた
ふーん
I KNOW IT'S NOT GOOD!
THAT'S NOT TRUE. I LIKE GIRLS WHO CAN MAKE THEIR OWN THINGS.
WAAH! WHY AM I BLUSHING?!
AH HA HA HA! WELL, IT DOESN'T LOOK GOOD ON ME.
IF I WAS AS PRETTY AS MISS SAWAMURA, IT WOULD LOOK A LOT BETTER.
びくっ
WHY DO YOU SAY THAT? YOU'RE CUTE. I BET YOU COULD DRESS UP EVEN PRETTIER THAN SAWAMURA.
AND THEN LET'S GO TO THE FORMAL TOGETHER, YEAH?
AT THAT MOMENT, I FELL IN LOVE WITH TSUKAMOTO.
I VOWED TO BECOME PRETTY SO I COULD FINALLY CONFESS MY FEELINGS TO HIM.

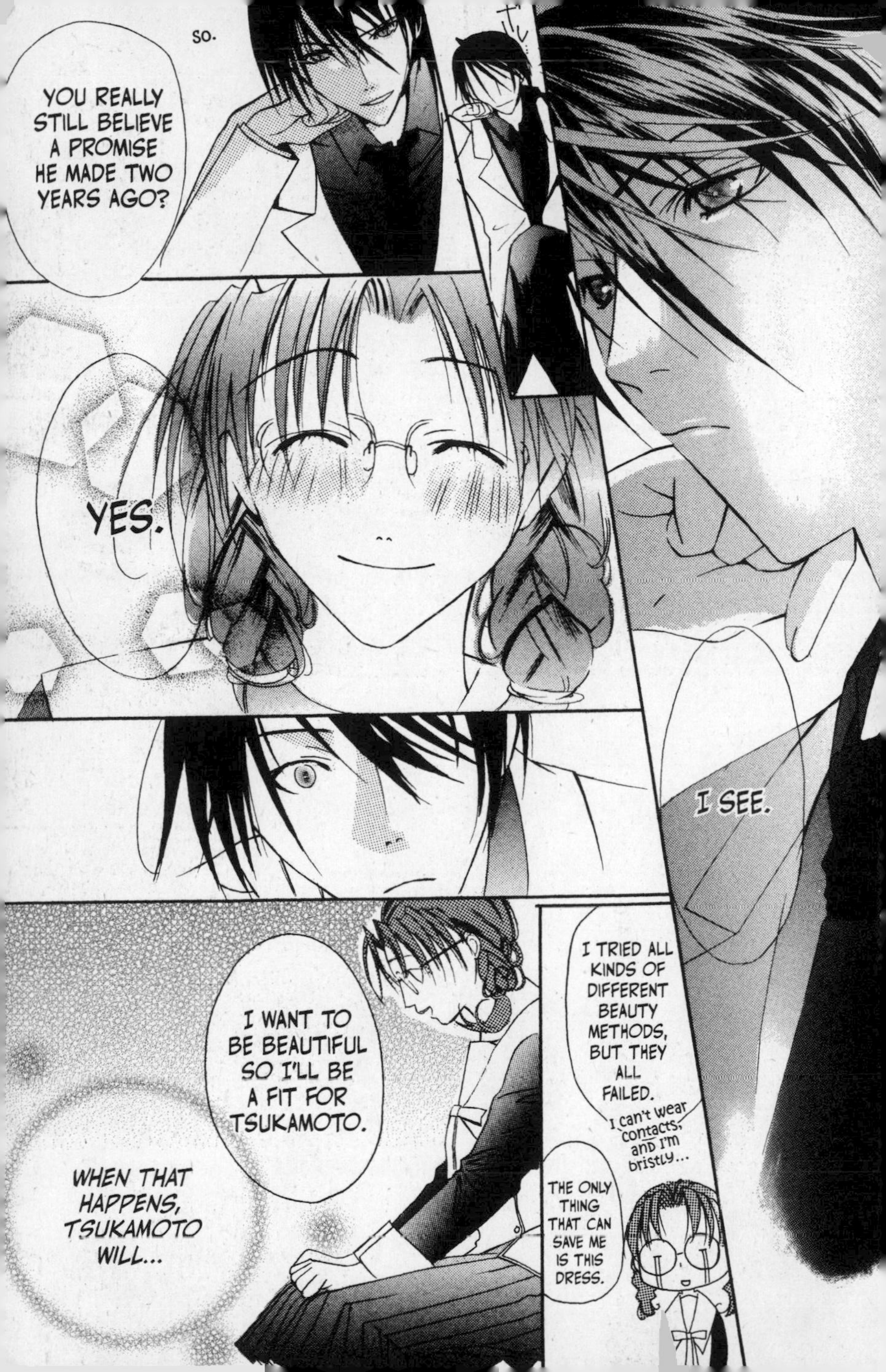
SO.
YOU REALLY STILL BELIEVE A PROMISE HE MADE TWO YEARS AGO?
YES.
I SEE.
I TRIED ALL KINDS OF DIFFERENT BEAUTY METHODS, BUT THEY ALL FAILED.
I can't wear contacts, and I'm bristly...
THE ONLY THING THAT CAN SAVE ME IS THIS DRESS.
I WANT TO BE BEAUTIFUL SO I'LL BE A FIT FOR TSUKAMOTO.
WHEN THAT HAPPENS, TSUKAMOTO WILL...

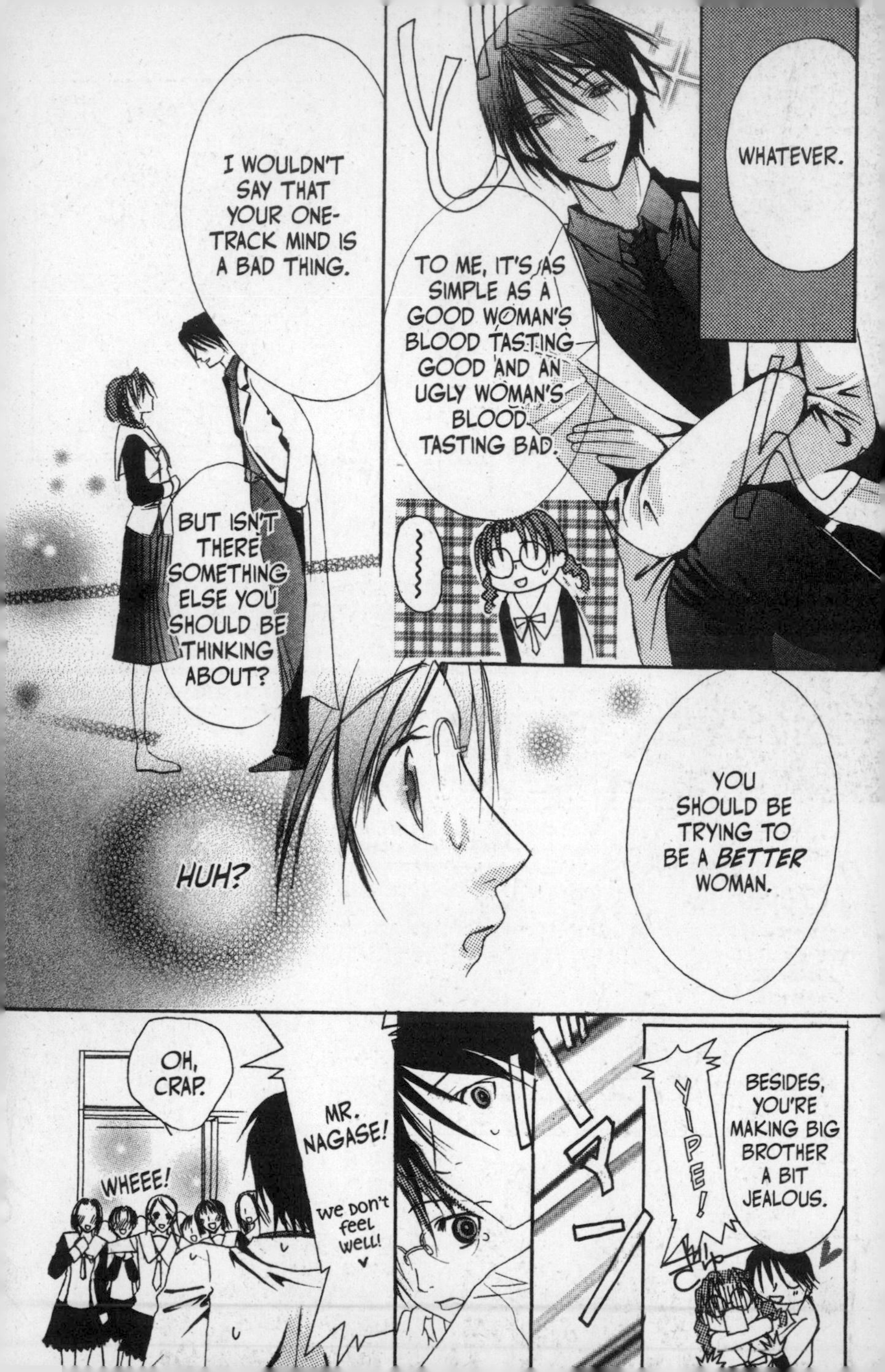
WHATEVER.
TO ME, IT'S AS SIMPLE AS A GOOD WOMAN'S BLOOD TASTING GOOD AND AN UGLY WOMAN'S BLOOD TASTING BAD.
I WOULDN'T SAY THAT YOUR ONE-TRACK MIND IS A BAD THING.
BUT ISN'T THERE SOMETHING ELSE YOU SHOULD BE THINKING ABOUT?
YOU SHOULD BE TRYING TO BE A *BETTER* WOMAN.
HUH?
BESIDES, YOU'RE MAKING BIG BROTHER A BIT JEALOUS.
YIPE!
MR. NAGASE!
OH, CRAP.
WHEEE!
We DON'T feel WELL!

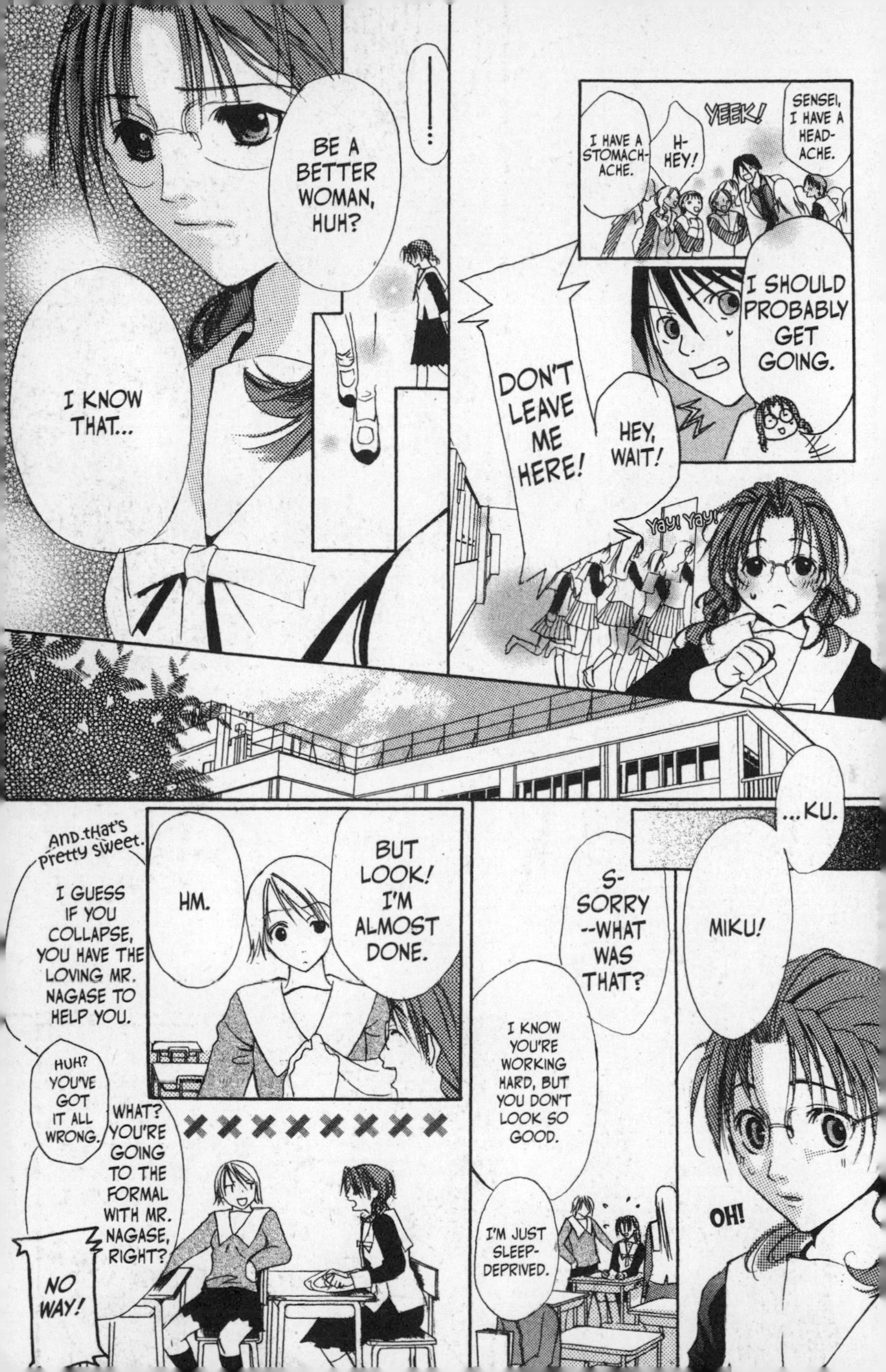
SENSEI, I HAVE A HEADACHE.
YEEK!
H-HEY!
I HAVE A STOMACHACHE.
I SHOULD PROBABLY GET GOING.
HEY, WAIT!
DON'T LEAVE ME HERE!
Yay! Yay!
...!
BE A BETTER WOMAN, HUH?
I KNOW THAT...
...KU.
MIKU!
OH!
S-SORRY--WHAT WAS THAT?
I KNOW YOU'RE WORKING HARD, BUT YOU DON'T LOOK SO GOOD.
I'M JUST SLEEP-DEPRIVED.
BUT LOOK! I'M ALMOST DONE.
HM.
I GUESS IF YOU COLLAPSE, YOU HAVE THE LOVING MR. NAGASE TO HELP YOU.
And that's pretty sweet.
WHAT? YOU'RE GOING TO THE FORMAL WITH MR. NAGASE, RIGHT?
HUH? YOU'VE GOT IT ALL WRONG.
NO WAY!

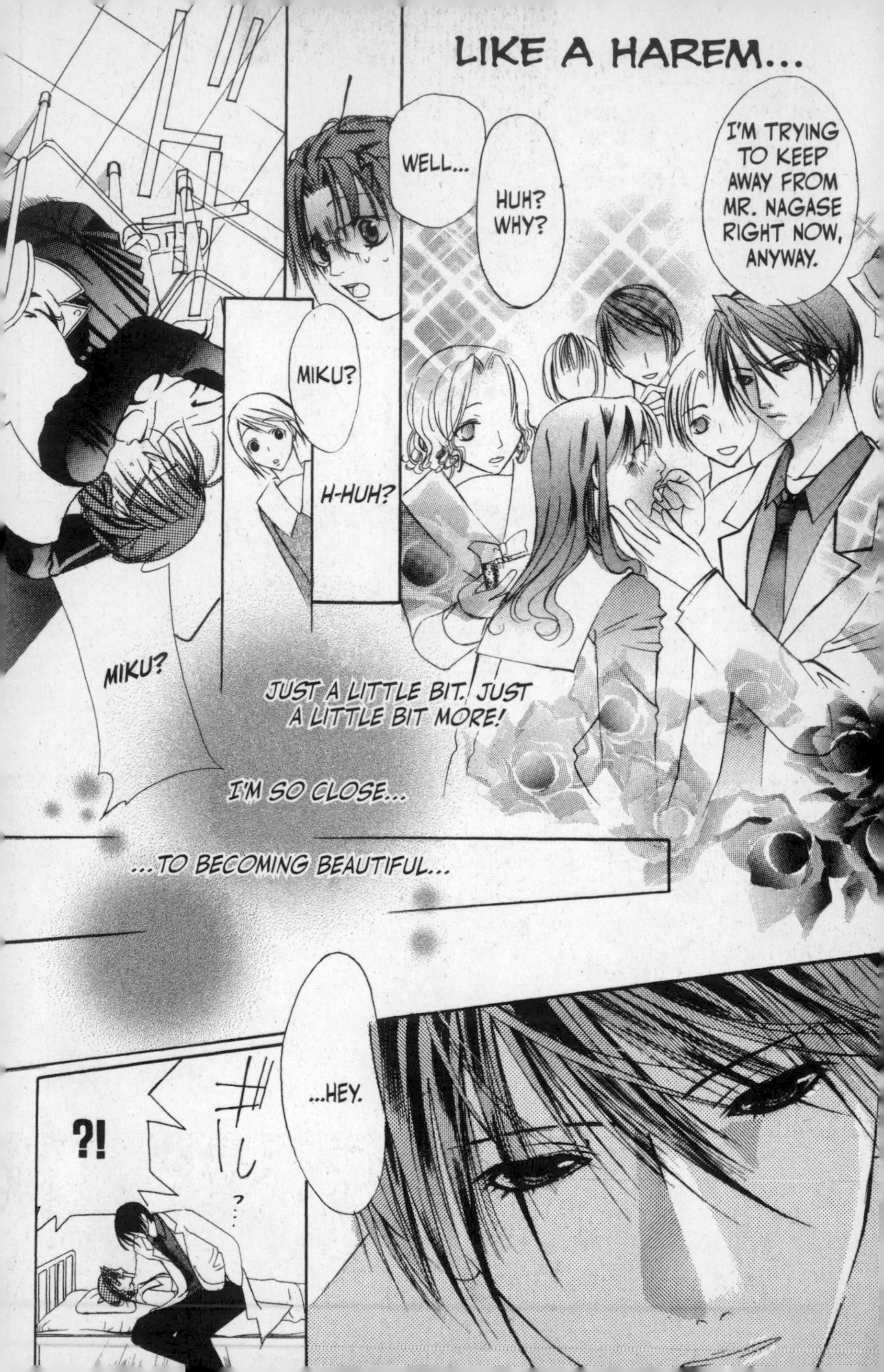
LIKE A HAREM...
I'M TRYING TO KEEP AWAY FROM MR. NAGASE RIGHT NOW, ANYWAY.
HUH? WHY?
WELL...
MIKU?
H-HUH?
MIKU?
JUST A LITTLE BIT. JUST A LITTLE BIT MORE!
I'M SO CLOSE...
...TO BECOMING BEAUTIFUL...
...HEY.
?!

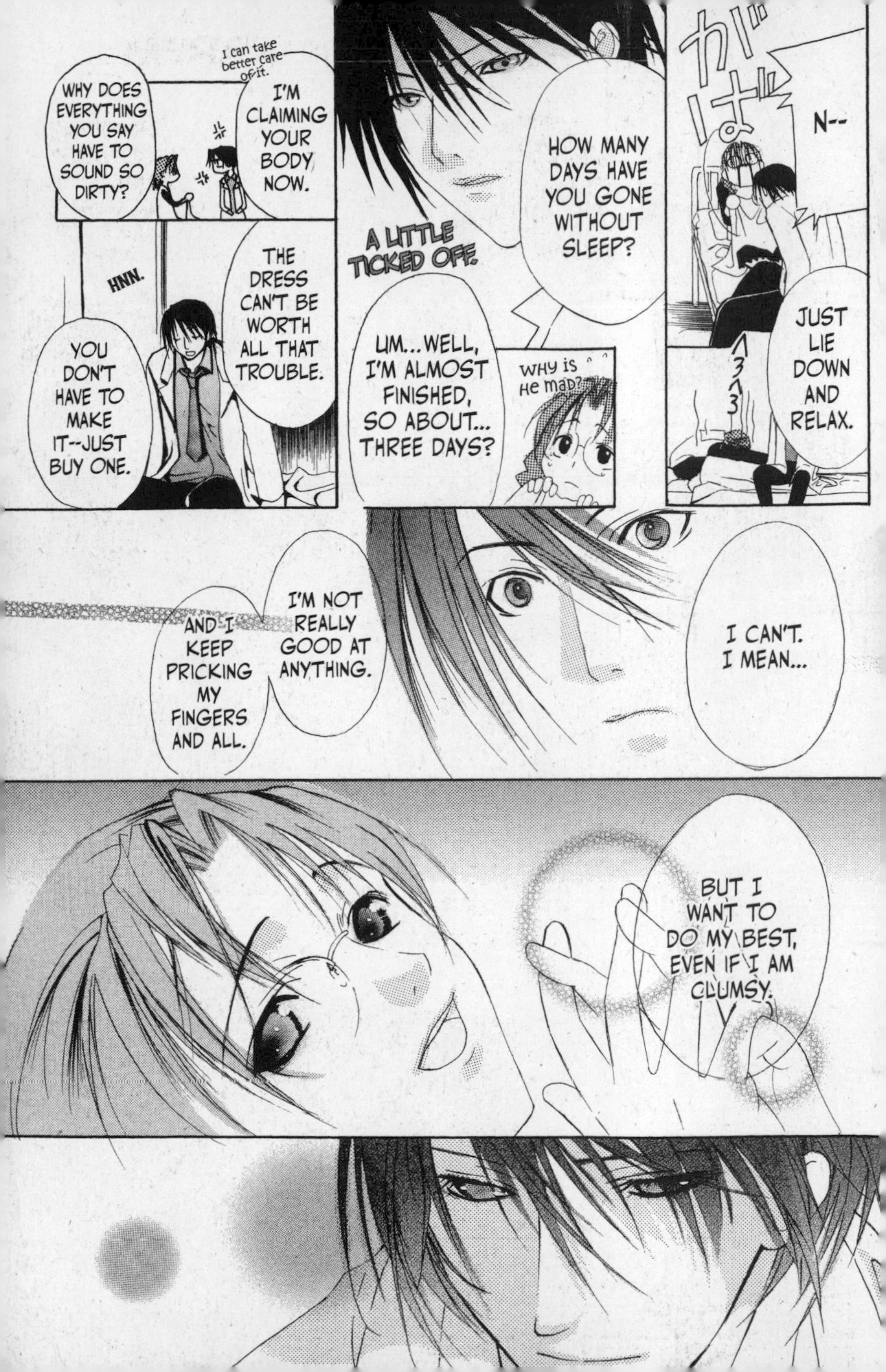
がば
N--
JUST LIE DOWN AND RELAX.
HOW MANY DAYS HAVE YOU GONE WITHOUT SLEEP?
A LITTLE TICKED OFF.
UM...WELL, I'M ALMOST FINISHED, SO ABOUT... THREE DAYS?
Why is he mad?
I'M CLAIMING YOUR BODY NOW.
I can take better care of it.
WHY DOES EVERYTHING YOU SAY HAVE TO SOUND SO DIRTY?
THE DRESS CAN'T BE WORTH ALL THAT TROUBLE.
HNN.
YOU DON'T HAVE TO MAKE IT--JUST BUY ONE.
I CAN'T. I MEAN...
I'M NOT REALLY GOOD AT ANYTHING.
AND I KEEP PRICKING MY FINGERS AND ALL.
BUT I WANT TO DO MY BEST, EVEN IF I AM CLUMSY.

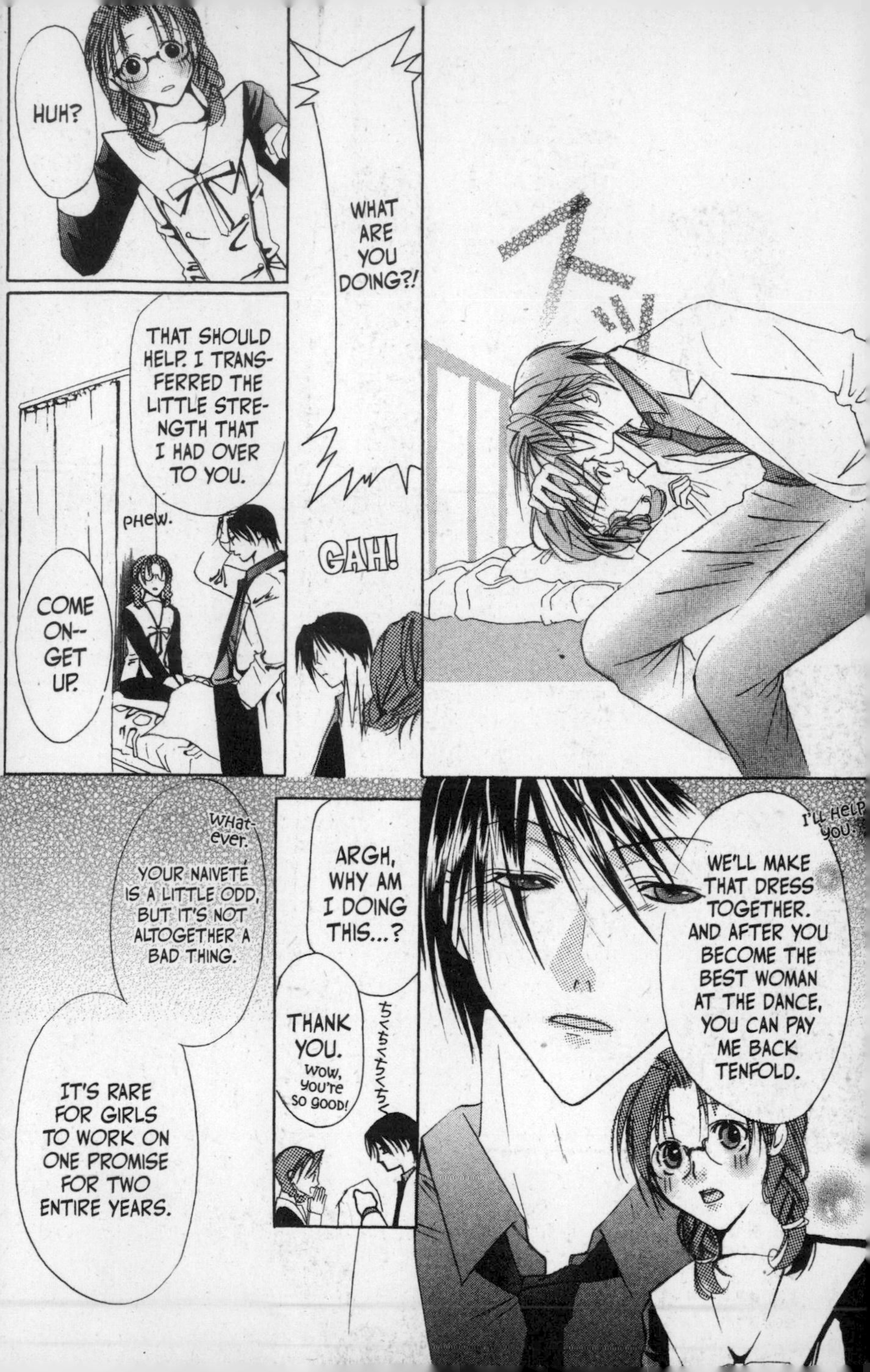
WHAT ARE YOU DOING?!
GAH!
HUH?
THAT SHOULD HELP. I TRANSFERRED THE LITTLE STRENGTH THAT I HAD OVER TO YOU.
phew.
COME ON-- GET UP.
I'll help you...
WE'LL MAKE THAT DRESS TOGETHER. AND AFTER YOU BECOME THE BEST WOMAN AT THE DANCE, YOU CAN PAY ME BACK TENFOLD.
ARGH, WHY AM I DOING THIS...?
THANK YOU.
wow, you're so good!
ちくちくちくちく
Whatever.
YOUR NAIVETÉ IS A LITTLE ODD, BUT IT'S NOT ALTOGETHER A BAD THING.
IT'S RARE FOR GIRLS TO WORK ON ONE PROMISE FOR TWO ENTIRE YEARS.

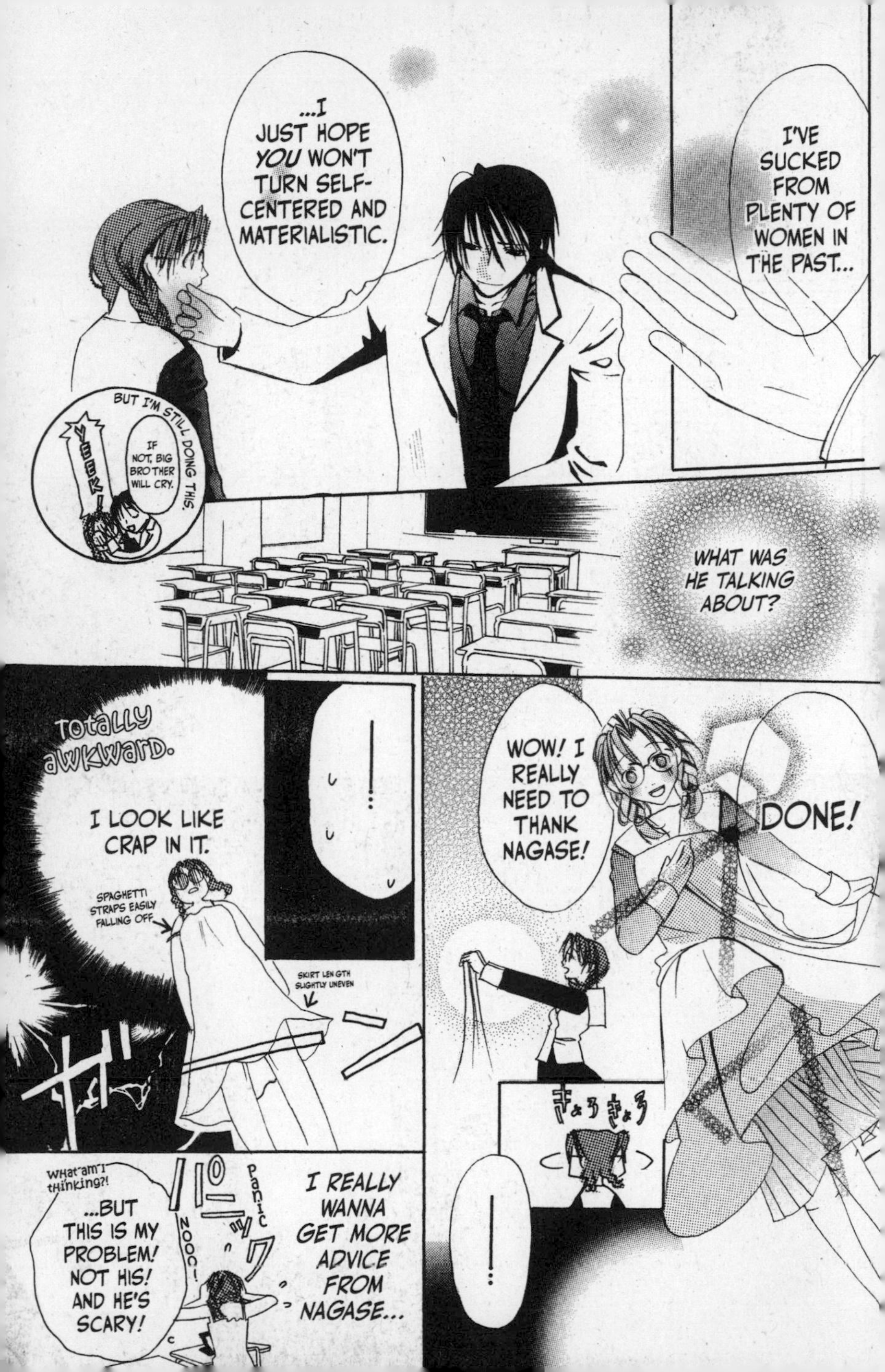
I'VE SUCKED FROM PLENTY OF WOMEN IN THE PAST...
...I JUST HOPE YOU WON'T TURN SELF-CENTERED AND MATERIALISTIC.
BUT I'M STILL DOING THIS.
IF NOT, BIG BROTHER WILL CRY.
YEEK!
WHAT WAS HE TALKING ABOUT?
DONE!
WOW! I REALLY NEED TO THANK NAGASE!
!...
Totally awkward.
I LOOK LIKE CRAP IN IT.
SPAGHETTI STRAPS EASILY FALLING OFF
SKIRT LENGTH SLIGHTLY UNEVEN
!...
I REALLY WANNA GET MORE ADVICE FROM NAGASE...
panic
NOOO!
What am I thinking?!
...BUT THIS IS MY PROBLEM! NOT HIS! AND HE'S SCARY!

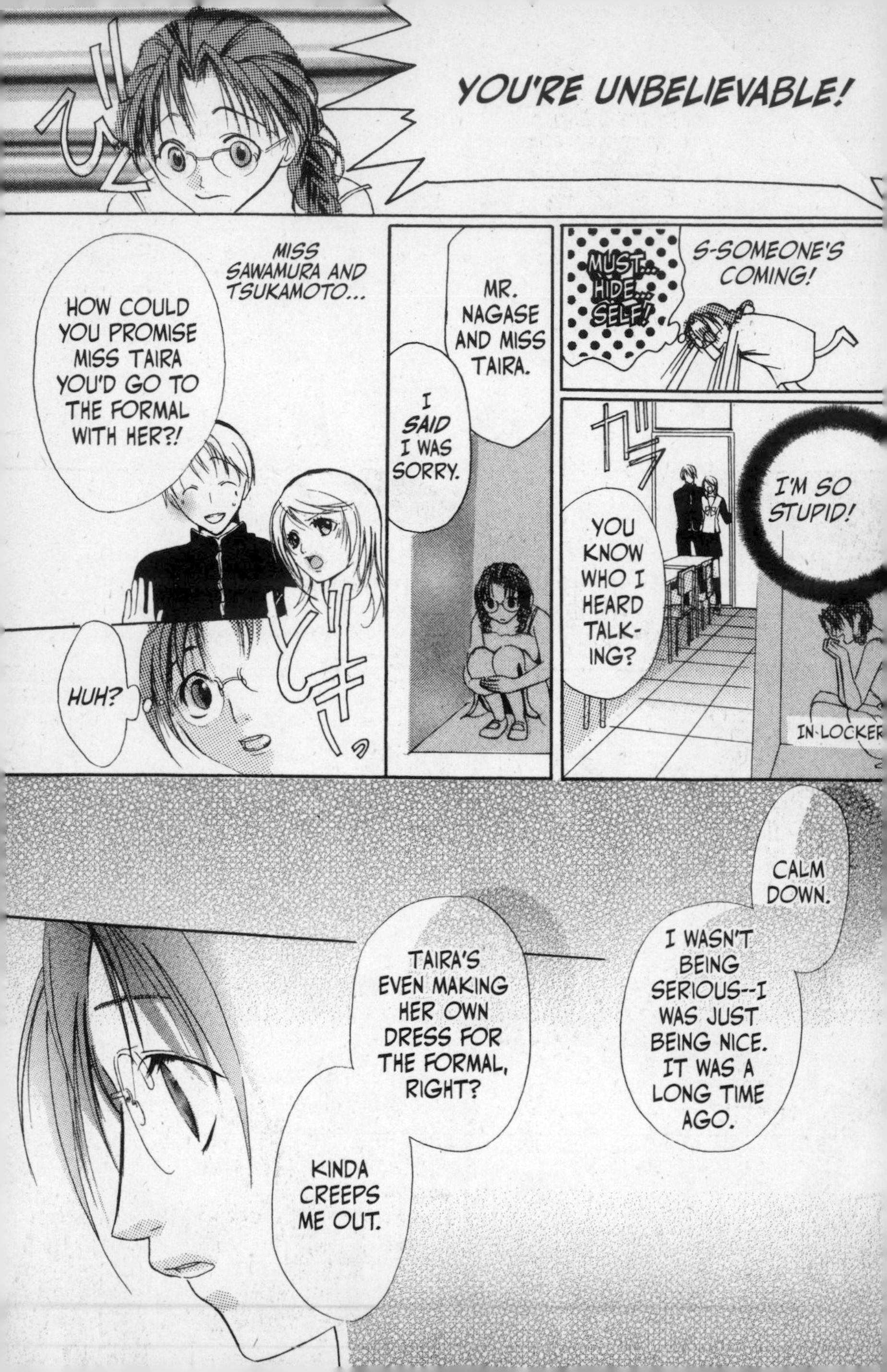
YOU'RE UNBELIEVABLE!
S-SOMEONE'S COMING!
MUST... HIDE... SELF!
I'M SO STUPID!
IN LOCKER
YOU KNOW WHO I HEARD TALK-ING?
MR. NAGASE AND MISS TAIRA.
I SAID I WAS SORRY.
MISS SAWAMURA AND TSUKAMOTO...
HOW COULD YOU PROMISE MISS TAIRA YOU'D GO TO THE FORMAL WITH HER?!
HUH?
CALM DOWN.
I WASN'T BEING SERIOUS--I WAS JUST BEING NICE. IT WAS A LONG TIME AGO.
TAIRA'S EVEN MAKING HER OWN DRESS FOR THE FORMAL, RIGHT?
KINDA CREEPS ME OUT.

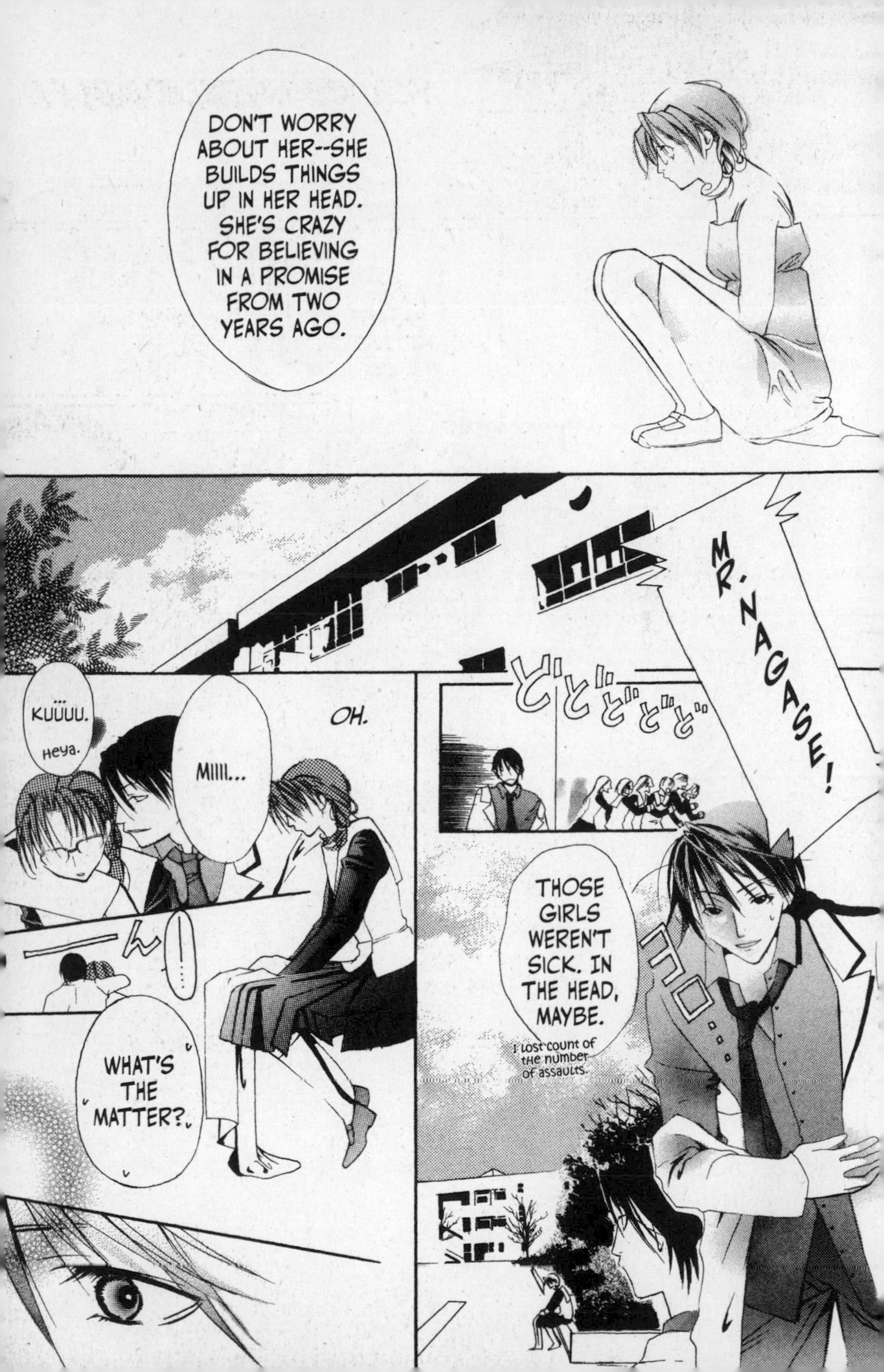
DON'T WORRY ABOUT HER--SHE BUILDS THINGS UP IN HER HEAD. SHE'S CRAZY FOR BELIEVING IN A PROMISE FROM TWO YEARS AGO.
MR. NAGASE!
THOSE GIRLS WEREN'T SICK. IN THE HEAD, MAYBE.
I lost count of the number of assaults.
OH.
MIIII...
KUUUU.
Heya.
WHAT'S THE MATTER?

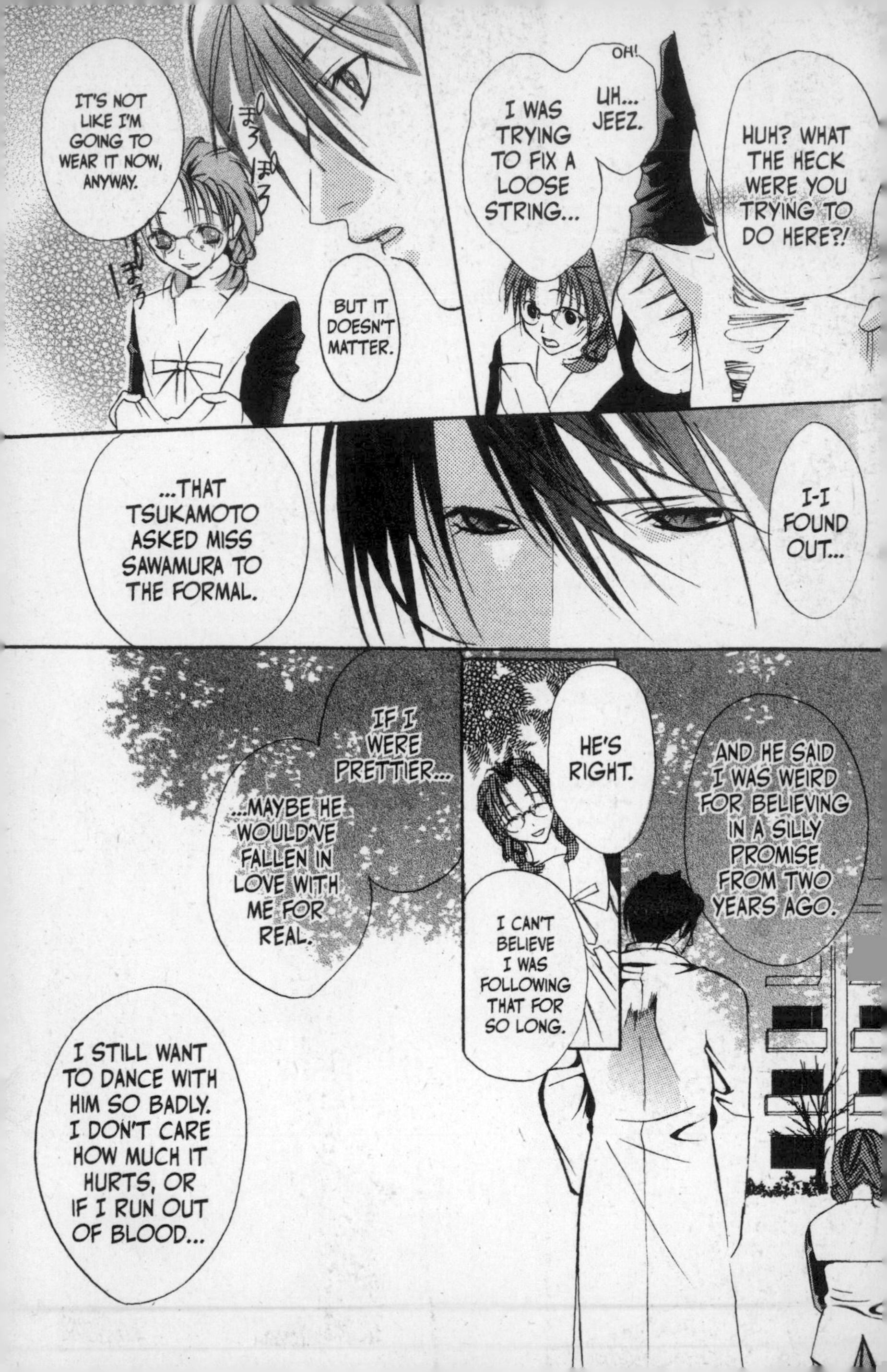
HUH? WHAT THE HECK WERE YOU TRYING TO DO HERE?!
OH!
UH... JEEZ.
I WAS TRYING TO FIX A LOOSE STRING...
BUT IT DOESN'T MATTER.
IT'S NOT LIKE I'M GOING TO WEAR IT NOW, ANYWAY.
I-I FOUND OUT...
...THAT TSUKAMOTO ASKED MISS SAWAMURA TO THE FORMAL.
AND HE SAID I WAS WEIRD FOR BELIEVING IN A SILLY PROMISE FROM TWO YEARS AGO.
HE'S RIGHT.
I CAN'T BELIEVE I WAS FOLLOWING THAT FOR SO LONG.
IF I WERE PRETTIER...
...MAYBE HE WOULD'VE FALLEN IN LOVE WITH ME FOR REAL.
I STILL WANT TO DANCE WITH HIM SO BADLY. I DON'T CARE HOW MUCH IT HURTS, OR IF I RUN OUT OF BLOOD...

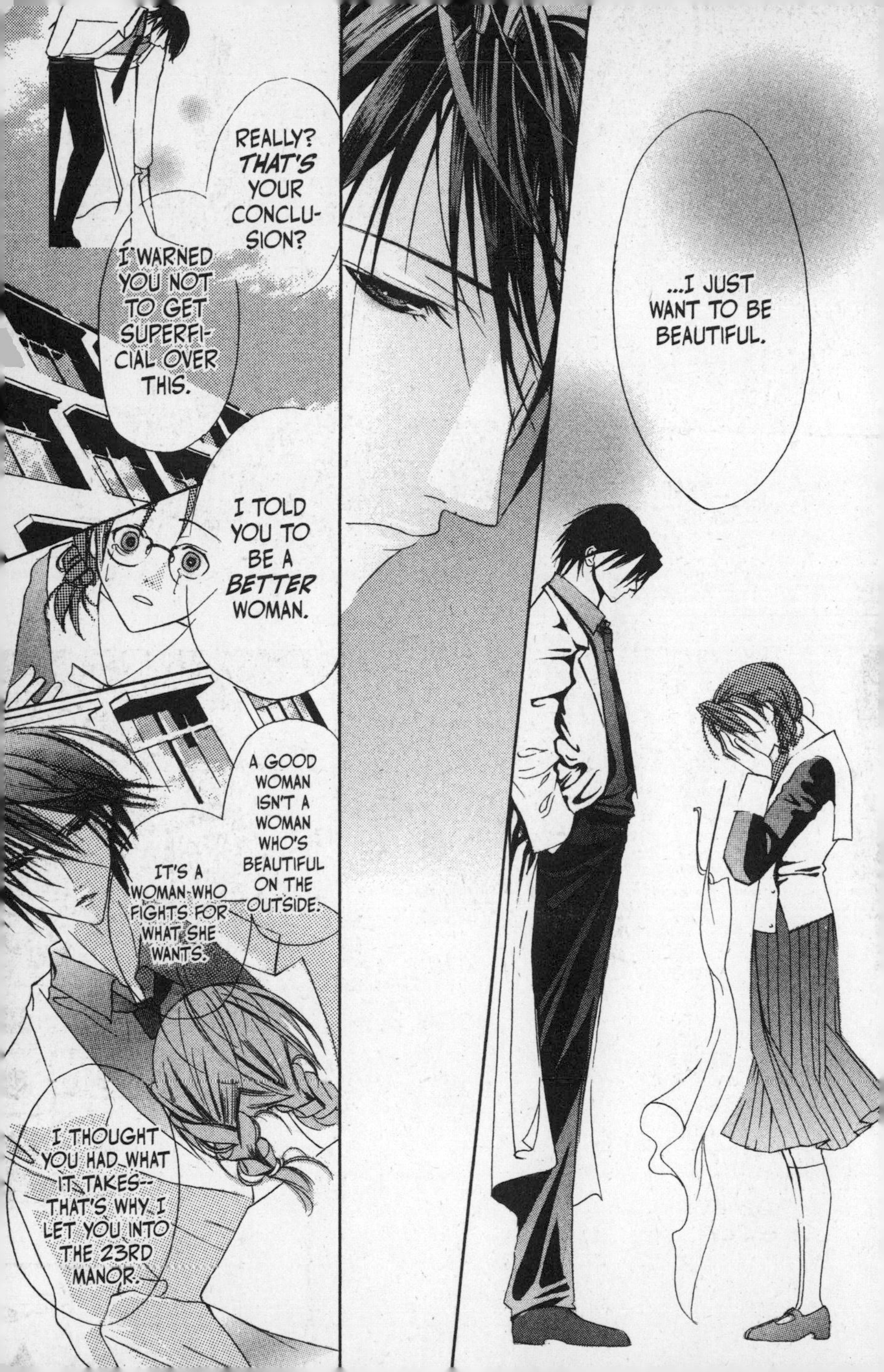

...I JUST WANT TO BE BEAUTIFUL.
REALLY? *THAT'S* YOUR CONCLUSION?
I WARNED YOU NOT TO GET SUPERFICIAL OVER THIS.
I TOLD YOU TO BE A *BETTER* WOMAN.
A GOOD WOMAN ISN'T A WOMAN WHO'S BEAUTIFUL ON THE OUTSIDE.
IT'S A WOMAN WHO FIGHTS FOR WHAT SHE WANTS.
I THOUGHT YOU HAD WHAT IT TAKES--THAT'S WHY I LET YOU INTO THE 23RD MANOR.

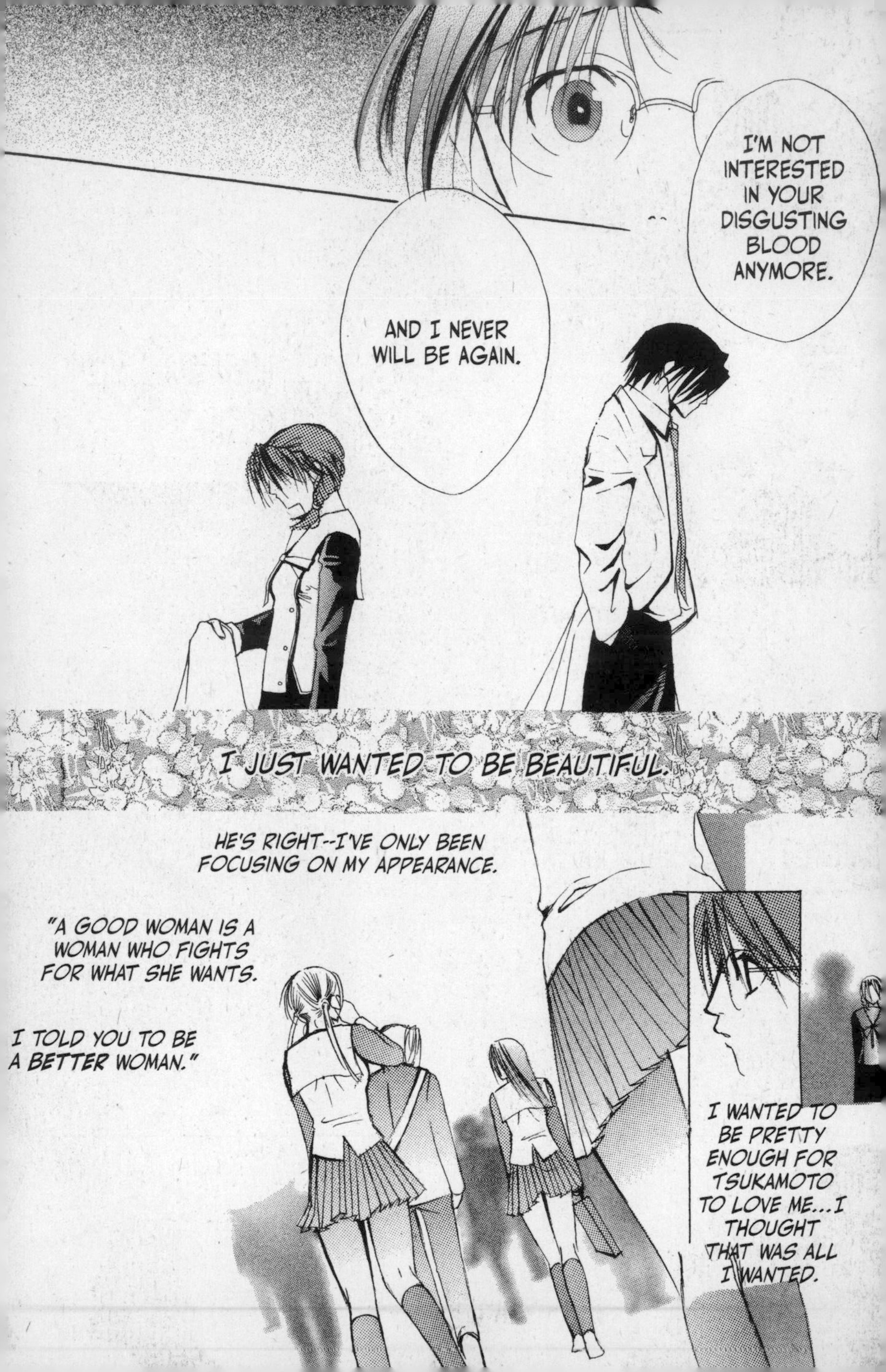
I'M NOT INTERESTED IN YOUR DISGUSTING BLOOD ANYMORE.
AND I NEVER WILL BE AGAIN.
I JUST WANTED TO BE BEAUTIFUL.
HE'S RIGHT--I'VE ONLY BEEN FOCUSING ON MY APPEARANCE.
"A GOOD WOMAN IS A WOMAN WHO FIGHTS FOR WHAT SHE WANTS.
I TOLD YOU TO BE A BETTER WOMAN."
I WANTED TO BE PRETTY ENOUGH FOR TSUKAMOTO TO LOVE ME...I THOUGHT THAT WAS ALL I WANTED.

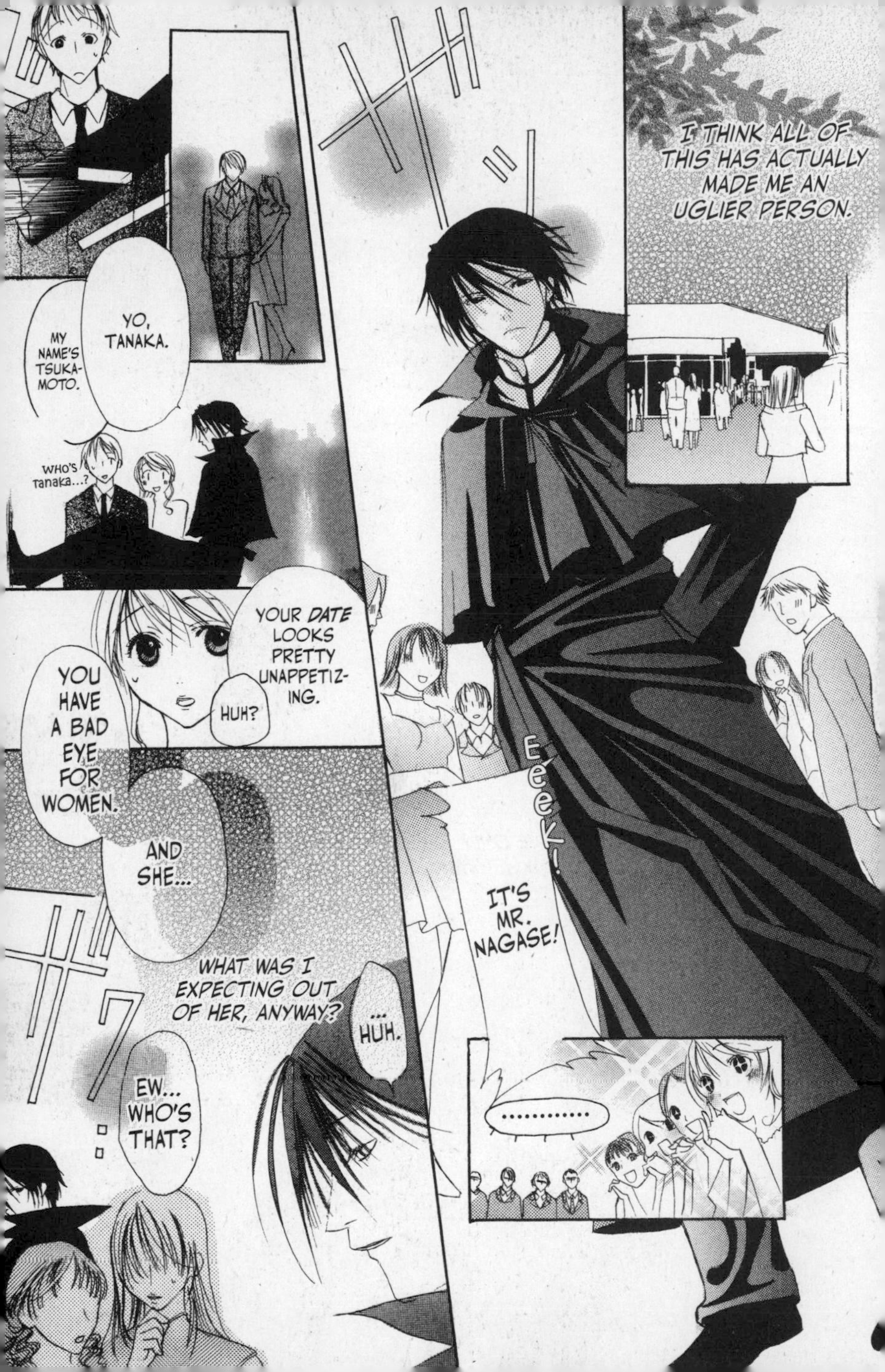
I THINK ALL OF THIS HAS ACTUALLY MADE ME AN UGLIER PERSON.
Eeek!
IT'S MR. NAGASE!
....
YO, TANAKA.
MY NAME'S TSUKA-MOTO.
WHO'S Tanaka...?
YOUR *DATE* LOOKS PRETTY UNAPPETIZ-ING.
HUH?
YOU HAVE A BAD EYE FOR WOMEN.
AND SHE...
WHAT WAS I EXPECTING OUT OF HER, ANYWAY?
...HUH.
EW... WHO'S THAT?

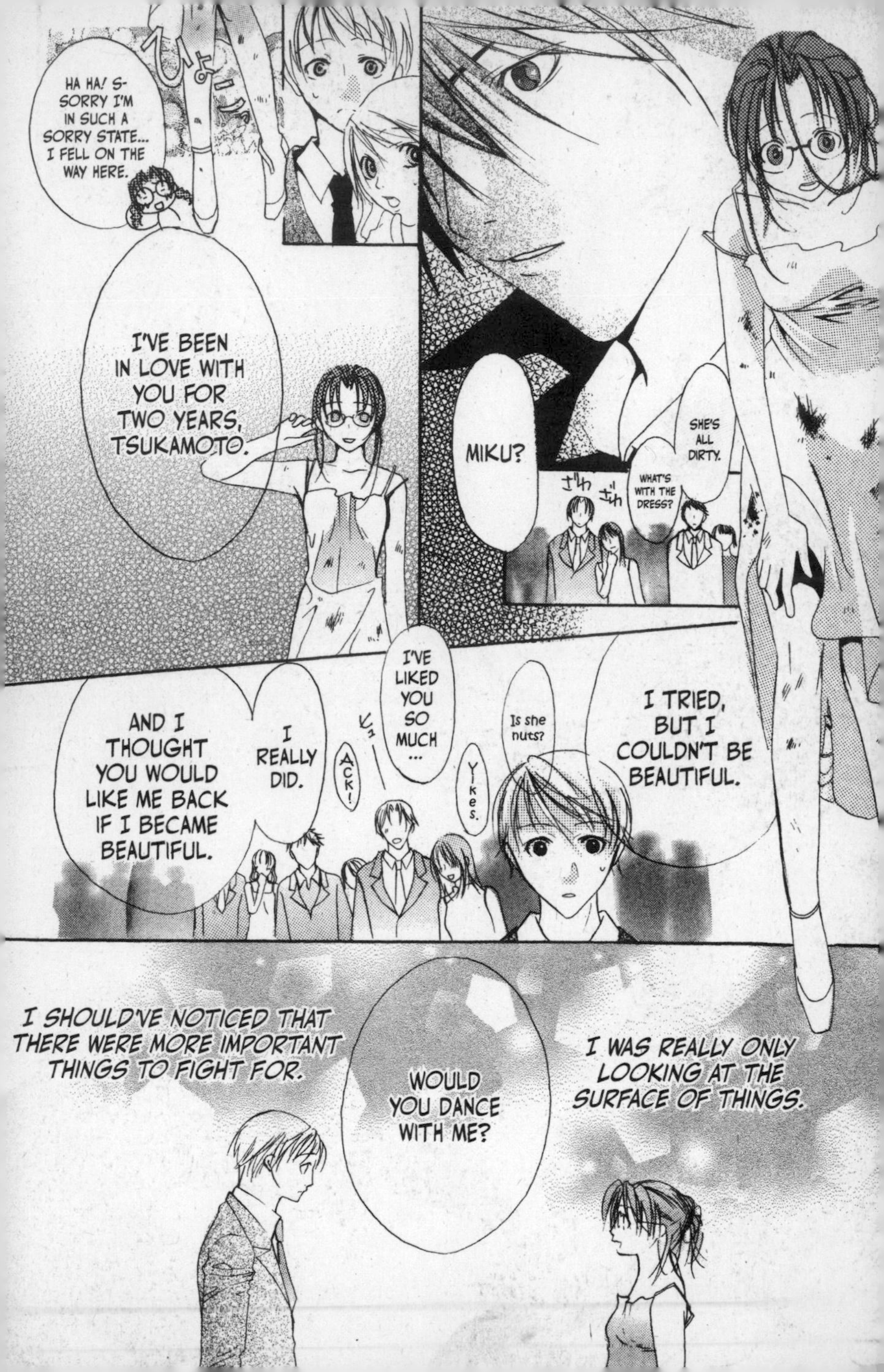
MIKU?
SHE'S ALL DIRTY.
WHAT'S WITH THE DRESS?
ざわ ざわ
HA HA! S-SORRY I'M IN SUCH A SORRY STATE... I FELL ON THE WAY HERE.
I'VE BEEN IN LOVE WITH YOU FOR TWO YEARS, TSUKAMOTO.
I TRIED, BUT I COULDN'T BE BEAUTIFUL.
Is she nuts?
Yikes.
I'VE LIKED YOU SO MUCH...
ACK!
I REALLY DID.
AND I THOUGHT YOU WOULD LIKE ME BACK IF I BECAME BEAUTIFUL.
I WAS REALLY ONLY LOOKING AT THE SURFACE OF THINGS.
WOULD YOU DANCE WITH ME?
I SHOULD'VE NOTICED THAT THERE WERE MORE IMPORTANT THINGS TO FIGHT FOR.

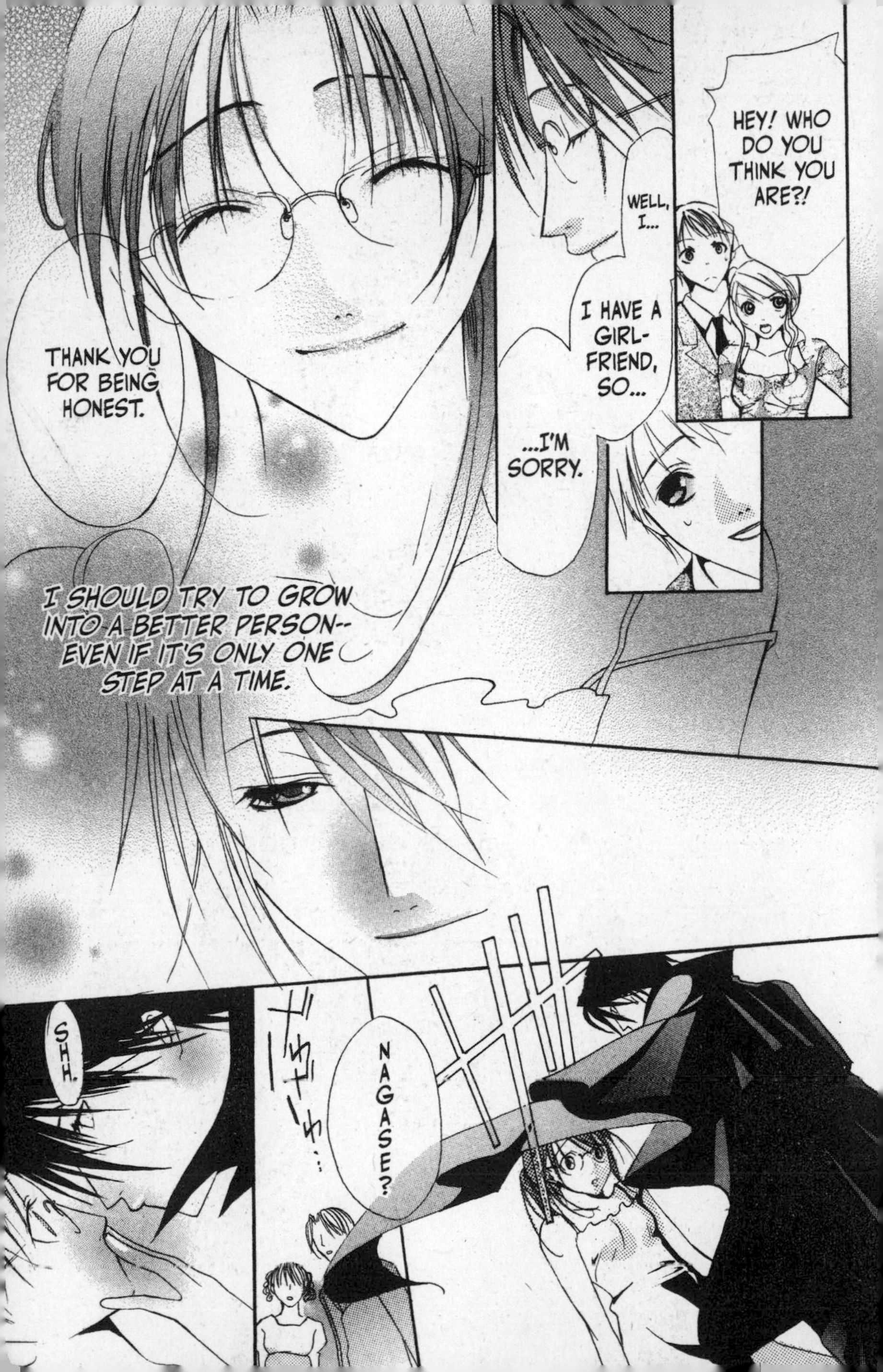
HEY! WHO DO YOU THINK YOU ARE?!
WELL, I...
I HAVE A GIRL-FRIEND, SO...
...I'M SORRY.
THANK YOU FOR BEING HONEST.
I SHOULD TRY TO GROW INTO A BETTER PERSON--EVEN IF IT'S ONLY ONE STEP AT A TIME.
NAGASE?
SHH.

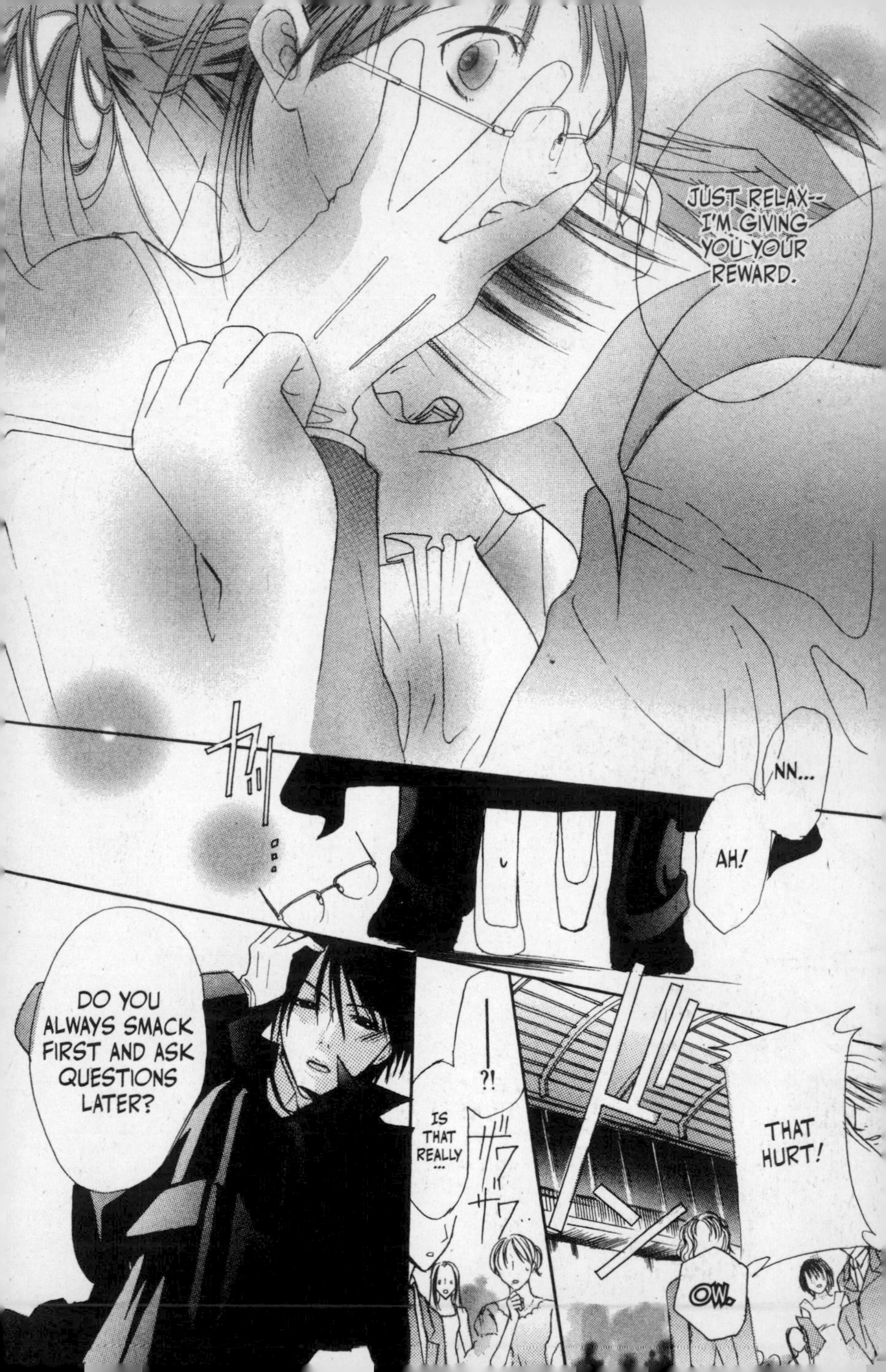
JUST RELAX-- I'M GIVING YOU YOUR REWARD.
NN...
AH!
...
THAT HURT!
OW.
?!
IS THAT REALLY...
DO YOU ALWAYS SMACK FIRST AND ASK QUESTIONS LATER?

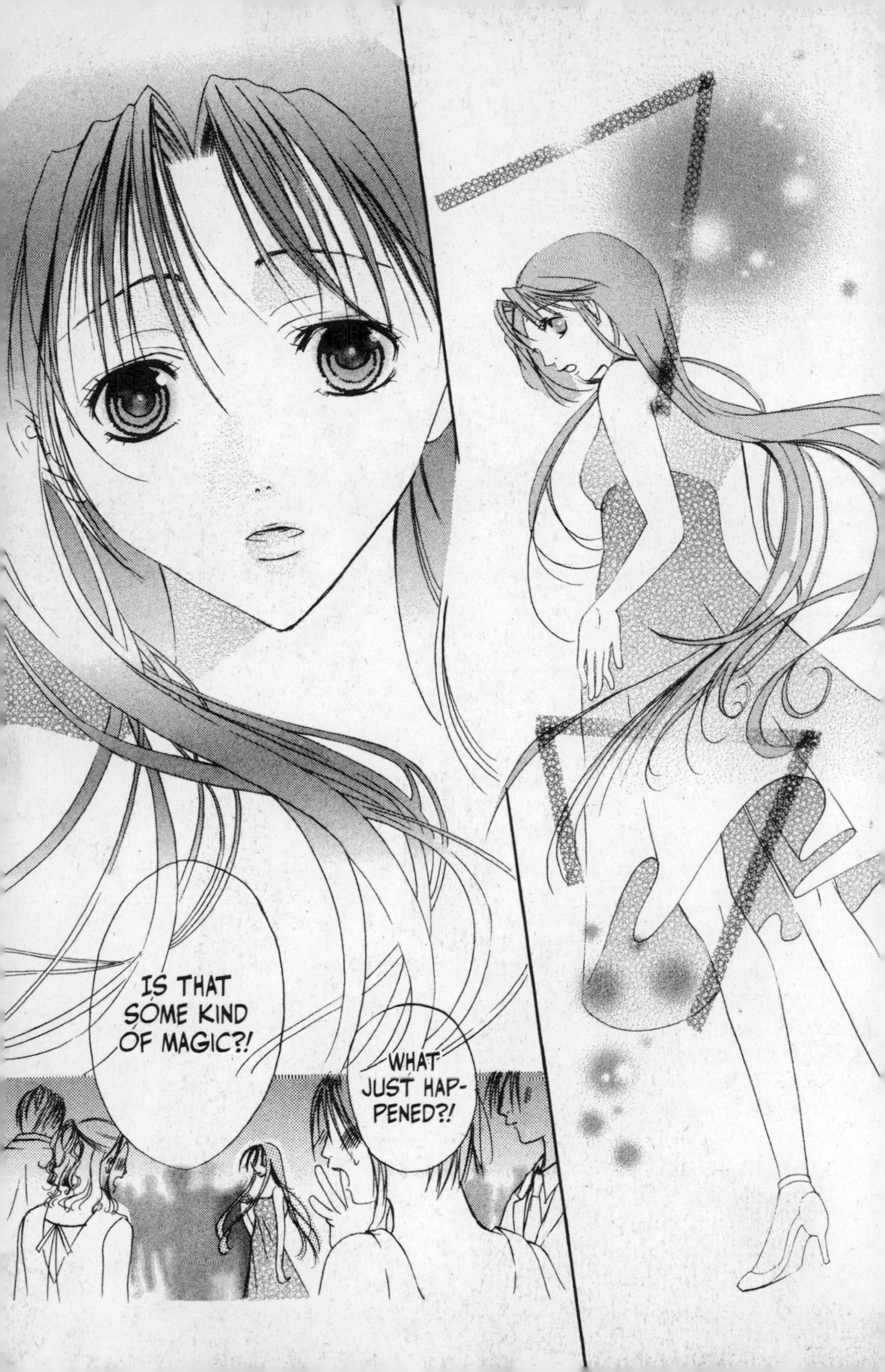
WHAT JUST HAP-PENED?!
IS THAT SOME KIND OF MAGIC?!

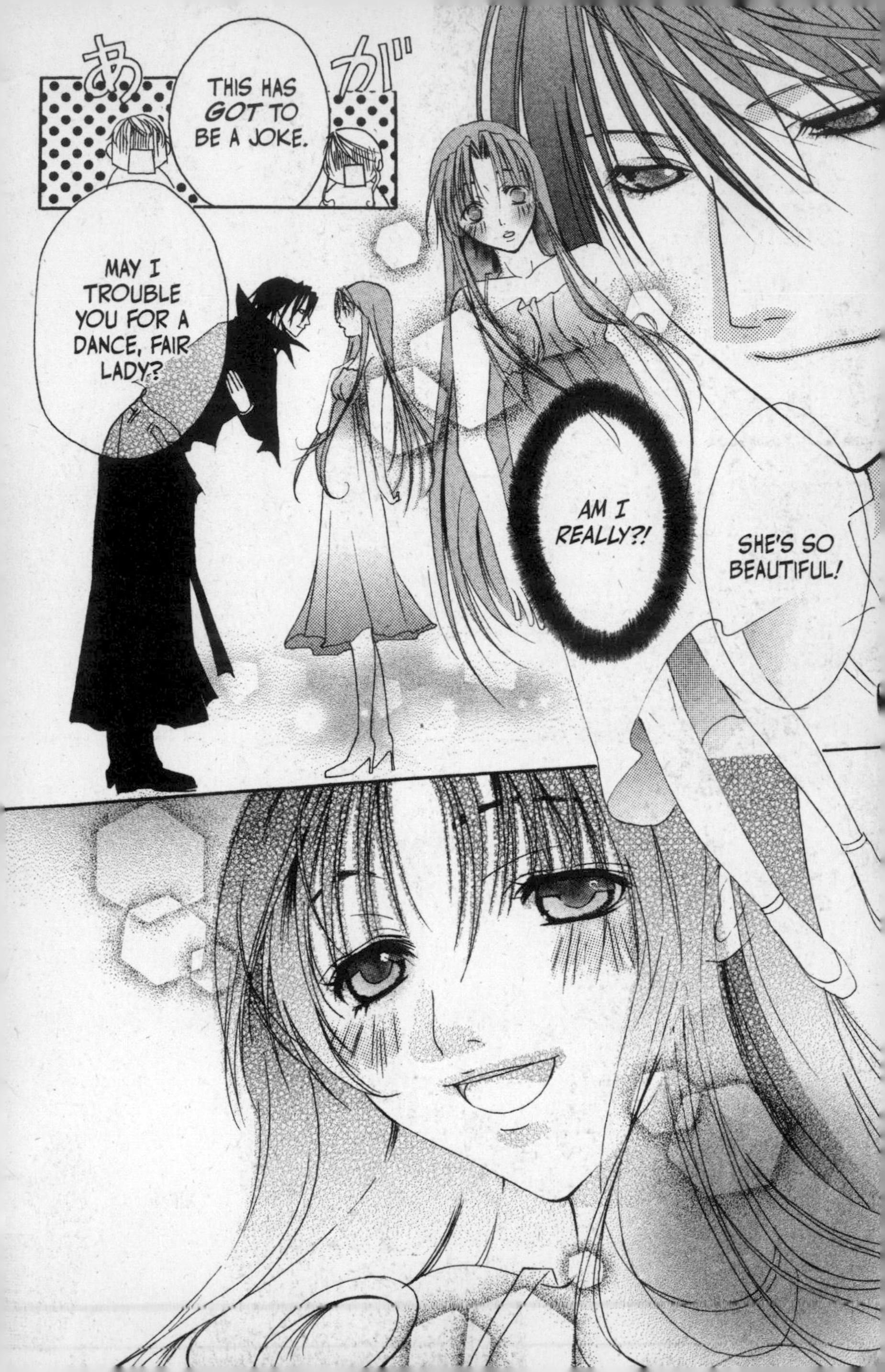
SHE'S SO BEAUTIFUL!
AM I REALLY?!
が
THIS HAS GOT TO BE A JOKE.
あ
MAY I TROUBLE YOU FOR A DANCE, FAIR LADY?

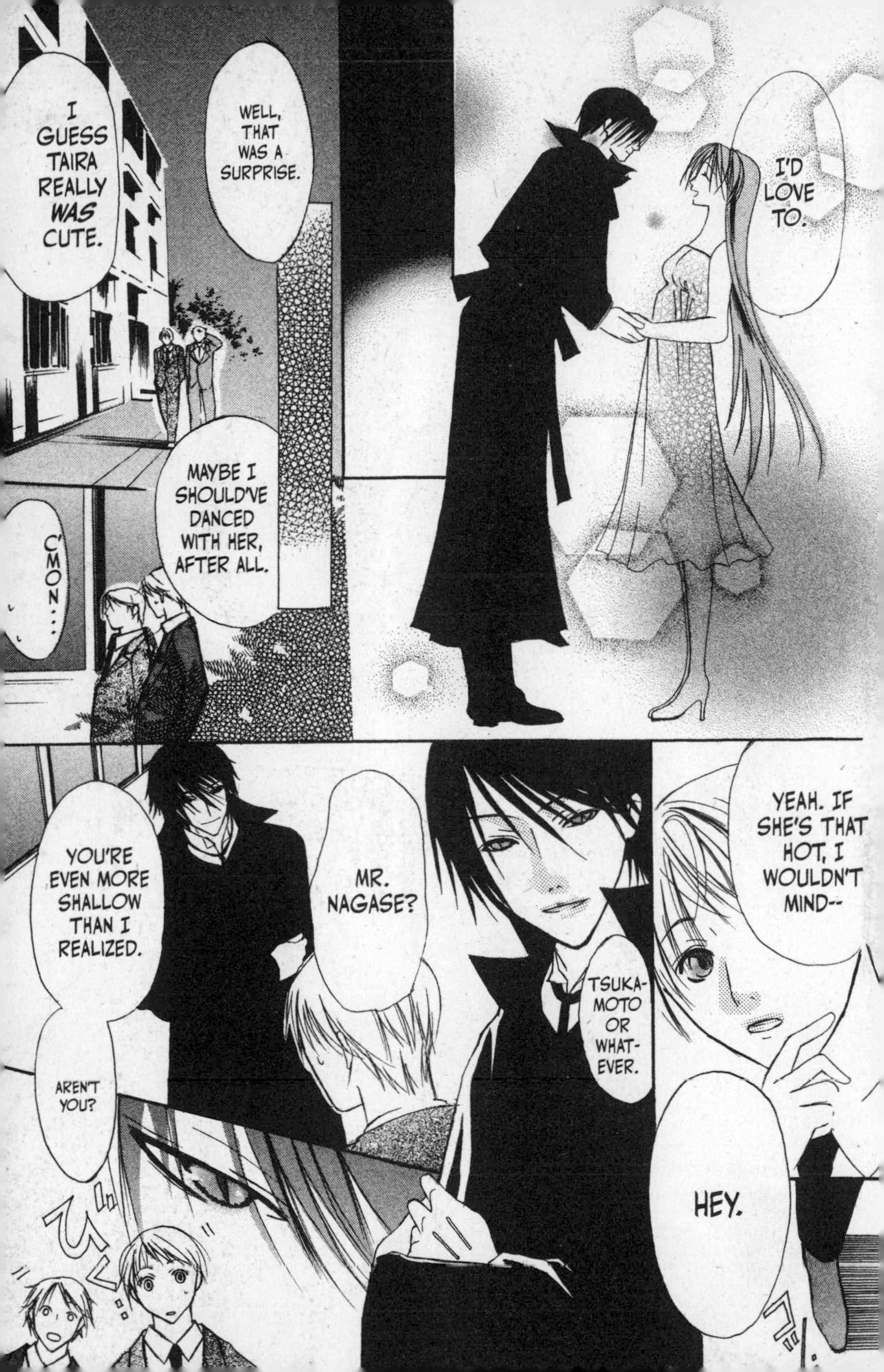
I'D LOVE TO.
WELL, THAT WAS A SURPRISE.
I GUESS TAIRA REALLY *WAS* CUTE.
MAYBE I SHOULD'VE DANCED WITH HER, AFTER ALL.
C'MON...
YEAH. IF SHE'S THAT HOT, I WOULDN'T MIND--
HEY.
TSUKA-MOTO OR WHAT-EVER.
MR. NAGASE?
YOU'RE EVEN MORE SHALLOW THAN I REALIZED.
AREN'T YOU?

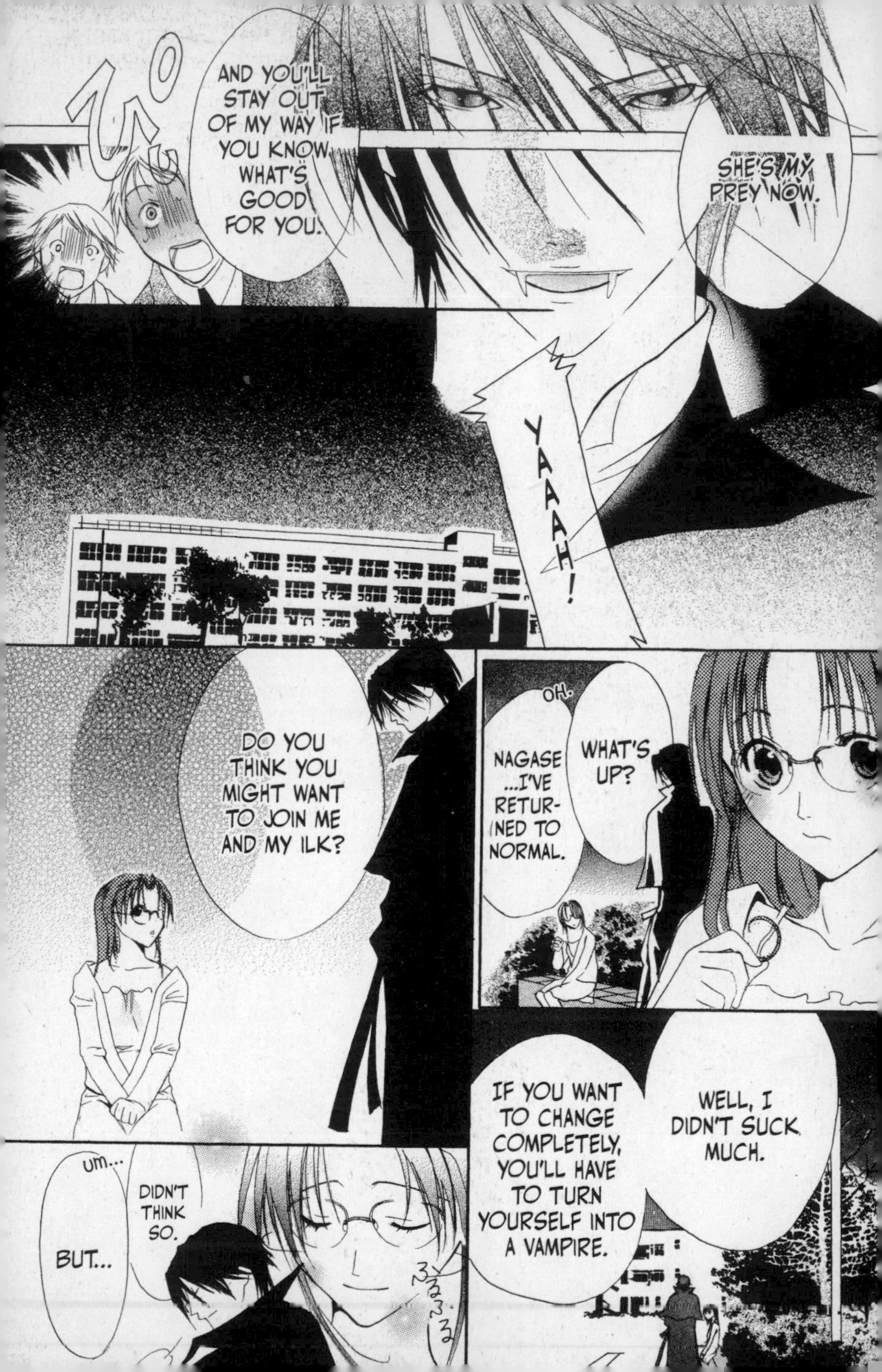
SHE'S MY PREY NOW.
AND YOU'LL STAY OUT OF MY WAY IF YOU KNOW WHAT'S GOOD FOR YOU.
YAAAAH!
OH.
WHAT'S UP?
NAGASE ...I'VE RETURNED TO NORMAL.
DO YOU THINK YOU MIGHT WANT TO JOIN ME AND MY ILK?
WELL, I DIDN'T SUCK MUCH.
IF YOU WANT TO CHANGE COMPLETELY, YOU'LL HAVE TO TURN YOURSELF INTO A VAMPIRE.
DIDN'T THINK SO.
UM... BUT...

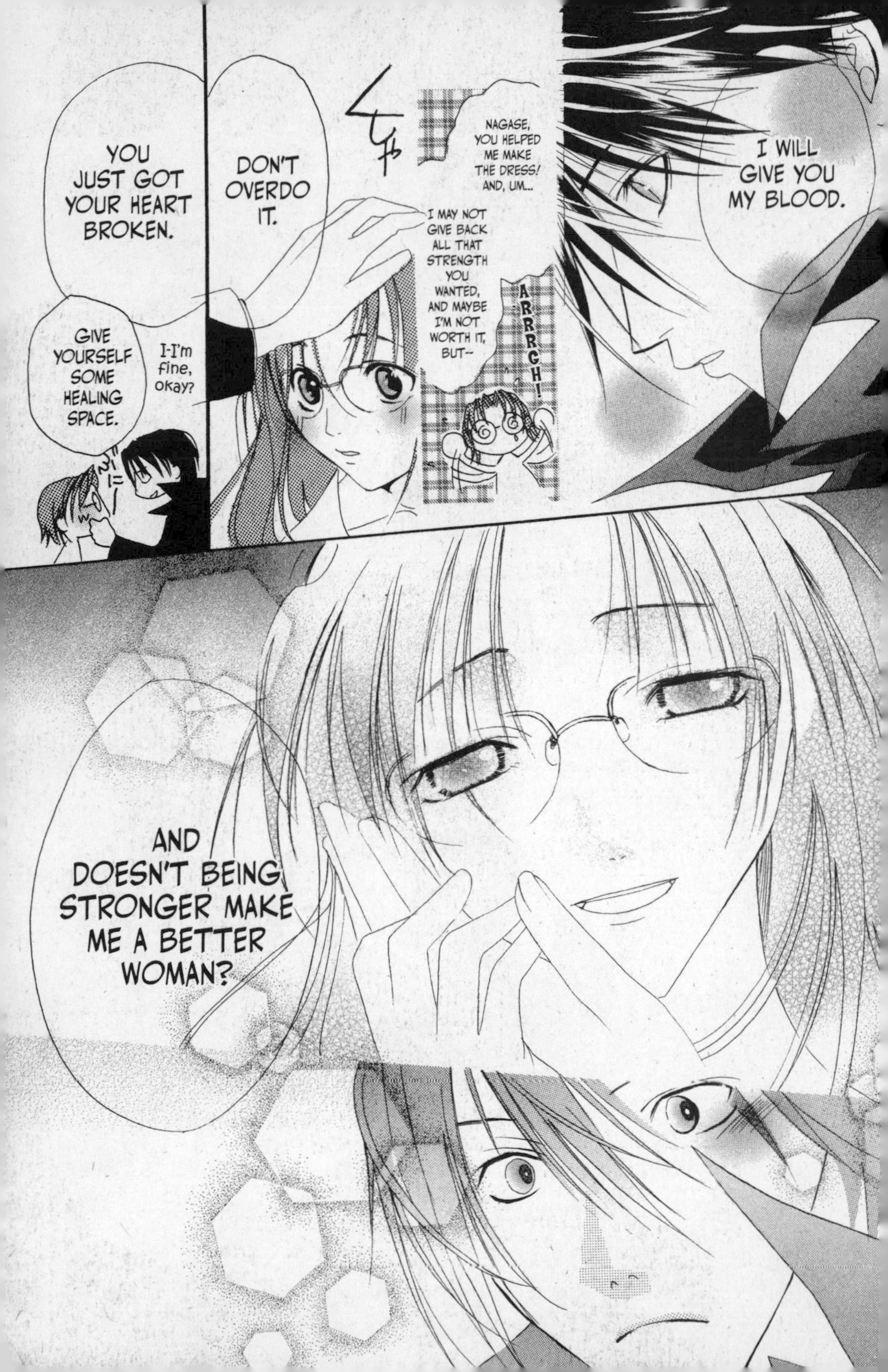
I WILL GIVE YOU MY BLOOD.
NAGASE, YOU HELPED ME MAKE THE DRESS! AND, UM...
I MAY NOT GIVE BACK ALL THAT STRENGTH YOU WANTED, AND MAYBE I'M NOT WORTH IT, BUT--
ARRRGH!
DON'T OVERDO IT.
YOU JUST GOT YOUR HEART BROKEN.
GIVE YOURSELF SOME HEALING SPACE.
I-I'm fine, okay?
AND DOESN'T BEING STRONGER MAKE ME A BETTER WOMAN?

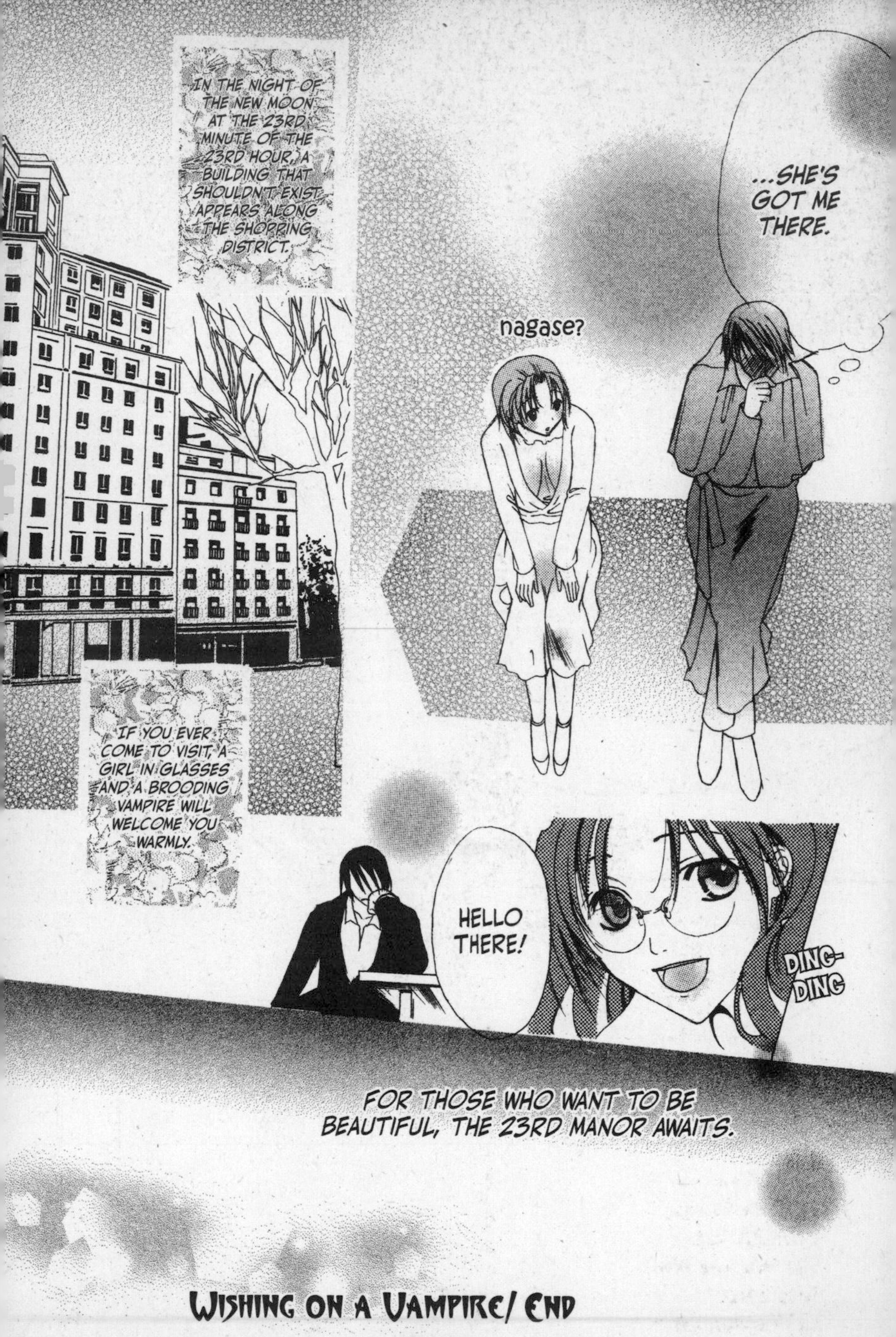
...SHE'S GOT ME THERE.
nagase?
IN THE NIGHT OF THE NEW MOON AT THE 23RD MINUTE OF THE 23RD HOUR, A BUILDING THAT SHOULDN'T EXIST APPEARS ALONG THE SHOPPING DISTRICT.
IF YOU EVER COME TO VISIT, A GIRL IN GLASSES AND A BROODING VAMPIRE WILL WELCOME YOU WARMLY.
DING-DING
HELLO THERE!
FOR THOSE WHO WANT TO BE BEAUTIFUL, THE 23RD MANOR AWAITS.

WISHING ON A VAMPIRE/ END

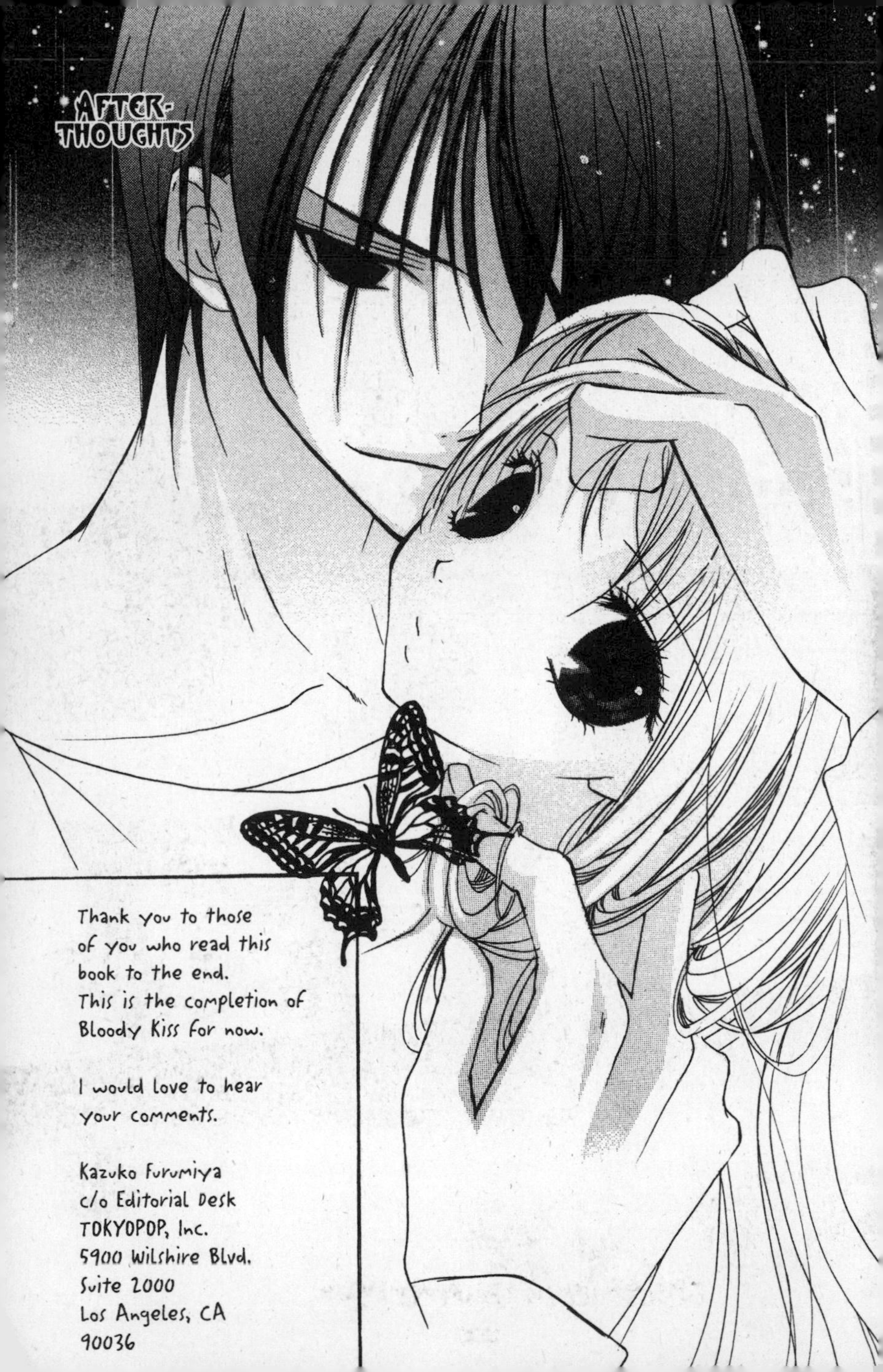
AFTER-THOUGHTS
Thank you to those of you who read this book to the end.
This is the completion of Bloody Kiss for now.
I would love to hear your comments.
Kazuko Furumiya
c/o Editorial Desk
TOKYOPOP, Inc.
5900 Wilshire Blvd.
Suite 2000
Los Angeles, CA
90036

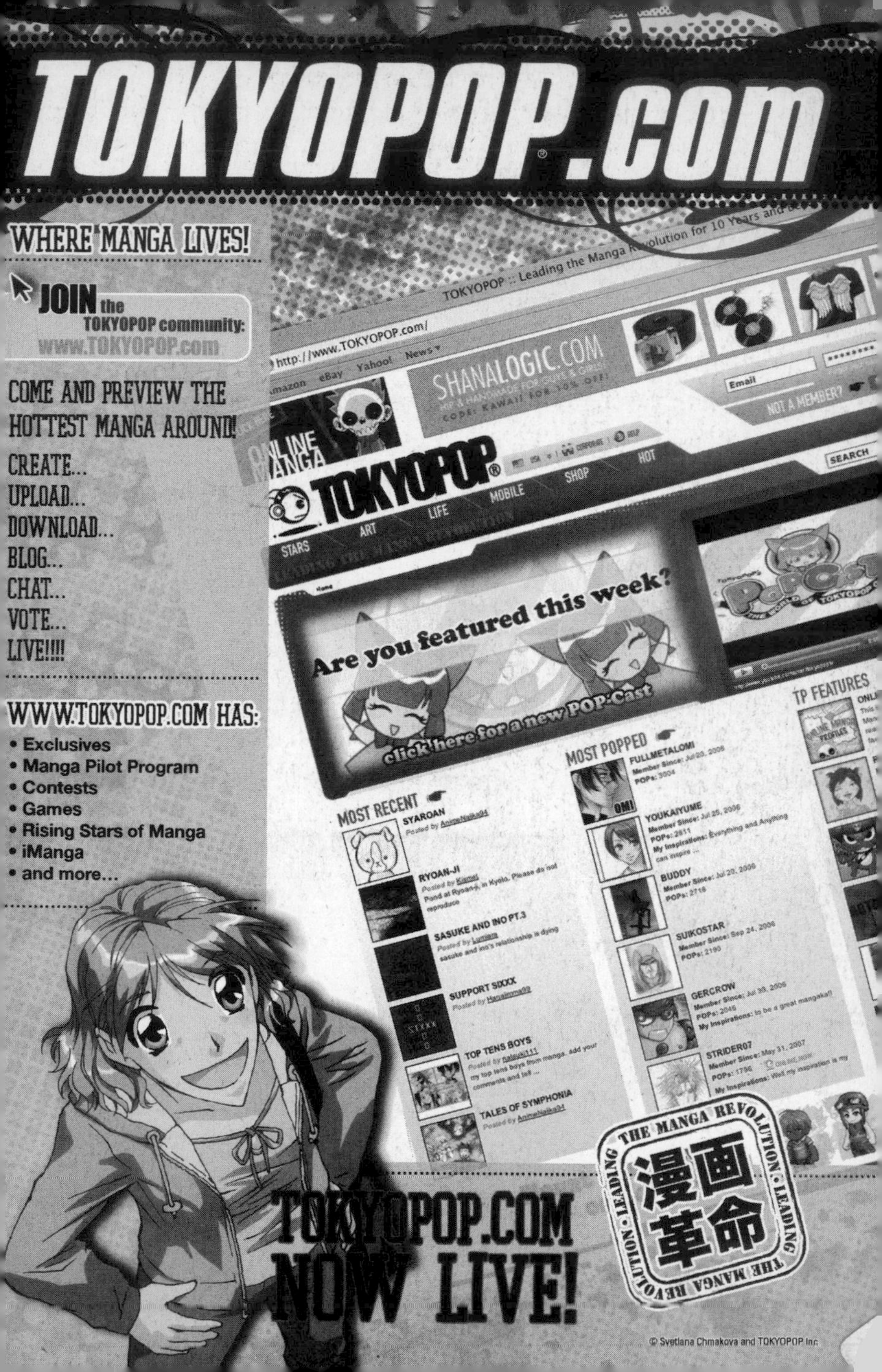
TOKYOPOP.com
WHERE MANGA LIVES!
JOIN the TOKYOPOP community:
www.TOKYOPOP.com
COME AND PREVIEW THE HOTTEST MANGA AROUND!
CREATE...
UPLOAD...
DOWNLOAD...
BLOG...
CHAT...
VOTE...
LIVE!!!!
WWW.TOKYOPOP.COM HAS:
• Exclusives
• Manga Pilot Program
• Contests
• Games
• Rising Stars of Manga
• iManga
• and more...
Are you featured this week?
click here for a new POP-Cast
MOST RECENT
MOST POPPED
TP FEATURES
TOKYOPOP.COM
NOW LIVE!
THE MANGA REVOLUTION • LEADING THE MANGA REVOLUTION • LEADING
漫画革命
© Svetlana Chmakova and TOKYOPOP Inc.

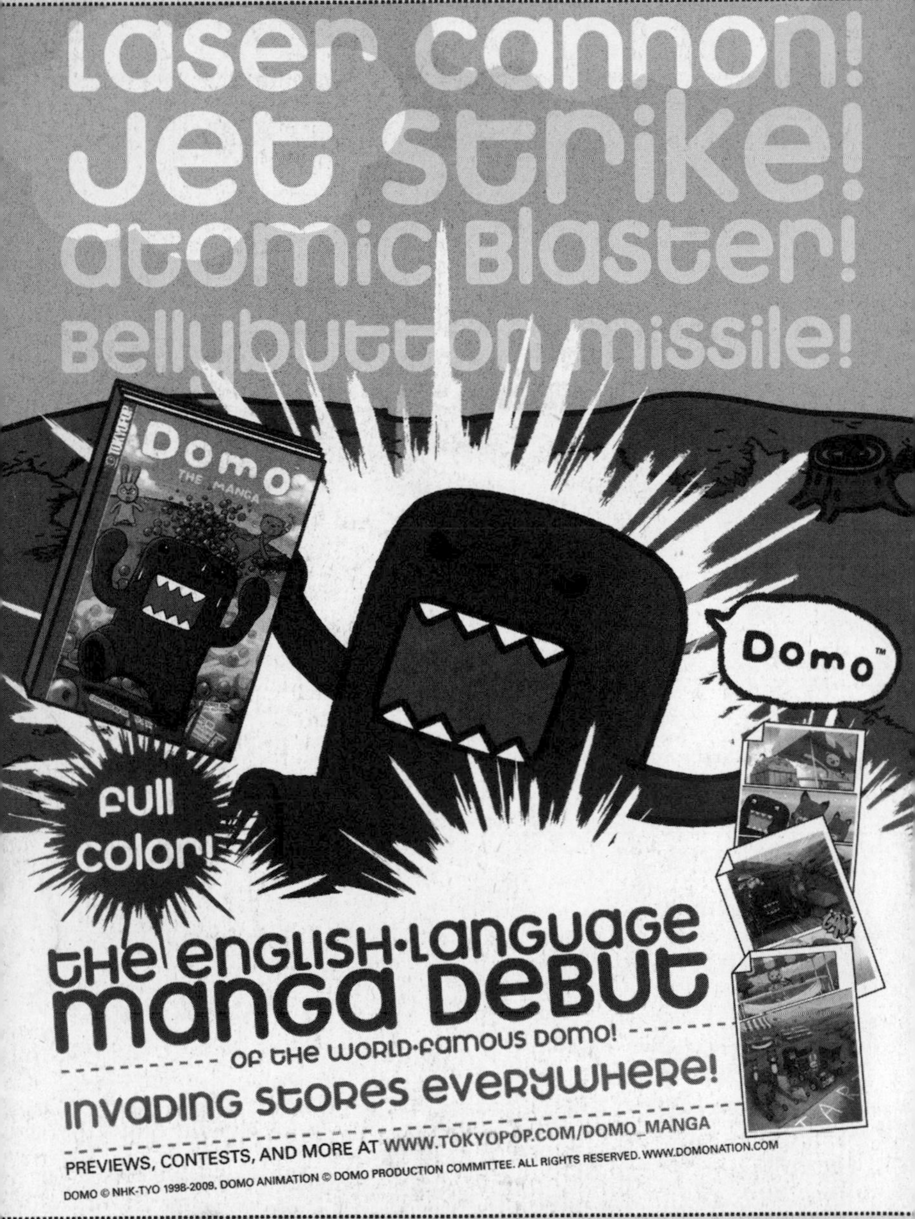
Laser Cannon!
Jet Strike!
Atomic Blaster!
Bellybutton missile!
Domo
THE MANGA
Domo™
full color!
THE ENGLISH-LANGUAGE MANGA DEBUT
OF THE WORLD-FAMOUS DOMO!
INVADING STORES EVERYWHERE!
PREVIEWS, CONTESTS, AND MORE AT WWW.TOKYOPOP.COM/DOMO_MANGA
DOMO © NHK-TYO 1998-2009. DOMO ANIMATION © DOMO PRODUCTION COMMITTEE. ALL RIGHTS RESERVED. WWW.DOMONATION.COM

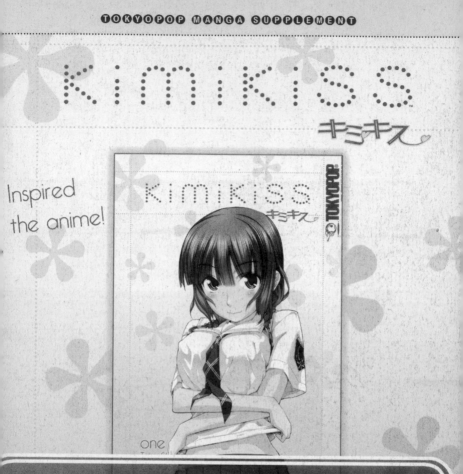

STOP!

This is the back of the book.
You wouldn't want to spoil a great ending!

This book is printed "manga-style," in the authentic Japanese right-to-left format. Since none of the artwork has been flipped or altered, readers get to experience the story just as the creator intended. You've been asking for it, so TOKYOPOP® delivered: authentic, hot-off-the-press, and far more fun!

DIRECTIONS

If this is your first time reading manga-style, here's a quick guide to help you understand how it works.

It's easy... just start in the top right panel and follow the numbers. Have fun, and look for more 100% authentic manga from TOKYOPOP®!